Famines in European Economic History

This volume explores economic, social and political dimensions of three catastrophic famines which struck mid-nineteenth and early-twentieth century Europe; the Irish Famine (*An Gorta Mór*) of 1845–1850, the Finnish Famine (*Suuret Nälkävuodet*) of the 1860s and the Ukrainian Famine (*Holodomor*) of 1932/1933.

In addition to providing new insights into these events on international, national and regional scales, this volume contributes to an increased comparative historiography in historical famine studies. The parallel studies presented in this book challenge and enhance established understandings of famine tragedies, including: famine causation and culpability; social and regional famine vulnerabilities; core–periphery relationships between nations and regions; degrees of national autonomy and self-sufficiency; as well as famine memory and identity.

Famines in European Economic History advocates that the impact and long-term consequences of famine for a nation should be understood in the context of evolving geopolitical relations that extend beyond its borders. Furthermore, regional structures within a nation can lead to unevenness in both the severity of the immediate famine crisis and the post-famine recovery.

This book will be of interest to those in the fields of economic history, European history and economic geography.

Declan Curran is Lecturer in Development Economics and Industrial Economics at Dublin City University Business School, Ireland.

Lubomyr Luciuk is Professor of Political Geography at the Royal Military College of Canada and Fellow of the Chair of Ukrainian Studies at the University of Toronto.

Andrew G. Newby is Senior Research Fellow of the Academy of Finland, University of Helsinki, Finland.

Routledge explorations in economic history

Edited by Lars Magnusson

Uppsala University, Sweden

1 **Economic Ideas and Government Policy**
Contributions to contemporary economic history
Sir Alec Cairncross

2 **The Organization of Labour Markets**
Modernity, culture and governance in Germany, Sweden, Britain and Japan
Bo Stråth

3 **Currency Convertibility**
The gold standard and beyond
Edited by Jorge Braga de Macedo, Barry Eichengreen and Jaime Reis

4 **Britain's Place in the World**
A historical enquiry into import controls 1945–1960
Alan S. Milward and George Brennan

5 **France and the International Economy**
From Vichy to the Treaty of Rome
Frances M.B. Lynch

6 **Monetary Standards and Exchange Rates**
M.C. Marcuzzo, L. Officer and A. Rosselli

7 **Production Efficiency in Domesday England, 1086**
John McDonald

8 **Free Trade and its Reception 1815–1960**
Freedom and trade: volume I
Edited by Andrew Marrison

9 **Conceiving Companies**
Joint-stock politics in Victorian England
Timothy L. Alborn

10 **The British Industrial Decline Reconsidered**
Edited by Jean-Pierre Dormois and Michael Dintenfass

11 **The Conservatives and Industrial Efficiency, 1951–1964**
Thirteen wasted years?
Nick Tiratsoo and Jim Tomlinson

12 **Pacific Centuries**
Pacific and Pacific Rim economic history since the 16th century
Edited by Dennis O. Flynn, Lionel Frost and A.J.H. Latham

13 **The Premodern Chinese Economy**
Structural equilibrium and capitalist sterility
Gang Deng

14 **The Role of Banks in Monitoring Firms**
The case of the Crédit Mobilier
Elisabeth Paulet

15 **Management of the National Debt in the United Kingdom, 1900–1932**
Jeremy Wormell

16 **An Economic History of Sweden**
Lars Magnusson

17 **Freedom and Growth**
The rise of states and markets in Europe, 1300–1750
S.R. Epstein

18 **The Mediterranean Response to Globalization before 1950**
Sevket Pamuk and Jeffrey G. Williamson

19 **Production and Consumption in English Households 1600–1750**
Mark Overton, Jane Whittle, Darron Dean and Andrew Hann

20 **Governance, the State, Regulation and Industrial Relations**
Ian Clark

21 **Early Modern Capitalism**
Economic and social change in Europe 1400–1800
Edited by Maarten Prak

22 **An Economic History of London, 1800–1914**
Michael Ball and David Sunderland

23 **The Origins of National Financial Systems**
Alexander Gerschenkron reconsidered
Edited by Douglas J. Forsyth and Daniel Verdier

24 **The Russian Revolutionary Economy, 1890–1940**
Ideas, debates and alternatives
Vincent Barnett

25 **Land Rights, Ethno Nationality and Sovereignty in History**
Edited by Stanley L. Engerman and Jacob Metzer

26 **An Economic History of Film**
Edited by John Sedgwick and Mike Pokorny

27 **The Foreign Exchange Market of London**
Development since 1900
John Atkin

28 **Rethinking Economic Change in India**
Labour and livelihood
Tirthankar Roy

29 **The Mechanics of Modernity in Europe and East Asia**
The institutional origins of social change and stagnation
Erik Ringmar

30 **International Economic Integration in Historical Perspective**
Dennis M.P. McCarthy

31 **Theories of International Trade**
Adam Klug
Edited by Warren Young and Michael Bordo

32 **Classical Trade Protectionism 1815–1914**
Edited by Jean Pierre Dormois and Pedro Lains

33 **Economy and Economics of Ancient Greece**
Takeshi Amemiya

34 **Social Capital, Trust and the Industrial Revolution**
1780–1880
David Sunderland

35 **Pricing Theory, Financing of International Organisations and Monetary History**
Lawrence H. Officer

36 **Political Competition and Economic Regulation**
Edited by Peter Bernholz and Roland Vaubel

37 **Industrial Development in Postwar Japan**
Hirohisa Kohama

38 **Reflections on the Cliometrics Revolution**
Conversations with economic historians
Edited by John S. Lyons, Louis P. Cain and Samuel H. Williamson

39 **Agriculture and Economic Development in Europe since 1870**
Edited by Pedro Lains and Vicente Pinilla

40 **Quantitative Economic History**
The good of counting
Edited by Joshua Rosenbloom

41 **A History of Macroeconomic Policy in the United States**
John H. Wood

42 **An Economic History of the American Steel Industry**
Robert P. Rogers

43 **Ireland and the Industrial Revolution**
The impact of the Industrial Revolution on Irish industry and society, 1801–1922
Andy Bielenberg

44 **Intra-Asian Trade and Industrialization**
Essays in memory of Yasukichi Yasuba
Edited by A.J.H. Latham and Heita Kawakatsu

45 **Nation, State and the Industrial Revolution**
The visible hand
Lars Magnusson

46 **A Cultural History of Finance**
Irene Finel-Honigman

47 **Managing Crises and De-globalisation**
Nordic foreign trade and exchange 1919–1939
Edited by Sven-Olof Olsson

48 **The International Tin Cartel**
John Hillman

49 **The South Sea Bubble**
Helen J. Paul

50 **Ideas and Economic Crises in Britain from Attlee to Blair (1945–2005)**
Matthias Matthijs

51 **Bengal Industries and the British Industrial Revolution (1757–1857)**
Indrajit Ray

52 **The Evolving Structure of the East Asian Economic System since 1700**
Edited by A.J.H. Latham and Heita Kawakatsu

53 **German Immigration and Servitude in America, 1709–1920**
Farley Grubb

54 **The Rise of Planning in Industrial America, 1865–1914**
Richard Adelstein

55 **An Economic History of Modern Sweden**
Lennart Schön

56 **The Standard of Living and Revolutions in Russia, 1700–1917**
Boris Mironov

57 **Europe's Green Revolution and Others Since**
The rise and fall of peasant-friendly plant breeding
Jonathan Harwood

58 **Economic Analysis of Institutional Change in Ancient Greece**
Carl Hampus-Lyttkens

59 **Labour-Intensive Industrialization in Global History**
Edited by Gareth Austin and Kaoru Sugihara

60 **The History of Bankruptcy**
Economic, social and cultural implications in early modern Europe
Edited by Thomas Max Safley

61 **The Political Economy of Disaster and Underdevelopment**
Destitution, plunder and earthquake in Haiti
Mats Lundahl

62 **Nationalism and Economic Development in Modern Eurasia**
Carl Mosk

63 **Agricultural Transformation in a Global History Perspective**
Edited by Ellen Hillbom and Patrick Svensson

64 **Colonial Exploitation and Economic Development**
The Belgian Congo and the Netherlands Indies compared
Edited by Ewout Frankema and Frans Buelens

65 **The State and Business in the Major Powers**
An economic history 1815–1939
Robert Millward

66 **Privatization and Transition in Russia in the Early 1990s**
Carol Scott Leonard and David Pitt-Watson

67 **Large Databases in Economic History**
Research methods and case studies
Edited by Mark Casson and Nigar Hashimzade

68 **A History of Market Performance**
From ancient Babylonia to the modern world
Edited by R.J. van der Spek, Jan Luiten van Zanden and Bas van Leeuwen

69 **Central Banking in a Democracy**
The Federal Reserve and its alternatives
John H. Wood

70 **The History of Migration in Europe**
Perspectives from economics, politics and sociology
Edited by Francesca Fauri

71 **Famines in European Economic History**
The last great European famines reconsidered
Edited by Declan Curran, Lubomyr Luciuk and Andrew G. Newby

Famines in European Economic History

The last great European famines reconsidered

Edited by Declan Curran, Lubomyr Luciuk and Andrew G. Newby

LONDON AND NEW YORK

First published 2015
by Routledge

2 Park Square, Milton Park, Abingdon, Oxfordshire OX14 4RN
52 Vanderbilt Avenue, New York, NY 10017

Routledge is an imprint of the Taylor & Francis Group, an informa business

First issued in paperback 2019

British Library Cataloguing in Publication Data
A catalogue record for this book is available from the British Library

Library of Congress Cataloging in Publication Data
Famines in European economic history: the last great European famines reconsidered / edited by Declan Curran, Lubomyr Luciuk and Andrew Newby.
pages cm
1. Famines–Europe–History. 2. Europe–Economic conditions–19th century. 3. Europe–Economic conditions–20th century. I. Curran, Declan. II. Luciuk, Lubomyr Y. III. Newby, Andrew G.
HC240.9.F3F36 2015
363.8094–dc23 2014044066

ISBN: 978-0-415-65681-8 (hbk)
ISBN: 978-0-367-86748-5 (pbk)

Typeset in Times New Roman
by Wearset Ltd, Boldon, Tyne and Wear

Contents

Figures

Maps

Tables

Contributors

Declan Curran lectures in Development Economics and Industrial Economics at Dublin City University Business School. He holds a PhD in Economics from University of Hamburg. He is also a contributor to the volume *Global Legacies of the Great Irish Famine* (2014). His research interests focus on industrial development and economic geography.

Henrik Forsberg received his MA degree in History in 2011 and is currently a doctoral candidate at the University of Helsinki. His ongoing research project compares Irish and Finnish historical cultures and specifically how famine has been incorporated into various national narratives from the 1850s to the 1960s. He has previously published on the politicisation of Finnish famine memory and actively engages in international collaborations within the fields of nationalism, politics of memory and famine studies.

Peter Gray is Professor of Modern Irish History at Queen's University Belfast. His research specialism is in the history of British–Irish relations *c.*1800 to 1870, especially the political history of the Great Famine of 1845 to 1850 and the politics of poverty and land in the nineteenth century. Notable publications include a history of the origins and implementation of the 1838 Irish Poor Law Act entitled *The Making of the Irish Poor Law 1815–43* (Manchester: Manchester University Press, 2009) and *Famine, Land and Politics: British government and Irish society 1843–1850* (Dublin: Irish Academic Press, 1999). He served as chair of the Royal Irish Academy's National Committee for Historical Sciences from 2007 to 2010 and was elected a Member of the Royal Irish Academy in 2013.

Andrea Graziosi is Professor of Contemporary History at the University of Naples 'Federico II' (Università di Napoli 'Federico II'), as well as Research Fellow at the Harvard Ukrainian Research Institute. He has also served as president (2011–2013) of the Panel for Research Evaluation in History, Philosophy, Geography, Anthropology, Psychology and Education, Italian State University System. He has authored numerous books and articles on modern East European, Soviet and Ukrainian history, including the influential *The Great Soviet Peasant War. Bolsheviks and Peasants, 1918–1934* (Harvard Ukrainian Research Institute, 1997).

Antti Häkkinen is Docent in Social History at the University of Helsinki, where he has worked as a researcher and senior lecturer at the Department of Political and Economic Studies the since the 1980s. His research fields cover the history of health, ethnic relations, social problems, economic and hunger crisis, and the intergenerational transmission of economic, social and human capital. He is currently managing 'Ten Generations – Three Centuries: A Finnish History as Family Stories', a project which will reconstruct 300 years of Finland's history through the life histories of hundreds of Finnish families, comprising more than 100,000 individual life stories.

Mary Kelly lectures in social and cultural geography at the Department of Geography, Geology and the Environment at Kingston University London. Her research interests are in nineteenth- and early twentieth-century Ireland. She has published on population change, literature and identity, and the Irish famine.

Bohdan Klid is Assistant Director of the Canadian Institute of Ukrainian Studies (CIUS), Faculty of Arts, University of Alberta. He is a historian who is also research director of the Holodomor Research and Educational Consortium (HREC) at CIUS. He is co-editor of the *Holodomor Reader: A Sourcebook on the Famine of 1932–1933 in Ukraine* (Edmonton, 2012), and has authored articles on Ukrainian historiography and on contemporary popular music and politics in Ukraine.

Nataliia Levchuk is Senior Researcher at the Ptoukha-Institute of Demography and Social Studies, National Academy of Sciences of Ukraine. She is involved in a research project estimating 1932 to 1934 famine losses in Ukraine, which is a part of the Harvard Ukrainian Research Institute's Holodomor Atlas Project. She has published on public health issues and their impact on the demography of Ukraine and the 1932/1933 Famine. Recent publications are: 'A Country Divided? Regional Variation in Mortality in Ukraine', *International Journal of Public Health* 58(6), 837–844, and 'Demography of a Man-made Human Catastrophe: The Case of Massive Famine in Ukraine 1932–1933', *Canadian Studies in Population* (forthcoming).

Lubomyr Luciuk is Professor of Political Geography at the Royal Military College of Canada. He is the author, editor and co-editor of a number of books dealing with twentieth-century Ukraine and the Ukrainian Diaspora, among them *The Foreign Office and the Famine: British Documents on the Great Famine of 1932–1933 in Soviet Ukraine* (Limestone Press, 1988), *Searching for Place: Ukrainian Displaced Persons, Canada and the Migration of Memory* (University of Toronto Press, 2000), *Holodomor: Reflections on the Great Famine of 1932–1933 in Soviet Ukraine* (Kashtan Press, 2008), *The Holy See and the Holodomor* (Toronto, Chair of Ukrainian Studies, 2011) and *Jews, Ukrainians and the Euromaidan* (Toronto, Chair of Ukrainian Studies, 2014). With Kyiv's Dr Volodymyr Viatrovych, he is currently working on a two-volume documentary collection, *Enemy Archives*, dealing with Soviet counterinsurgency efforts in western Ukraine before, during and after the Second World War.

Timo Myllyntaus is Professor of Finnish History at the University of Turku. He gained his first two degrees from the University of Helsinki and a PhD in Economic History from the London School of Economics. His research interests stretch from social history and environmental history to the development of everyday technology. His edited volumes include the special issue of *ICON* (no. 16) entitled *Technology in Everyday Life* (2012), and *Pathbreakers, Small European Countries Responding to Globalisation and De-globalisation* (co-edited with Margret Müller (2008)). He is President of the Committee for the History of Technology (ICOHTEC).

Andrew G. Newby is Senior Research Fellow of the Finnish Academy, and Associate Professor (Docent) in European Area and Cultural Studies at the University of Helsinki. He is principal investigator of the research project '"The Terrible Visitation", Famine in Finland and Ireland, *c.*1845–1868: Transnational, Comparative and Long-Term Perspectives'. He is the author of many articles on different aspects of Northern European history, society and culture, of *Ireland, Radicalism and the Scottish Highlands* (2007) and *The Life and Times of Edward McHugh* (2004). He is also co-editor of *Michael Davitt: New Perspectives* (2009), and *Language, Space and Power: Urban Entanglements* (2012).

Omelian Rudnytskyi is Senior Researcher at the Ptoukha-Institute of Demography and Social Studies, National Academy of Sciences of Ukraine. His area of research is the historical demography of Ukraine and, specifically, the estimation of population losses of Ukraine in the twentieth century. He is the author of a comprehensive reconstruction of the population of Ukraine in the eighteenth to twentieth centuries. His latest publication is 'Demographic Aspects of the 1932–1933 Famine in Ukraine' in *Proceedings of the Conference on Famines in Ukraine during the First Half of the XXth Century: Causes and consequences* (1921–1923, 1932–1933, 1946–1947) (Kyiv, 20–12 November 2013, pp. 281–289).

Pavlo Shevchuk is Research Fellow at the Department for Demographic Modelling and Forecasting, National Academy of Sciences of Ukraine. He graduated from Taras Shevchenko National University of Kyiv in 1997. He obtained his PhD in 2002 at the Council of Productive Forces of Ukraine. His research interests include population projections, population ageing, demographic methods and models.

Miikka Voutilainen holds an MA in Economic History and an MSc in Economics, and is a doctoral student at the University of Jyväskylä. His doctoral thesis concerns the long-term socio-economic background of the Finnish famine of the 1860s, with other research interests dealing with long-term economic growth and social and economic inequality.

Oleh Wolowyna is Research Fellow at the Center for Slavic, Eurasian and Eastern European Studies, University of North Carolina-Chapel Hill. He is also Director of the Center for Demographic and Socioeconomic Research on Ukrainians in the United States. He is a contributor to the *Holodomor Reader: A Sourcebook on the Famine of 1932–1933 in Ukraine* (Edmonton, 2012), and has published articles in the *Journal of Ukrainian Studies* and *The Ukrainian Quarterly*.

Famines in European economic history

Introduction

Declan Curran, Lubomyr Luciuk and Andrew G. Newby

> The young laughing full faces, and brilliant eyes, and buoyant limbs, had become walking-skeletons of death! When I saw one approaching, with his emaciated fingers locked together before him, his body in a bending position, as all generally crawled along, if I had neither bread nor money to give, I turned from the path; for, instead of the 'God save ye kindly,' or 'Ye look wary, lady,' which had ever been the salutation to me on the mountains, I knew it would be the imploring look or the vacant sepulchral stare, which, once fastened upon you, leaves its impress for ever.[1]
>
> (Asenath Nicholson (American Evangelist) on famine in Ireland, 1851)

> Bread has also been made of hay, of stems of peas, and of husks of malt, but these wretched substitutes have failed to stay the progress of the famine, and it has swept before it the inhabitants of whole villages, whose lifeless and emaciated bodies have alone remained to memorialise at once their past existence and their suffering. This state of things continues, and help is urgently needed.[2]
>
> (Thomas Harvey (English Quaker) on famine in Finland, 1868)

> We have arrived at the station. My God! what a sight! I shall never forget it. Poverty, filth, disease and hunger everywhere. Women in rags and tatters are lying about in the dust and dirt half asleep with emaciated little babies sucking their empty breasts. I can see one poor woman with four small children … I see a little girl who looks about ten years old to judge from her skinny little body but her face looks like that of a woman thirty years old. She is taking care of a baby whose face is purple with cold … I smiled at the child but she didn't smile back; I'm wondering if she has ever learned to smile.[3]
>
> (Zetta Wells (American traveller and TV presenter) on famine in Ukraine, 1933)

The testimonies of foreign witnesses to famine often reproduce familiar tropes in order to convey the extent of the suffering, ensuring that descriptions have a global resonance. And yet, famines have regularly been treated as distinctive national calamities, reinforcing the unity of a people through a shared calamitous experience, or 'othering' an imperial power or outside agency. The chapters in this volume explore various aspects of three catastrophic famines which struck mid-nineteenth- and early twentieth-century Europe: the Great Irish Famine (*An Gorta Mór*) of 1845 to 1850, the Finnish Famine of the late 1860s (referred to in this volume by the Finnish phrase *Suuret Nälkävuodet* – 'Great Hunger Years'), and the Ukrainian Famine (commonly known as the *Holodomor*, 'Death by Starvation') of 1932 to 1933. In addition to providing new insights into these events, on international, national and regional scales, the overall volume contributes to an increased comparative historiography in historical famine studies, and responds in particular to calls from Irish scholars to ensure that the Great Irish Famine is set in a broader international context.[4] As is often the case with comparative history, the contrasts between the cases, rather than the similarities, can be the most instructive in reassessing national narratives or in overcoming exceptionalism or path-dependency.

Recognising comparisons and contrasts

Irish scholars have recognised the Ukrainian famine of 1932/1933 as a tragedy of comparable proportions to that experienced in Ireland in the 1840s. For example, Peter Gray, in the context of the 150th anniversary of the Great Irish Famine, noted the Ukrainian famine experience: 'no peacetime European social crisis since the seventeenth century, with the possible exception of the Ukrainian famine of the early 1930s, has equalled it in intensity of scale.'[5] The Finnish case has also been noted in Irish work. Cormac Ó Gráda, for example, has emphasised the social and spatial disparities and vulnerabilities inherent in both the Irish and Finnish famine experiences – features explored in this volume: 'there are obvious parallels and contrasts worth pursuing: differential impact by region, the causes of death and the variation in deaths by age and sex, functioning of markets and communications networks.'[6] More recently, Niall Ó Ciosáin's review of the *Atlas of Great Irish Famine* noted a dearth of comparative work, particularly between Ireland, the Scottish Highlands and Finland in the nineteenth century.[7]

From a Finnish perspective, Varpu Ikonen's broad comparative overview of the Finnish and Irish famines (1991) highlights Ó Gráda's assertion that the Finnish case is 'internationally relatively unknown', and discusses the shared problems of rapid population growth and a lack of pre-famine economic diversity.[8] A start towards addressing the historiographical gaps highlighted by Ó Ciosáin has been made recently with some of output from the Academy of Finland's project, 'The Terrible Visitation: Famine in Finland and Ireland *c.*1845–68'.[9] In the early twenty-first century, the 'transnational turn' in historical research has started to make an impact in both Finland and Ireland. Recent years have seen the formation of the *Transnational Ireland* research cluster, and the Finnish Centre of Excellence in Historical Research features a regular *Finland in Comparison* seminar, based at the University of Tampere.[10] The International Network of Irish Famine Studies, based in Nijmegen and established in 2014 with funding from the Dutch Research Council, also symbolises the willingness to analyse these catastrophes from interdisciplinary but also international perspectives.[11] An international perspective also forms part of the mission statement of Harvard Ukrainian Research Institute, whose recent *Atlas of the Holodomor* project is discussed further below.[12] Although the national paradigm seems to remain dominant in historical research and teaching, these research groups demonstrate an increased willingness to adopt a comparative approach.

Bilateral and trilateral comparisons

The Finnish and Irish famines were relatively close in time, which allows for comparison within a context of emerging nationalist (and eventually separatist) movements in the two countries, as well as the relationship with the imperial powers and the effect this had on the famine relief efforts. Newby and Myllyntaus' chapter in this volume, in particular, forms an agenda for the comparative studies of the famines in Ireland and Finland. Here, the authors warn that despite the superficial similarities between the two countries in the nineteenth century, there were important constitutional and social differences which affected how the famines were tackled and remembered.

In seeking bilateral comparisons, it is arguably Ireland and Ukraine that are more comparable from the point of view of the politicisation of famines, and their appropriation in collective memory and national identity formation. Recent research presented by Noack, Janssen and Comerford has initiated a strand of comparative study of the Great Irish Famine and Ukrainian *Holodomor*, which probes the competing national narratives that have sought to interpret the famine experiences of both Ireland and Ukraine.[13] What emerge are complex pictures of economic, social, cultural, and institutional structures and transformations, both on the eve of famine and in its aftermath. The literary critic, Terry Eagleton, referred to the Great Irish Famine as 'the greatest social disaster of nineteenth-century Europe, an event with something of the characteristics of a low-level nuclear attack'.[14] The Ukrainian *Holodomor* has also formed the basis for evocative narratives. In discussing Ukraine, Heorhiy Kasianov writes: 'the 1932–33 famine emerged as a topic in Ukrainian political and public discourse during the mid-1980s and formed part of an overall critique of the Soviet past', which characterised the Holodomor as a 'tragedy of global dimensions, no less tragic than the Holocaust'.[15] A comparative context provides a basis for challenging established, often evocative, explanations of famine-era phenomena such as the workings of government relief efforts – and the underlying political processes which shaped such responses, famine-induced migration, post-famine demographic patterns, as well as the wide-ranging social and cultural ruptures brought about by the famine-era suffering and dislocation.

Death-tolls

Although many of the comparative elements to be found within this volume may be considered 'bilateral', there are nevertheless some common elements in all three cases. For example, the relative death-tolls can be examined – not as a means of instigating a competition of grief, or grievance, but because of the ways in which the figures in all cases defy precise enumeration, even though consensus may be reached on the general order of magnitude. Casualty figures for the Irish and Ukrainian famines, in particular, remain contested, subject to different methodologies (such as the time-span for the calamities) and, often, politically oriented perspectives.

Statistically, there are stark differences in the sheer numbers of deaths caused by starvation or famine-related disease in the three case studies. Nevertheless, when examining the relative percentages of the national populations implicated in the crises, it seems fair to conclude that the contemporary designations of the three events as 'Great' famines withstand scrutiny. In a more general comparative sense, a number of trilateral comparisons are evident between the Irish, Finnish and Ukrainian famine experiences: in each case famine conditions led to devastating loss of life and social dislocation. This study sees us move beyond comparison as a means of benchmarking the relative death-toll of a particular famine, towards a discussion of the spatial and socio-economic processes and relationships that characterised the onslaught of each famine crisis.

While the most striking parallel across these three famine tragedies is their appalling level of death and dislocation, the extent of famine-related mortality has not been resolved in all three cases. A certain level of consensus does appear to have emerged in recent years regarding estimates of the death-toll resulting from the Irish and Finnish famines. Excess mortality due to the Irish famine is believed to be in the region of one million famine-related deaths from a population of 8.5 million, compared to the Finnish famine's death-toll of between 100,000 and 150,000 from a population of 1.6 million.[16] Nevertheless, figures remain contested and there are still adherents to a higher death toll. In his *Famine Plot* (2012), Tim Pat Coogan argues that the under-reporting of victims during the Irish famine, and the inclusion of averted births in the statistics, would mean that nearly two million deaths would be a more accurate figure.[17] In the Ukrainian context, Donald Rayfield has argued that the 'death toll from the famine in 1932–33 seems to depend upon the methodology and trustworthiness of the demographer', even while accepting that the *Holodomor* was genocidal.[18] David Marples refers to 'between three [million] and ten million' victims, depending on the source.[19] Olga Papash has argued 'in current discussions on the 1932–33 famine, figures of up to ten million victims are quoted', noting that while these figures are 'excessive', they are nonetheless 'taken for granted in the current Ukrainian historiographical mainstream'.[20] Papash then claims that 'any significant reduction [of the figure of ten million] would not alter the situation much, as we would still be dealing with millions of premature deaths'.[21] Lubomyr Luciuk makes a similar point, observing that the *Holodomor* was arguably 'an act of genocide without parallel in European history', given that 'many millions' perished of hunger in Soviet Ukraine over a period of some six months in 1932/1933.[22]

While the total extent of famine-related mortality in Soviet Ukraine is still debated, with estimates of excess famine deaths ranging from 2.6 million[23] to five million, or higher,[24] the contribution to this volume by Omelan Rudnytskyi, Nataliia Levchuk and Pavlo Shevchuk (Institute for Demography and Social Studies, Kyiv) with Oleh Wolowyna (University of North Carolina at Chapel), as part of the *Atlas of the Holodomor* project undertaken by the Harvard Ukrainian Research Institute, represents a pioneering initiative to estimate famine mortality in Ukraine over the period 1932 to 1934.[25] Their analysis, based on reconstructed population data, reveals the variation in famine mortality across all former Soviet republics, from extremely high levels in Ukraine and Kazakhstan to very low levels in the Russian and Transcaucausian republics. Analyses of direct population losses by region (*oblast*) within Soviet Ukraine show large regional variations, from very high relative values in the Kyiv and Kharkiv *oblasts* to very low values in the Donetsk *oblast*. This contribution yields an estimate of total famine losses in Soviet Ukraine of 4.5 million, with 3.9 million direct losses and 0.6 million indirect losses out of a population of approximately 30 million. They have estimated rural and urban excess deaths at equivalent to 16.5 and 4.0 per cent of the respective 1933 populations. Even more telling, and one of the unique characteristics of the *Holodomor*, compared to all other famines, is the extremely high concentration of deaths due to starvation in a very short time period. Of the 3.9 million deaths during 1932 to 1934, 90 per cent occurred in 1933, and among all rural deaths 83 per cent took place between March and August of 1933. At the peak of this six-month period, June, the rate of deaths by starvation averaged 31,000 per day, with more than 20,000 per day in July and August 1933.[26]

In Finland, it was estimated that over 100,000 died in 1868, a figure that, while much lower than the Ukrainian and Irish cases, nonetheless approached 10 per cent of the total population.[27] Even in a country with excellent statistical information, and a much less politicized historiography of the famine, however, the figures for Finland can diverge considerably, mainly because of the different interpretations of famine's time-span. It should also be noted that the Finnish historiography's treatment of the 1860s famine is remarkable when approaching it from an Irish or Ukrainian perspective, supporting Mary Daly's more general point about the Finns' national 'amnesia' around the catastrophe. Some general histories do not mention the famine years and the excess deaths at all, whereas others deal with it cursorily.

This volume moves away, consciously, from a description of 1868 as an isolated, remarkable year, and rather builds upon Kari Pitkänen's earlier characterisation of the period as a 'decade of misery'.[28] From an Irish perspective, of course, the idea that successive disastrous harvest years led to escalating crisis seems axiomatic. However, the idea that the Finns were visited by a single disastrous year precludes full analysis of the post-Crimean economic crisis, the role of government in easing or exacerbating the crisis, or the application of 'entitlement theory' more broadly to the case. This long-term problem of recurrent famine was well known to contemporaries, both in Finland and abroad. In 1857, for example, one English newspaper reported on 'hundreds of fellow creatures dwindling away into moving skeletons and at length staggering to their graves the victims of a general starvation'.[29] Foreign audiences also read in 1862 of how 'hosts' of Finns were dying 'lingering, fearful' deaths, and how they would 'perish on the road, to be devoured by dogs and wolves'.[30] As may be seen in the population graph provided in Häkkinen and Forsberg's chapter in this volume, there was a notch in the year 1868, just as there had been during the 'Finnish War' between Sweden and Russia in 1808 to 1809, but overall the upward population trend in Finland continued unaltered by the famine.

Of course, the human cost of such a tragedy greatly exceeded that conveyed by estimated mortality rates. In the Irish case, estimates of excess mortality often preclude averted births (a bone of contention, as noted above, with commentators such as Tim Pat Coogan), believed to be in the region of 300,000, or famine-related deaths abroad. The Irish famine also triggered a wave of mass emigration, with over a million people emigrating from Ireland from 1846 to 1851.[31] In the Finnish case, migration was internal in nature and reached a peak in 1868 when approximately 100,000 individuals (5 per cent of the total population) left their home parishes. Large-scale transatlantic emigration from Finland commenced two decades after the worst of the famine years, and although Finns did form an active political group in North America, they did not agitate to any great extent against Russian rule up until Finnish independence in 1917.[32] In the Ukrainian case emigration was not an option, as Soviet Ukraine's borders were sealed, with no relief allowed in and no one allowed out, another striking difference between Ukraine's famine and the Irish and Finnish experiences.[33]

Autonomy, causation and culpability

The events which directly triggered the Irish and Finnish famines are also well established: both were subsistence crises, in the Irish case caused by the arrival of the fungus *phythophtera infestans* to Irish shores in autumn 1845 and decimating the potato crop in 1845, 1846 and 1848. In the Finnish case adverse weather conditions led to widespread cereal crop failure in 1866 to 1867, which put pressure on a society with grain stores already depleted by several bad harvests in the 1850s and early 1860s. Thus, the year of greatest mortality, 1868, cannot be understood without the context of the previous years of dearth: 1857 to 1858, 1862 and 1865 to 1866.[34] The calamity of 1867 to 1868 was not perceived as a fully 'national' emergency by the politicians in Helsinki, and the narrative developed around the idea of a general economic setback. This crisis was deemed to have been caused in part by Finland's readjustment in the 1860s to playing a full role in the international economic system, as part of its fiscal autonomy under Russian rule. As a result, Finns perceived their own plight as rather different from that suffered two decades earlier by the Irish. By examining Finland along with Ireland and Ukraine, it is possible to demonstrate that even in the event of famine in an imperial context, it is not inevitable that the imperial power will be made culpable for the catastrophe. Clearly, the existence of a Home Rule Parliament in Helsinki offset some of the potential for blaming the Russians for the 1860s famine, but there was also a strong element of self-sufficiency within the national identity that was being constructed for the Finns. Antti Häkkinen and Henrik Forsberg's chapter in this volume notes that the famine highlighted other social cleavages within Finland – cleavages which have often been erased under a narrative of common struggle – but blaming the authorities in St Petersburg was not on the agenda. There was no contemporary recollection of the biblical term 'holocaust', as happened in Ireland, and nor has there been any subsequent thought of there being an attempted 'genocide'.

The issue of culpability has also been a contentious one in interpretations of the Great Irish Famine. In documenting the historiography of the Irish Famine, Lee and Donnelly note that academic scholarship had long been dismissive of the genocidal interpretation embodied by John Mitchel's *The Last Conquest of Ireland (perhaps)*, published in 1861.[35] This divergence in famine narratives is clearly illustrated by the contrast between the two most prominent book-length studies of famine to emerge prior to the 1990s: *The Great Hunger: Ireland, 1845–1849* by Woodham-Smith (1962),[36] which shared many of Mitchel's sentiments, and *The Great Famine: Studies in Irish History, 1845–52* by Edwards and Williams (1957), a revisionist work which eschewed the traditional nationalist view of the famine. Since the 1980s a more nuanced characterisation of the Irish Famine has emerged which challenges both nationalist and revisionist narratives. Terry Eagleton noted that, although it was 'misguided', a nationalist cry of genocide over the Great Famine was understandable, and that the 'zealous sanitizing' of the revisionist school was 'as tendentious as any nationalist polemic'.[37]

'Post-revisionist' studies have been influenced conceptually by contemporary studies of hunger and poverty and methodologically by the emergence of new statistical and econometric techniques (see e.g. the quantitative study of Mokyr, and Ó Gráda's discussion of Amartya Sen's food entitlement view in the Irish context). One notable contribution is that of Gray, who analyses the response of British government and public opinion to the famine, in the context of famine-era debates about the nature and future of Irish society. Gray, drawing on archival material and the personal correspondence of famine-era policy-makers, examines the prevailing ideologies among elite British politicians and civil servants during the famine years. What emerges is a dogmatic disdain among British policy-makers for publicly funded relief efforts, predicated on ideas of moralism, a providentialist view of the famine and laissez-faire economics, which had deadly consequences for those enduring the deteriorating famine conditions. This debate regarding famine culpability can be enriched by comparative perspectives, as illustrated by Noack, Janssen and Comerford, who contend that a distinction should be made between culpability which centres on adequacy of government relief efforts and humaneness of intentions in the face of the crisis, and culpability in which the government is the instigator of the crisis.[38]

In Ireland, the Great Famine was also constructed within a 'less influential militant socialist narrative, associated especially with James Connolly', where it was portrayed as a 'class crime perpetrated against a peasant proletariat by capitalist exploiters, domestic and foreign'.[39] Where critique emerges in Finnish historiography, it comes from a similar perspective. During the 1890s, the rapidly expanding Finnish proletariat was starting to mobilise itself under the banner of socialism, and in the parliamentary elections in 1907 the social-democratic party won an astounding majority. Finland's political division was starting to form along the lines of socialists and bourgeois, which eventually clashed in the Civil War of 1918. This political demarcation is particularly interesting when we look at the interpretations of the famine in the 1860s. While the bourgeois side saw the famine as a heroic struggle, as an example of high moral self-sacrifice for future generations,[40] the socialist camp on the other hand saw it as the starting point of capitalist oppression.[41] In Ukraine's case, the argument over whether the famine was an act of genocide continues. However, recent scholarship, notably the work of an interdisciplinary group mapping famine losses and studying the further consequences of the famine for Ukrainian society, corroborates the views of Raphael Lemkin, who coined the term *genocide*, and subsequently described the famine in Ukraine as an act of genocide.[42]

Famine vulnerabilities

One theme which recurs throughout this volume is that of 'famine vulnerabilities' – the role played by social and spatial disparities in exacerbating the impact of famine, be it in Ireland, Finland or Ukraine. In analysing this issue, concepts emanating from economic geography have been particularly informative. Economic geography is an interdisciplinary field which emphasises both the role of ongoing processes of economic change, which occur unevenly across a given geographical or spatial scale, as well as the economic, social, cultural and institutional relationships among regions.[43] A prominent theme of economic geography is the diversity of economic life, with the heterogeneity of people and places being seen as paramount – in contrast to the tendency of mainstream economics to seek universal principles of economic behaviour. The intellectual foundations of economic geography are strongly contested by economists and geographers. Within the discipline of economics, economic geography focuses on incorporating into international trade theory the concepts of agglomeration economies, increasing returns to scale and imperfect competition.[44] In this volume, processes of economic and social change, and the spatial unevenness with which these transformations were experienced, are discussed in the context of specific incidences of famine-induced death, human misery and social upheaval experienced in Ireland, Finland and Ukraine.

Long-term and multi-scale perspectives

The contribution of Declan Curran considers the spatiality of the Great Irish Famine, advocating an analysis that situates distinct local and regional dimensions in their national and international context. In this way, the evolving structure of pre-famine Ireland's economy and society in which social and spatial disparities were perpetuated, the devastation wrought by the famine across an Ireland of uneven 'famine vulnerabilities', as well as the long-term socio-economic consequences for post-famine Ireland, may be seen as taking place across many geographical scales simultaneously.

Bohdan Klid discusses the famine experienced in Ukraine in 1932 to 1933 in the context of the 15 years of social and political upheaval which preceded it – a period in which Soviet rule was established in Ukraine, Ukrainian agriculture was collectivised, and grain procurement quotas were implemented. While situating the Ukrainian famine in the context of the party-state's policies towards the peasantry, Klid also explores the role played by Soviet policies aimed at quelling Ukrainian nationalist resistance in exacerbating and exploiting famine conditions, and the connections between the social and national questions in Ukraine.

Antti Häkkinen and Henrik Forsberg's chapter sets the famine years of the 1860s into a longer nineteenth-century context, highlighting the economic and social challenges and opportunities which the Finns experienced after their imperial rulers changed from Sweden to Russia in 1809. Often associated with the birth of modernity in Finland, Häkkinen and Forsberg argue that there was not a straightforward causal relationship between the famine and the subsequent modernisation and economic progress made in Finland towards the end of the nineteenth century. Furthermore, they challenge the narrative set out by the founding fathers of the nation, which promoted the idea of communality and self-enlightenment, and which erased social and regional cleavages within the country. The famine was presented as a national calamity as a means of uniting a previous disparate people, but famine mortality was not shared equally, a point which is further elucidated by Miikka Voutilainen in this volume.

Regional variations

Comparative studies also have the potential to uncover local details which have perhaps been masked by grand national master-narratives, and this volume provides a detailed local- and regional-level spatial analysis of the disparities inherent in how each respective famine unfolded, as well as a consideration of the subsequent long-run development of the famine-stricken regions, in terms of population dynamics and socio-economic indicators. Mary Kelly presents and interprets the geography of famine vulnerabilities emergent in pre-famine Ireland, utilising Geographic Information Systems (GIS) methodologies. The social geography of pre-famine Ireland is shown to be one of mounting destitution and impoverishment, as well as one of complex but weak social structures. Mid-nineteenth-century Ireland was characterised by an intricate mosaic of east–west and north–south socio-economic and cultural-environmental configurations. These pre-existing local conditions influenced how the ensuing distress was experienced by individuals and households. This local- and regional-level social complexity and spatial variation is crucial to understanding the extent of famine suffering, mortality and emigration flows, as well as obstacles hampering both effective local responses to famine and the adequacy of official relief efforts at a local level. As Mary Kelly vividly demonstrates, it was often in those very regions where deprivation was greatest and famine conditions most severe that local agency and relief infrastructure were in shortest supply. The contribution of Omelan Rudnytskyi, Nataliia Levchuk, Oleh Wolowyna and Pavlo Shevchuk, outlined above, further develops this discussion of regional variation of famine mortality. Their detailed reconstruction of population data yields new estimates of famine mortality, and reveals the marked variation in mortality rates, both at the level of Ukrainian regions (*oblast*) and across all former Soviet republics for the period 1932 to 1934.[45] In the Finnish case, Miikka Voutilainen takes an economic perspective and uses archival data to outline the considerable class and regional variations which occurred in the levels of suffering during the worst year of the Finnish famine. Voutilainen supports Antti Häkkinen's assertion that social divisions in Finland were much greater than has been acknowledged in the general historiography, and that although frost-induced harvest failures triggered the famine, these natural events were exacerbated by man-made social conditions.

Memory and identity

In *Holdomor and Gorta Mór*, the editors quite rightly argue that 'an obvious parallel' between the Irish and Ukrainian cases would be 'the centrality of the two famines for the development of modern Ireland and modern Ukraine'. This led to both feeling 'estranged from humanity', and basing a national identity on otherness and a key traumatic event in the development of the nation.[46] However, in the case of the Ukrainian Famine of 1932 to 1933 details have only begun to emerge in recent decades and the events surrounding that famine have not yet been fully resolved. It was not until 1956 that historians in the USSR were permitted to use the term 'food difficulties' in reference to this period and, even then, there was a prohibition against using the word 'famine'. Until the late 1980s, the famine of 1932 to 1933 was officially denied by Soviet scholars and officials. Outside of the Soviet Union, relatively little was known about the *Holodomor* until the appearance of Robert Conquest's *The Harvest of Sorrow* in 1986, which characterised the famine as an act of mass murder deliberately inflicted upon Ukraine in order to repress Ukrainian nationalism. Further publications supporting a genocide interpretation of the *Holodomor* followed, from Serbyn and Krawchenko to more recent examples, such as those by Naimark and Kulchytskyi.[47] This genocide thesis has been challenged by Davies and Wheatcroft,[48] Ellman[49] and Kuromiya[50] among others, who contend that the famine was the unplanned result of Stalin's catastrophic anti-peasant policies rather than a deliberate attempt to inflict famine on Ukraine, even though Raphael Lemkin, who coined the term 'genocide', applied it to the famine in Soviet Ukraine, describing it as a 'classic example of Soviet genocide'.[51]

Clearly, the Great Irish Famine has played a role in the identity of the nation. Indeed, Vanessa Pupavac has called it 'a founding myth of Irish nationalism'.[52] Pupavac juxtaposes Ireland with the 'virtually unknown' Finnish crisis:

> Strikingly, the later devastating Finnish famine of the 1860s did not lead to political crisis and remains virtually unknown outside Finland; instead, the traumatic experience prompted the Finnish state to industrialise its economy and to shift from its reliance on subsistence farming. Such capacity for progressive social change seems anathema in today's prevailing disaster models.[53]

Arguably, Pupavac could have gone even further – some histories of Finland do not mention the famine at all, despite Arne Reunala's assertion that the events of 1868 are 'indelibly marked in the memory of the Finns'.[54] Antti Häkkinen's assertion that 'the impact of the [1868] famine on the economy was of short duration, and better times soon compensated for the losses' exemplifies the standard Finnish economic historical narrative.[55] The elision of the famine years into a narrative of general economic crisis, the birth pangs of a nation, have certainly been one reason why the 1860s do not have the same resonance in Finland as the 1840s in Ireland. A further reason is the rather different core–periphery relationship between Finland and the Russian Empire. In today's Ukraine, meanwhile, the *Holodomor* has increasingly come to be seen in the context of a Soviet legacy that undermined, demographically, perhaps even spiritually, the *corpus* of the nation, this understanding echoing James Mace's description of Ukraine as a 'post-genocidal society'.[56]

Core and periphery

One of the comparisons which is highlighted in Newby and Myllyntaus' chapter is that between the constitutional relationships of Ireland and Finland to their respective empires. As a largely self-governing Grand Duchy of the Russian Empire, Finland took ever-increasing control over its own political and economic affairs during the nineteenth century, at least until the imposition of 'Russification' in 1899 and afterwards. The centralised control exercised by London over Ireland was generally absent from the Finnish case. Peter Gray's chapter builds upon the provocative assertion made by William J. Smyth in the *Atlas of the Great Irish Famine*, when he argued that 'the proper geographical and political unit for the analysis of the Great Famine is Britain and Ireland'.[57] Moreover, in stressing the imperial–colonial relationship between Great Britain and Ireland, Smyth emphasised that 'an outstanding feature' of the famine period 'was the exercise of centralised political and administrative control over Ireland and the Irish people, which increased after the passing of the union'.[58] Gray expands upon this concept by outlining the 'Great British Famine', which never existed in the minds of the British or Irish public, but which, arguably, would have been the correct constitutional framing of the events of the 1840s. Gray argues that Charles Trevelyan, who oversaw the Irish relief efforts, held a view that Ireland's difference from Britain was 'essentially moral' rather than 'socio-economic or even political'. In formulating famine relief policy in Finland, J.V. Snellman, as outlined by Myllyntaus, may have held the view that 'what is rotten may collapse', but this attitude had none of the religious or ethnic overtones implied by Trevelyan's attitude towards the Catholic, Celtic, Irish. Snellman was seeking to crystallise a nation – his economic policies were presented as guarding the nation's long-term survival by eschewing Russian intervention.

Thus, Myllyntaus and Gray demonstrate the existence of very different constitutional situations in Finland and Ireland in the nineteenth century, reflected in their diverging historiographies. As Andrew G. Newby has argued, the core–periphery relationship between Finland and Russia differed considerably from Ireland (and Britain) and Ukraine (and the Soviet Union) during these famines.

In a European context, arguably all three case studies here deal with peripheries. In an 'imperial' context, the issue is rather more complex – with Ireland and Finland both being relatively close to the imperial core (London and St Petersburg respectively), but Finland operating with a devolved 'home rule' administration. Thus, explains Newby,

> even if Snellman's policies failed, it was considered important that Finland should be left to fail alone, rather than be saved by Russian intervention. The Russians were not subsequently blamed for failing to come to Finland's rescue, nor for creating conditions in which famine could occur by treating Finland as a colony.[59]

In Ireland and Ukraine the famines 'othered' the imperial power. In Finland it bound the Finns in a national cause. Midway through the 'decade of calamities', in the face of another harvest failure, one influential Finnish newspaper expanded on the perceived link between hunger, self-sufficiency and nation building:

> Let us busy ourselves as one in providing aid, it really should not burden anyone and indeed the feelings awakened in the helpers will be a marvellous and adequate reward, the sense that the Finns have been able to help Finns out of hunger and destruction, and aid would help the overall spirit of our nation, demonstrating that the inhabitants of our country feel that they are brothers, who suffer misfortune together just as they share good times, and are faithful towards each other. This assistance binds together the children of the fatherland with an iron grip, and through this it is possible to see that they can rely on each other's help in times of hardship.[60]

Andrea Graziosi reconstructs pre-famine events in Ukraine from a comparative perspective, making reference both to overall Soviet political developments and to 'regional' or, more precisely, to national tensions. Grazioisi argues that while the famine may have initially been the inadvertent consequence of Soviet policy responses to the resistance of the peasantry to collectivization and the threat of an agricultural collapse, it subsequently in Ukraine became a politically orchestrated weapon of state power. According to Grazioisi, a fuller understanding the *Holodomor* necessitates a recognition of the overlapping nature of social (that is, the peasant) and national (that is, the Ukrainian) factors, bridging the divide between those scholars who offer an interpretation based largely on one or the other perspective.

Any study of the onset and consequences of famine is inevitably a study of death and despair. In that context, it may well be impossible to adequately convey the depths of suffering experienced by those caught up in such a maelstrom, be it at an individual level, within family units, or across localities. That said, seeking to comprehend why famine-induced death, human misery and social upheaval occur and how these shocking developments unfold remains a worthwhile endeavour. It is hoped that the parallel studies presented in this volume will challenge and enhance established understandings of famine tragedies along a number of lines, including: famine causation and culpability; social and regional famine vulnerabilities; core–periphery relationships between nations and regions; degrees of national autonomy and self-sufficiency; as well as famine memory and identity. Beyond contributing to contemporary scholarship, it is hoped that this volume will help to keep alive the memory of the many millions who suffered and perished due to famine in Finland, Ireland, and Ukraine.

Notes

1 Asenath Nicholson, *Annals of the Famine in Ireland in 1847, 1848, and 1849* (New York, 1851), 82–83.

2 *Leeds Mercury*, 14 April 1868.

3 Zetta Wells was the wife of the American explorer, author and radio commentator Carveth Wells. She went on to present the TV Show *Geographically Speaking* on NBC after 1946. This extract from her diary is recorded in Carveth Wells, *Kapoot: The Narrative of a Journey from Leningrad to Mount Ararat in Search of Noah's Ark* (London: Jarrolds, 1933), 139–140. It is also quoted in 'Memorandum: The United Ukrainian Organisation of the United States', *Svoboda*, 12 June 1934; and in *Famine in Ukraine* (New York: United Ukrainian Organizations of the United States, 1934), 15.

4 Niall Ó Ciosain, 'Cartography and Commemoration: the Atlas of the Great Irish Famine', *Irish Historical Studies* 38 (2013), 705; Gerry Kearns (ed.), 'Debating The Atlas of the Great Irish Famine', *Irish Geography* 46(3) (2013), 240, 242, 254; Cormac Ó Gráda, *Ireland's Great Famine: Interdisciplinary Perspectives* (Dublin: UCD Press, 2006), 22, 76.

5 Peter Gray, 'Famine Relief Policy in Comparative Perspective: Ireland, Scotland, and Northwestern Europe, 1845–1849', *Eire–Ireland* 32:1 (1999), 86–108. Ó Gráda has also highlighted the high death rates in Moldova during the Soviet famine of 1946–1947, which he calls 'the last famine to strike Europe'. Cormac Ó Gráda, *Famine: A Short History* (Princeton: Princeton University Press, 2009), 241.

6 Cormac Ó Gráda, *Ireland: A New Economic History* (Oxford: Clarendon Press, 1994), 208.

7 Ó Ciosain, 'Cartography and Commemoration', 705.

8 Varpu Ikonen, 'Kaksi 1800-luvun nälkäkriisiä – Suomi ja Irlanti', in *Kun Halla Nälän Tuskan Toi*, ed. Antti Häkkinen, Vappu Ikonen, Kari Pitkänen and Hannu Soikkanen (Porvoo: WSOY, 1991), 273–282.

9 See, *inter alia*, Andrew G. Newby, '"The Cold Northern Land of Suomi": Michael Davitt and Finnish Nationalism', *Journal of Irish and Scottish Studies* 6:1 (2012), 71–92; Andrew G. Newby, '"Neither Do These Tenants or their Children Emigrate": Famine and Transatlantic Emigration from Finland in the Nineteenth Century', *Atlantic Studies: Global Currents*, 11:3 (2014), 383–402; Andrew G. Newby, '"Rather Peculiar Claims Upon Our Sympathies": Britain and Famine in Finland, 1856–68', in *Global Legacies of the Great Irish Famine: Transnational and Interdisciplinary Perspectives*, ed. Marguérite Corporaal, Christopher Cusack, Lindsay Janssen and Ruud van den Beuken (London: Peter Lang, 2014), 61–80.

10 See http://transnationalireland.com (accessed 19 September 2014); www.uta.fi/yky/coehistory/index.html (accessed 19 September 2014).

11 See www.nwo.nl/en/research-and-results/research-projects/56/2300187256.html (accessed 19 September 2014).

12 The Harvard Ukrainian Research Institute's mission statement includes the study of the diverse religious and ethnic groups that make their home in Ukraine, as well as

acting as a bridge between Ukrainian studies and the study of Russia, Poland, Turkey, Belarus and Moldova. See www.huri.harvard.edu/about-huri/mission.html (accessed 22 October 2014).

13 Christian Noack, Lindsay Janssen and Vincent Comerford (eds), *Holodomor and Gorta Mór: Histories, Memories and Representations of Famine in Ukraine and Ireland* (London: Anthem Press, 2012).

14 Terry Eagleton, *Heathcliffe and the Great Hunger: Studies in Irish Culture* (London: Verso, 1995), 23.

15 Heorhiy Kasianov, 'Holodomor and the Politics of Memory in Ukraine after Independence', in *Holodomor and Gorta Mór: Histories, Memories and Representations of Famine in Ukraine and Ireland*, ed. Christian Noack, Lindsay Janssen and Vincent Comerford (London: Anthem Press, 2012), 168. For the findings of the Commission on the Ukraine Famine (22 April 1988) see Appendix A in L. Luciuk, ed., *Holodomor: Reflections on the Great Famine of 1932–1933 in Soviet Ukraine* (Kingston: Kashtan Press, 2008). Appendix B reproduces the findings of the International Commission of Inquiry into the 1932 to 1933 Famine in Ukraine (10 March 1990). On 28 November 2006 Ukraine's Parliament, the *Verkhovna Rada*, promulgated a law defining the *Holodomor* as an act of genocide.

16 Phelim P. Boyle and Cormac Ó Gráda, 'Fertility Trends, Excess Mortality, and the Great Irish Famine', *Demography* 23:4 (1986), 543–562; Joel Mokyr, *Why Ireland Starved: a Quantitative and Analytical History of the Irish Economy*, 1800–1850 (2nd edn) (London: George Allen & Unwin, 1983), 265–266; Cormac Ó Gráda, 'Mortality and the Great Famine', in *Atlas of the Great Irish Famine*, ed. John Crowley, William J. Smyth and Mike Murphy (Cork: Cork University Press, 2012), 170.

17 Coogan here uses figures from Ó Gráda and Mokyr. Tim Pat Coogan, *The Famine Plot: England's Role in Ireland's Greatest Tragedy* (New York: Palgrave Macmillan, 2012), 10.

18 Donald Rayfield, 'The Ukrainian Famine of 1933: Man-made Catastrophe, Mass Murder or Genocide?', in *Holodomor: Reflections on the Great Famine of 1932–33 in Soviet Ukraine*, ed. Lubomyr Luciuk (Kingston: Kashtan Press, 2008). This does, however, reinforce the extent to which the events of 1932 to 1933 remain contentious, particularly in a context in which some states, such as Canada, and several international organisations have classed the *Holodomor* as genocide, despite the concerted efforts of the Russian Federation. For a succinct English-language overview of the Ukrainian famine historiography, see Paul R. Magocsi, *A History of Ukraine: The Land and Its Peoples* (2nd edn) (Toronto: University of Toronto Press, 2010), 799–801. More recently Naimark has made the case for the *Holodomor* being an example of genocide. See Norman M. Naimark, *Stalin's Genocides* (Princeton, NJ: Princeton University Press, 2011).

19 David Marples, 'Ethnic Issues in the Famine of 1932–33 in Ukraine', in *Holodomor and Gorta Mór: Histories, Memories and Representations of Famine in Ukraine and Ireland*, ed. Christian Noack, Lindsay Janssen and Vincent Comerford (London: Anthem Press, 2012), 45.

20 Olga Papash, 'Collective Trauma in a Feature Film: Golod-33 As One-Of-A-Kind', in *Holodomor and Gorta Mór: Histories, Memories and Representations of Famine in Ukraine and Ireland*, ed. Christian Noack, Lindsay Janssen and Vincent Comerford (London: Anthem Press, 2012), 197.

21 Ibid.

22 Lubomyr Y. Luciuk, 'What was Sown Shall be Reaped', Foreword to *Holodomor: Reflections on the Great Famine of 1932–33 in Soviet Ukraine* (Kingston: Kashtan Press, 2008).

23 See Jacques Vallin, France Meslé, Sergei Adamets and Serhii Pyrozhkov, 'A New Estimate of Ukrainian Population Losses During the Crises of the 1930s and 1940s', *Population Studies* 56:3 (2002), 249–264; and France Meslé, Jacques Vallin, Vladimir Shkolnikov and Serhii Pyrozhkov, *Mortality and Causes of Death in 20th Century Ukraine* (Dordrecht: Springer, 2012).

24 Robert Conquest, *The Harvest of Sorrow: Soviet Collectivization and the Terror – Famine* (Oxford: Oxford University Press, 1986), 249. Conquest made a passing reference to a 1953 address by Raphael Lemkin, who coined the term 'genocide' and applied it to the famine in Soviet Ukraine. This speech, along with a foreword by Douglas Irvin-Erickson, has been reissued as Raphael Lemkin, *Soviet Genocide in the Ukraine* (Kingston: Kashtan Press, 2014).

25 See Omelan Rudnytskyi, Nataliia Levchuk, Pavlo Shevchuk and Oleh Wolowyna, 'Demography of a Man-made Human Catastrophe: The Case of Massive Famine in Ukraine 1932–1933', *Canadian Studies in Population* 42:1–2 (2015, forthcoming); and Воловина, Олег, 'Щомісячний розподіл демографічних втрат в наслідок голоду 1933 року в Україні'. *Голод в Україні у першій половині XX століття: причии та наслідки (1921–1923, 1932–1933, 1946–1947).* Матеріали Міжнародної Наукової Конференції. (Київ, 2013), 233–242.

26 James E. Mace, 'Is the Ukrainian Genocide a Myth?', *Canadian American Slavic Studies Journal* 37:3 (2003), 45–52, reprinted in L. Luciuk (ed.), *Holodomor: Reflections on the Great Famine of 1932–1933 in Soviet Ukraine* (Kingston: Kashtan Press, 2008).

27 Kari J. Pitkänen, *Deprivation and Disease. Mortality During the Great Finnish Famine of the 1860s* (Helsinki: Suomen Väestötieteellisen Yhdistyksen Julkaisuja, 1993), 116; Antti Häkkinen, 'Nälkä, Valta ja Kylä 1867–1868', in *Talous Valta ja Valtio: Tutkimuksia 1800-luvun Suomesta*, ed. Pertti Haapala (Tampere: Vastapaino, 1990), 125; John Lefgren, 'Nälänhätä Suomessa 1867–68', *Historiallinen Aikakauskirja* 72:3 (1974), 198–201.

28 Pitkänen, *Deprivation and Disease*, 51.

29 *Ladies' Newspaper*, 11 April 1857.

30 Quoted in *Glasgow Herald*, 17 January 1863.

31 S.H. Cousens, 'The Regional Variations in Emigration from Ireland Between 1821 and 1841', *Transactions and Papers of the Institute of British Geographers* 37 (1960), 15–30; David Fitzpatrick, *Irish Emigration 1820–1914* (Dublin: Irish Economic and Social History Society, 1984).

32 Newby, 'Neither Do These Tenants', 395.

33 Naimark, *Stalin's Genocides*, 73.

34 As distinct from the *Suuret Kuolonvuodet* ('Great Death Years') of the late seventeenth century.

35 James S. Donnelly, *The Irish Potato Famine* (London: Stutton, 2001); Joseph J. Lee, 'The Famine as History', in *Famine 150: Commemorative Lecture Series*, ed. Cormac Ó Gráda (Dublin: Teagasc and University College Dublin).

36 Cecil Woodham-Smith, *The Great Hunger: Ireland, 1845–1849* (New York and London: Hamish Hamilton, 1962).

37 Terry Eagleton, *Heathcliffe and the Great Hunger: Studies in Irish Culture* (London: Verso, 1995), 16, 23.

38 Noack *et al.*, 'Introduction', 12.

39 Ibid., 5.

40 See Senator August Hjelt's presentation held on 5 August 1918 at the Suomen Historiallinen Seura (Finnish Historical Society). This was published as A. Hjelt, 'Surmavuosista Suomessa 1860-luvulla', *Historiallinen Aikakauskirja* 16 (1918), 70–71. Hjelt argued that 'Unforgettable was the beauty of the virtuous strength and sublime submissiveness with which our nation stood up to its misfortunes. It did so without any grumble or tremble from the path of honesty.'

41 Edvard Gylling, 'Nälkävuodet 1867–68: Puolivuosisatamuisto', *Työväen Kalenteri* 11 (1918), 110–121; Samuli Paulaharju, 'Kun Petäjäinen Taas Pyrkii Pöydälle', *Nuori Suomi Joulualbumi* 27 (1917), 133–141.

42 See Graziosi (Chapter 9, this volume), 223–260.

43 Gordon L. Clark, Meric S. Gertler and Maryann P. Feldman, *Oxford Handbook of Economic Geography* (Oxford: Oxford University Press, 2000), 3–18.

44 Paul R. Krugman, *Geography and Trade* (Cambridge, MA: MIT Press, 1991); Masahisa Fujita, Paul Krugman and Anthony J. Venables, *The Spatial Economy: Cities, Regions and International Trade* (Cambridge, MA: MIT Press, 1999).
45 For more information on the Harvard University Ukrainian Research Institute project, MAPA, go to http://gis.huri.harvard.edu/map-gallery/demography/population-losses.html. A map of the political geography of the Great Famine was presented in Marco Carynnyk, Lubomyr Y. Luciuk and Bohdan S. Kordan, *The Foreign Office and the Famine: British Documents on Ukraine and the Great Famine of 1932–1933 in Soviet Ukraine* (Kingston: Kashtan Press, 1988). A recent publication, edited by A. Graziozi, L.A. Hajda and H. Hryn, *After the Holodomor: The Enduring Impact of the Great Famine on Ukraine* (Cambridge, MA: Harvard University Press, 2013) explores the short- and long-term consequences of the famine for Ukrainian society.
46 Noack *et al.*, 'Introduction', 1–2.
47 Stanislav V. Kulchytskyi, '*Holodomor* in Ukraine 1932–1933: An Interpretation of Facts', in *Holodomor and Gorta Mór: Histories, Memories, and Representations of Famine in Ukraine and Ireland*, ed. Christopher Noack, Lindsay Janssen and Vincent Comerford (London: Anthem Press, 2012).
48 R.W. Davies and S.G. Wheatcroft, *The Years of Hunger: Soviet Agriculture, 1931–1933* (New York: Palgrave Macmillan, 2004).
49 Michael Ellman, 'Stalin and the Soviet Famine of 1932–33 Revisited', *Europe-Asia Studies* 59 (2007), 663–693.
50 Hiroaki Kuromiya, 'The Soviet Famine of 1932–33 Reconsidered', *Europe-Asia Studies* 60 (2008), 663–675.
51 'Soviet Genocide in the Ukraine', New York Public Library, Manuscripts and Archives Division, Raphael Lemkin Papers, Raphael Lemkin ZL-273, Reel 3, Box 2, Folder 16. From the point of view of the British Foreign Office 'the fundamental ill is communism, not the weather; & famine will be more or less chronic in Russia until either communism goes or the population is greatly reduced by nature's cruel and drastic methods'. Cited in L. Luciuk, *Searching for Place: Ukrainian Displaced Persons, Canada, and the Migration of Memory* (Toronto: University of Toronto Press, 2000), fn. 2, p. 413 (from 'Famine in Russia', FO 371/8150). This prescient comment was penned on 18 August 1922. During and after the famine of 1932 to 1933 the British government covered up news about the causes and consequences of what has been described as a 'politically engineered famine'. See 'Choosing Not to See', in Marco Carynnyk, Lubomyr Y. Luciuk and Bohdan S. Kordan, *The Foreign Office and the Famine: British Documents on Ukraine and the Great Famine of 1932–1933 in Soviet Ukraine* (Kingston: Kashtan Press, 1988), and the Foreword to this volume by Michael Marrus.
52 Vanessa Pupavac, 'Natural Disasters: Trauma, Political Contestation and Potential to Precipitate Social Change', in Erica Resende and Dovile Budryte (eds), *Memory and Trauma in International Relations* (Abingdon: Routledge, 2013), 82.
53 Ibid., 82.
54 Aarne Reunala, 'The Forest and the Finns', in *Finland: People, National, State*, ed. Max Engman and David Kirby (London: Hurst, 1989), 45.
55 Antti Häkkinen, 'On Attitudes and Living Strategies in the Finnish Countryside in the Years of Famine 1867–68', in *Just a Sack of Potatoes? Crisis Experiences in European Societies, Past and Present*, ed. Antti Häkkinen (Helsinki: SHS, 1992), 150.
56 Mace, 'Is the Ukrainian Genocide a Myth?', 45–52.
57 William J. Smyth, 'The *longue durée* – Imperial Britain and Colonial Ireland', in *Atlas of the Great Irish Famine*, ed. John Crowley, William J. Smyth and Mike Murphy (Cork: Cork University Press, 2012), 46.
58 Ibid., 61.
59 Newby, 'Neither Do These Tenants', 394.
60 *Suometar*, 19 September 1862.

Part I

The Great Irish Famine [*An Gorta Mór*], 1845 to 1850

Map PI.1 Provinces and counties of Ireland.

1 From the 'haggart' to the Hudson

The Irish famine across many geographical scales

Declan Curran

Introduction

Where does the *local* end and the *regional*, *national* or *international* begin? When the impact of a natural disaster, such as an epidemic or famine, or a man-made calamity, such as armed conflict or an economic crisis, is characterised as being, say, *localised* or *regional*, does this adequately capture the manner in which this event unfolds across places and over time? Similarly, does the notion of a *national* or *international* emergency convey the variation in how such a widespread development might be experienced 'on the ground'? While what follows is ostensibly an overview of socio-economic aspects of the Great Irish Famine, this chapter highlights the fact that the impacts of such a disaster are felt across many geographic scales simultaneously and that pre-existing local and regional differences, both spatial and social, influence how the ensuing distress is experienced by individuals and households.[1] This chapter discusses pre- and post-famine Ireland in an international context, while at the same time acknowledging the local and regional distinctions within Ireland that had become firmly established in the years prior to the famine.[2]

Ireland before the famine

During the late 1700s and early 1800s, Ireland experienced a period of rapid social and economic change. In an international context, a series of technological improvements in textiles and a major geopolitical event, the Napoleonic Wars of 1793 to 1815, provided a great stimulus to Irish economic development and, through their interaction with existing social and economic structures within Ireland, these developments had far-reaching consequences for Irish living standards. The Napoleonic Wars, in particular, brought about a wartime boom in farm prices, which benefited not only large dairy farmers but also smallholders involved in tillage and pig production. At the same time, textiles had emerged as an important cottage industry, supplementing rural farm incomes. These economic developments were accompanied by an unprecedented population explosion, particularly in Connaught and Munster whose greater proportion of small farmers reaped the benefits of the wartime boom.[3] However, the end of the war in 1815, along with the collapse of the domestic textile industry, ushered in an era of economic turbulence between 1815 and the eve of the famine.

Pre-famine economic development

As the 1700s progressed, increased British industrialisation led to a strengthening in demand for Irish agricultural exports and ushered in an era of prolonged agriculture price increases. Crotty points to the repeal of the Cattle Acts in 1760 as the embodiment of Britain's changing economic orientation from finding markets for its own agricultural output to finding food supplies for its manufacturers and commercial consumers.[4] The Cattle Acts, enacted in the 1680s, placed an embargo on the British importation of livestock from Ireland. In Crotty's view, these acts had inadvertently served as the catalyst for Ireland's one great industry of the eighteenth century: the provisions trade. Trade in salted meats emerged in place of the export of livestock, and these foodstuffs were exported to Britain, its colonies, and mainland Europe. Subsidiary trades such as cooperage, tanning and tallow manufacturing also emerged, and the resultant increase in employment and income created a strong domestic demand for dairy produce and corn.

Irish agriculture was further boosted by Britain's involvement in the Napoleonic wars (1793–1815). These wars were characterised by economic warfare between Britain and France, as each tried to restrict the other country's trade.[5] The outlook for Irish agriculture remained positive as long as Britain continued to wage war. War necessitated the suspension of the Gold Standard (the convertibility of paper currency notes into a fixed quantity of gold) and ushered in a period of price inflation, it conferred near-monopoly status on Ireland as supplier of British foodstuff due to the blockade of continental food supplies, and it presented Irish Agriculture with the lucrative requirements of the British army and navy for provisions.[6] However, Cullen notes that Irish prosperity during this period may have owed more to price increases than to increased volumes of exports: Irish exports rose by 120 per cent in monetary terms over the duration of the Napoleonic wars, while the volume of exports rose by only 40 per cent over this period.[7]

It was grain exports, in particular, that benefited from the surge in British wartime demand and this gave impetus to a restructuring of Irish agricultural production from pasture to tillage.[8] Tillage gave a higher gross output per acre than either dairy farming or grazing.[9] Legislation providing government bounties to grain exporters in 1758 and 1784 reinforced this trend.[10] The emergence of the potato in Irish society in the 1750s, with its appeal both as a high-yield root crop and as a nutrition-rich subsistence food for labourers, also contributed to both economic growth and rapid population growth. According to Crotty, the labour-intensive nature of tillage encouraged the subdivision of landholdings in order to provide additional labourers with a means of subsistence through potato cultivation.[11] Cullen, on the other hand, contends that the expansion of the potato crop was a response to, rather than a cause of, Irish population growth: the growing population reduced the price of labour and thus made a shift into more labour-intensive arable crops more attractive.[12] As Mokyr notes, arable production as a whole benefited from a technological improvement in the shape of accelerating diffusion of potatoes after 1750.[13] Taken together, the wartime boom and the potato's emergence as the ultimate subsistence crop brought about a vast agricultural expansion in the form of increased tillage acreage.

The end of the war in 1815 brought with it severe difficulties for Irish agriculture, particularly for tillage farming.[14] The reopening of the British market to grain imports from continental Europe, demobilisation of the British army and navy, and the falling prices associated with the return to the gold standard all combined to create a more challenging environment for Irish agriculture. A banking crisis in 1820, due to Bank of Ireland's efforts to restrict credit in the face of Britain's deflationary return to the gold standard, and again in 1826, as a currency union between Ireland and Britain was being implemented as part of the 1800 Act of Union, prolonged the difficulties of the agricultural industry.[15] Irish agriculture did overcome this post-war slump, as prices of grain, livestock and livestock products began to recover in the 1830s, and export volumes of livestock, grain and butter expanded once again.[16] However, the domestic textiles industry, which had been the second major area of economic expansion in eighteenth-century Ireland, entered into a terminal decline during this period.

Towards the end of the eighteenth century, exports of non-agricultural goods, particularly linen, cotton and woollen goods, increased significantly relative to agricultural exports. By the 1790s, the Irish Customs Ledger indicated that textiles accounted for 60 per cent of the value of total Irish exports, almost double the value of all Irish agricultural exports combined.[17] O'Malley attributes the burgeoning Irish textile industry at this time to the labour-intensive nature of the work and relatively low Irish wages, while he traces the origins of the Ulster's strength in this industry to the seventeenth-century influx of Hugoenot and British immigrants skilled in textile manufacturing.[18] Linen was the most successful of the Irish textile industries and by 1800 linen had developed into a major rural cottage industry, emerging in northeast Ulster and spreading across the northern half of the country and into isolated parts of the west.[19] The principal export markets for Irish linen were Britain and North America.[20] The textile industry provided an additional source of employment and income, with many families working in both agriculture and domestic textile production. Many landless labourers and smaller tenant farmers earned additional income, either by spinning yarn or weaving coarser fabrics, while many weavers rented a plot of land where they grew potatoes but paid the rent from weaving earnings.[21]

In the early 1800s, the linen industry was adapting to mechanised technology at a slower pace than the cotton industry. Belfast experienced a move away from linen to cotton, and cotton spinning mills began to concentrate in the Belfast area. Outlying districts of Ulster and beyond remained active in the linen industry, particularly in fine linen where they had established a strong competitive position.[22] Eventually, technological advances were incorporated into Irish linen production. Wet spinning, devised in France in 1810, was introduced in Britain and Ireland in the 1820s.[23] Now powered spinning of fine linen was possible and, in the face of competitive pressures, many Belfast cotton mills changed over to linen production. Belfast's large population of skilled weavers and existing mills put it in a strong position to capitalise on the new linen technology and establish itself as an early centre of mechanised fine linen spinning.[24] However, the domestic textile industry that had provided supplementary income to the rural poor could not compete in the face of large-scale mechanised production. Landless labourers, cottiers and smaller tenant farmers were now almost exclusively dependent on farming, and in particular the potato crop, for subsistence.

While there appears to be a consensus that Ireland experienced a process of deindustrialisation in the first half of the nineteenth century, a divergence of views has emerged with respect to the extent and cause of this deindustrialisation.[25] Regarding the extent of deindustrialisation, Cullen argues that deindustrialisation was confined to the textile industry, and that other domestic industries such as milling, brewing, iron founding, shipbuilding, rope making, paper and glass making benefited from large-scale production and centralisation.[26] Both Mokyr and Solar, on the other hand, speak of a wider deindustrialisation process.[27] As for the causes of deindustrialisation, the traditional nationalist view, as articulated by O'Brien, held that the removal of protective tariffs brought about by the Act of Union left Irish industry exposed to free trade with Britain's larger, more advanced industries.[28] Ó Gráda, however, questions whether or not the 10 per cent tariffs (Union dues) removed in the 1820s as a consequence of the Act of Union would have been sufficient to protect Irish industry from competitive pressures exerted by British industry, given the dramatic decline in the prices of British industrial output.[29] Mokyr attributes Irish deindustrialisation to weak trading performance in the face of competition arising from proximity to newly industrialised Britain.[30] Lee points to the transport improvements that exposed Irish rural industries to competition from British large-scale producers, and attributes the absence of Irish large-scale producers to the lack of Irish entrepreneurship, as well as a dearth of natural resources.[31] However, O'Malley argues that deindustrialisation may not have been primarily due to internal inadequacies in local social or economic conditions, such as deficiencies in entrepreneurship, capital availability or education levels, but to the existence of a strong competitor in the form of Britain, who benefited from being a pioneer of large-scale, specialised and geographically concentrated production processes.[32] Bielenberg characterises the impact of British industrialisation upon Ireland as a mixed story: while it presented Irish industry with enhanced opportunities in terms of technology, capital, markets, trade networks and consumer goods, British competition brought about the decline of a number of Irish industries and contributed to regional economic decline and emigration.[33]

Ó Gráda cautions against painting an overly pessimistic picture of Irish economic development in the decades prior to the famine.[34] Advances took place in road and sea transport, as well as in carriage of mail and goods, and the Irish banking sector developed in a similar manner to its English counterpart.

However, the decline of Irish industry and fluctuations in Irish agriculture led to a deterioration of the position of the poor, who accounted for at least half of the population prior to the famine, and left them particularly vulnerable to the famine onslaught when it struck.[35]

Pre-famine economic geography and land ownership

The changing economic fortunes of the pre-famine decades were played out in the context of a broader social transformation, which exacerbated Ireland's susceptibility to the oncoming famine crisis. Inherent in this social transformation were spatial and social differences that created distinct vulnerabilities to famine across the country.

Mokyr notes that, in terms of economic geography, pre-famine Ireland has tended to be characterised as comprising three main regions: (1) the eastern, central and southeastern counties, including Leinster and east Munster, which included much of the land held as large tenant farms, with landless labourers and smallholders providing the supply of labour; (2) the northern counties, including most of Ulster and north Connaught, where farming was combined with rural industry, and smallholders held a large proportion of the land, and (3) the west and southwest, which contained features similar to those of the other two regions, but was relatively more backward and less prosperous.[36] Daly provides further detail on the regional dispersion of agriculture across the country, noting that commercial farming was prominent on the better and drier land of the east and southeast, which was also nearer to the British market, while the transport of grain from the midlands was facilitated by a network of canals.[37] The more remote areas of the west, northwest and southwest suffered from poorer soil quality, a wetter climate, and from greater difficulties in gaining access to export markets due to high transport costs.

These regional and social differences in pre-famine agricultural commercialisation are also highlighted by Ó Gráda, who points first to the west of the country as undertaking less commercial farming, due to farm sizes being smallest and dependence on the potato as a subsistence crop being greatest, and second to smallholders and labourers nationwide undertaking less commercial farming, partly because they consumed the subsistence potato crop produced on their plot of land and paid their rent mostly in labour.[38]

An indication of the socio-economic variation within pre-famine Ireland may be gleaned from the 1841 census. The 1841 census classifies families according to their means into four categories: (1) property owners, and farmers of more than 50 acres; (2) artisans, and farmers of 5 to 50 acres; (3) labourers and smallholders of up to five acres; and (4) a 'means unspecified' category. For rural districts of the country as a whole, the first two categories accounted for 30 per cent of families.[39] A further 68 per cent of rural families consisted of labourers, smallholders with less than five acres, and less prosperous artisans, while 2 per cent of families were unspecified. However, these first two categories of larger landholdings combined ranged from 40 to 42 per cent in some eastern counties to below 23 per cent in the western counties of Donegal, Sligo, Leitrim, Roscommon, Mayo, Galway and Clare. These percentages actually understate the variation within these counties, as sharp contrasts existed between better-off and poorer districts. Districts of impoverished smallholders were also to be found in peninsular Kerry and southwest Cork.[40]

Land ownership in pre-famine Ireland largely resided in the hands of several thousand landlords, most of whom were descendants of families granted land either by Cromwell or the British Crown in the seventeenth century. Landlords were typically of Anglo-Irish stock and Protestant religion, though some traditional Irish landlords had survived.[41] Few landlords were actively involved in managing their estates. Instead they rented their land on long-term leases in order to receive a secure fixed income. These leases were often granted to large tenants, known as middlemen, who then sublet portions of land to numerous smaller tenants. However, the fluctuations in agricultural prices from the late 1700s onward, initially rising during the Napoleonic wars and then declining in the period after 1815, led many landlords to reconsider their leasing practices. The inflation of the late 1700s reduced the real value of landlords' rental income from long-term leases, and long-term leases also left landlords unable to benefit from rising land values. As a result, landlords increasingly came to favour shorter leases.[42] The turbulent economic conditions after 1815 brought about a situation whereby grazing, rather than tillage, began to generate higher yields. This created an incentive for landlords to consolidate holdings and led to a deterioration in the tenant–landlord relationship.[43]

As well as the subdivision of land undertaken by middlemen, the labour requirements of tillage farming also led to the division of land into smaller plots. Commercial famers made agreements with permanent labourers, known as cottiers, whereby the cottier provided his labour to the farmer for a fixed daily rate. The cottier would also rent a portion of land (*conacre*) from the farmer for a fixed annual sum on a short-term lease. On this parcel of land, the cottier could build a cabin and grow the subsistence potato crop. The rent on this plot of land was paid through days of labour provided to the farmer. Casual labourers (*spalpeen*) also rented *conacre* plots, but their employment was less secure than that of cottiers. These casual labourers often received monetary payment, although potatoes, turf and other provisions were also used as a means of payment.[44]

Subdivision of land also took place on smaller non-commercial farms. In some cases, small and medium-sized farmers supplemented their income by subletting small plots of land to labourers. More often, subdivision took place within families to provide for a son or act as a dowry for a daughter's marriage.[45] This process of subdivision led to the formation of ever smaller landholdings as families were pushed on to marginal land suitable only for potato cultivation.

Pre-famine living standards and demographics

Irish living standards in the decades leading up to the famine compared poorly with the rest of the United Kingdom and were characterised by increasing inequality and regional disparity.[46] Irish income per capita in the early 1840s have been estimated to be approximately half that of the prevailing British wage level, and O'Rourke concludes that unskilled wages were stagnant, if not falling, in pre-famine Ireland.[47]

Mokyr and Ó Gráda, in a detailed analysis of Irish living standards in the half-century prior to the famine, conclude that while the urban and middle classes may have seen some moderate increase in their incomes, the landless poor experienced increasing impoverishment.[48] Although the nutritional content of the potato and widespread access to heating fuel in the form of turf may have ameliorated conditions somewhat for landless labourers and cottiers, the collapse of the cottage textile industry had a devastating impact in many rural areas and led to an increased dependence on the potato crop as a means of subsistence. The marked regional disparities in living standards are evident from the illiteracy data reported in the 1841 census, which put illiteracy in the 16- to 25-year age cohort at 27.6 per cent and 29.5 per cent for Ulster and Leinster, respectively, compared to 48.5 per cent and 62.5 per cent for Munster and Connaught, respectively. The proportion of illiteracy for older age cohorts in Munster and Connaught was within a range of 60 to 80 per cent. In the words of Mokyr and Ó Gráda, 'Leinster and Ulster were relatively literate, while throughout Connaught and Munster one of the last mainly pre-literate cultures in north-western Europe was to be found'.[49]

The deteriorating conditions of the Irish poor brought about by economic turmoil, dependence on the potato crop and subdivision of landholdings occurred in an era of rapid population growth. In the century preceding the famine, the Irish population increased at a rate unparalleled anywhere else in Western Europe (see Table 1.1). On the eve of the famine, Ireland's population stood at 8.5 million.

Pre-famine population growth had both a social and spatial dimension. Population grew most rapidly among labourers as a class generally and in counties where large regions of smallholders existed, such as Galway, Clare, Mayo and Donegal.[50] In these regions, the continued subdivision of landholdings and movement of families on to marginal, poorer quality plots of land which yielded little beyond potatoes had coincided with the decline of the cottage textile

Table 1.1 Comparison of European population growth rates (% per annum), 1750 to 1845

Country	*Population growth (%)*
France	0.4
England	1.0
Ireland	1.3
Scotland	0.8
Sweden	0.7

Source: J. Mokyr and C. Ó Gráda, 'New Developments in Irish Population History, 1700–1850', *Economic History Review* (1984, p. 476, table 2).

industry. Together, these factors exerted pressure on the living standards of the pre-famine rural poor and contributed to the mounting regional and spatial inequalities. Table 1.2 documents provincial population growth rates in the decades prior to the famine.

The expanding Irish population in the first half of the nineteenth century withstood the impact of two other prominent pre-famine demographic adjustments: a fall in birth rates and a sharp increase in emigration. Boyle and Ó Gráda provide estimates of falling Irish birth rates in the 20 years before the famine, declining from an estimated crude birth rate of 42 per 1,000 in 1822 to 36 per 1,000 in 1841.[51] As Boyle and Ó Gráda note, these birth rates and their downward trajectory bear strong similarities to British birth rate trends for the same period.[52] While large-scale emigration may be regarded as a defining characteristic of the famine years, the phenomenon had already become firmly established in the decades prior to the famine. In the three decades after 1815 over one million emigrants left Ireland, as the country became the largest European source of long-distance emigrants relative to home population.[53]

Movement between Ireland and Britain had long been commonplace, particularly in the context of the seasonal migration of labourers. Irish emigrants to Britain were not registered at any port, but the British Census of 1841 reported the number of persons born in Ireland residing in Britain as 419,256.[54] Transatlantic movement had been impeded by the Napoleonic wars, but it resumed on a large scale when hostilities ceased in 1815. Emigration to North America is estimated to have risen from 13,000 per annum in the early 1820s to well in excess of 50,000 per annum on the eve of the famine.[55] The majority of early emigrants to North America were from Ulster, of Scots Presbyterian heritage, whose departure was triggered by the deterioration of the linen industry. Daly points to New York emigration statistics which show that, for the period 1820 to 1834, Ulster and Leinster had around equal shares, together accounting for almost 80 per cent of emigrants, whereas Connaught accounted for a mere 6.7 per cent of emigrants. However, in the decade leading up the famine the Connaught share of Irish emigrants to New York almost doubled and it doubled again during the famine years.[56]

Table 1.2 Provincial population growth rates (% per annum), 1791 to 1821 and 1821 to 1841

Province	*Population growth (%)*	
	1791–1821	*1821–1841*
Leinster	1.3	0.6
Munster	1.6	1.1
Ulster	1.1	0.9
Connaught	2.0	1.2

Source: C. Ó Gráda, *Ireland: A New Economic History* (p. 6, table I.I), based on W.E. Vaughan and A.J. Fitzpatrick (eds) *Irish Historical Statistics: Population 1821–1971* (Royal Irish Academy, Dublin, 1978).

Cousens posits that a number of interrelated factors influenced the regional distribution of emigration between 1821 and 1841: the decline of the textile industry; tenant rights that facilitated emigration, such as the 'Ulster Custom' whereby an outgoing tenant was entitled to payment for improvements made to landholdings; religious and cultural minority groups fearful of hostility; and the expiry of old leases that had previously been held under favourable terms.[57] The deteriorating economic conditions of the pre-famine decades brought about a change in the emigrant profile. According to Daly, the poorest parts of Ireland were underrepresented among the early emigrants, possibly due to prohibitive travel costs, lack of information regarding opportunities abroad, or the barrier posed by the Irish language.[58] But Fitzpatrick notes that 'from the 1840s onwards, emigration was not only intensive from virtually every county but also most heavily concentrated in the regions of greatest poverty and least off-farm employment'.[59]

The famine onslaught

The blight that decimated the Irish potato crop for three harvests over the period 1845 to 1848 was the catalyst for one of the last major famines to be seen in the Western world. Despite being unsuited to storage or transportation, the potato's high nutritional content, relatively dependable yield even in poor soil during the pre-famine years, and its suitability as a foodstuff for both man and livestock led to an over-dependence on the crop, particularly among the poorer layers of Irish society. By 1845, according to Ó Gráda, the potato's share in tilled acreage was little short of one-third and about three million people were largely dependent on it for food.[60] As Kinealy notes, 'the Great Irish Famine remains unsurpassed, in relative terms, in terms of demographic decline with the Irish population falling by approximately 25% in just six years, due to a combination of excess mortality and emigration'.[61] While the devastation of the potato crop may have triggered the famine, the interaction of the complex set of economic and social issues discussed in the previous section exacerbated Irish vulnerability to famine and ultimately contributed to the shocking levels of distress witnessed during the famine years.

The onset of potato blight

The direct cause of the Great Irish Famine was the fungus *Phytophthora infestans*, which decimated the Irish potato crop in the harvesting seasons of 1845, 1846 and 1848. The introduction of the pathogen to Europe has been well documented by Bourke and Dowley.[62] *Phytophthora infestans* was recorded in the northeastern area of the USA between 1843 and 1845, with initial theories suggesting that it may have originated in the northern Andes region of South America and more recent research pointing to Mexico.[63] As European potato crops had endured problems with dry rot in the preceding years, large quantities of more resistant potato varieties were brought into Belgium from the USA for the 1844 planting season. The disease appears to have entered Europe with these imports, as its presence was detected in Belgium by the end of June 1845. The fungus had spread from Belgium to the Netherlands by mid-July, and on to France, Germany and southern England by mid-August. By late August *Phytophthora infestans* had arrived in Ireland, where it was first observed in the Dublin area. When the potato blight struck Ireland in autumn 1845, it destroyed about one-third of that year's potato crop and nearly the entire potato crop of 1846. After a respite in 1847, the potato blight returned with a vengeance in 1848, destroying most of that year's harvest.

From its introduction into Ireland in the mid-seventeenth century, the potato crop established itself as the mainstay of the Irish diet prior to the famine. The progress of the potato in pre-famine Ireland is chronicled by Bourke, who tracks the crop's role from being a supplementary food in a diet comprising cereal and milk, as well as being a fall-back foodstuff in case of famine in the early 1700s to a standard winter food of the poor later in the mid-1700s.[64] It eventually became the staple diet of small farmers over the greater part of the year, and an important part of the diet of all classes in the late 1700s. In the decades prior to the famine this progression culminated in an over-dependence on inferior potato varieties. By the early 1800s, superior potato varieties such as the Black Potato and the Apple had given way to the infamous Lumper potato, which was high yielding but low in nourishment and better suited to use as animal fodder. The significance of the potato crop reverberated through the social and demographic development of pre-famine Ireland. For example, Daly contends that as potato cultivation removed the need to invest in cattle, it may have facilitated earlier marriages, a higher birth rate and greater population density.[65] Potatoes could be cultivated in soil which was unsuitable for other tillage crops, particularly wetter, poorer quality lands of the west of Ireland. As a nutritious source of subsistence food whose cultivation required smaller plots of land than either milk or grain production, the potato crop facilitated the subdivision of landholdings into ever smaller plots and ultimately contributed to pre-famine Ireland's rapid population expansion.

As mentioned above, Ireland was not alone in being struck by potato blight in 1845. The disease was prevalent across many European countries. However, the experiences of other European countries differed markedly from the Irish experience, as social and economic structures and development differed markedly both between and within European countries. For example, the Netherlands boasted the highest levels of GDP per capita of the Western European countries in the 1850s (more than twice that of Ireland), as well as greater levels of non-agricultural employment and urbanisation.[66]

The role of the potato in the average Irish diet was far greater than in the rest of Western Europe, with Irish daily potato consumption per capita more than double the Prussian or Netherlands equivalent.[67] Within Ireland the share of the average diet accounted for by potatoes exhibited a marked social variation. Ó Gráda estimates that, on the eve of the famine, Irish labourers – 40 per cent of the Irish population – accounted for over 60 per cent of human annual potato consumption. Cottiers (17 per cent of the population) and small farmers (6 per cent of the population) accounted for 13 per cent and 5 per cent of annual potato consumption, respectively.[68] When the potato blight struck in autumn 1845, potato yields in Ireland and regions of northern France declined by 20 to 30 per cent, whereas Belgium and the Netherlands suffered losses of closer to 80 per cent. However, in 1846 the potato crop in both Ireland and the Scottish Highlands was decimated, with yields down by over 80 per cent. Potato yields improved in Belgium and the Netherlands in 1846, though yields in these countries and in Prussia were still around 50 per cent less than normal yields. It was the failure of the rye harvest and the greatly reduced wheat harvest that exacerbated the situation in these countries in 1846, as bread from these crops was more prominent than potatoes in the continental European diet.[69] As cereal yields improved after 1846, the impact of the potato blight was considerably less in continental Europe relative to the Irish experience.

Famine mortality

While precise enumeration of the famine death-toll is impossible, estimates place the level of excess mortality due to the famine at one million deaths, nearly one-eighth of the entire population.[70] This figure does not include births which did not take place due to the famine, estimated to be in the region of 300,000, or famine-related deaths abroad. Boyle and Ó Gráda also find that famine mortality was particularly heavy on the young (under five) and the old (over 60) age cohorts.[71] Daly speculates that these groups probably had the greatest difficulty in gaining access to food or relief, were the least capable of earning a living, and were the least mobile in the search for food. Furthermore, according to Daly: 'the young had the least resistance to dysentery or infectious diseases, while typhus, which was extremely prevalent during famine years, caused many deaths among the elderly because it affected the heart'.[72] The vast majority of those who perished succumbed to dysentery, typhus, typhoid fever, and other hunger-induced infectious diseases. Outright starvation was not a major cause of death during the famine years.[73]

While the famine's grip extended across the whole of Ireland, its death-toll was distributed very unevenly across the country. Donnelly reports the provincial breakdown of excess mortality as follows: Connacht accounted for 40.4 per cent, Munster for 30.3 per cent, Ulster for 20.7 per cent, and Leinster for 8.6 per cent.[74] Mokyr's county-level estimates of excess mortality resulting from the famine (Table 1.3), as well as earlier county-level estimates of Cousens, illustrate that, rather than being uniform across provinces, mortality levels varied markedly from county to county.[75] Excess mortality was highest in the western counties of Galway, Leitrim Mayo, Roscommon and Sligo. High excess mortality was also evident in the Munster counties of Cork, Kerry and Tipperary, as well as in south Ulster (Cavan and Monaghan). In contrast, excess mortality rates were relatively lower in east Leinster (particularly Dublin) and in northeast Ulster (Antrim, Down and Derry). The protracted

Table 1.3 Average annual excess death rates, 1846 to 1851, by county (per 1,000)

County	*Upper bound*	*Lower bound*	*County*	*Upper bound*	*Lower bound*
Antrim	20.3	15.0	Limerick	20.9	10.0
Armagh	22.2	15.3	Londonderry	10.1	5.7
Carlow	8.8	2.7	Longford	26.7	20.2
Cavan	51.8	42.7	Louth	14.6	8.2
Clare	46.5	31.5	Mayo	72.0	58.4
Cork	41.8	32.0	Meath	21.2	15.8
Donegal	18.7	10.7	Monaghan	36.0	28.6
Down	12.5	6.7	Queen's	29.1	21.6
Dublin	0.7	−2.1	Roscommon	57.4	49.5
Fermanagh	39.1	29.2	Sligo	61.1	52.1
Galway	58.0	46.1	Tipperary	35.0	23.8
Kerry	36.1	22.4	Tyrone	22.3	15.2
Kildare	12.0	7.4	Waterford	30.8	20.8
Kilkenny	18.1	12.5	Westmeath	26.3	20.0
King's	24.9	18.0	Wexford	6.6	1.7
Leitrim	50.2	42.9	Wicklow	14.6	10.8

Source: Mokyr, *Why Ireland Starved* (1983, p. 267, table 9.2).

nature of the famine is also borne out in the regional mortality rates. The south and west of the country is thought to have been hit particularly hard by the amendment of the Poor Law in 1847 (discussed below), which placed the full burden of financing poor relief on the Irish rate payer and facilitated large-scale eviction by landlords.[76]

Mokyr's quantitative analysis points to a number of explanatory variables which may account statistically for variation in excess mortality across Irish counties: income levels – higher income facilitated greater dis-saving or borrowing and made emigration less of an obstacle; literacy – which Mokyr speculates may have been correlated with other socio-economic characteristics such as personal hygiene, ability to adapt to other foods such as Indian corn, and knowledge about emigration opportunities; and farm size of under 20 acres, which includes both the smallest farmers and somewhat larger holdings.[77] The Devon Commission, established by the British Parliament to undertake an examination of Irish landholding practices, reported in 1845 that only a quarter of Irish farm holdings prior to the famine exceeded 20 acres.[78]

A more palpable sense of the horrors of the famine emerges from the recollections and 'memories' passed in oral tradition from famine survivors to the following generations. Oral histories, such as those gathered by the Irish Folklore Commission in the 1940s have been studied by McHugh and Póirtéir, among others.[79] Below are a number of extracts which convey the manner in which suffering and trauma had become commonplace during the famine:

> The beginning of 1847 saw want and hunger all over the country. The poor were the worst. They had nothing. What made matters very trying and hard

in these districts was the number of starving creatures that having left their homes in the Skibbereen and Bantry districts travelled around these parts looking for a bite to eat.

(Séamus Reardon, b.1873, Boulteen, Eniskeane, Co. Cork [IFC 1071:77–154, as reported in Póirtéir (1995, p. 111)])

The 'black fever' followed. This appeared in black spots which gradually crossed the body, lips became bloodless. Death followed at home if they were not removed to the workhouse and there seems to be no tradition that anyone catching the disease survived.... It was dreaded more than actual hunger and when persons were found dead in the fields or along the road, their own kith and kin often denied knowing them.

(Thomas Flynn, John Melody, Attymass, Ballina, Co. Mayo [IFC 1069: 351–378, as reported in Póirtéir (1995, p. 105)])

1847 was a worse year here than the previous two. People in general were weaker from the effects of the two previous years of scarcity, and less able to resist the attack of any epidemic. There were more deaths in 1847 than in 1845–46 due more to fever than starvation.

(Michael Gildea, b. 1872, Dromore, Ballintra, Co. Donegal [IFC 1074: 441–454, as reported in Póirtéir (1995, p. 96)])

Relief efforts

A national system of poor relief had been established in Ireland prior to the famine by the Irish Relief Act of 1838. The Irish Poor Law differed from the English model in that relief was to be provided within the workhouse, rather than outdoors.[80] The Act established a system of 130 administrative unions, each to have a workhouse where the destitute would work for their keep. However, this workhouse system was only designed to deal with levels of destitution experienced in normal times, and with a capacity of 100,000 it was not adequate to cope with the distress levels witnessed during the famine.[81] With the onset of the famine, the earliest measure taken by the Tory government of Sir Robert Peel was the procurement of £100,000 worth of Indian corn and meal from the United States, with the supplies arriving in Ireland from February to June 1846. Local relief committees and a network of food depots were set up to distribute the food, though with some delay. A scheme of public works, mostly involving road improvements, was established in order to provide employment so that the destitute could purchase food. The public works schemes were overseen by either county grand juries, in which case the entire cost of the works was borne by the county, or a local Board of Works, whereby half of the funds advanced were to be repaid to the British Treasury and half chargeable to a consolidated fund.[82] By March 1847 the public works employed 700,000 people (one-twelfth of the Irish population) but this did not succeed in containing the famine, as the public works schemes did not target the neediest, paid too low a wage, and exposed the malnourished and poorly clothed to harsh weather conditions.[83]

In spring 1847 the new Whig administration of Sir John Russell replaced the public works scheme with a system of soup kitchens. These soup kitchens were also financed by local ratepayers and private subscriptions from local landowners, and provided meal-based gruel for three million people daily.[84] The soup kitchen scheme was brought to an end in September 1847, as mortality rates appeared to wane, food prices fell, and demand for seasonal work was anticipated. However, a further season of complete potato crop failure was to follow in 1848. The British government's relief policy from September 1847 onward was predicated on shifting the burden of financing relief from the British Treasury to Irish landlords and tenants, with the workhouse system becoming the main thrust of subsequent relief efforts.[85] The Poor Law Amendment of 1847 placed the financing of relief fully on the Irish ratepayer at a local level and the infamous Gregory Clause prohibited tenants with landholdings of more than a quarter of an acre from accessing relief. The Gregory Clause led to a wave of land clearances and evictions, as landlords sought to remove impoverished cottiers from their propery.[86] Estimates of the number of evictions over the course of the famine vary greatly: Vaughan estimates that over 70,000 families were evicted over the period 1846 and 1853, while analysis undertaken by O'Neill puts the number of evicted families at 144,759 for the period 1846 to 1854.[87] Both evictions and incidences of agrarian violence were most prevalent within the provinces of Munster and Connaught. Many smallholders were forced to give up their land in order to qualify for relief, losing their homes in the process and swelling the numbers dependent on the workhouse system. The numbers seeking relief within the workhouses rose to 932,284 in 1849, with a further 1,210,482 seeking outdoor relief.[88] The overcrowded workhouse system, with its regime of hard labour and conditions that spread contagious diseases, led to very high mortality rates within workhouses. Acording to Ó Gráda, about a quarter of all excess famine mortality occurred within the workhouse system.[89]

The emigration exodus

From 1846 to 1851, over one million people emigrated from Ireland.[90] Irish emigration was not immediately impacted by the failure of the potato crop in the autumn of 1845.[91] It was the second, more widespread, season of blight in 1846 that triggered an immediate large-scale exodus in which travellers embarked on risky winter transatlantic crossings with little or no food provisions. The first wave of emigrants were mainly poor cottiers, but were soon followed by smallholders of all types. Daly notes that farmers with holdings of 20 acres or more and businessmen dependent on the rural market were well represented among the 1847 transatlantic emigrants.[92] Only a small minority of emigrants were facilitated through state-assisted emigration. According to Cousens, assisted emigration to North America between1846 and 1852 accounted for less than 5 per cent of the total movement.[93] Any sponsored schemes proposed by the British government faced numerous obstacles, such as the necessity of securing colonial approval, logistical difficulties in organising such a project, the prevailing *laissez-faire* attitude towards public expenditure, as well as the vast voluntary emigration that was already occurring. Proposals drawn up by the British Whig administration for systematic emigration to Canada were defeated in 1846 and again in 1848.[94]

Internal migration within Ireland took place also, though it remains an under-researched aspect of the famine. Cousens characterised internal movement during the famine as a short-lived influx into larger urban centres, which was mitigated by the fact that relief efforts at a local level were restricted to local individuals who resided in a given area.[95] Donnelly describes a surge in famine-era vagrancy and medicancy, with large crowds from the countryside congregating in urban areas and at workhouses, food depots and soup kitchens. These population movements, of course, facilitated the spread of 'famine fevers' such as typhus.[96]

While the relatively less severe potato failure of 1847 led to a brief lull in emigration flows, the total failure of the potato crop in 1848 saw emigration levels return to the heights witnessed in 1846 and early 1847.[97] This third season of blight appears to have broken the morale of those cottiers and small farmers who had held on to their landholdings. Tales of high incidences of mortality on the 1847 transatlantic 'coffin ship' crossings, the prevalence of disease at the landing posts, as well as increased sea fares, did little to dampen this outflow.[98]

The consecutive seasons of potato blight brought about a profound change in attitudes towards emigration, weakening the Irish tenants' prejudice against giving up their holdings and forcing them to regard emigration as a genuine alternative to the persistent struggle for survival at home.[99] Fitzpatrick, Ó Gráda and O'Rourke, among others, characterise the distress levels of the famine as a 'push factor', with emigration occurring as a reaction to the threat of imminent destitution or death for the bulk of those who had formerly relied upon the potato crop for subsistence.[100] In the decades following the famine, however, the urgency of emigration diminished and pull factors such as employment opportunities and wage differentials in the destination country, as well as the self-perpetuating effect of chain emigration, came to the fore.[101]

The role played by friends and relatives in developing emigration chains has been well established.[102] In the Irish context, a key transmission mechanism for both information and funds for prospective emigrants was the 'emigrant's letter', particularly in the case of transatlantic emigration. Johnson notes that the main theme of these letters was the possibility of obtaining high wages in the destination, but the need to work hard to attain prosperity.[103] Remittances and prepaid tickets to facilitate the emigration of immediate relatives were also distributed by means of these letters. Johnson also posits that the localised word-of-mouth nature in which migration information was disseminated contributed to the tendency of informal migration streams to emerge between a given local area and a specific destination.[104] The spread of basic literacy after the 1830s and the widespread proliferation of shipping propaganda also contributed to emigration levels.[105]

Pre-famine emigration had developed its own distinctive regional character, social composition and demographic profile. While the famine exodus exerted great influence on the nature of the Irish emigration process, it is still unclear whether the famine itself reinforced or transformed these established emigration characteristics. Based on passenger lists from transatlantic crossings to the United States over the period 1819 to 1848, Ó Gráda characterises pre-famine emigration flows as being dominated by family units rather than individuals, comprising a greater proportion of children and over-35s, and, of those unaccompanied travellers, the number of unaccompanied men greatly exceeded unaccompanied women.[106] Ó Gráda finds that the profile of the arrivals in New York in 1847 and 1848 differed less markedly from those of the late 1830s and early 1840s than might have been expected. They were somewhat more likely to be under 15 and over 35 years of age, and less likely to travel alone. The share of females in the emigration flow remained unchanged during the famine, but would increase significantly in post-famine years.[107] Ó Gráda also finds support for Adams' contention that a lowering of the socio-economic status of transatlantic emigrants had begun in the decade prior to the famine.[108] Regarding occupational groups, Ó Gráda finds that servants and labourers accounted for 60 per cent of arrivals in 1847 to 1848, which was in line with the previous decade.[109] That said, MacDonagh cites 1849 as a high point of famine-era prosperous emigration, though he acknowledges the concurrent rise in remittances and pauper emigration.[110]

Origins and destinations of famine emigrants

The origins of emigrants during the famine years also bore a distinct spatial pattern, though again it may be that the famine reinforced, rather than disrupted, this pattern. According to Fitzpatrick,

> earlier emigration had been most intensive from northern and midlands counties, but from the famine onwards depletion tended to be greatest in the Connaught region, with a gradual extension down the length of the western seaboard. Broadly speaking, emigration was heavier from poorer and more agricultural counties, and relatively light in the more anglicized and commercial south-east and north-east.[111]

However, Daly notes that this change in the origins of emigration from Ulster to the south and west had already established itself in counties such as Sligo prior to the famine, indicating that the famine brought about an exacerbation, rather than a disruption, of pre-famine patterns.[112]

Irish emigration in the second half of the nineteenth century developed distinct streams between Irish places of origin and overseas destinations, as links were created through 'family and friends' effects. Based on an analysis of 1876 to 1914 emigration statistics, Fitzpatrick identifies a number of these streams: Irish emigrants who settled in America were more likely to emanate from Connaught and the west, while those settling in Canada were predominantly from Ulster; permanent emigrants to Scotland tended to come from the northeast and those to England from eastern and southern coastal regions; seasonal migrants to Britain were increasingly from the northwestern counties of Mayo, Donegal, Galway and Roscommon; Australian Irish tended to come from southwestern and north midlands counties while New Zealand, which had a strong Scottish tradition, also attracted emigrants from Ulster.[113] Notwithstanding these destination patterns, the scale of Irish emigration ensured that virtually all Irish counties were represented in all prominent destinations mentioned above. Fitzpatrick also links disparities in regional origin with differences in the social composition of the various emigrant streams, characterising Irish emigrants to Britain as townspeople circulating in the wider urban employment market of the British Isles. The American Irish, though they became concentrated in urban centres, were drawn from the surplus of the rural population who had subsisted on potato cultivation prior to the famine, while Irish emigrants to Australia were more likely to be semi-skilled farm workers rendered unemployable by the rapid contraction of Irish tillage farming. That said, specific famine-era factors may also have led to divergences from these trends: relatively lower fares to Canada and the criteria for assisted emigration to Australia may have drawn unskilled and unattached emigrants to these destinations.[114]

In the decades prior to the famine, Canadian ports were the least expensive transatlantic destination due to relatively lax regulations on passenger numbers and conditions.[115] The onset of the famine triggered a surge in demand for this route, culminating in over 100,000 Irish emigrants arriving in Canadian ports in 1847 alone. Emigrants disembarked at quarantine stations such as Grosse Isle in Quebec and Partridge Island near St John, New Brunswick. While about one-third of emigrants left for the United States when they disembarked, the majority moved north or west of the Great Lakes to join friends and relatives.[116] The vast influx of Irish emigrants to Canadian ports in 1847, and the appalling levels of death and disease evident when they disembarked the 'coffin ships' at Grosse Isle and the other quarantine stations, prompted the Canadian authorities to introduce stricter passenger regulations and higher surcharges before the onset of the 1848 shipping season. As a result, fares to Canada rose steeply and this led to a change of shipping destinations in favour of New York and Boston. The number of Irish arrivals in Canada in 1848 fell to a quarter of the preceding year's inflow and was lower than that of the pre-famine period.[117]

MacDonagh estimates that, over the course of the famine years, 75 per cent of Irish emigrants to the New World settled in the United States. Irish immigrants settled in compact groups in urban areas, concentrated on the east coast – in a coastal belt running south from Maine to Long Island; upper New York state, south and west of the Great Lakes; and in the industrial regions of Pennsylvania. By 1867, almost half a million people of Irish origin were living in the 13 principal cities in the United States, with over 200,000 in New York, 100,000 in Philadelphia and nearly 50,000 in Boston.[118] The paradox of Irish rural emigrants eschewing rural life in the American prairies for concentration in urban settlements has been considered by Shannon and McCaffery among others.[119] The unwillingness of Irish emigrants to settle in rural areas has been attributed to limited experience with large-scale farming, lack of capital and the unattractiveness of isolation in the vast frontier regions. Miller's explorations of cultural aspects of Irish adjustment to life in America emphasise an Irish mindset in which emigration was viewed as exile. Miller argues that this mindset contributed to the Catholic Irish in particular being more communal and more prone to accept conditions passively than to take initiatives, notwithstanding a minority of Irish emigrants from urban, educated, business backgrounds who proved to be better attuned to the challenges of commercial or industrial America.[120] Campbell, however, stresses the importance of local conditions in determining patterns of Irish adjustment and argues that Irish settlements in rural areas in Minnesota, Wisconsin, the mountain states and the West 'point to the tremendous colours and hues in the experiences of the Irish in America'.[121] Fitzpatrick also disputes the notion that the vast majority of Irish emigrants invariably settled in major cities. While true of the Irish in Britain by 1851, Fitzpatrick notes that even by 1870 less than two-fifths of Irish Americans were living in cities of over 50,000 people.[122]

Irish permanent – as opposed to seasonal – migration to Britain was predominantly urban and industrial in nature. Lawton notes that the distribution of Irish settlers in Britain was stable throughout the pre- and post-famine period, with prominent destinations for Irish emigrants being the cities of Glasgow, Liverpool, Manchester and London, as well as the coalfields of northeast England and South Wales, the textile districts of East Lancashire and West Yorkshire, and the West Midlands coal and iron manufacturing region.[123]

Famine-era emigration to Australia occurred on a much smaller scale than that to Britain or America. The length of the journey involved, high rates of passage, the relatively undeveloped conditions of the colonies and the absence of a remittance system prevented Irish emigration flows from being perpetuated in the same way as American emigration.[124] In 1847 a number of small-scale government-assisted emigration projects were initiated which sent the wives and children of former settlers, as well as pardoned and 'ticket-of-leave' convicts, to Australia. Further assisted emigration of 4,000 orphaned girls occurred between 1847 and 1849. Fitzpatrick notes that most Irish settlers destined for Australia received some form of government subsidy from the colonial land funds, and that by 1872 up to 140,000 Irish emigrants had been assisted in their relocation to the Australian colonies. These state-assisted initiatives were initially met with dissatisfaction in Australia, due to opposition to what was perceived as pauper emigration.[125] Irish emigration to Australia re-emerged later in the century with the advent of rising Irish living standards, the discovery of gold in the colonies, steam transport, and civil war and depression in the United States. Campbell notes that, contrary to the American experience, nineteenth-century Irish settlers in Australia were more evenly distributed throughout the entire country, they enjoyed a relatively easier adjustment to their new surroundings, and their preferred habitat was the rural agricultural settlement.[126]

Consequences of the Great Irish Famine

The Great Irish Famine was a catastrophe of proportions that are difficult to comprehend. The sheer scale of mortality arising from the famine, an estimated one million famine-related deaths over a six-year period from a population of 8.5 million in 1845, has seen the famine's death-toll recognised internationally as being proportionately larger than any other subsistence famine on record.[127] Together with an emigration exodus in excess of one million Irish inhabitants, the suffering unleashed by the famine culminated in a 20 per cent population decline over the period 1845 to 1851. Beyond its immediate Irish impact, the Great Irish Famine has also come to be regarded as a significant event in global history, with far-reaching and enduring economic and political consequences. This is exemplified by the subsequent involvement of famine emigrants and their descendants in the economic, social, and political life of the countries in which they settled, particularly the United States: 'Individual memories of the famine, coupled with "collective memory" of the event in later years, influenced the political culture of both Ireland and Irish-America, and indeed still play a role.'[128]

The famine was followed by a century of Irish population decline, during a period in which other European countries experienced robust population growth. This occurred despite the Irish post-famine birth rate being unremarkable by European standards, albeit a birth rate generated by an unusual combination of large families and low marriage rates.[129] It was continued emigration flows rather than low birth rate growth that principally caused this persistent post-famine depopulation. However, as Daly notes, Irish population growth had begun to slow down in the decades prior to the famine and emigration had already risen to substantial levels prior to the 1840s.[130]

Aside from the immediate devastation experienced during the crisis years, there has been much debate in recent decades as to extent to which the famine constituted a watershed event, changing the course of Irish history, as opposed to a catalyst which exacerbated or accelerated social and economic transformations already under way in pre-famine Ireland. To what extent then can long-run Irish post-famine demographic trends be attributed to the famine? Watkins and Menken, in a study of long-run demographic effects of South Asian famines, indicate that as 'normal' demographic patterns resumed in the post-famine environment, the demographic vacuum created by famine was quickly filled.[131] However, in the Irish case the population fell by 21 per cent between 1851 and 1881 and the decline continued into the twentieth century, falling a further 5 per cent between 1891 and 1926 – the first year in which a census was held for the newly independent 26-county state which would become the Republic of Ireland – and remaining relatively stable until the 1960s (see Appendix, Figures A1.2 and A1.3). Guinnane attributes this prolonged depopulation to the role played by the famine in altering the decision-making of future generations about migration and household formation.[132] Large-scale famine-induced emigration facilitated future waves of emigration through remittance flows and the formation of chain emigration patterns among siblings, and these developments also enhanced the attractiveness of larger family units among those remaining in Ireland.

The structure of Irish agriculture changed dramatically in the aftermath of the famine, as post-famine farming switched from labour-intensive tillage to land-intensive pasture. The share of crops fell from 55 per cent of agricultural output prior to the famine to 36 per cent a decade later, to only 12 per cent at the beginning of the twentieth century.[133] Irish agricultural employment fell significantly as a result of this change in agricultural output, contracting to 55 per cent of famine-era employment levels by 1870.[134] This post-famine agricultural restructuring may be placed in a broader international context: the 1846 repeal of the Corn Laws opened up Irish grain farming to unrestricted competition from continental and American producers, and from the late 1850s onward grain prices declined while livestock prices increased.[135] However, simulation modelling undertaken by O'Rourke indicates that international market and price trends alone cannot account for the scale of agricultural unemployment and output declines experienced in the post-famine decades.[136]

The sluggish nature of post-famine industrialisation has also been well documented, though its causes have not been resolved.[137] Both Bielenberg and Ó Gráda document only slight post-famine industrial growth at a time when UK industrial output increased fourfold.[138] That said, these accounts note that Irish progress in textiles, shipbuilding, brewing and distilling may have offset declines in other sectors. Competing explanations for the poor Irish post-famine industrial performance focus on either the loss of skilled workers due to famine-era emigration or the technological externalities and resource abundance that allowed British manufacturing regions to industrialise first and establish a productivity advantage over other regions.[139] Bielenberg points to regional and sectoral disparities in Irish post-famine industrial development in the face of British competition: industries dependent on processing raw materials produced by the agricultural sector remained more concentrated in the south, while relatively higher value, labour-intensive industries such as textiles and shipbuilding became progressively concentrated in Ulster in the post-famine decades.[140]

However, taken as a whole, Irish living standards actually improved in the post-famine decades. Geary and Stark estimate that Ireland's GDP per capita grew at an average of 0.9 per cent per annum over the period 1871 to 1911 (see Appendix, Figure A1.1), with GDP per worker averaging at 1.1 per cent over the same period. The corresponding figures for Great Britain are 0.8 per cent, both in per capita and per worker terms.[141] These positive developments are supported by Ó Gráda, who notes that average life expectancy rose from 40 years on the eve of the famine to 50 years by the early 1870s, and 58 years by the 1920s, while post-famine literacy levels and housing standards also improved.[142]

What brought about this increase in post-famine living standards? Competing theories tend to fall into two broad categories. The first draws parallels with medieval Europe after the Black Death, as surviving labourers may have secured higher wages due to the contraction of the labour force.[143] In a similar vein, Williamson attributes increased living standards for those remaining in

Ireland to the large-scale famine-induced emigration, as it 'severed the ties between subsistence costs and wages, generating links between Ireland and the rest of the world which ensured that foreign-labour market conditions would have a far greater impact on Irish labour costs than the Irish potato'.[144] The second attributes rising living standards predominantly to real economic gains accrued from structural change, access to a common UK-wide pool of technology, capital and labour as well as enhanced international trade, which facilitated a 'catching-up' process with other developed countries.[145] Cullen, in particular, highlights the role of the existing institutional and infrastructural base – established foreign trade, export-orientated industries, railway infrastructure, highly developed banking and commerce institutions, and attractiveness to foreign investment – in facilitating this 'catching-up' process.[146] While these competing theories may dispute the dominant force behind Irish post-famine economic development, both place Ireland's post-famine experiences firmly in an international context.

Despite an overall increase in living standards in the post-famine decades, at a local and regional level social and spatial variations colour the post-famine experience. Daly points to the smallholders and landless labourers as the major casualties of the famine.[147] Landholdings of fewer than five acres fell from around 442,000 in 1841 to 126,000 in 1851, or by about 70 per cent, while employment in agriculture fell by 392,700 from 1841 and 1851, with labourers, servants and ploughmen accounting for 84 per cent of the job losses.[148] It was smallholders and landless labourers who endured the heaviest death-toll during the famine years and they faced further difficulties in the years after the famine, as efforts to consolidate landholdings meant that farmers were increasingly reluctant to provide them with *conacre* leases or permit them to build cabins on their land. Furthermore, the agricultural shift to pasture, as well as the mechanisation of agriculture, reduced their employment opportunities and forced many labourers to emigrate.[149] Western counties, with a prevalence of smallholdings and a lack of capital, were less suited to making the shift from crops to livestock and, as a result, were less capable of keeping pace with rising Irish living standards.[150] As Gray notes:

> The post-famine social order was characterised by the predominance of larger holdings and the decline, outside the west, of the smallholder. Much of the surviving agricultural labour class continued to depend on conacre and cottier plots, but it was steadily attenuated in numbers, and became increasingly differentiated from the farming community.[151]

That the heaviest burden fell on smallholders and landless labourers both during and after the famine is a recurring theme, characterised by Ó Gráda as a 'hierarchy of suffering' in which the rural poor, landless, or near-landless were most likely to perish.[152] A more pointed synopsis of famine mortality was delivered by Karl Marx (1867, p. 774): the Great Irish famine 'killed poor devils only'.[153]

Appendix

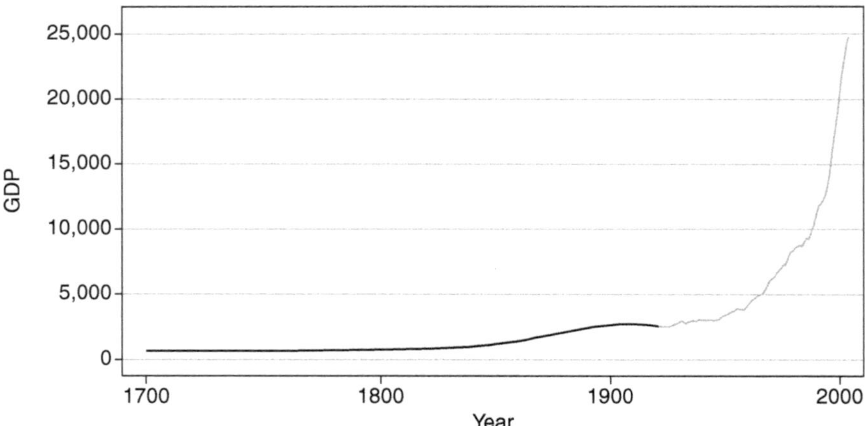

Figure A1.1 Irish GDP per capita, 1700 to 2004 (source: GDP per capita data for 1700 to 2004 (in 1990 international Geary-Khamis dollars) is available from www.ggdc.net/maddison/ (Angus Maddison homepage). Pre-1921 data points joined using a median spline).

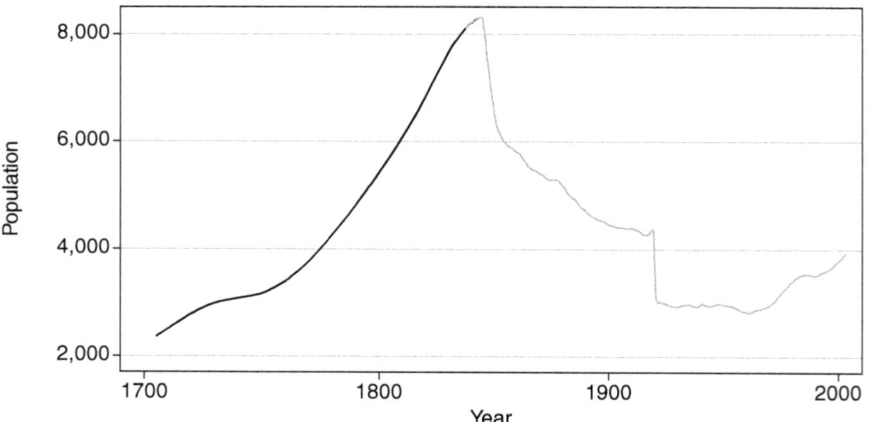

Figure A1.2 Irish population trends, 1700 to 2000 (in 000s) (sources: The Irish population data presented above come from a variety of different sources: 1712 to 1791 O'Connell estimates and Irish Census data 1821 to 1841 reproduced in J. Mokyr and C. Ó Gráda, 'New Developments in Irish Population History, 1700–1850', *Economic History Review* 37 (1984), 37, 473–488; 1838 to 1900 data available from ESRC quantitative database. Irish population data are also available in W.E. Vaughan and A.J. Fitzpatrick (eds), *Irish Historical Statistics: Population 1821–1971* (Dublin: Royal Irish Academy, 1978). Irish population data for 1900 to 2000 are available from www.ggdc.net/maddison/ (Angus Maddison homepage). Pre-1838 data points joined using a median spline. Post-1921 data refer to what is now the Republic of Ireland).

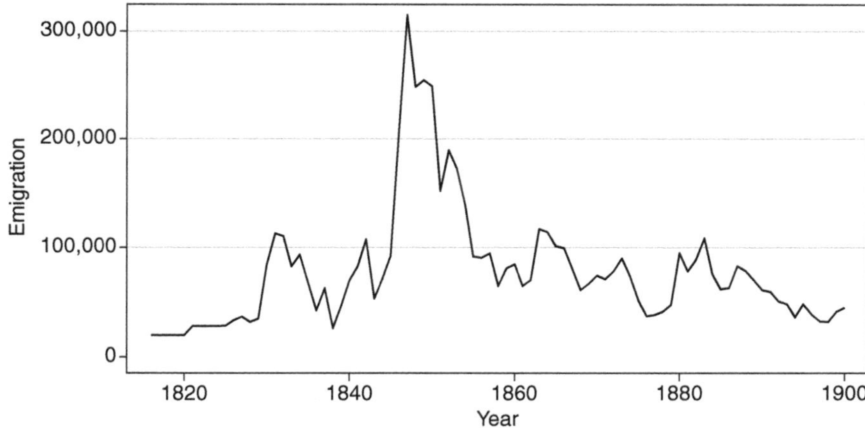

Figure A1.3 Total Irish emigration, 1821 to 1900 (sources: Estimates of Irish emigration to North America and Britain 1821 to 1850 available from Boyle and Ó Gráda, 'Fertility Trends, Excess Mortality, and the Great Irish Famine'; estimates of total Irish emigration 1851 to 1900 available from Vaughan and Fitzpatrick, *Irish Historical Statistics: Population 1821–1971*).

Notes

1 A haggard or 'haggart' refers to an enclosure beside a farmhouse in which crops were stored. According to the *Collins Dictionary*, the word is derived from the Norse term *heygarthr*, which comprises *hey* meaning hay and *garthr* meaning yard.

2 One well-known international manifestation of the Great Irish Famine was large-scale emigration, with an estimated one million people leaving Ireland during the famine and a further four million leaving between 1850 and 1914. Such was the extent of the exodus that French writer Louis Paul-Dubois wrote: 'emigration will soon cause it to be said that Ireland is no longer where flows the Shannon, but rather beside the banks of the Hudson River' (Louis Paul-Dubois, *Contemporary Ireland* (Dublin: Maunsel & Co, 1908), 350–351. Quoted in Cormac Ó Gráda, 'A Note on Nineteenth-century Irish Emigration Statistics', *Population Studies* 29:1 (1975), 143).

3 James S. Donnelly, *The Irish Potato Famine* (London: Stutton, 2001).

4 Raymond D. Crotty, *Irish Agricultural Production: Its Volume and Structure* (Cork: Cork University Press, 1966), 26–28.

5 Milton Briggs and Percy Jordan, *Economic History of England* (London: University Tutorial Press, 1934).

6 Mary E. Daly, *Social and Economic History of Ireland since 1800* (Dublin: Educational Company, 1981).

7 Louis M. Cullen, *An Economic History of Ireland since 1660* (London: Batsford, 1972), 103.

8 The increase in Irish salted beef exports following the repeal of the Cattle Acts in the 1760s was not maintained, with its position being undermined by an Act of 1783 which permitted the colonies to import provisions from the United States; Crotty, *Irish Agricultural Production*, 19–24.

9 Crotty, *Irish Agricultural Production*, 24.

10 Cullen, *Economic History of Ireland*, 95–96; Joel Mokyr, *Why Ireland Starved: a Quantitative and Analytical History of the Irish Economy, 1800–1850* (London: George Allen & Unwin, 2nd edn, 1983), 114. O'Donovan notes that, in terms of physical geography and climate, Irish land is relatively better suited to pastoral agriculture than tillage, due to its grass coverage, humidity, high rainfall, as well as low summer and high winter temperatures; John O'Donovan, *An Economic History of Livestock in Ireland* (Cork: Cork University Press, 1940).

11 Crotty, *Irish Agricultural Production*, 30–33.

12 Cullen, *Economic History of Ireland*, 118–120.

13 Mokyr, *Why Ireland Starved*, 7–9. Crotty notes that soil quality deteriorates rapidly when broken out of pasture and tilled. This may be counteracted by periodically sowing the land with grass ('ley-farming'), by leaving land fallow for a year or longer, or by growing a root crop such as potato or turnip to restore soil and break the cycle of cereal diseases and pests; Crotty, *Irish Agricultural Production*, 24–25.

14 Mary E. Daly, *The Famine in Ireland* (Dundalk: Dundalgan Press, 1986), 21–24.

15 Cullen, *Economic History of Ireland*, 100–110. The Act of Union (1800) abolished the Irish Parliament and established a new political unit known as the United Kingdom of Great Britain and Ireland. The economic consequences of the Act of Union involved the following steps: abolition of intra-Union trade barriers, the establishment of a common external tariff, consolidation of the exchequers, and the merger of the two currencies. The first two steps were implemented in 1801, the exchequers were consolidated in 1817, and the currencies merged in 1826. Frank Geary and Thomas Stark, 'Examining Ireland's Post-famine Economic Growth Performance', *The Economic Journal* 112 (2002), 919–935.

16 Cormac Ó Gráda, *Ireland: A New Economic History, 1780–1939* (Oxford: Oxford University Press, 1994), 162–163.

17 Crotty, *Irish Agricultural Production*, 21.

18 Eoin O'Malley, 'The Decline of Irish Industry in the Nineteenth Century', *Economic and Social Review* 13:1 (1981), 21–42.

19 Eric L. Almquist, 'Labour Specialisation and the Irish Economy in 1841: An Aggregate Occupational Analysis', *Economic History Review* 36:4 (1983), 4; Cormac Ó Gráda, *Ireland Before and After the Famine: Explorations in Economic History 1800–1925* (Manchester: Manchester University Press, 1988), 27.

20 Jane Gray, 'The Irish, Scottish and Flemish Linen Industries During the Long Eighteenth Century', in *The European Linen Industry in Historical Perspective*, ed. Brenda Collins and Philip Ollershaw (Oxford: Oxford University Press, 2003), 159–186.

21 Daly, *The Famine in Ireland*, 29–30.

22 O'Malley, 'The Decline of Irish Industry', 32.

23 Mokyr, *Why Ireland Starved*, 176–177.

24 O'Malley, 'The Decline of Irish Industry', 32–33.

25 Frank Geary, 'The Act of Union, British–Irish Trade, and Pre-famine Deindustrialization', *The Economic History Review* 48:1 (1995), 68–88.

26 Cullen, *Economic History of Ireland*, 108–109.

27 Mokyr, *Why Ireland Starved*, 13–14; Peter M. Solar, 'The Irish Linen Trade 1820–1852', *Textile History* 21:1 (1990), 57–85.

28 George O'Brien, *The Economic History of Ireland in the Eighteenth Century* (Dublin: Maunsell, 1918).

29 Ó Gráda, *Ireland Before and After the Famine*, 27–28.

30 Mokyr, *Why Ireland Starved*, 288.

31 Jospeh J. Lee, *The Modernisation of Irish Society, 1848–1918* (Dublin; Gill & McMillan, 1973), 1–36.

32 O'Malley, 'The Decline of Irish Industry', 41.

33 Andy Bielenberg, *Ireland and the Industrial Revolution: The Impact of the Industrial Revolution on Irish Industry, 1801–1922* (London: Routledge, 2009), 175–179.
34 Ó Gráda, *Ireland: A New Economic History*, 131–152.
35 Donnelly, *Irish Potato Famine*, 7–11.
36 Mokyr, *Why Ireland Starved*, 17. See also Cullen, *Economic History of Ireland*, 111.
37 Daly, *The Famine in Ireland*, 10–11.
38 Ó Gráda, *Ireland Before and After the Famine*, 51.
39 Cullen, *Economic History of Ireland*, 112–113; Mokyr, *Why Ireland Starved*, 17–18.
40 Cullen, *Economic History of Ireland*, 112–113.
41 Daly, *Social and Economic History of Ireland*, 13.
42 Ibid.
43 Crotty, *Irish Agricultural Production*, 42–43.
44 Mokyr, *Why Ireland Starved*, 21; Daly, *The Famine in Ireland*, 17–19.
45 Daly, *The Famine in Ireland*, 17–19.
46 Cormac Ó Gráda, 'Ireland's Great Famine: An Overview', in *When the Potato Failed: Causes and Effects of the Last European Subsistence Crisis*, ed. Cormac Ó Gráda, Richard Paping and Eric Vanhaute (Turnhout: Brepols, 2007), 46.
47 Mokyr, *Why Ireland Starved*, 10, Table 2.1; Ó Gráda, 'Ireland's Great Famine: An Overview', 43; Kevin O'Rourke, 'Rural Depopulation in a Small Open Economy: Ireland 1856–76', *Explorations in Economic History* 28 (1991), 409–432. Estimates of pre- and post-famine real wages were originally constructed in A.L. Bowley, 'Statistics of Wages in the United Kingdom During the Last Hundred Years (Part IV) Agricultural Wages – Concluded. Earnings and General Averages', *Journal of the Royal Statistical Society* 62 (1899), 555–570. For a discussion of the limitations inherent in this data, see Ó Gráda, *Ireland: A New Economic History*, 236–237.
48 Joel Mokyr and Cormac Ó Gráda, 'Poor and Getting Poorer? Living Standards in Ireland Before the Famine', *Economic History Review* 41 (1988), 209–235. The analysis by Mokyr and Ó Gráda draws on a number of sources: the Poor Inquiry Commissioners, a body appointed by the British Parliament in 1835 which collected responses from 1,590 Catholic and Protestant clergymen on the conditions facing the Irish poor; consumption data of sugar, tea and tobacco; as well as indicators of human capital formation such as illiteracy and school attendance.
49 Mokyr and Ó Gráda, 'Poor and Getting Poorer', 226.
50 Cullen, *Economic History of Ireland*, 118–119; Mokyr, *Why Ireland Starved*, 30–38; Ó Gráda, *Ireland Before and After the Famine*, 6–8.
51 Phelim P. Boyle and Cormac Ó Gráda, 'Fertility Trends, Excess Mortality, and the Great Irish Famine', *Demography* 23 (1986), 543–562.
52 Ibid.
53 Mokyr, *Why Ireland Starved*, 230; Boyle and Ó Gráda, 'Fertility Trends', 547–548; David Fitzpatrick, *Irish Emigration 1801–1921*(Dublin: Irish Economic and Social History Society, 1984), 3.
54 Mokyr, *Why Ireland Starved*, 230.
55 Boyle and Ó Gráda, 'Fertility Trends', 560 (Table A.1); Daly, *The Famine in Ireland*, 34–38.
56 Daly, *The Famine in Ireland*, 34–38.
57 S.H. Cousens, 'Regional Death Rates in Ireland during the Great Famine, from 1846 to 1851', *Population Studies* 14:1 (1960), 55–74.
58 Daly, *The Famine in Ireland*, 37.
59 Fitzpatrick, *Irish Emigration*, 9.
60 Ó Gráda, *Ireland Before and After the Famine*, 9.
61 Christine Kinealy, *This Great Calamity: The Irish Famine, 1845–52* (2nd edn) (Dublin: Gill & Macmillan, 1996), xvi.
62 Austin Bourke, *The Visitation of God? The Potato and the Great Irish Famine* (Dublin: Lilliput Press, 1993); L.J. Dowley, 'The Potato and Late Blight in Ireland',

in *Famine 150: Commemorative Lecture Series*, ed. Cormac Ó Gráda (Dublin: Teagasc, 1997).
63 John S. Neiderhauser, 'International Cooperation in Potato Research and Development', *Annual Review of Phytopathology* 48 (1993), 274–277.
64 Bourke, *The Visitation of God?*
65 Daly, *The Famine in Ireland*, 8.
66 Eric Vanhaute, Richard Paping and Cormac Ó Gráda, 'The European Subsistence Crisis of 1845–1850: A Comparative Perspective', in *When the Potato Failed: Causes and Effects of the Last European Subsistence Crisis*, ed. Cormac Ó Gráda, Richard Paping and Eric Vanhaute (Turnhout: Brepols, 2007), 20–21.
67 Ibid.
68 Ó Gráda, 'Ireland's Great Famine: An Overview', 46 (Table 2.1).
69 Vanhaute *et al.*, 'European Subsistence Crisis of 1845–1850', 23.
70 Mokyr, *Why Ireland Starved*, 265–266; Daly, *The Famine in Ireland*, 98; Boyle and Ó Gráda, 'Fertility Trends', 554.
71 Boyle and Ó Gráda, 'Fertility Trends', 554.
72 Daly, *The Famine in Ireland*, 100.
73 Frank Geary, 'Regional Industrial Structure and Labour Force Decline in Ireland between 1841 and 1851', *Irish Historical Studies* 30:118 (1996), 167–194.
74 Donnelly, *Irish Potato Famine*, 176.
75 Mokyr, *Why Ireland Starved*, 267; S.H. Cousens, 'The Regional Variations in Emigration from Ireland between 1821 and 1841', *Transactions and Papers of the Institute of British Geographers* 37 (1960), 15–30.
76 Ó Gráda, *Ireland: A New Economic History*, 97–98; Donnelly, *Irish Potato Famine*, 70–72.
77 Mokyr, *Why Ireland Starved*, 261–276; see also Daly, *The Famine in Ireland*, 113. Ó Gráda highlights a number of limitations of county-level analysis: (1) county-level data should be treated with caution, as county boundaries may be unsuited to separating regions of cluster and disperse rural settlement; (2) settlement origins and inheritance customs may not be related to the set of economic variables that Mokyr introduces; and (3) Mokyr's estimates of county-level excess mortality should be regarded as tentative, as they are based on estimates of 1851 county-level emigration, which underrepresent southern and western migration; Ó Gráda, *Ireland: A New Economic History*, 183–184.
78 Donnelly, *Irish Potato Famine*, 8.
79 Cathal Póirtéir (ed.), *Famine Echoes* (Dublin: Gill & MacMillan, 1995); Roger J. McHugh, 'The Famine in Oral Tradition', in *The Great Famine*, ed. Ruth Dudley Edwards and T. Desmond Williams (Dublin: Lilliput, 1966), 391–435.
80 Mary E. Daly, 'Something Old and Something New: Recent Research on the Great Irish Famine', in *When the Potato Failed: Causes and Effects of the Last European Subsistence Crisis*, ed. Cormac Ó Gráda, Richard Paping and Eric Vanhaute (Turnhout: Brepols, 2007), 68.
81 Daly, *The Famine in Ireland*, 92.
82 Donnelly, *Irish Potato Famine*, 54.
83 Ó Gráda, 'Ireland's Great Famine: An Overview', 47–49.
84 Cormac Ó Gráda, *The Great Irish Famine* (London: Macmillan, 1989), 46.
85 Daly, *The Famine in Ireland*, 92–98.
86 Donnelly, *Irish Potato Famine*, 101–112.
87 William E. Vaughan, *Landlord and Tenant 1850–1904* (Dublin: Irish Economic and Social History Society, 1984), 24–26; Tim P. O'Neill, 'Famine Evictions', in *Famine, Land and Culture in Ireland*, ed. Carla King (Dublin: UCD Press, 2000), 29–58.
88 Daly, *The Famine in Ireland*, 94.
89 Ó Gráda, 'Ireland's Great Famine: An Overview', 47–49.

90 S.H. Cousens, 'The Regional Pattern in Emigration during the Great Irish Famine,1846–1851', *Transactions and Papers of the Institute of British Geographers* 28 (1960), 119–134; Boyle and Ó Gráda, 'Fertility Trends', 555.
91 Oliver MacDonagh, 'Irish Emigration to the United States of America and the British Colonies during the Famine', in *The Great Famine*, ed. Ruth Dudley Edwards and T. Desmond Williams (Dublin: Lilliput, 1966), 319–388.
92 Daly, *The Famine in Ireland*, 106.
93 Cousens, 'The Regional Pattern in Emigration', 121.
94 MacDonagh, 'Irish Emigration', 340–352.
95 Cousens, 'The Regional Pattern in Emigration', 119–120.
96 Donnelly, *Irish Potato Famine*, 172–173.
97 MacDonagh, 'Irish Emigration', 322–324.
98 Mortality was particularly high in 1847 crossings to Canada, and Miller estimates that at least 30,000 emigrants may have died on the Canadian route or in fever hospitals on their arrival. Mokyr attributes the high mortality rates to overcrowding, poor nutrition, the already emaciated condition of many emigrants, as well as exposure to contagious diseases prior to departure. Kerby A. Miller, *Emigrants and Exiles: Ireland and the Irish Exodus to North America* (Oxford: Oxford University Press, 1985), 292; Kerby A. Miller, *Ireland and Irish America; Culture, Class, and Transaction Migration* (Dublin: Field Day, 2008), 67; Mokyr, *Why Ireland Starved*, 267.
99 MacDonagh, 'Irish Emigration', 325–326.
100 Fitzpatrick, *Irish Emigration*, 26–30; Ó Gráda and O'Rourke discuss the extent to which famine-era emigration served as a crude form of disaster relief; Cormac Ó Gráda and Kevin H. O'Rourke, 'Migration as a Disaster Relief: Lessons from the Great Irish Famine', *European Review of Economic History* 1 (1997), 3–25.
101 As Hatton and Williamson illustrate, push factors may also have played a role in post-famine emigration, such as the lack of inheritance opportunities for children of large families; Timothy J. Hatton and Jeffrey G. Williamson, 'After the Famine: Emigration from Ireland, 1850–1913', *Journal of Economic History* 53 (1993), 575–600.
102 Hatton, and Hatton and Williamson provide comprehensive studies of the factors influencing the emigration decision. Based on the contributions of Sjaastad and Borjas, among others, Hatton and Williamson observe that emigration from Europe in the late nineteenth century was driven by a number of key factors: demographic forces reflecting the deteriorating employment conditions in the source country; the purchase power parity adjusted real wage of the source country relative to the destination; a 'friends and relative effect' attracting migrants to the destination; and, to a lesser extent, the differential mobility between urban and rural populations in the source country; Timothy J. Hatton, 'The Age of Mass Migration: What We Can and Can't Explain', in *Migration and Mobility*, ed. Subrata Ghatak and Anne Showstack-Sassoon (London: Macmillan, 2001); Timothy J. Hatton and Jeffrey G. Williamson, 'What Fundamentals Drive World Migration?', CEPR Discussion Papers 3559 (2002); George J. Borjas, 'Self-selection and the Earnings of Immigrants', *American Economic Review* 77:4 (1987), 531–553.
103 J.H. Johnson, 'The Context of Migration: The Example of Ireland in the Nineteenth Century', *Transactions of the Institute of British Geographers* 15:3 (1990), 259–276.
104 Ibid.
105 Fitzpatrick, *Irish Emigration*, 24.
106 Cormac Ó Gráda, 'Across the Briny Ocean: Some Thoughts on Irish Emigration to America 1800–1850', in *Ireland and Scotland 1600–1850: Parallels and Contrasts in Economic and Social Development*, ed. Thomas M. Devine and David Dickson (Edinburgh: John Donald, 1983), 119.

107 Ibid.
108 William F. Adams, *Ireland and the Irish Emigration to the New World from 1815 to the Famine* (New Haven, CT: Yale University Press, 1932). Many of these characteristics changed in the post-famine decades. In post-famine emigration flows, females were the majority. While reasons for the marked increase in post-famine female emigration are not entirely clear, Ó Gráda points to increased demand for domestic servants in America during the second half of the nineteenth century, the relatively harsh lives of women in post-famine Ireland, and the scale of the emigration exodus itself. Irish post-famine emigrants were less inclined to travel in family groups, with family emigration peaking in the 1840s and declining thereafter. The post-famine age structure of emigrants also changed: during 1855 to 1914, the 20- to 24-year age group alone accounted for between 33 and 44 per cent of emigrants, whereas prior to the famine those travelling to North America were far less concentrated within this narrow age band; Fitzpatrick, *Irish Emigration*, 21; Ó Gráda, 'Across the Briny Ocean', 119–120.
109 Ó Gráda, 'Across the Briny Ocean', 119.
110 MacDonagh, 'Irish Emigration', 326.
111 Fitzpatrick, *Irish Emigration*, 9.
112 Daly, *The Famine in Ireland*, 108–109.
113 Fitzpatrick, *Irish Emigration*, 32–34.
114 Ibid.
115 Daly, *The Famine in Ireland*,107.
116 MacDonagh, 'Irish Emigration', 369.
117 Cecil J. Houston and William J. Smyth, *Irish Emigration and Canadian Settlement: Patterns, Links, and Letters* (Toronto: University of Toronto Press, 1990).
118 MacDonagh, 'Irish Emigration', 383.
119 William V. Shannon, *The American Irish* (New York: University of Massachusetts Press, 1963); Lawrence J. McCaffery, *The Irish Diaspora in America* (Bloomington: Indiana University Press, 1976).
120 Miller, *Emigrants and Exiles*, 107.
121 Malcolm Campbell, 'The Other Immigrants: Comparing the Irish in Australia and the United States', *Journal of American Ethnic History* 14:3 (1995), 9.
122 Fitzpatrick, *Irish Emigration*, 33.
123 R. Lawton, 'Irish Immigration to England and Wales in the Mid-nineteenth Century', *Irish Geography* 4 (1959), 35–54.
124 MacDonagh, 'Irish Emigration', 352.
125 Fitzpatrick, *Irish Emigration*, 18.
126 Campbell, 'The Other Immigrants', 3–4.
127 This international recognition is exemplified in Amartya Sen's comments: '[in] no other famine in the world [was] the proportion of people killed ... as large as in the Irish famines in the 1840s'; Amartya K. Sen, 'Starvation and Political Economy: Famines, Entitlement, and Alienation', address to the NYU/Ireland House Conference on Famine and World Hunger, New York, 1995, cited in Ó Gráda, 'Ireland's Great Famine: An Overview', 54.
128 Ó Gráda, 'Ireland's Great Famine: An Overview', 55.
129 Timothy W. Guinnane, *The Vanishing Irish: Households, Migration and the Rural Economy in Ireland, 1850–1914* (Princeton, NJ: Princeton University Press, 1997).
130 Daly, *The Famine in Ireland*, 48.
131 Susan C. Watkins and Jane Menken, 'Famines in Historical Perspective', *Population and Development Review* 11 (1985), 647–675.
132 Guinnane, *Vanishing Irish*, 3–18.
133 O'Rourke, 'Rural Depopulation', 409–432.
134 Ó Gráda, 'Ireland's Great Famine: An Overview', 54.
135 Daly, *The Famine in Ireland*, 118–119.

136 O'Rourke, 'Rural Depopulation', 409–432.
137 Karl Whelan, 'Economic Geography and the Long-run Effects of the Great Irish Famine', *The Economic and Social Review* 30:1 (1999), 1–20.
138 Andy Bielenberg, *Cork's Industrial Revolution 1780–1880* (Cork: Cork University Press, 1991); Ó Gráda, *Ireland: A New Economic History*, 309.
139 On the loss of skilled workers due to famine-era emigration see: O'Rourke, 'Rural Depopulation', 409–432; Timothy W. Guinnane, 'The Great Irish Famine and Population: the Long View', *American Economic Review* 84:2 (1994), 303–308. On technological externalities see O'Malley, 'The Decline of Irish Industry', 21–42; Ó Gráda, *Ireland: A New Economic History*, 343–347.
140 Bielenberg, *Ireland and the Industrial Revolution*, 175–180.
141 Geary and Stark, 'Examining Ireland's Post-famine Economic Growth Performance', 919–935.
142 Ó Gráda, *Ireland: A New Economic History*, 249–250. Daly speculates that increased literacy rates observed in the aftermath of the famine may have been due to heavy mortality among the poor and that the continuation of the literacy trend may have owed as much to the subsequent decline of the labouring population, rather than to improvements in the education system. Daly, *The Famine in Ireland*, 121–122.
143 Kieran A. Kennedy, Thomas Giblin and Deirdre McHugh, *The Economic Development of Ireland in the Twentieth Century* (London: Routledge, 1988).
144 Jeffrey G. Williamson, 'Economic Convergence: Placing Post-famine Ireland in Comparative Perspective', *Irish Economic and Social History* 21 (1994), 312.
145 Cullen, *Economic History of Ireland*, 134–170; Geary and Stark, 'Examining Ireland's Post-famine Economic Growth Performance', 919–935.
146 Cullen, *Economic History of Ireland*, 170.
147 Daly, *The Famine in Ireland*, 119–121.
148 Crotty, *Irish Agricultural Production*, 49; Geary, 'Regional Industrial Structure', 167–194.
149 Donnelly, *Irish Potato Famine*, 161–162.
150 Daly, *The Famine in Ireland*, 119–121.
151 Peter Gray, *Famine, Land, and Politics: British Government and Irish Society 1843–1850* (Dublin: Irish Academic Press, 1999), 335.
152 Ó Gráda, 'Ireland's Great Famine: An Overview', 52.
153 Karl Marx, *Capital* (Vol. I), trans. Ben Fowkes (Harmondsworth: Penguin Books, 1990 [1867]), 774.

2 Tracing 'the march of the enemy'

Regional and local experiences of the Irish famine

Mary Kelly

Introduction

While the famine decade saw an island-wide population decline of almost 20 per cent, the impacts of the disaster were not shared evenly among the populace nor distributed uniformly across the Irish landscape. The west suffered more severely than the east, the south more than the north. The poorer classes suffered most and consequently areas that contained the greatest concentrations of pre-famine poverty suffered severely in terms of excess deaths.[1] These hardest-hit areas were heavily concentrated in the west, although there were pockets of destitution spread to varying degrees all over the country. William Wilde's tables of death, for example, indicate that while pre-famine starvation deaths were more prevalent in the remoter western counties there were also instances of pre-famine starvation elsewhere in the country.[2]

Tracing the varied impacts of the famine as they unfolded across the countryside, this chapter begins by examining growing destitution in pre-famine Ireland because it is along the deepening fault lines of impoverishment and vulnerability that the disaster left its earliest and most severe imprint on the human landscape. However, as the famine wore on, more families, and in particular those occupying small to medium-sized holdings, fell into destitution. This meant that the impact of the famine, measured in terms of different kinds of human suffering, gradually reached into the higher echelons of society and across a wider geographical area. Those who had access to sufficient funds were able to emigrate, and while they may not have suffered in the same way as those who remained in Ireland during the famine years, they too were famine victims.[3] Others pawned their belongings, gave up their holdings, took to the roads or resorted to the workhouse. Many of those who chose this latter option did not survive, particularly when the famine was at its peak.[4] As one west of Ireland relief inspector reported, between March and December 1847 one local workhouse there 'emptied itself into the grave-yard'.[5]

Moreover, the social geography of mid-nineteenth-century Ireland was not just one of increasing impoverishment; it was also a geography of complex but weak social structures. In spite of being a small island, mid-nineteenth-century Ireland was an intricate mosaic of east–west and north–south socio-economic and cultural-environmental configurations, the result of a complicated settlement history upon a landscape of fertile lowlands broken up by rough uplands, drumlins, moorlands, boglands and uncultivable rock land. The west of Ireland contained the greatest amount of poor land and the most unbalanced social structure with overwhelming numbers of impoverished families living among a sparse network of gentry elites. The east contained the greatest quantity of fertile land, the least proportions of impoverishment, and the greatest proportions of affluence. The east also had a well-developed economic structure and contained many market towns. The north and south had more mixed land values and more complex social structures, albeit distributed in different ways across both provinces. Ulster's better-quality land was concentrated in the east which was more densely populated, more urbanised and more industrialised than the west. Munster's fertile land was more dispersed vis-à-vis intermittent uplands and lowlands, although its southern and western peninsulas contained extensive areas that were of poor quality. Any examination of the regional impact of the famine must consider therefore not only the levels of vulnerability to famine particular to each region but also the nature of the existing resource base, the manner in which it was divided among classes and the kinds of relationships that tied communities together. This is important because in times of crisis societies can survive if equipped with adequate resources, systems of shared distribution, social cohesion and political will. Unfortunately, the duration of the famine meant that gradually the ability of people, who in a less protracted crisis may have been able to support those around them either by spending money, providing employment, making goods available on credit, donating to charitable organisations or soliciting external help, had by 1847 been exhausted. Moreover, in the absence of rental incomes, increasingly burdened by poor law taxation, feeling guilty or frustrated about not being able to do more, and often in receipt of threats and abuse from the local peasantry, many gentry families withdrew from community life, barricaded themselves in, or left the country. In addition, in the absence of an autonomous political administration in Dublin, local political agency in many parts of Ireland was compromised as, since the union of the Irish and British Parliaments in 1801, Irish representatives had become disillusioned, fewer in number and increasingly London-based. This undermined their ability to witness local distress levels and to lobby for, or act on behalf of, Irish interests. Pre-existing social conditions within regional and local contexts therefore played a part in determining how the distress unfolded and affected different social groups.

Finally, while the geography of the famine may be traced along the deepening poverty lines and weak social relationships of pre-famine Ireland, it may also be examined as a geography of varied responses. As the effective organisation of relief was dependent on the availability of local agents to initiate and administer schemes and on levels of infrastructural development through which relief could be channelled, those areas in which local agency was scarce and infrastructures weak struggled to deal with the scale of the disaster.[6] Unfortunately, it was often in regions of greatest deprivation and most in need that both local agency and relief infrastructure were in shortest supply. In the town of Lanesboro, for example, it was reported that while a local fund of £20 had been raised for relief, there was not ‘a priest, a parson, church, a chapel, a resident landlord, a magistrate, a policeman, a soldier or a relief committee’ in the district to distribute it to those in need.[7] Moreover, given the manner in which relief funding was dependent on local subscriptions before 1847 and on local taxation thereafter, it was areas most in distress which were least financially equipped to deal with the disaster. However, as news of the suffering reached international audiences, donations from places as far away as India and the Caribbean started to arrive, as did volunteer relief workers from Britain and the United States. This assistance, along with the independent work of the Society of Friends who channelled resources into impoverished areas in the south and west, helped to some extent to offset the social and economic disadvantage that undermined the effectiveness of a poor law that saw all places as being responsible for their own impoverishment.[8]

In tracing the expanding fissures of pre-famine destitution, the varied but problematic social structures and the uneven geography of response, this chapter outlines that while the famine unfolded in multiple and varied ways across the Irish landscape, leaving distinctive marks on each region, no place was beyond the famine’s reach. Witnessing the gradual spread of destitution from the poorer to the better-off neighbourhoods in 1848, one relief inspector reported:

> Many townlands exhibit strong marks of the march of the enemy, in the multitudes of ruined cottages or cabins, the absence of every description of cattle, and the neglected state of the land; yet these contain less destitution, and stand less in need of relief, than the most favoured townlands.[9]

While all the cards may have been stacked against the west of Ireland, this chapter details how interrelated factors operated to various degrees in all parts of the country which, over a prolonged period, resulted in this particular famine escalating to the level of a national disaster.

Pre-famine destitution

Pre-famine destitution, most visible along roadsides, bogsides, mountainsides as well as on commons, town parks and village greens, was well documented in travellers’ accounts of 1800s Ireland. Such images lent support to the Malthusian argument that mid-nineteenth-century Ireland was over-populated and that the famine was a disaster waiting to happen. These images also fed into providentialist discourses that regarded the famine as a punitive ‘visitation of God’ on the Irish for their indolence.[10] In these characterisations, Irish people brought the famine on themselves. Such visible tracts of poverty, however, had a very distinct geography and were the outcome of a number of processes that had become particularly acute in the decades leading up to the famine. As the better-quality land had become occupied, marginal lands – mostly in the west but also in uplands, boglands and coastal fringes elsewhere – became the domain of the less well-off.[11] In these areas restrictions on subdivision were lax as landlords were often not interested in the goings-on in remote and unprofitable districts. Moreover, the keeping of large numbers of rent-paying tenants was often more feasible and more lucrative in such areas than either cattle or crop production.[12] Landowners, middlemen and agents benefited from the practice of letting to multiple occupiers, while for subsistence-based families – concentrated in areas where employment was scarce – partible inheritance was a way to ensure that all sons had some form of livelihood. Commons or land with uncertain ownership also became places into which expanding communities could settle.[13] The availability of land for children, regardless of how small in size, encouraged early marriage. Consequently, population pressure increased but landholding sizes decreased, resulting in more people subsisting on less and less land. The high calorific potato, which produced good yields on limited acreages and more importantly on poor soils, became the staple foodstuff of these communities and it was on this single crop that they came to depend for survival.[14] It was in the west of Ireland that this situation became most acute. The extent of poor land in the west, some of which was still available for settlement, facilitated continued pre-famine population growth among subsistence-based communities. Moreover, the poor quality of the soil and patchiness of fertility in this region had resulted in the evolution of a more complicated and fragmented estate system. The limited productive capacity of the land also meant that wealthy landlords were few. Many were heavily indebted and many spent their time elsewhere. Thus the availability of poor land for settlement facilitated natural population increases and, where further settlement expansion was no longer possible, subdivision went unchecked.

The emergence of settlements on bogland in County Roscommon was noted as early as 1814. Reporting to the Bogs Commission, John Longfield stated:

> the population of the county of Roscommon (although generally considered as a grazing county) is exceedingly great, so much so, that every little island or peninsula in the bogs contains more than an ordinary proportion of inhabitants; as an instance of which, I shall mention one island near Lough Glynn of 107 acres, called Cloonborny, that contains no less than 21 families, being little more than five acres to each house.[15]

However, pressure on these settlements was exacerbated by land management policies then being introduced on some of the better-run estates. Recognising the unsustainable nature of existing practices, some landlords encouraged the gradual removal of excess tenants to make way for more economically viable farm sizes or to facilitate the expansion of grazing. The aesthetics of the restructured but depopulated landscapes that result from such policies is recorded by Weld in 1830. Describing part of the countryside not far from the colonised bog that Longfield had commented on some decades earlier, he states:

> The country in the vicinity of Tulsk is reputed to afford some of the richest pastures in this fertile part of Ireland.... The farms [here] are considerable from three hundred acres Irish, a quantity of land very commonly held by a single individual, up to one thousand acres and more.... Sometimes the

> traces of ancient hawthorn hedges, marked by insulated bushes in even lines, but at very remote intervals, afford proof that in former times the subdivisions of the land were more numerous … vast herds may [now] be observed together, spread over the hills, where scarcely tree or even a bush is to be seen. Habitations are few.[16]

Those tenants cleared from their smallholdings relocated to poorer uplands or wasteland, thus creating new enclaves or exacerbating existing ones. Others were put to the roads where they proceeded to seek out their own spaces in ditches, on unsettled bogs or commons, or by moving in with already overcrowded kinspeople. The Devon Commission Report (1845) is replete with unashamed accounts by landlords and agents on the manner in which clearances were effected. Henry Kelly from Galway reported that he had 'not the slightest difficulty' in 'getting rid of the rundale' that existed on an estate which was 'covered with a pauper population'. He divided the land among those who could keep it in a good state of cultivation. With respect to the paupers for whom he could not make room, he explained:

> I set aside a proportion which they called Ballybeggarman; and instead of throwing them on the road side I sacrificed a few acres and let them go there; many of them have since either emigrated to America or got holdings elsewhere.[17]

Another reported that in clearing his estate he divided the land between 'those who had the most land in possession, those who had the best characters, those who were most solvent, and those who had been longest living on the land'.[18] The remainder, 33 families, were sent on their way. The move towards grazing and other kinds of commercial farming also meant that there was less land available for small cottier farmers and fewer employment opportunities for rural labourers. One Connemara priest referred to graziers as a 'tuberculosis on the constitution … spreading out on the vitals of the people'.[19] In the absence of land to produce food or a money wage with which to procure it, country people became increasingly dependent on the potato. Weld had witnessed squatter settlements being erected among the ruins of a medieval abbey in the town of Roscommon, the grounds of which were already planted with potatoes, while the enclosure of its castle was completely under potatoes.[20] However, this was not just a west of Ireland phenomenon. Increasing impoverishment in marginal areas stretched eastward across the Shannon into east-Leinster.[21] As recorded in the 1841 Ordnance Survey Field books for Moyglare in fertile Co. Meath:

> Nine-tenths of this land is down in grazing and is occupied by non-resident graziers who stock it with their own cattle and keep herds and caretakers on the land.… The inhabitants, with the exception of four or five families are wretchedly poor. Their food is potatoes or salt, and it is only with much difficulty that they procure as much fuel as will boil the potatoes.[22]

Similarly, the return to pastoral grazing in the fertile lowlands of Munster forced rural labourers to settle peripheral mountain areas where they eked out an existence on potatoes.[23] Ulster also had its share of rural destitution; an outcome of estate rationalisation and the decline of domestic spinning industries. As Ulster's textile production industrialised, it contracted northward and eastward. As a result home spinning and weaving which kept many families in south and west Ulster afloat went into decline. Textiles produced in homes here could not compete with those being produced in the towns, where economies of scale afforded competitive advantage. In the absence of domestic incomes which supplemented what was produced by farming, families resorted to the potato and thus became as vulnerable to disaster as their southern and western counterparts.[24]

Connaught counties, along with those on the western seaboard, however, were most severely affected by the famine because these counties contained the highest proportions of unprofitable land and the greatest proportions of impoverished communities. Moreover, while population growth had slowed down on the better-managed estates of the east, population numbers in the west continued to rise. Examination of population growth between 1821 and 1841 illustrates that counties on the western side of the island had increased by over 30 per cent, while increases on the eastern side were as low as 10 per cent (Map 2.1). The population of County Roscommon, regarded by Longfield as being 'exceedingly great' in 1814, was to increase by a further 40 to 50 per cent before the outbreak of the famine. Analysis of pre-famine population change at parish level reveals that in parts of the extreme west increases were of a similar magnitude.[25]

An insight into the geography of this pre-famine vulnerability, which was heavily concentrated in the west of the country, may be gleaned from an examination of population density per acre of crop land[26] (Map 2.2). As illustrated in Map 2.2, over much of the island there were about 2.5 people for every acre of crops. In the east, however, there was less than one person per acre of crops, while in Connaught more than five people depended on each acre of crop land and in some places the figure was over 7.5. The population pressure evident here corresponds closely to the distribution of potato acreages in 1851, which is presented in Map 2.3 as an indicator of the geography of potato cultivation (though not the intensity of cultivation). These heavily populated potato dependent regions felt the full force of the famine both in terms of population decline and excess mortality (Map 2.4).

Social structures

As outlined above, Connaught was the province that contained the greatest amount of impoverishment on the eve of the famine. Almost half of the population were living in one-roomed cabins made of mud and a further 40 per cent were living in houses of a similar standard, albeit with two to four rooms and windows. Less than 1 per cent of the housing in this western region was of the first-class category (dwellings regarded as better than a good farmhouse or townhouse) while less than 10 per cent were categorised as second-class houses

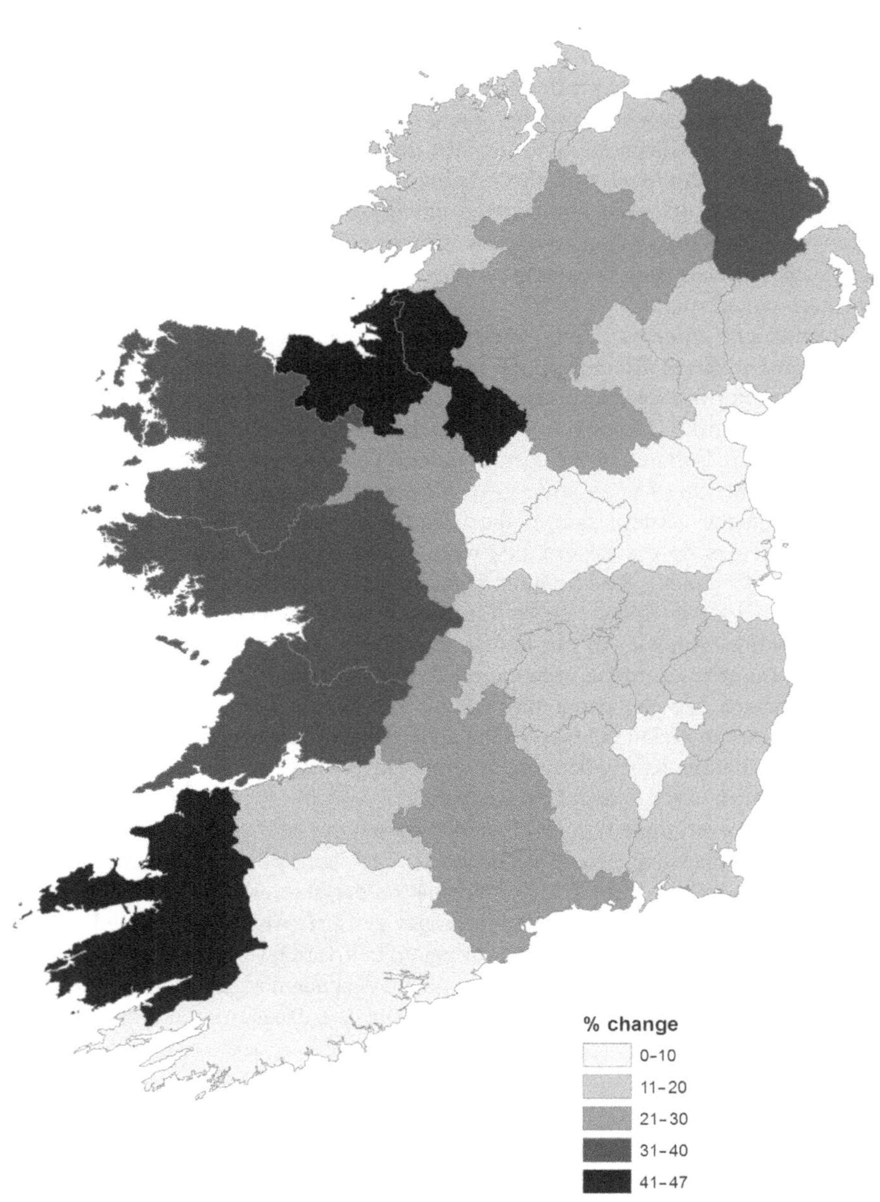

Map 2.1 Population change, 1821 to 1841.

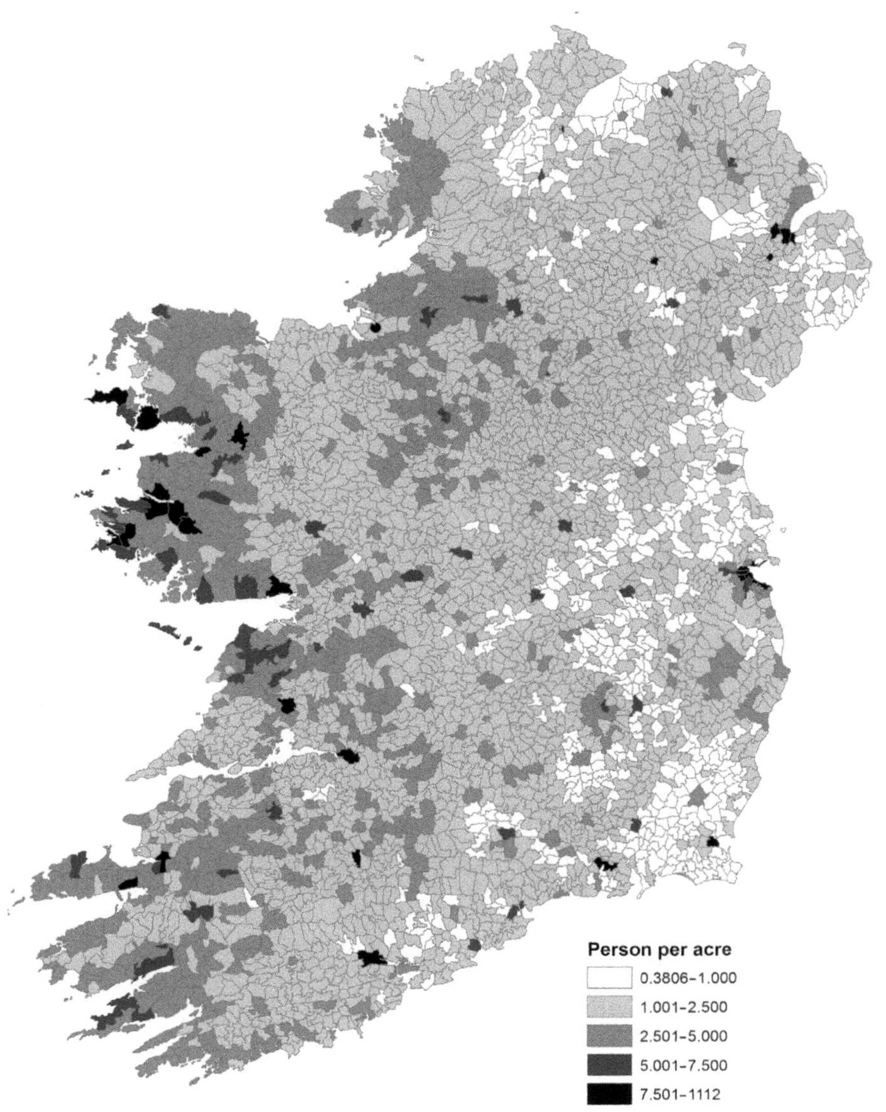

Map 2.2 Population density per acre of crop land, 1841.

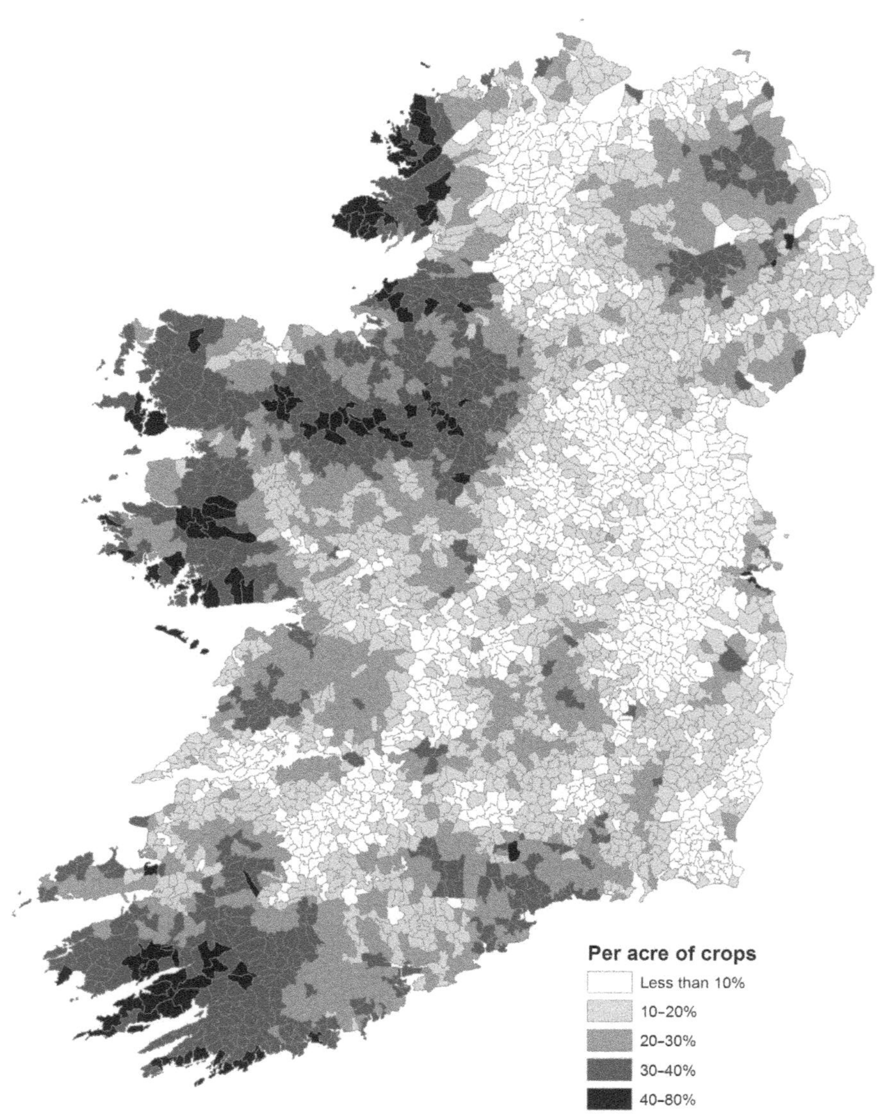

Map 2.3 Potato acres per acre of crops, 1851.

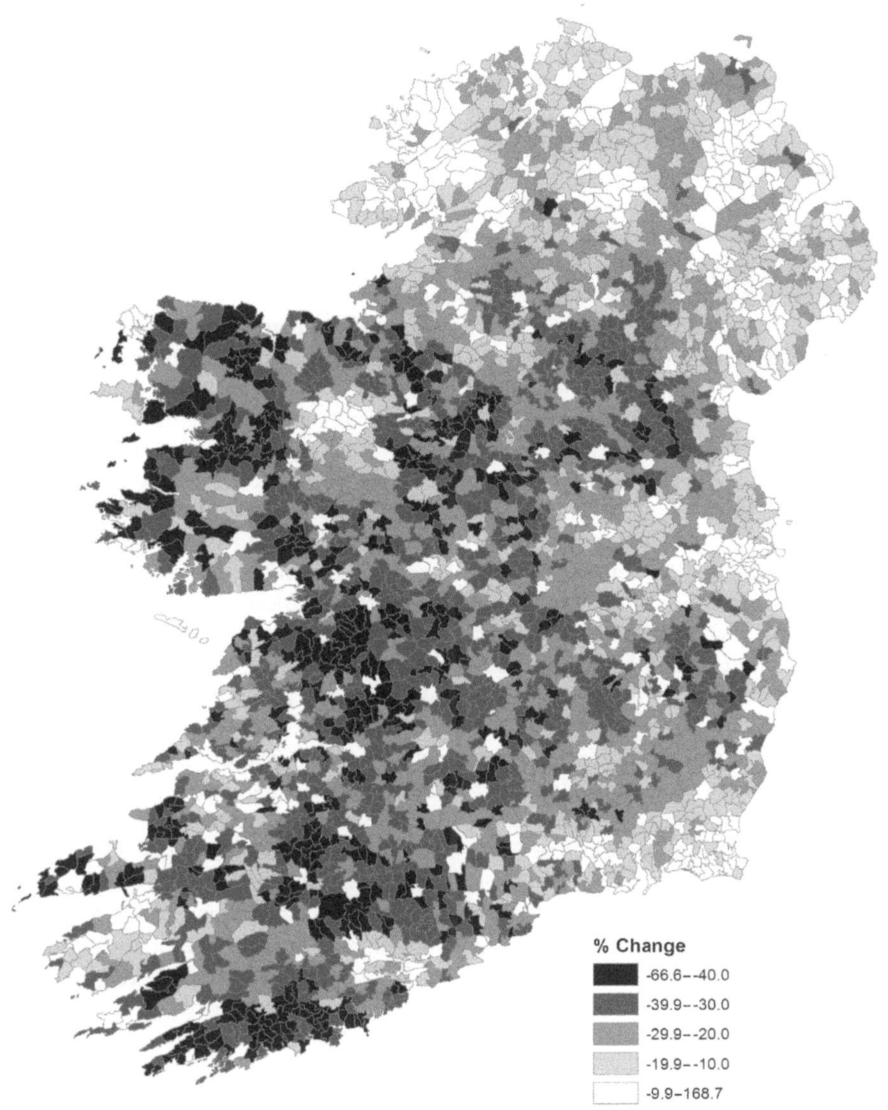

Map 2.4 Population change, 1841 to 1851.

(a good farmhouse or townhouse). Moreover, not only were wealthy landlords not as numerous here as they were in other parts of Ireland, but in this region of marginal profitability landlords often lived beyond their means and were heavily mortgaged. The fragility of this social structure, whereby gentry families, limited in number and not very well-off, were surrounded by impoverished tenants upon whom they were dependant for their income, became apparent when the potato blight struck.

While Connaught contained the greatest concentrations of poverty and the least amount of wealth, Munster was a more complex social world made up of a more mixed class structure. This province, which comprised 'good land, poor land, wet land, moorland, extensive coastlands, remote rural regions and sophisticated port cities', had a settlement history that was different to that of Connaught and it contained better proportions of fertile soil and more balanced resource allocations.[27] While the western and southern fringes resembled the west of Ireland generally, the rest of the province was characterised by a series of uncultivated uplands – many of which had recently been settled – interspersed with long-settled fertile lowlands. This diversified landscape is illustrated in Map 2.5, which shows valuation per acre in 1851. Along the western fringes, land values were less than 10 pence per acre. Here population pressure per acre of crop land was as high as in Connaught (Map 2.2). The rest of the province was characterised by a better and more varied pattern of land values and by more balanced population densities per acre of crops. This more diversified landscape provided the context for a social structure that was more complex than that of Connaught, where more families occupied less land. In Connaught, 64.3 per cent of farms were classified as being between one and five acres, 29.1 per cent were between five and 15 acres while only just over 6 per cent were over 15 acres. In Munster, 35.4 per cent were between one and five acres, 38 per cent were between five and 15 acres and 26 per cent were over 15 acres.[28] This variation in farm sizes may be seen in Map 2.6. Significant disparities are evident among the overwhelming numbers of farms between one and five acres in Galway, Mayo and Roscommon as opposed to Cork, Waterford, Limerick or Kerry where there was a more equal distribution of each category – and in some instances more farms of five to 15 acres than there were below five acres. Many of the occupiers of farms of five to 15 acres were nonetheless poor farmers. Respondents to the Devon Commission reported that a family of five needed about ten acres to survive in Ireland in the mid-1840s. However, the gap between wealth and poverty evident in Connaught was bridged in Munster by the existence of a sizeable middle-income group. This is also evident in the better mix of first-, second-, third- and fourth-class house types in Munster being 2.8 per cent, 17.8 per cent, 24.3 per cent and 45 per cent, respectively, and by the fact that a greater proportion of the population in Munster had access to some kind of capital. In Connaught, 79 per cent of people were classified as being 'without capital, in either money, land or acquired knowledge', having their physical labour as their only means. In Munster, 67.3 per cent were without capital – lower than that for Connaught although higher than in Ulster or Leinster. In addition to its more

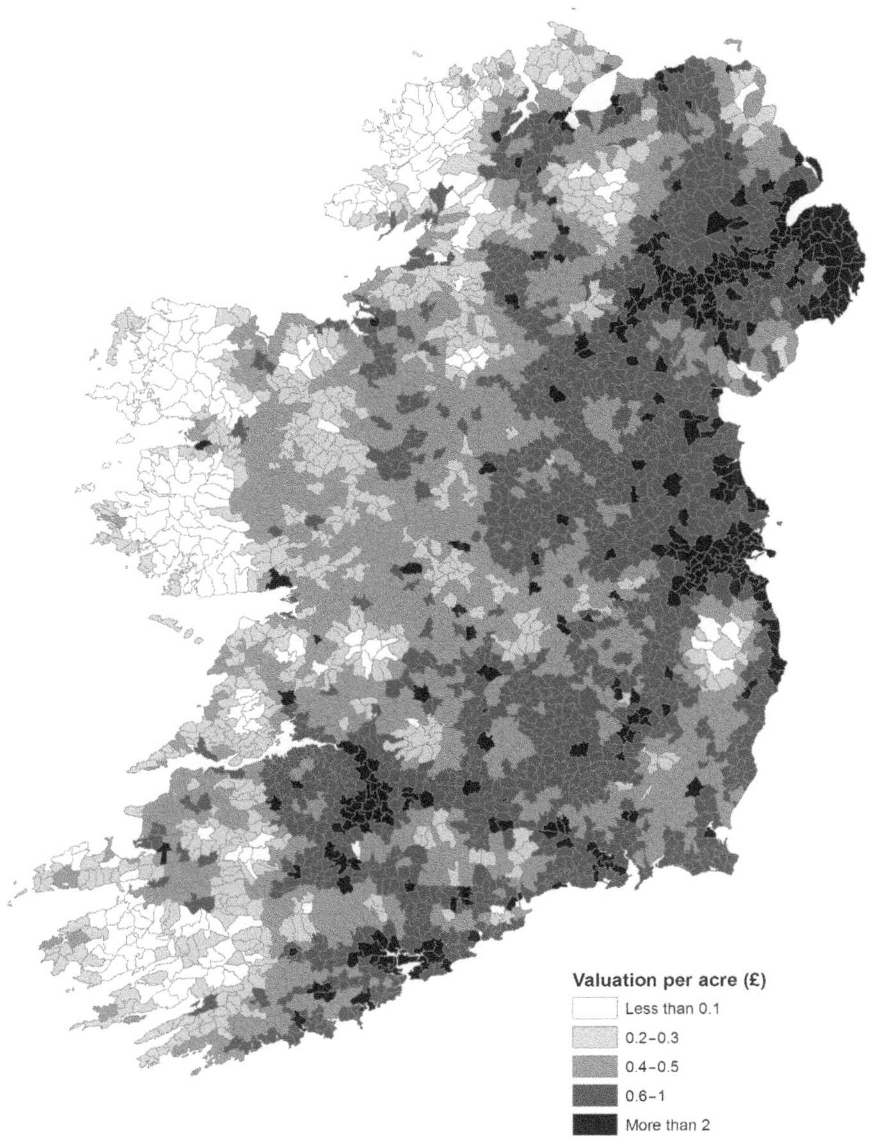

Map 2.5 Land valuation per acre, 1851.

complex social structure, its higher proportion of good land and larger average farm sizes, Munster also had a good urban network, contained a number of port towns, and had an occupational structure that was more varied than in Connaught.

However, a number of characteristics of Munster's social landscape meant that suffering here was only marginally less than that experienced in Connaught. First, this was a province where large numbers of labourers were paid in

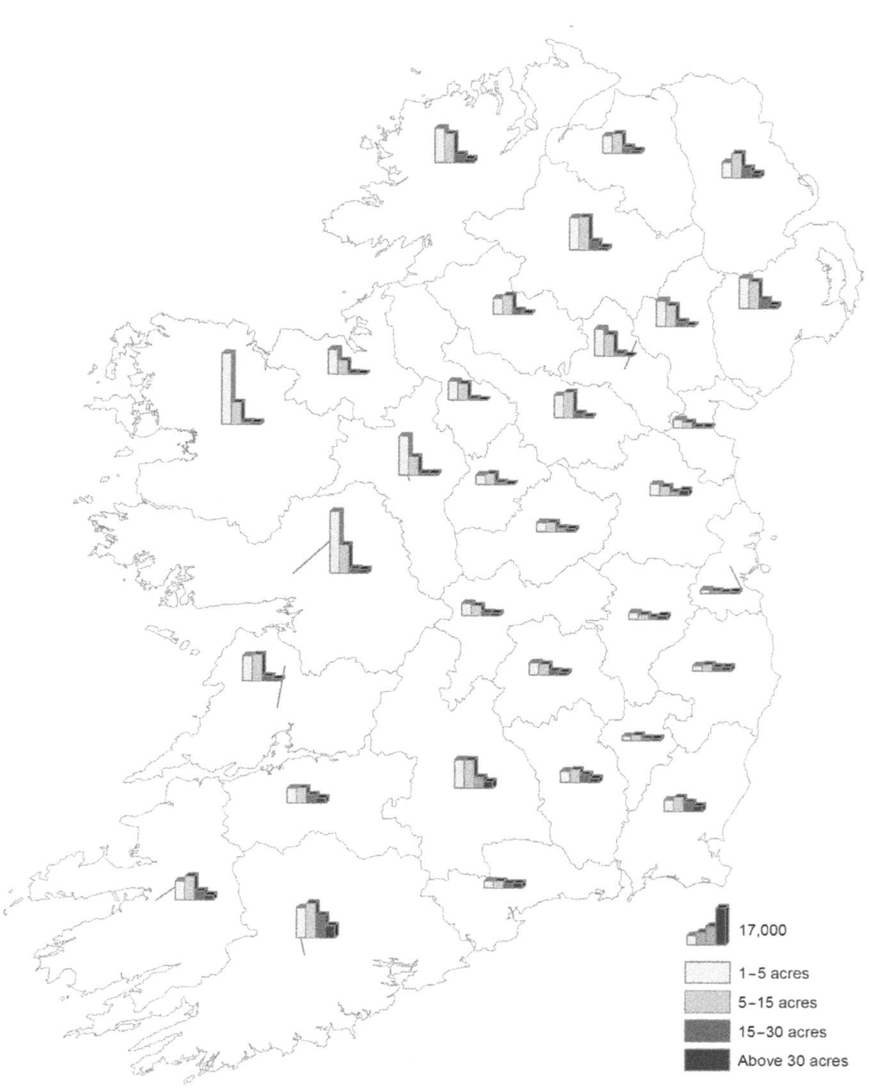

Map 2.6 Farm sizes at county level, 1841.

conacre. Munster labourers were twice as likely to be paid in *conacre* than their Connaught counterparts.[29] In the absence of a money wage, these labourers were heavily dependent on their potato crop and consequently, in spite of having more land and more employment opportunities than the people of the west, suffered greatly when their crops were destroyed. Moreover, without a monetary income or land of their own to sell and to some extent more tied to local landowners from whose land they produced their own food, emigration was not an option for many Munster labourers. Excess mortality in this southern province was therefore higher than in either Ulster or Leinster (Map 2.7). Moreover, witnessing the increasing destitution around them, many of those who had the means to emigrate did so.[30] While 6.6 per cent of Munster's 1841 population died from famine or famine-related disease over the subsequent decade, 16 per cent emigrated. This exodus may have been fuelled not only by the greater relative wealth of Munster's middle-sized farmers who could take flight, but also by the fact that Munster was characterised by a high incidence of eviction, a legal method of removing troublesome or insolvent tenants from the land. Constabulary reports from this province indicate that approximately 45,000 Munster families (250,000 people) were put to the roads between 1846 and 1852, constituting 43.1 per cent of all evictions carried out in Ireland during this period.[31] The high incidence of ejectments in Munster may partly be explained by the fact that Munster had been the heartland of much pre-famine agrarian agitation and famine-related unrest, and eviction was an established solution to this problem. However, the poor law which forced landowners to pay the tax of tenants occupying holdings valued below £4 also incentivised clearances. Moreover, many of Munster's smallholders who may have been on the threshold of this category, recognising the deteriorating state of the country and the already widespread culture of eviction around them, did not wait for their time to come. Thus, while Munster cottiers and labourers were in general better off than those in Connaught, they too lived on a precarious margin which, during a period of prolonged crisis, could not sustain them. The scars of its population loss, primarily the result of the flow of emigration from Munster's many ports, is visible in Map 2.4. As may be seen here, significant stretches of rural Cork, Tipperary, Limerick and Clare suffered losses in excess of 40 per cent.

If Connaught was least well equipped to cope with famine, Leinster was in the best position to withstand the famine onslaught.[32] This province had the highest land values, the greatest proportion of wealthy people and the lowest levels of impoverishment. Like Munster, Leinster had a complex social structure with substantial numbers of middle-income people living on moderate farm sizes (Map 2.6). Overall, 43 per cent of the population had over 15 acres, and 25 per cent had over 20 acres. These farming families participated in commercial agriculture and were a more monetised class. Moreover, partible inheritance, which resulted in ever-increasing numbers subsisting on ever-decreasing farm sizes in other parts of Ireland, had largely been replaced here by single inheritance. This served to maintain the viability of farm sizes and freed those not in line for inheritance to seek employment elsewhere. As a result, Leinster had a more

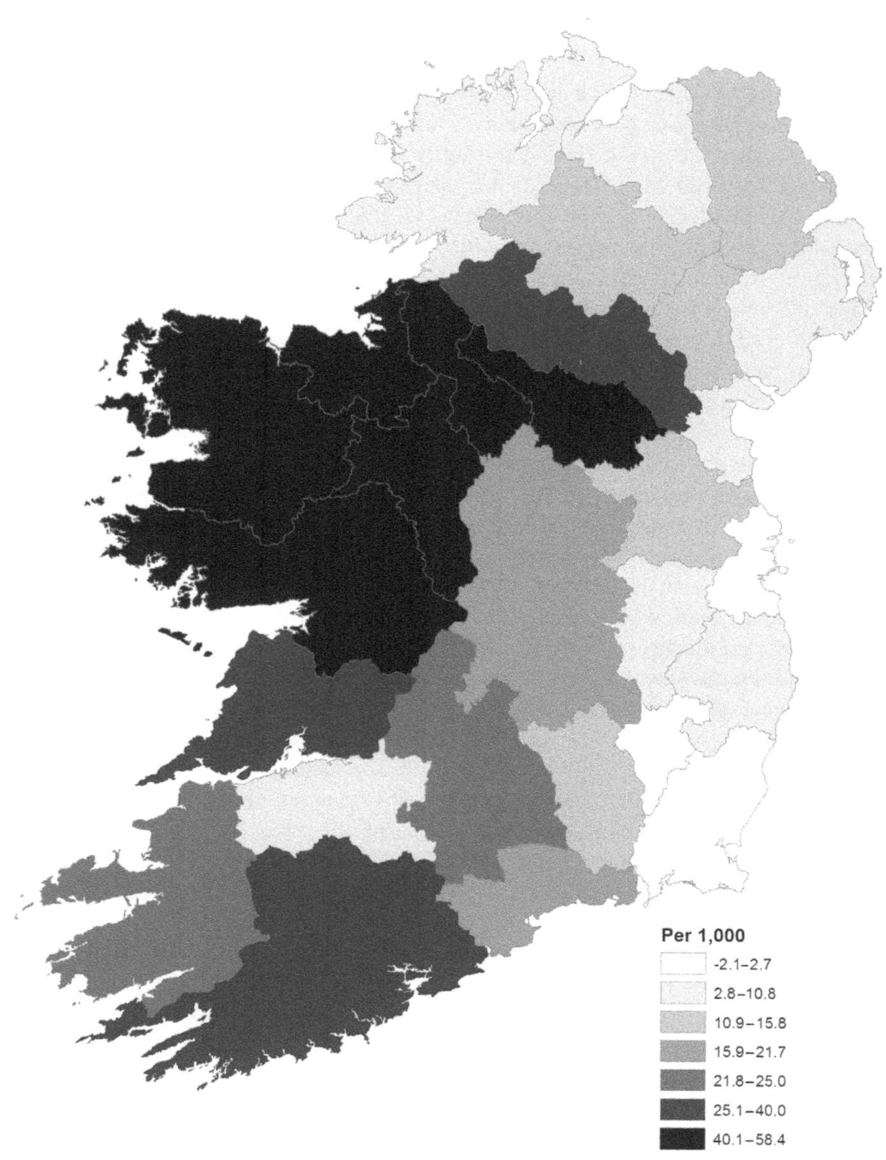

Map 2.7 Excess mortality, 1841 to 1851

complex occupational structure with more people engaged in non-agricultural activities than in other parts of Ireland. Leinster also had a well-developed urban network that contained numerous market as well as port towns, with Dublin, the administrative capital, providing an outlet for goods and services from the surrounding areas as well as providing employment opportunities for an increasingly migrant population.

While on the surface Leinster's socio-economic structure appeared to exhibit stark contrasts with that of Connaught, the affluent east was also undercut by local disparities. Indeed, Leinster was as much a land of extremes, with wealth and poverty existing side by side, as was the west of Ireland. While 25 per cent of the farms in Leinster were over 20 acres, 36 per cent were between one and five acres. Those who occupied these smallest of farms, coupled with those on less than one acre and those without land, constituted the underclass whose labour serviced the larger commercial farms. These people, like the poor in Connaught, occupied the marginal interstices, and while they could be found to varying degrees across the province, they were more densely concentrated in the west which was characterised by more extensive, though fragmented, stretches of poor land alongside good land. The communities who occupied these areas sold their labour to the larger commercial farmers in return for money wages which were often used to pay the rent. Some labourers, however, were paid in *conacre*. As a result, they lived by subsistence or partial subsistence and did so in increasingly congested conditions. As outlined by Jones-Hughes, population density in Leinster was highest on the poorest of land and, as in the west of Ireland, pressure on these communities was mounting.[33] The expansion of grazing, particularly in the north of the province, forced many to seek refuge in the unregulated enclaves where subdivision was still practised. The potato, which enabled these ever-increasing numbers to survive on small plot sizes, was also the response to these pressures here.[34] As might be expected, it was these Leinster communities (not as widespread as in Connaught but significant none the less) who felt the full force of the catastrophe and, while Leinster experienced a level of famine mortality lower than the national average, in some of the poorer and more densely populated regions of west Leinster excess mortalities were as high as in parts of the west of Ireland. Moreover, due to the more monetised nature of the Leinster economy, coupled with the existence of a significant proportion of farmers occupying five to 15 acres (burdened by poor law taxation if occupying land valued at over £4 but living under the threat of distrain[35] and possibly eviction if unable to pay), small Leinster farmers, like those in Munster, seeing the deteriorating conditions of those around them and having the means and the freedom to emigrate, did so. Their proximity to ports may also have made the decision to depart somewhat easier. As estimated by Cousens, up to 70 per cent of those who disappeared from this province during the famine years did so as emigrants.[36]

In 1841, Ulster was the most densely settled and intensively cultivated province on the island. Here, population density was 406 people per square mile of arable land, higher than in any of the other three regions, while the proportion of land classified as arable was greater than in either Connaught or Munster. However, Ulster was also a province of contrasts, with much regional variation in the distribution of good-quality land, farm sizes, population densities per acre of crops, house classifications, work patterns and social relationships. The west of the province was more impoverished and characterised by traditions and practices similar to those of the west of Ireland in general. Only one-third of Donegal and just over half of Tyrone was classified as arable and in both of these counties land devoted to crop production was limited. Across large areas of Donegal, for example, less than 10 per cent of the land surface was under crops. Thus, while overall crop densities were low, densities per crop acre were high (Map 2.2). However, while the people in west Ulster depended on potatoes to the same extent as impoverished communities elsewhere, seasonal migration to Scotland provided many families with supplementary incomes which helped tide them over during the hungry months before crops were harvested.[37] Moreover, relations between landlords and tenants were somewhat different in Donegal than they were in the other northern counties. The Ulster custom, a practice whereby landowners provided occupiers with fairer rents, some measure of fixity of tenure, and the opportunity to sell their holdings if they so wished, strengthened the bond between landlords and tenants.[38] The Ulster custom also gave occupiers more financial power and freedom of mobility. Thus the social structure in this part of Ireland resembled that in the impoverished west in general but the strong tradition of seasonal migration, coupled with better landlord–tenant relationships and to some extent better tenant rights, meant that people here were not as vulnerable when the famine struck.

In the east of the province, population densities were higher but, with better-quality soils and more land under crop cultivation, this region could sustain higher numbers. Moreover, east Ulster's expanding textile industry stimulated local domestic craft industries such as lace making and embroidery. This meant that rural communities here were not as dependent on subsistence farming as were those to the west or south of the province. Overall, 33 per cent of Ulster workers were engaged in manufacturing (as opposed to 26 per cent in Leinster, 19 per cent in Munster and 15 per cent in Connaught) and these producers were predominantly concentrated in the east. Thus, while farm sizes in the province were similar to the west of Ireland, with large numbers of families living on smallholdings (Map 2.6), the overall better land quality and the availability of secondary sources of employment gave people here a better standard of living and more choices in terms of what they could grow, eat and work at.

However, as outlined above, to the south and west of the province, remoter cottage industries, unable to compete with the better textiles being produced in the east, had fallen into decline. As a result, small farming families here had become increasingly reliant on potatoes in the run-up to the famine. Moreover, while Ulster labourers were not as dependent on *conacre* as a form of payment as elsewhere – making them less dependent on the potato crop, more familiar with the use of money, and better placed to escape from their smallholdings – *conacre* was still practised in parts of Cavan, Monaghan and Armagh. Labourers from these areas therefore had fewer options. However, the effects of the Ulster custom, albeit expressed in different ways in different places, may have saved some communities from the kind of widespread suffering and death experienced in the west. The Shirleys, for example, assisted large numbers of people to emigrate from their estate in Co. Monaghan, thereby increasing their chances of survival but leaving a significant scar on the human landscape locally.[39] Excess deaths were, however, high in parts of Armagh, Cavan, Monaghan, Tyrone and Fermanagh.

The better-off position of the people of this province overall, notwithstanding significant local variation, is borne out in their housing classifications. Only 30 per cent of Ulster people were living in fourth-class accommodation, with the greatest bulk (43%) living in third-class houses. However, the heaviest concentrations of better-quality housing were to be found in east Ulster. Forty-three per cent of people in Donegal were living in fourth-class houses, while Cavan, Fermanagh, Londonderry and Tyrone also had higher proportions of people living in the poor one-roomed cabins than the national average. Thus the fissures of poverty, population pressure and potato dependency evident all over the country, while not as prevalent in a province characterised by different socio-economic structures, work patterns and social relationships, were visible on Ulster's southern and western fringes. Cavan, Monaghan and Fermanagh suffered population losses as high as those experienced on the western seaboard. However, the better-off and more monetised position of people here, coupled with established traditions of seasonal migration and assisted migration from landlords, meant that a large proportion of the population losses here was a result of emigration rather than excess mortality. Population decline over the rest of the province was in general lower (Map 2.4), albeit with localised variations. Thus, while Ulster as a whole did not suffer to the same extent or in the same way as the rest of the country, areas of severe destitution and suffering could also be found in this province.[40]

Geography of famine relief

The final issue to be considered in this chapter is the geography of famine relief because the unevenness of the famine relates not only to the varied levels of poverty and vulnerability that existed in pre-famine Ireland, but also to the kinds of responses that were initiated in local acres to deal with the disaster. The Poor Law was introduced into Ireland in 1838 to deal with destitution in the Irish countryside. This legislation called for the division of the island into 130 unions which would each contain a workhouse. Workhouses were to be managed by a board of locally elected representatives and paid for through local taxation.[41] There were a number of problems with the introduction of an English-style poor law to Ireland. First, it had been recognised that the English system was not suitable in Ireland because of the high levels of poverty on the island and, as was to become abundantly clear, areas characterised by concentrated poverty would not have the resources to deal with it.[42] At the outbreak of the famine only 123 workhouses had been completed and it was in the most impoverished unions in the west where they would soon be most needed that they were scarcest (Map 2.8). Moreover, the taxation system upon which the Poor Law was based, whereby landowners were liable for the taxes rated on holdings of less than £4, meant that in the parts of the country characterised by high numbers of people living on smallholdings, the burden of the poor rate was carried by the landowners. Examination of the imbalance between ratepayers and non-ratepayers as recorded in April 1846 shows that overall, 42 per cent of the population were not liable for their own rates, but that the proportions of those not liable were far greater in western unions where up to 80 per cent did not pay their own rates (Map 2.9).[43] The indebted nature of many landowners in the west of Ireland, coupled with the fact that they were few in number in this region, meant that the heaviest burden on the island was levied on a community least capable of dealing with it. As a consequence, many landowners sought to 'disencumber' their estates by evicting tenants occupying holding sizes so small that the landlord would be liable for taxes, thereby turning the rural poor into paupers.[44] From the outset therefore, the Poor Law as implemented in Ireland was not only undermined by regional poverty but in fact exacerbated by it.

By November 1845, it had become clear that additional measures would be needed to deal with the unfolding crisis, and a Temporary Relief Commission was established to oversee the administration of relief operations. Boards of guardians around the country were instructed to set up local relief committees. These committees were to be responsible for raising subscriptions locally, which could be used to purchase Indian corn. This corn could then be sold cheaply to those in need. Whatever was raised by local efforts was matched by a government grant. Such a system was again wholly dependent on the existence, willingness and ability of local agents to establish committees, to raise funds and to manage schemes. As outlined above, in some parts of the country such people were in short supply. In other places local relief efforts were hindered by bureaucracy. A request for a grant made by the Tisrara Relief Committee in the barony of Athlone, for example, was denied due to the fact that the committee had spent the funds it had raised on gratuitous relief. Providing free food to the poor was against relief commission regulations which stipulated that food had to be sold, albeit at a low cost, but could not be given for nothing.[45] In other places committees were slow to get started.[46] Moreover, rioting around corn depots, the delayed arrival of stocks, reports of corruption and objections against the sale of cheap food from local provisions traders hindered the effectiveness of this scheme.

Relief committees were also responsible for the establishment of public work schemes which would provide employment for those without the means to purchase cheap corn. Such schemes were also problematic as projects had again to be initiated by local agents, the criteria for eligibility were ambiguous and open to abuse, and schemes were criticised by potential employers for creating a culture of dependency locally. In addition, the weakened and malnourished state of labourers meant that deaths on the roads were common and the Board of Works often received bills for coffins and burials from the families of those who

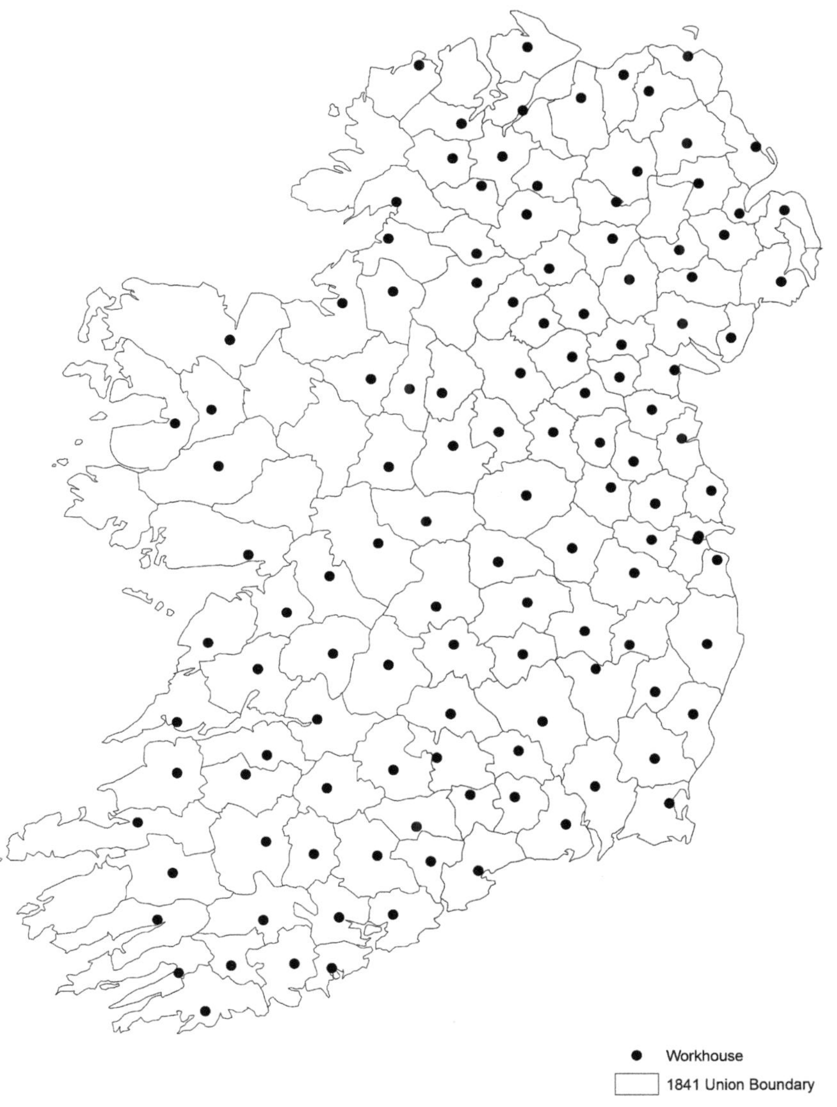

Map 2.8 Workhouses in operation, 1845.

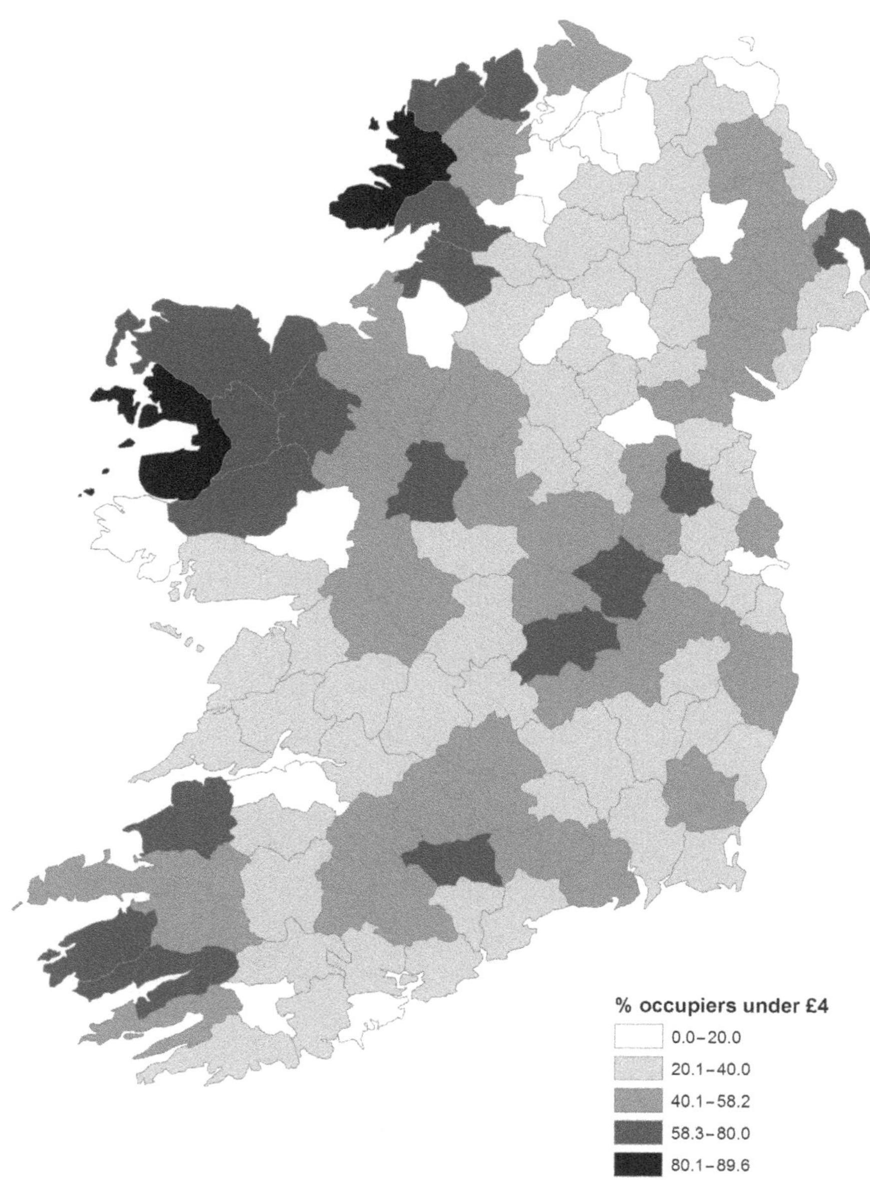

Map 2.9 Proportion of people not paying rates, 1846.

had died while employed on public work schemes. Another problem was that the public works, like the food depots, were places of contagion.[47] In spite of these weaknesses, large numbers of people were employed on the schemes and, notwithstanding the limited infrastructure in place in the west, far greater numbers of people from Clare, Galway, Mayo, Sligo and Roscommon were employed on them than from other counties.[48] This reflects the uneven geography of need, which was heavily concentrated in the west. The numbers employed in Ulster were also low and some counties did not participate in the schemes. This was again due in part to the overall lower levels of destitution in this province but also to the existence of a philosophy of self-reliance that characterised northern outlooks. The absence of official relief schemes in Ulster, however, was offset by unofficial schemes, as landlords here sought to manage destitution on their own estates without public assistance.[49]

By early 1847 the inadequacies of the public works and the need for free food had become apparent. Following the success of charitable organisations like the Society of Friends, who had established soup kitchens independently of the relief committees, the government passed the Temporary Relief Act (or Soup Kitchen Act). This called for the setting up of soup distribution points in every electoral division in Ireland, from which free food could be given to the poor.[50] This measure met with some success. By the summer of 1847 soup stations had been established all over the country and 700,000 people were being fed daily. Analysis of ration distribution in July 1847, when the soup kitchen scheme was at its peak, illustrates that it was again in the western unions of Connaught and Munster that the greatest proportions of people were in receipt of food rations. Over much of Galway, Mayo, Clare, Limerick and Kerry, over 45 per cent of the population were in receipt of rations, although in the far west the figure was as high as 80 per cent.[51] Over much of Ulster less than 15 per cent of people were receiving rations. The low figures here were once again partly due to the reluctance of Ulster landowners to operate under the terms of the Act, some seeing it as a 'disgrace to the province'.[52]

In Leinster, ration distribution was also lower in the east of the province – between 15 and 25 per cent of the population were in receipt of food – while unions in the west of Leinster were higher. However, believing that the famine would end in September 1847, when the harvest of that year was gathered, the government terminated the Soup Kitchen Act at the end of August and responsibility for destitution again fell on the Poor Law guardians of each union. After two years of famine, during which little rent had been paid, employment had dried up, surplus provisions had been depleted, and valuables had been sold or pawned, local areas were less well equipped to deal with existing levels of distress or with any further calamities. Not only was there still an enormous imbalance between the numbers of those liable for rates and those dependent on it, but rate collection was now almost impossible – particularly in the remoter and hardest hit areas. Map 2.10 shows the amount of rates collected in 1848 as a percentage of the amount due, illustrating the geography of shortfall heavily concentrated in the west.[53] Moreover, the Poor Law Amendment Act (1847) called

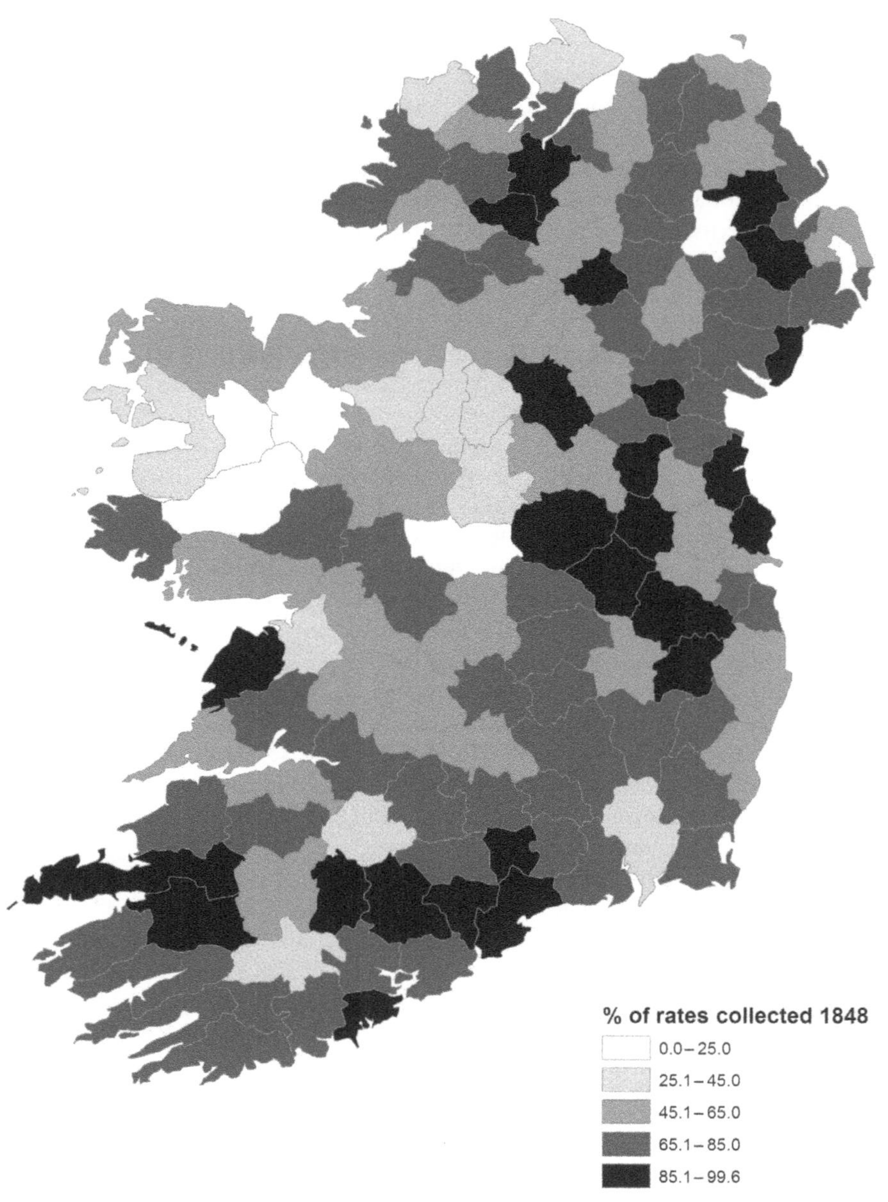

Map 2.10 Proportion of rates not collected, 1848.

for the taxation of each electoral division on the basis of its level of distress as opposed to distributing it across the union. This served to further concentrate the burden on areas least able to cope with it. In response landlords carried out localised removals either in the form of ejectments for non-payment of rent or as assisted migration. Ejectments served to swell pauper numbers locally which resulted in heavier taxation. Assisted migration was cheaper than paying for paupers in the workhouse and it removed the burden from the area. While such schemes account for only about 5 per cent of overall emigration they did have a very real impact on population numbers locally.[54]

One section of the 1847 Act, the Gregory clause, had particularly serious consequences for smallholders. This clause stipulated that families occupying more than a quarter of an acre were not eligible for relief. This resulted in thousands of families giving up their land so as to be eligible. The clause also provided legitimacy to landlords to evict tenants on the basis that eviction would render families eligible. The huge numbers crowding into Carrick-on-Shannon in search of relief, as explained by a relief officer there, was the direct outcome of this policy. In November 1847 he reported that:

> there are now wandering about the Union almost 1,600 persons, most of whom have given up their houses and land and are only waiting for admittance [to the workhouse].[55]

While the 1847 potato harvest was blight-free, it was a year of severe food scarcity. With little seed for planting in the early part of the year, potato acreages were a fraction of what they had been prior to 1845.[56] However, blight struck again in 1848, resulting in a 50 per cent failure in some areas, and both 1849 and 1850 were years of partial potato crop failure. This led to prolonged destitution in many areas, particularly so in Munster, where, as illustrated in Smyth's analysis of the data on workhouse admissions, outdoor relief, excess mortalities, starvation deaths and continued emigration, famine distress lingered well into the 1850s and beyond. By 1848 the inadequacy of the poor law union system was becoming clear. Boards of Guardians had become exhausted and over the course of the year most were dissolved and replaced by paid officials. The futility of a blanket policy of local property paying for local poverty had also become apparent. In 1848 the government declared that 22 unions, mostly in the west of Ireland, were officially in distress and required external assistance. In 1850 the existing union network was revised to facilitate the creation of 33 new unions. Again, many of the new unions were in the west where the existing ones had covered geographical areas too vast and too impoverished to be adequately serviced by a single central workhouse (Map 2.11). These changes in policy, while implemented too late for those who had already died, illustrate that eventually there was a recognition on the part of government that however rational and egalitarian the poor law system was in design and principle, the reality was that not all places were equal, and that the level of distress experienced and types of assistance required in particular areas needed to be taken into consideration for any relief operation to be effective.

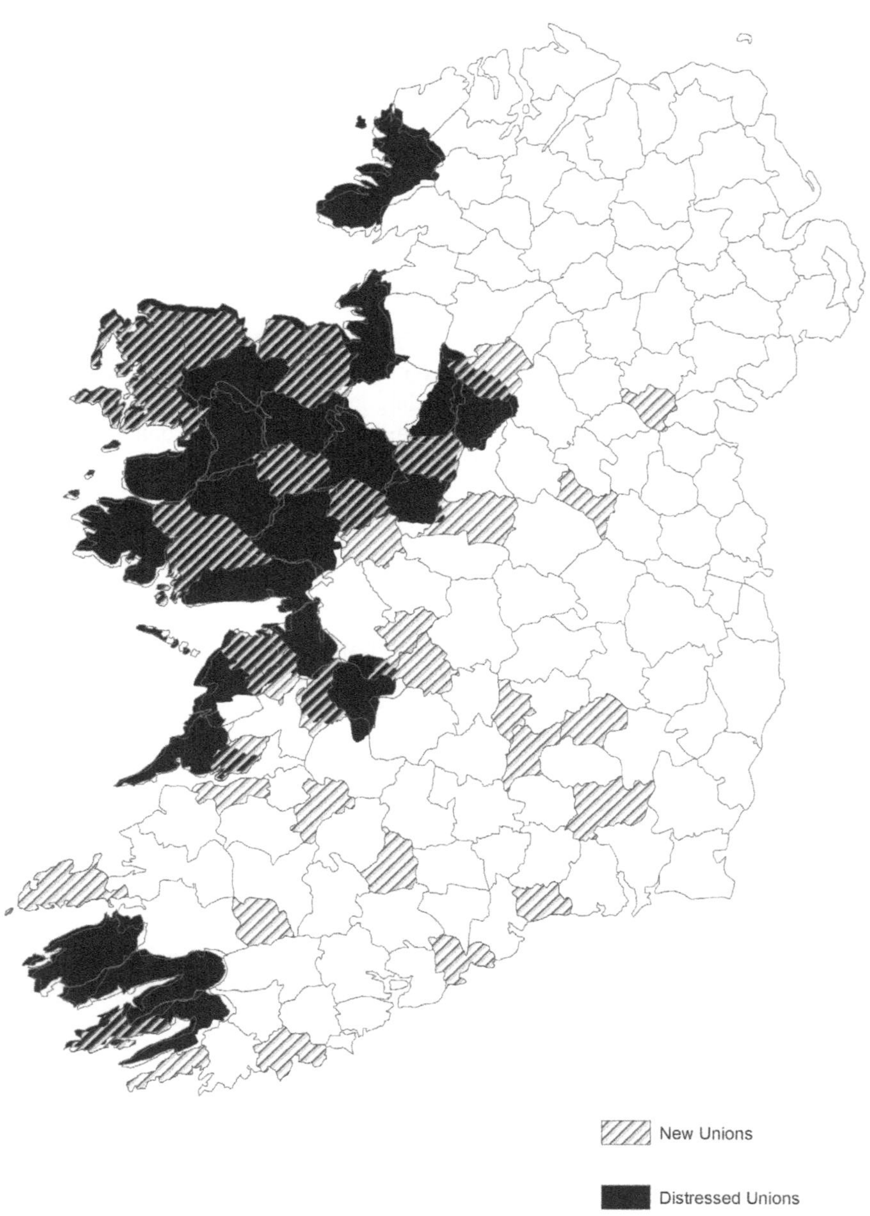

Map 2.11 Distressed unions and new unions.

Impacts of the famine

The devastation wreaked by the famine upon Irish society included both the immediate famine-related population loss as well as the prolonged post-famine population decline which ensued as Irish people continued to follow their friends and relatives to Britain, the USA, and to other parts of the world. The heaviest famine-related population losses and highest levels of excess mortality were in the west of Ireland, north Connaught and south Ulster, where both populations and land quality were poorer than in the rest of the country (Map 2.7). However, as illustrated in Map 2.4, areas of higher than average losses were to be found nationwide. Emigration was the main driver of population loss in the more affluent areas where people had the means to escape. In 1846 the *Meath Herald* reported that:

> the spirit of emigration was never known to have arrived at the height it is at present. Numbers who can muster sufficient funds are wending their way towards the shipping ports towards America.[57]

In 1849 the *Downpatrick Recorder* reported that:

> within the last few weeks, upwards of two thousand individuals have left the district of Newtownards, Lecale, and other parts of this county ... in one emigrant ship alone, which sailed from Belfast the other day, more than three fourths of the passengers were from the county of Down.[58]

While newspaper reports shed light on the levels of emigration from local areas, in the absence of population numbers for 1845 or exact mortality and emigration figures for each district, the actual human cost may never be known with any certainty. Recognising the gradual but silent disappearance of people from the district around Castlerea in February 1847, one public works official stated that:

> lists were supplied: but comparatively few of those who were called answered their names, a great many of them having to England, Scotland or elsewhere, some (as I was informed) being dead, others sick, and some in the workhouse. All the relief committees of the barony are now engaged in revising their registers.[59]

The tireless collector of data, William Wilde, also recognised the impossibility of establishing the true extent of population loss:

> no pen has recorded the numbers of the forlorn and starving who perished by the wayside or in the ditches, or of the mournful groups, sometimes of whole families, who lay down and died, one after another, upon the floor of their miserable cabin.[60]

Longer term population loss was most pronounced in Munster and Leinster.[61] It was from these regions that many famine emigrants originated, and as a result, the pull of those already in Britain and America were strongest here. Thus, while overall population loss on the island in the four decades after the famine was greater than during it, post-famine declines in parts of Leinster and Munster were twice – and in some instances three times – as high (Map 2.12). By contrast, western counties experienced population recovery during the post-famine decades. In spite of having suffered the most extensive losses during the famine crisis, many west of Ireland people returned to their pre-famine traditions of having large families, marrying early, cultivating with the spade and in some instances subdividing property. While large numbers did emigrate from the west, large numbers also continued to take seasonal work in Scotland and England. This source of supplementary income enabled them to maintain their position on the land in Ireland.[62] However, farm labouring opportunities in Britain gradually declined. This, coupled with the onset of agricultural depression in Ireland in the 1880s, encouraged increasing numbers from the west of Ireland to make the permanent journey across the Irish Sea or the Atlantic Ocean. For those who stayed behind, families became smaller and fewer, and marriages occurred at a later age. This resulted in a gradual but prolonged decline in population from the turn of the century onward.

While the famine left a large social vacuum in rural Ireland, the material quality of life for the reduced numbers now living on the land improved.[63] The famine removed the most destitute from the human landscape, resulting in the disappearance of smallholdings and fourth-class house accommodation either through death, eviction or abandonment. However, the kind of poverty described by pre-famine travellers to Ireland was still visible in some local areas, particularly in those places that had been identified as sites of destitution. The entry for Frenchpark, recorded in Fraser's *Handbook for Travellers in Ireland* published in 1854, reads:

> scattered over the face of the district here, as in common with the whole bleak country from Longford to Ballina, may be seen those miserable groups of cabins surrounded by the accompanying osier hedge.[64]

The consolidation of the smallholdings of those who had disappeared resulted in an overall increase in farm sizes, while the disappearance of people meant that the kind of competition for land that characterised pre-famine Ireland, particularly in marginal areas, was much reduced.[65] Map 2.13 shows farm sizes by county in 1851. As illustrated here, the enormous disparity that had existed between the numbers of smallholders and large landowners, particularly in the west (Map 2.6), had now disappeared. In Mayo, for example 72 per cent of farms in 1841 were classified as being between one and five acres. In 1851 only 14.6 per cent of farms were in this size category. Moreover, excluding all farms under one acre, between 1841 and 1851 the number of farms recorded for county Mayo had decreased by over 12,000. Over the subsequent decades, the practice

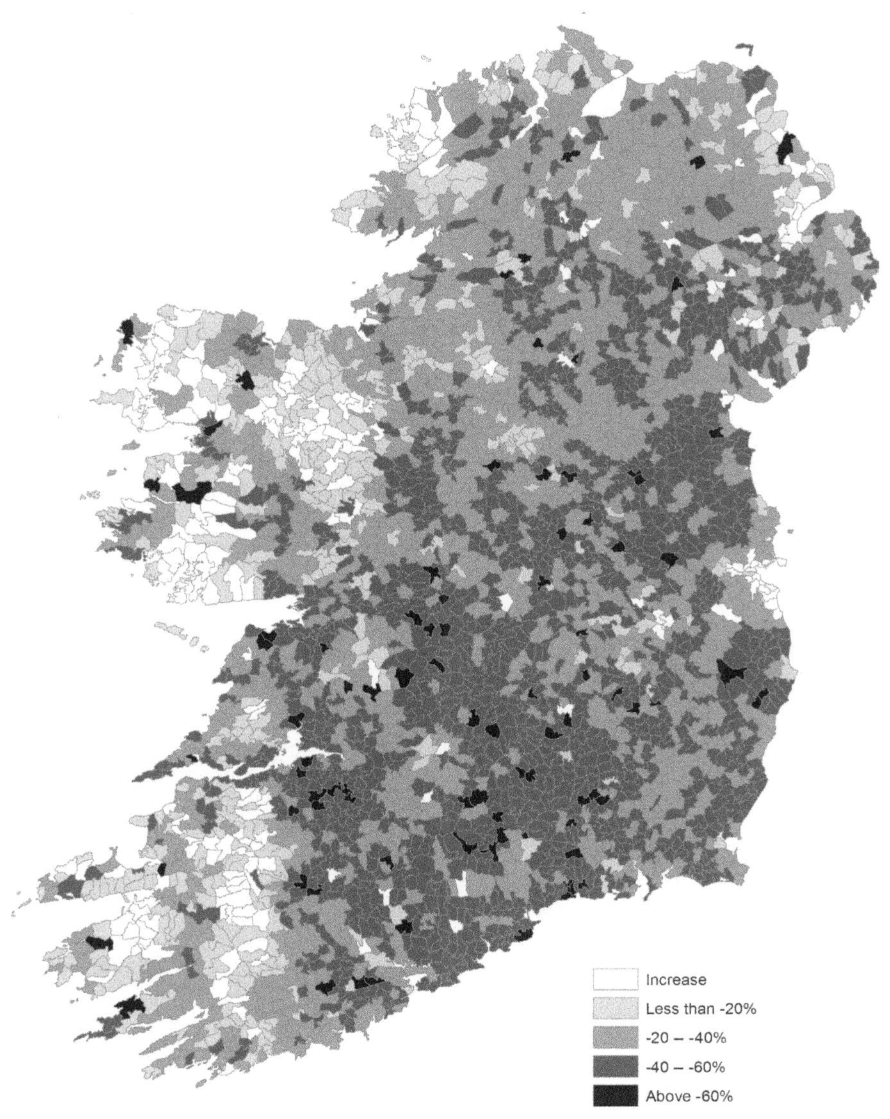

Map 2.12 Population change, 1851 to 1891.

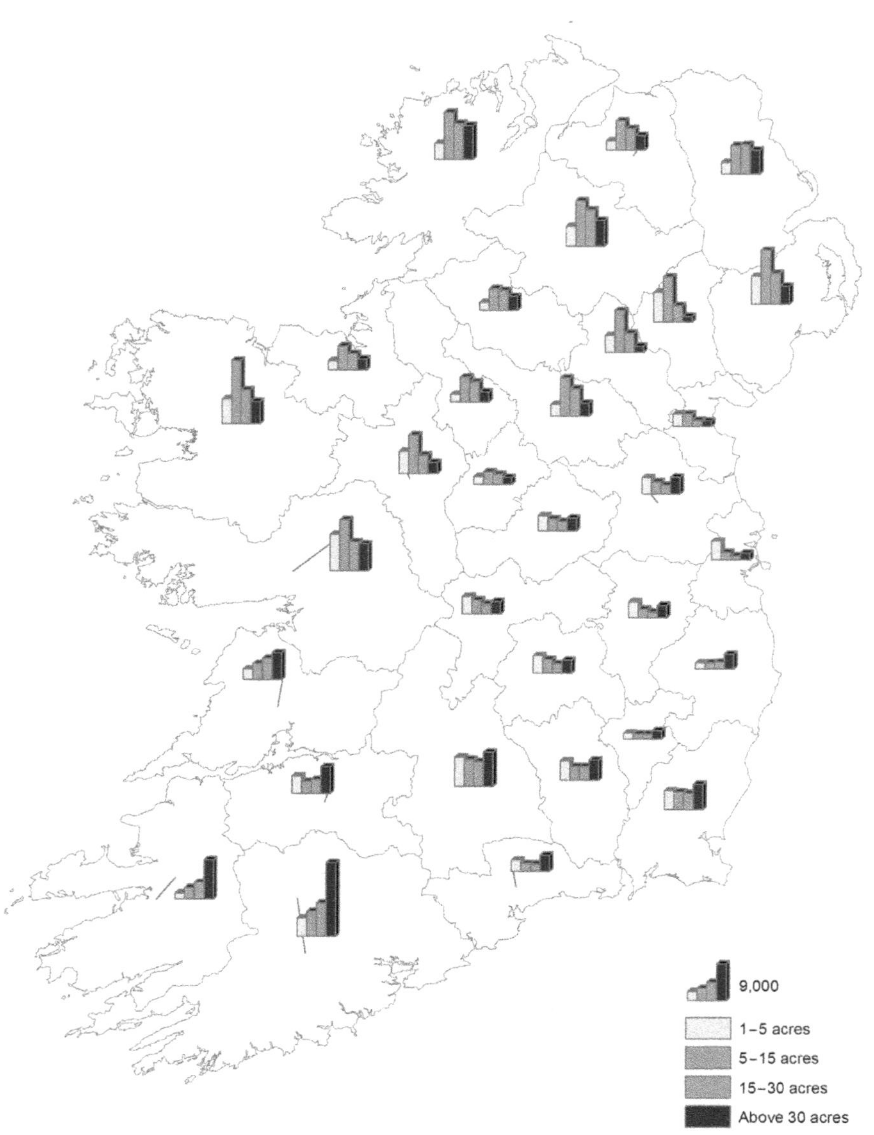

Map 2.13 Farm sizes at county level, 1851.

of partible inheritance that had continued to some extent in the west of Ireland following the famine was gradually replaced by primogeniture. This enabled inheriting sons to maintain newly enlarged farm sizes and/or to expand their holdings through marriage, while emigration provided an outlet for those not in line for inheritance. However, the prospect of marrying into a house where the inheriting son may have been the only sibling remaining to care for elderly parents, did not appeal to many potential young wives. One Irish emigrant who arrived at Elis Island in 1923 explained what life was like in rural Ireland:

> Well, we didn't have anything to do in Ireland there was no work. And you didn't want to be poor all your life. You could have married an old farmer if you wanted to and stay there and work on that old farm. But I wasn't about to do that. He had a father and a mother and I'd have to go in and live with them.[66]

The disappearance of thousands of Irish speakers through death or emigration also had a major impact on the cultural and linguistic geography of the island, clearing them, along with their customs, from their native landscape. As a result, the young people of post-famine Ireland became increasingly English speaking, literate and outward looking. By the turn of the century there were more Irish people living outside the country than in it.[67] At home and abroad the memory of the famine's death-toll, and its impact on all those who survived – whether they remained in Ireland or were exiled abroad – was kept alive in folklore, balladry and literature.[68] Again, local stories from places such as Skibbereen fed into this ballad history and geography of Ireland, albeit in often selective ways, usually attributing blame to landlords and the British government. Such stories were to shape Irish historical imaginations for generations to come.

Conclusion

The famine left an indelible imprint on the human and physical landscape of Ireland and did so in very diverse ways. As outlined in this chapter, the heaviest and most extensive scars were left primarily on the west of Ireland, where land was poorest and vulnerable subsistence-based communities most numerous. Scars were also left, though to a lesser extent, on the ribbons, pockets and mountainsides of poverty that stretched across the entire island. The geography of pre-famine vulnerability and its impact may be seen in Maps 2.2 and 2.7. The protracted duration of the famine, however, meant that over time groups who may have been able to withstand a one- or two-year shortage – either through their own resources or with the help of others – fell into destitution. Thus, while the different socio-economic structures that characterised each region enabled different kinds of response, by 1847 there were few communities which could deal with a crisis that now seemed to be without end. The whole situation, however, was worsened by the Poor Law Amendment Act of 1847, which forced increasing numbers of smallholders into complete destitution in order to be eligible for relief. This turned people who lived by subsistence or semi-subsistence, and for whom the famine may have been a short-term crisis, into a new social class characterised by total and permanent dependency.[69] Forcing local taxpayers, growing fewer in number, to support this new class eventually exhausted local resources, capabilities and, in some instances, will. As a consequence, the island-wide famine management policy exacerbated poverty everywhere and undermined regional capabilities to cope with it. This is not to deny that many people were sustained on relief and that the greatest concentration of relief was distributed in the areas that needed it most. However, the poor law contributed to the destitution in these impoverished areas least able to cope with it, and in effect produced the throngs that witnesses saw walking the roads or streets towards workhouses and relief schemes. Finally, the fact that large numbers of people left from Ireland's ports further complicates the famine as a local, regional or national story by adding to population decline but doing so in a different way. The flow of emigration was predominantly from counties on the more accessible eastern side of the island, where people had the means to leave, and from north Connaught and south Ulster where some communities were assisted. However, emigrants did originate from all parts of the island and, as illustrated above, these local exoduses had a significant impact upon population numbers in local areas.

Examining the famine, therefore, in terms of the extent of human suffering, the numbers of excess deaths, the flow of emigration, and the levels and kinds of local response illustrates that its impacts were complex and spatially varied. However, the crisis lasted much longer than anyone had expected and many of its impacts were mutually reinforcing – seeing local death-tolls rise convinced many to take flight and initial emigration flows stimulated further out-migration while the burden of poor law taxation incentivised land clearances and encouraged those with means to retreat from social responsibility or to leave. Thus, between 1845 and 1851, people from all over the country had witnessed and/or experienced suffering, death and emigration, and knew that no person, house or place on the island was beyond 'the march of the enemy'.

Notes

1 S.H. Cousens, 'Regional Death Rates in Ireland during the Great Famine, from 1846 to 1851', *Population Studies* 14(1) (1960), 55–74; James S. Donnelly, Jr., 'Excess Mortality and Emigration', in *A New History of Ireland V: Ireland Under the Union 1801–1870*, ed. William E. Vaughan (Oxford: Oxford University Press, 1989), 350–356; Liam Kennedy, Paul S. Ell, E. Margaret Crawford and Leslie A. Clarkson, *Mapping the Great Irish Famine: A Survey of the Famine Decades* (Dublin: Four Courts Press, 1999); John Crowley, William J. Smyth and Mike Murphy (eds), *Atlas of the Great Irish Famine* (Cork: Cork University Press, 2012).

2 Census of Ireland, 1841, *Report of the Commissioners Appointed to Take the Census of Ireland for the Year 1841*. 1843, XXIV [504].

3 Kerby A. Miller, *Emigrants and Exiles: Ireland and the Irish Exodus to North America* (New York: Oxford University Press, 1985); David Fitzpatrick, 'Emigration 1801–70', in *A New History of Ireland V: Ireland Under the Union 1801–1870*, ed. William E. Vaughan (Oxford: Oxford University Press, 1989), 562–622.

4 Timothy W. Guinnane and Cormac Ó Gráda, 'The Workhouses and Irish Famine Mortality' (Dublin: UCD Department of Economics Centre for Economic Research, Working Paper Series WP100/10, 2000); John O'Connor, *The Workhouses of Ireland: the Fate of Ireland's Poor* (Dublin: Anvil Books, 1995).

5 *Papers Relating to Proceedings for the Relief of the Distress, and the State of Unions and Workhouses in Ireland.* Eighth Series, 1849, XLVII [1042], 139.

6 Mary E. Daly, 'The Operation of Famine Relief, 1845–57', in *The Great Irish Famine: The Thomas Davis Lecture Series*, ed. Cathal Póirtéir (Cork: Mercier Press, 1995), 123–134; James S. Donnelly, Jr., 'The Administration of Relief, 1846–7', in *A New History of Ireland V: Ireland Under the Union 1801–1870*, ed. William E. Vaughan (Oxford: Oxford University Press, 1989), 294–306; James S. Donnelly, Jr., 'The Administration of Relief, 1847–51', in *A New History of Ireland V: Ireland Under the Union 1801–1870*, ed. William E. Vaughan (Oxford: Oxford University Press, 1989), 316–317; Thomas P. O'Neill, 'The Organisation and Administration of Relief', in *The Great Famine: Studies in Irish History, 1845–52*, ed. Ruth D. Edwards and T. Desmond Williams (Dublin: The Lilliput Press (republished 1994)), 209–260.

7 *The Nation*, 13 March 1847, 13.

8 Patrick Hickey, *Famine in West Cork: the Mizen Peninisula Land and People, 1800–1852* (Cork: Mercier Press, 2002); Christine Kinealy, 'Potatoes, Providence and Philanthropy: The Role of Private Charity during the Irish Famine', in *The Meaning of the Famine*, ed. Patrick O'Sullivan (Leicester: Leicester University Press, 1997), 140–171.

9 *Papers Relating to Proceedings for Relief of Distress, and State of Unions and Workhouses in Ireland*, Sixth Series, 1847–48, [955], 730.

10 Bourke, *Visitation of God?*; Peter Gray, *Famine, Land, and Politics: British Government and Irish Society, 1843–1850* (Dublin: Irish Academic Press, 1999); David Lloyd, 'The Political Economy of the Potato', *Nineteenth Century Contexts* 29(2–3) (2007), 311–335.

11 S.H. Cousens, 'The Regional Pattern of Emigration During the Great Irish Famine 1846–51', *Transactions of the Institute of British Geographers* 28 (1960), 128–134.

12 E.R.R. Green, 'Agriculture', in *The Great Famine: Studies in Irish History, 1845–52*, ed. Ruth D. Edwards and T. Desmond Williams (Dublin: The Lilliput Press (republished 1994)), 89–128.

13 Patrick J. Duffy, 'Mapping the Famine in Monaghan', in *Atlas of the Great Irish Famine*, ed. John Crowley, William J. Smyth and Mike Murphy (Cork: University Cork Press, 2012), 440–459; Peter Connell, *The Land and People of County Meath* (Dublin: Four Courts Press, 2004).

14 Louis M. Cullen, 'Irish History without the Potato', *Past and Present* XL (1968), 72–83; Lloyd, 'Political Economy of the Potato', 311–335; Kevin Whelan, 'Pre- and Post-famine Landscape Change', in *The Great Irish Famine: The Thomas Davis Lecture Series*, ed. Cathal Póirtéir (Cork: Mercier Press, 1995), 19–33.

15 *The Third Report of the Commissioners Appointed to Enquire into the Nature and Extent of the Several Bogs in Ireland, and, the Practicability of Draining and Cultivating Them*, 1813–14 [130], 16.

16 Isaac Weld, *Statistical Survey of the County of Roscommon* (Dublin: Royal Dublin Society, 1830), 250–251.

17 Rundale was a system of landholding whereby multiple families held the land in common. For this example of the breakup of rundale, see *Evidence Taken before Her Majesty's Commissioners of Inquiry into the State of the Law and Practice in Respect to the Occupation of Land in Ireland. Part II*, 1845 [616], 340.

18 *Evidence Taken before Her Majesty's Commissioners of Inquiry into the State of the Law and Practice in Respect to the Occupation of Land in Ireland. Part II*, 1845 [616], 262.
19 Whelan, 'Pre- and Post-famine Landscape Change', 33.
20 Weld, *Survey of the County of Roscommon*, 250–251.
21 Tom Jones-Hughes, 'East Leinster in the Mid-nineteenth Century', *Irish Geography* 3(5) (1958), 227–241; Cousens, 'Regional Death Rates', 55–74.
22 Quoted in Connell, *The Land and People of County Meath 1750–1850* (Dublin: Four Courts Press), 162.
23 James S. Donnelly, Jr., *The Land and the People of Nineteenth-century Cork: The Rural Economy and the Land Question* (London: Routledge & Keegan Paul, 1975); William J. Smyth, 'Landholding Changes, Kinship Networks and Class Transformation in Rural Ireland: A Case Study from County Tipperary', *Irish Geography* 16(1) (1983), 16–35.
24 Christine Kinealy and Trevor Parkhill (eds), *The Famine in Ulster: The Regional Impact* (Belfast: Ulster Historical Foundation, 1997); Duffy, 'Famine in Monaghan', 440–459.
25 William J. Smyth, 'Mapping the People: The Growth and Distribution of the Population', in *Atlas of the Great Irish Famine*, ed. John Crowley, William J. Smyth and Mike Murphy (Cork: University Cork Press), 13–22.
26 In the absence of crop data at ED level for pre-famine Ireland I have used the crop data for 1851 as a surrogate. As outlined by Bourke, there were 14 million acres of crops in Ireland in 1841, a number similar to that in 1831 and 1851. This map is based on population numbers of 1841 with crop data for 1851.
27 William J. Smyth, 'The Province of Munster and the Great Famine', in *Atlas of the Great Irish Famine*, ed. John Crowley, William J. Smyth and Mike Murphy (Cork: University Cork Press), 361.
28 *Report of the Commissioners Appointed to Take the Census of Ireland, for the Year 1841* [1843 [504], 454.
29 *Conacre* was a system whereby tenants were given the use of a plot of land in return for their labour. They then lived off what they could grow on their plot. For a discussion on the impact of this system in Munster, see Smyth, 'Province of Munster and the Great Famine', 368–370.
30 Cousens, 'Regional Pattern of Emigration', 128–134.
31 Smyth, 'Province of Munster and the Great Famine', 368–370.
32 W.J. Smyth, 'The Province of Leinster and the Great Famine', in *Atlas of the Great Irish Famine*, ed. John Crowley, William J. Smyth and Mike Murphy (Cork: University Cork Press, 2012), 325–333.
33 Jones-Hughes, 'East Leinster', 227–241.
34 Cullen, 'Irish History without the Potato', 72–83.
35 To seize (someone's property) to obtain payment of rent or other money owed.
36 Cousens, 'Regional Pattern of Emigration', 128–134.
37 J.H. Johnson, 'Harvest Migration from Nineteenth-century Ireland', *Transactions of the Institute of British Geographers* 41 (1967), 97–112. This practice was also common in County Mayo.
38 William E. Vaughan, *Landlords and Tenants in Mid-Victorian Ireland* (Oxford: Clarendon Press, 1994).
39 Duffy, 'Famine in Monaghan', 440–459.
40 Kinealy and Parkhill, *Famine in Ulster*; William J. Smyth, 'The Province of Ulster and the Great Famine', in *Atlas of the Great Irish Famine*, ed. John Crowley, William J. Smyth and Mike Murphy (Cork: University Cork Press, 2012), 417–425.
41 Virginia Crossman, *The Poor Law in Ireland, 1838–48* (Dublin: Dundalgan Press, 2006); Gerard O'Brien, 'The Establishment of Poor Law Unions in Ireland, 1838–1943', *Irish Historical Studies* 23 (1982), 97–120; O'Connor, *Workhouses of Ireland.*

42 Peter Gray, *The Making of the Irish Poor Law, 1815–43* (Manchester: Manchester University Press, 2009); David Nally, *Human Encumbrances: Political Violence and the Great Irish Famine* (Notre Dame, IN: University of Notre Dame Press, 2011).
43 *A Return from the Poor Law Unions (Ireland), Showing the Name of Each Union in Ireland, the Name of the County in which Situated, and of Each Electoral Division; the Extent of Statute Acres, Bog or Waste, &c. &c.*, 1846 [262].
44 Patrick J. Duffy (ed.), *To and From Ireland: Planned Migration Schemes* c.*1600–2000* (Dublin: Geography Publications, 2004).
45 *Correspondence from July 1846 to January 1847 Relating to the Measures Adopted for the Relief of the Distress in Ireland.* Commissariat Series 1847 [761], 319.
46 James Grant, 'Local Relief Committees in Ulster 1845–7', in *The Hungry Stream: Essays on Emigration and Famine*, ed. M. Crawford (Belfast: Institute of Irish Studies, 1997), 185–198; Mary Kelly, 'The Famine in County Roscommon', in *Atlas of the Great Irish Famine*, ed. John Crowley, William J. Smyth and Mike Murphy (Cork: University Cork Press, 2012), 308–317.
47 Frank Geary, 'Regional Industrial Structure and Labour Force in Ireland between 1841 and 1851', *Irish Historical Studies* 30(118) (1996), 167–194.
48 Kennedy *et al.*, *Mapping the Great Irish Famine.*
49 Grant, 'Local Relief Committees in Ulster 1845–7'.
50 Donnelly, Jr., 'Excess Mortality and Emigration', 350–356.
51 Kennedy, *Mapping the Great Irish Famine*, 135; William J. Smyth, 'Classify, Confine, Discipline and Punish – the Roscrea Union!: A Microgeography of the Workhouse System during the Famine', in *Atlas of the Great Irish Famine*, ed. John Crowley, William J. Smyth and Mike Murphy (Cork: University Cork Press, 2012), 143.
52 William J. Smyth, 'The Province of Ulster and the Great Famine', 418.
53 *Poor Law (Ireland). Abstract of returns of each Poor Law Union in Ireland, specifying the electoral divisions, and the valuation thereof; rates made during the year ended 25 March 1848, and amount thereof collected:–also, return of the liabilities and expenses of each union on and for the year ending 25 March 1848.* 1847–48 [707].
54 Cousens, 'Regional Pattern of Emigration', 128–134; Duffy (ed.), *To and From Ireland*; Patrick J. Duffy, 'Emigrants and the Estate Office: A Compassionate Relationship?', in *The Hungry Stream: Essays on Emigration and Famine*, ed. M. Crawford (Belfast: Institute of Irish Studies, 1997), 71–86; Fitzpatrick, 'Emigration 1801–70', 562–622; Gerard J. Lyne, 'William Stuart Trench and Post-Famine Emigration from Kenmare to America 1850–55', *Journal of the Kerry Archaeological and Historical Society* 25 (1992), 51–137.
55 *Papers Relating to Proceedings for the Relief of the Distress, and State of the Unions and Workhouses, in Ireland.* Fourth series – 1847–48 [896], 113–114.
56 P.M. Austin Bourke, 'The Extent of the Potato Crop in Ireland at the Time of the Famine (with Discussion by Thomas P. O'Neill, Kevin B. Nowlan, Ruth Dudley Edwards)', *Journal of the Statistical and Social Inquiry Society of Ireland* 20 (1959–1960), 31–35.
57 *Meath Herald*, 13 October 1846.
58 John Killen, *The Famine Decade: Contemporary Accounts, 1841–1851* (Dublin: Blackstaff Press, 1995), 221.
59 *Correspondence from January to March 1847, Relating to the Measures Adopted for the Relief of the Distress in Ireland.* Board of Works Series. [Second part.] 1847 [797], 266.
60 *The Census of Ireland for the year 1851. Part V. Tables of Deaths. Vol. II. Containing the Tables and Index.* 1856 [2087-I], 243.
61 Mary Kelly and A. Stewart Fotheringham, 'The Online Atlas of Irish Population Change 1841–2002: A New Resource for Analysing National Trends and Local Variations in Irish Population Dynamics', *Irish Geography* 44 (2011), 215–244.

62 Cormac Ó Gráda, 'Seasonal Migration and Post-famine Adjustment in the West of Ireland', *Studia Hibernica* 13 (1973), 48–76.

63 Kennedy *et al.*, *Mapping the Great Irish Famine.*

64 James Fraser, *Handbook for Travellers in Ireland: Descriptive of its Scenery, Towns, Seats, Antiquities, etc.* (Dublin: James McGlashan, 1854), 460.

65 Cormac Ó Gráda, *Ireland Before and After the Famine: Explorations in Economic History 1800–1925* (Manchester: Manchester University Press, 1993); Michael Turner, *After the Famine: Irish Agriculture 1850–1914* (Cambridge: Cambridge University Press, 1996).

66 Extract taken from Bertha Devlin, 'Journeys: The Peopling of America® Center, 1550–1890', exhibit, Ellis Island Museum, New York City (April 2012).

67 Miller, *Emigrants and Exiles.*

68 Niall O'Ciosáin, 'Famine Memory and the Popular Representation of Scarcity', in *History and Memory in Modern Ireland*, ed. Ian McBride (Cambridge: Cambridge University Press, 2001), 95–117; Melissa Fegan, *Literature and the Irish Famine 1845–1919* (Oxford: Clarendon Press, 2002); Roger J. McHugh, 'The Famine in Oral Tradition', in *The Great Famine: Studies in Irish History, 1845–52*, ed. Ruth D. Edwards and T. Desmond Williams (Dublin: Brown & Nowlan, 1956), 392–430; Cathal Póirtéir, 'Folk Memory and the Famine', in *The Great Irish Famine: The Thomas Davis Lecture Series*, ed. Cathal Póirtéir (Cork: Mercier Press, 1995), 219–232.

69 Nally, *Human Encumbrances.*

3 'The Great British Famine of 1845 to 1850'?

Ireland, the UK and peripherality in famine relief and philanthropy

Peter Gray

The political context of the Great Irish Famine of 1845 to 1850 was established by Ireland's incorporation into the United Kingdom of Great Britain and Ireland in 1801, and the failure of the UK state to prevent mass mortality during the 1840s was consequently identified by Irish nationalists at the time and subsequently as proof of the failure of that union and hence of the necessity of Irish independence.[1] The extent to which nationalists' causal association of British rule and the union state with the horrors of famine in Ireland is justified was and remains highly contested. At the same time it is surely right, as one recent commentator has observed, that 'the proper geographical and political unit for the analysis of the Great Famine is Britain and Ireland'.[2]

In seeking to address one aspect of this question, this chapter considers the shifting dynamics of the debates on the moral and political peripherality of Ireland within the UK state and society in the later 1840s, and the relationship between these perceptions and state famine relief measures and private philanthropy. It argues that despite Ireland's geographical isolation from Great Britain by the Irish Sea as well as its long record of historical difference and colonial subordination, the political and cultural construction of Ireland as peripheral to the UK fluctuated significantly during the famine years. These fluctuations in moral, emotional and political engagement with the Irish crisis in Britain led to significantly different public policy and private philanthropic outcomes at different stages of the Famine – varying from large-scale charitable donations and a highly interventionist food ration-based relief policy in spring to summer 1847, to a radical alienation of political and public sympathy from an Ireland deemed increasingly to be the author of its own misfortunes, which paralleled the virtually total withdrawal of public and private resource transfers to Ireland in 1848 to 1849.

This chapter will also consider the highly controversial imposition of a double-peripheralisation relief model upon Ireland in 1849, in the shape of a 'rate in aid' initiative that threw all additional relief on to Irish resources, by taxing the poor law unions of the recovering east and north of the country to relieve the continuing hunger crisis in the internally peripheral west and southwest of the island. Following King and Stewart's categorisation, Ireland as a whole may be said to have constituted a structural 'welfare periphery', with a history of limited and contingent poor relief interventions. However, its welfare relationship with the UK 'core' (England and, to a lesser extent, Scotland) and relationships among the Irish regions fluctuated, especially in periods of crisis.[3]

The socio-economic crisis that precipitated the excess deaths of over one million of the island's inhabitants between 1845 and 1850 is generally referred to by historians as the 'Great Irish Famine' (distinguishing it more from the lesser famines of the early nineteenth century than from the major demographic catastrophes of 1739 to 1741 and the 1650s, which were probably as 'great' in terms of proportional mortality). However, given the fact that this famine occurred in the 1840s within the unitary political state of the United Kingdom of Great Britain and Ireland, there may be some merit, if only as a heuristic device, to consider it under the title of 'the Great British Famine' of 1845 to 1850. It is worth noting that famine, arising from the impact of potato blight on the equally vulnerable socio-economic structure of the western Highlands and Islands, afflicted Scotland at the same time (albeit without the same proportionate mortality toll but accompanied by heavy emigration), and the Irish crisis spilled across the narrow Irish Sea to bring a refugee crisis, and epidemic outbreaks, to cities such as Liverpool and Glasgow. The financial crash of 1847 and the industrial recession that followed brought the return of hunger, if not outright famine, to many English urban centres, a situation worsened by a cholera epidemic in 1848 to 1849.[4]

Ascribing territorial limits to historical famines is problematic and inevitably politicised. There remains an acutely contested historical dispute, for example, between many historians focusing on the Ukrainian *Holodomor* and those preferring to emphasise the alternative frame of reference of the 'Soviet Famine' of 1932 to 1933 (especially regarding geographical focus, the agency of the Soviet regime and excess mortality figures).[5] If the UK rather than Ireland is taken as the relevant territorial unit for the 1840s famine, the proportional excess death rate falls from around 12 per cent of the population of Ireland to just over 4.1 per cent of that of the UK (taking the 1841 census as the baseline). This is still cognate with the upper bounds of mortality for both the Soviet famine of 1932 to 1933 and the Chinese Great Leap Forward famine of 1959 to 1961, in each case taking the aggregate state as the territorial entity within which famine occurred and ignoring marked regional variations in intensity, although it was significantly less than the Finnish famine of 1867 to 1868 (taking autonomous Finland and not the Russian Empire of which it was a part as the territorial unit).

There are of course numerous reasons why the 'Great British Famine' has never acquired traction in describing the crisis of the 1840s. Both during and more especially in the decades after the catastrophe, Irish nationalist commentators constructed an interpretive narrative that stressed the culpability and even the malevolent intent of the British state for the scale of deaths, while Catholic historians emphasised national 'martyrdom' at the hands of British Protestant persecution. Whether using the term 'Great Famine' or the (for radical nationalists preferable) labels 'the great hunger' or 'the last conquest', or indeed the Irish phrase 'an gorta mór', the catastrophe was depicted as a distinctly Irish tragedy, imposed upon the people of that island by a hostile or indifferent colonial metropolis, but appropriated as further evidence of Ireland and its people's (and its diaspora's) suffering under British rule and the need for its redemption through the acquisition of independence from Britain and its empire (or, at the very least, autonomy in the form of Home Rule). For their part, British commentators, although quick to stress the extent of 'imperial' (i.e. UK) generosity towards Ireland in the later 1840s, also tended over time to use distancing techniques to categorise the crisis as a specifically 'Irish' one, arising from that country's distinct socio-economic backwardness that had been manifest in over-population and resistance to integration into perceived British behavioural traits of entrepreneurialism and work discipline.[6]

During the crisis itself, however, attitudes towards the relationship between Ireland and the UK and where responsibility rested fluctuated for a number of participant groups: Irish and British political and social commentators, political activists and administrators and ministers. These shifting ambiguities may be discerned and explored with reference to a statement made in an Irish monthly journal, the *Dublin University Magazine*, in April 1847:

> What can be more absurd, what can be more wicked, than for men professing attachment to an imperial constitution to answer claims now put forward for state assistance to the unprecedented necessities of Ireland, by talking of Ireland being a drain upon the English treasury? The exchequer is the exchequer of the United Kingdom.... If the Union be not a mockery, there exists no such thing as an English treasury.... How are these expectations to be realized, how are these pledges to be fulfilled, if the partnership is only to be one of loss and never of profit to us? if, bearing our share of all imperial burdens – when calamity falls upon us we are to be told that we then recover our separate existence as a nation, just so far as to disentitle us to the state assistance which any portion of a nation visited with such a calamity has a right to expect from the governing power? If Cornwall had been visited with the same scenes that have desolated Cork, would similar arguments have been used?[7]

This howl of outrage at how Ireland was being treated (in contradistinction to how it should have been treated under the constitutional structure established in 1801) was made by a leading Dublin unionist, Isaac Butt. Butt's background and political trajectory are relevant: from a Protestant family in Co. Donegal and trained in law, he emerged as one of the leading conservative and unionist voices in 1830s to 1840s Dublin, a regular sparring partner for the Catholic constitutional nationalist leader Daniel O'Connell in civic debates, and the founding editor of the conservative *Dublin University Magazine*. At the same time, he was sympathetic to some aspects of cultural nationalism, and was friendly with some of the Young Ireland group before the famine. Already suspicious of the political manoeuvrings of British governments towards Ireland before 1845, Butt's reaction to what he saw as the denial of the 'British' character of the famine by English commentators in press and Parliament placed him on a personal trajectory that would eventually see him renounce his previously fervent unionism, and embrace and then lead the cause of Home Rule for Ireland in the 1870s.[8]

The central problem for Butt and for those like him who sought to assert the 'Britishness' of Ireland and hence the 'imperial' character of its famine crisis was the strongly entrenched perception of Irish national distinctiveness, of otherness, that dominated British thinking about Ireland long after the introduction of the Union. This in turn reflected the strength of popular Irish nationalism and resurgent Catholicism manifest in the decades preceding 1845. Whatever hopes may have existed for Irish integration into the British body politic after 1801 (predicated by the Union's more optimistic advocates on the model of Scotland, which had retained its cultural distinctiveness while surrendering its political autonomy in 1707), were dashed by the intense politicisation of religious difference over the following decades. In a context of growing doctrinal antagonisms between evangelical Protestants and ultramontane Catholics, the royal veto on the proposed political emancipation of Catholics in 1801 destroyed a nascent accommodation with the moderate Catholic clerical and political leadership of the period and created a political vacuum soon filled by O'Connell's more radical politics of mass mobilisation in pursuit of Catholic emancipation, quickly followed (when this was grudgingly granted in 1829) by agitation for the repeal of the Act of Union and the restoration of an Irish Parliament with powers of self-government over Irish affairs.

British economists and politicians, as well as most of the Irish landed interest, denied the legitimacy of the nationalist case that Ireland's socio-economic malaise arose from the loss of political autonomy after 1801, and continued to advocate the integrative power of the union (so long as this was not disrupted by 'agitation') to act as the vehicle for socio-economic modernisation. However, after the first wave of fiscal and administrative integration, which saw the merger of the Irish currency and exchequer with Britain's, and the abolition of most tariff barriers between the islands by 1826, the unresponsiveness of much of Ireland to the 'Scottish solution' began to provoke more doubts, with greater state experimentation in the Irish socio-economic sphere in the 1830s (in such domains as education, public works, the poor law and policing), directed from the devolved executive at Dublin Castle and tending to erode the local powers of the landed elite.

Irish policy during this period was part of a complicated pattern of inter- and intra-party conflict in the UK, and, as an integral part of the wider 'condition of Britain' debate, attracted the attention of an increasingly vociferous and powerful British middle-class public opinion. Extensive analyses of the problems of Irish land and agriculture were published in numerous pamphlets and in leading London newspapers both before and during the famine.[9] Public debate about the 'Irish problem' in Britain drew not only upon economic arguments and upon prejudice against Catholic-Irish improvidence and violence (countered by the reformist case that British misgovernment had engendered this), but also upon more pervasive popular and Christian concepts of economic laws, which were in turn heavily laden with moral, religious and political presuppositions and concerns. Some of these elements had long existed at the policy-making level, but with the mobilisation of middle-class political activity in the 1840s, popular opinion became an important force in the making of Irish policy. The repeated potato failures from 1845 and the ensuing famine drew these developments to a head and added a new dimension of urgency; policy decisions could no longer be deferred when thousands began to perish. With both famine-era governments politically weak (Sir Robert Peel's due to the irrevocable split in his Conservative Party in early 1846, his successor Lord John Russell's due to his government's minority support in Parliament and radical restiveness following the inconclusive 1847 general election), 'public opinion' as expressed through the press, and those political factions best placed to exploit it, were particularly influential in shaping policy outcomes in Ireland.

These tensions may be seen in the response to the first onset of the potato blight in 1845 to 1846. The incumbent prime minister, Sir Robert Peel, had significant experience of dealing with previous Irish subsistence crises, and had adopted a strategic approach to Irish policy which sought to balance acknowledgement of Irish exceptionalism to British socio-economic and political norms with the application of stimuli to promote the 'natural' assimilation of the country into the British body politic. His pre-famine Irish policy had focused on concessions to moderate propertied Catholic opinion in Ireland, especially through a generous grant to the seminary at Maynooth, along with some financial assistance and encouragement to 'improving' proprietors. Having laid this foundation for stability, he hoped that British economic growth and the geographical integration of the islands promoted by the 'wonderful applications of science' such as steam-powered transport would develop Irish markets and lead to an unprecedented improvement in Irish living conditions, undermining the appeal of nationalist politicians and agrarian agitators.[10]

The threat of famine in 1845 to 1846 led Peel not to abandon these hopes for Irish amelioration, but to invest them further in what he regarded as the transformative power of the repeal of the UK Corn Law to promote a 'high farming' revolution in both Ireland and Britain, associated with the weaning of the Irish labourer off reliance on self-cultivated potatoes and on to subsistence on grain purchased through wage labour in more efficient and productive agriculture. Emergency transitional aid to Ireland – in the form of state-imported Indian meal, public relief works providing employment and grants in aid of local relief committees – were intended to carry Ireland over the short-term crisis while avoiding any permanent enhancement of the state's socio-economic role and bolstering the charitable and developmental initiatives to be undertaken by the Irish landed elite.[11] Arguably, then, the famine policy adopted by the Peel government was a predominantly 'British' one, combining an economically integrationist objective (however unrealistic this may have been) with 'special measures' of a strictly temporary nature reflecting Ireland's developmental backwardness: 'we have a nation to carry, as it were, in our arms,' Home Secretary

James Graham advised the Prime Minister, 'and no very great assistance on which we can rely.'[12] Although the relief structures of 1845 to 1846 were set up in such a way as to ensure a measure of central surveillance from the Irish administration at Dublin Castle (and behind that from the Treasury in London), the government was relatively quick to override its own regulations to head off popular disturbances related to employment and food supply in the spring of 1846. Looking back from June 1846, Peel congratulated himself on the positive political outcome of the relief campaign of that season:

> These measures, as might have been expected in a generous and kind hearted people, have produced a corresponding good. I believe that there does pervade amongst the people in the wilds of Connaught, and in Munster … a feeling of grateful acknowledgement towards Her Majesty's Government.[13]

The Irish west in particular might remain geographically peripheral to the UK, but in the first phase of the Great Famine, its assimilation, both political and social, remained a central concern of government.

This 'imperial' approach to the crisis provoked something of a counter-reaction. Influential voices in the British press had long stressed the otherness of Ireland and by implication its unassimilability into the metropolitan UK (while retaining the security case for the Union of 1800). This was reflected in a *Punch* editorial cartoon in late 1845 satirising Daniel O'Connell (and, by implication, the nationalist movement he embodied) as the 'Real potato blight of Ireland'.[14] Responding to Peel's Irish relief policy, *The Times* described those poor Irish dependent on the potato for subsistence as existing in a debased and savage state similar to the 'untutored Indian' and 'ocean islander'. In a version of the cargo-cult, the Irish peasant had, the newspaper asserted in 1846, adopted the impious delusion that the 'deity' bringing 'goodly manna and salient waters' to their localities was government through its needlessly generous relief measures.[15] If this reinforced dependency on the state was deemed to be self-evidently true for the predominantly Catholic and often Irish-speaking lower orders, much of the British press extended the attack to what it regarded as (despite their overwhelmingly British Protestant origins) the culpable Irish landowning class. In spring 1846 *The Times* denounced the relief measures as simply channelling British funds into the pockets of the Irish landlords, while the *Illustrated London News* posited the outrage of its British readers at the estate-clearing behaviour of Irish proprietors and demanded the state make them bear the consequences:

> Englishmen cannot see such barbarities practiced at the very moment that they are paying enormous sums out of the taxes to support those whom the landlords thus plunge into destitution … if the landlord makes paupers he must also maintain them.[16]

The incoming minority Whig government of Lord John Russell faced a dilemma on how to respond to the second (and much greater) potato crop failure of summer

1846. Although it could not afford to alienate Peel and his supporters, now in opposition, it had at the same time to accommodate the numerous critics of the previous ministry's 'over-generous' relief of Ireland in 1845 to 1846. These included a number of the new government's own members, as well as the Assistant Secretary to the Treasury, Charles Trevelyan, nominally a subordinate civil servant, but with doctrinaire opinions on how the Irish crisis should be managed newly empowered through political alliances with incoming ministers. In seeking to balance these competing forces, Russell prefaced a new Irish poor employment bill in August 1846 with the 'British' assertion that 'the whole credit of the Treasury and the means of the country are ready to be used as it is our bounden duty to use them … to avert famine, and to maintain the people of Ireland'.[17] At the same time as making this public commitment to laying out British resources to aid British subjects, the government severely retrenched on grants to the relief committees, suspended state grain imports and moved to a public works policy whose purpose was more overtly to pressurise Irish landowners into undertaking their own 'remunerative' employment schemes, while imposing 'less eligibility' on the Irish poor through imposing piece-work and pegging pay levels rigorously below the 'market' rates of wages (at a time of rapidly escalating food prices and the collapse of private employment). These penal amendments were both a sop to impatient British opinion and a reflection of a more dogmatic administrative attitude towards obliging the Irish of all classes to 'help themselves'.

Lecturing the Irish landowner Lord Monteagle, who had complained that this new policy essentially withdrew support from proprietors seeking to improve the productive powers of their country through state-aided relief works, Charles Trevelyan articulated a 'moralist' position that still posited the aim of the integration of Ireland, but now stressed the absolute necessity of harsh moral mechanisms, operating on landowners and peasant alike through centrally directed relief structures, as the required means to attain this end. As so often his rhetoric likened Ireland to a diseased body separate from and subject to the ministrations of a 'British' surgeon following a divinely inspired diagnosis:

> A remedy has been already applied to that portion of the maladies of Ireland which were traceable to political causes.… The deep and inveterate root of Social evil remained, and … this being altogether beyond the power of man, the cure has been applied by a direct stroke of an all wise Providence in manner as unexpected and unthought of as it is likely to be effectual. God grant that we may rightly perform our part and not turn into a curse what was intended for a blessing.[18]

For Trevelyan and those who shared his interpretation, Ireland's difference from England was essentially moral rather than socio-economic or even political; this was remediable, but only through permitting the 'shock' of the famine to work its beneficial effects on Irish society.

Although not unchallenged within the administration, this harsher attitude towards Irish relief, based as it was on a moral conviction of its remedial desirability, dominated policy making during the hunger winter of 1846/1847. With much of the British press still demanding that Ireland bear the principal burden of relief, even less ideologically certain ministers chose not to question the subordination of Irish interests to British. As the Prime Minister warned the restive Lord Lieutenant in Dublin, politically Ireland was peripheral and there was electoral danger in being seen to favour its elites through over-generous assistance from the 'British' exchequer: 'our defence must be before Englishmen and Scotchmen – who will complain of their taxes being laid out on private estates and demand the same benefits'.[19]

However, towards the end of 1846 and into the early months of 1847 a change occurred in British understandings of the Irish crisis, and a more 'national' response took hold for a time in both private philanthropy and public policy. Arriving in England in late 1846 to request assistance, a delegation of Skibbereen clergy found 'a very exasperated state of public feeling ... against us', not least because of the perception of the widespread 'abuse' of English generosity, but that this antagonism dissipated as the facts of Irish suffering were put before audiences.[20] A growing awareness of the appalling human consequences of the potato failure engendered by emotive accounts of mass suffering in the press and charitable pamphlets altered (if temporarily) the context in which political decisions were made. Responding to perceptions of a shifting public mood, the government (through the established churches) issued a Queen's Letter for charitable relief for Ireland and the Scottish Highlands in December 1846 and endorsed the establishment of the British Association for the Relief of Distress in Ireland and Scotland early the following month. A widely observed National Day of Fast and Humiliation in March 1847 further added weight to the UK-wide campaign for charitable donations and its charitable revenues were added to the (suitably named) British Association's coffers. Although ultra-Protestants sought to equate the potato blight with a specific visitation against Catholicism, the Queen's letter and national fast day promoted reflection on the UK's 'national sin' and the national obligation to atone through (among other things) charitable giving for the relief of 'fellow citizens' in the distressed regions. The response to this was both widespread and substantial, with over £400,000 being raised for the British Association's use alone (with one-sixth of this sum reserved for Scotland).[21]

The spring of 1847 saw a temporary shift in the iconography of the famine in Britain. In March the *Illustrated London News*, which had previously published James Mahony's illustrated articles on the conditions of Skibbereen, accompanied William Harvey's pictorial 'Allegory of the National Fast' (which conflated the lamenting UK trinity of female representations of England, Scotland and Ireland below with the merciful divine Trinity above) with an emotive allegorical poem that was both strongly unionist and providentialist in tone. This described the 'Three Sisters throned on the freeborn wave', whose gallant sons 'guard the unstained Union shield', before proceeding to evoke the horror of famine and pestilence in Ireland, and ending with a call for national unity throughout the UK in prayer and supplication.[22]

This position was given greater intellectual substance by the leading evangelical Thomas Chalmers's essay on famine and political economy published in May 1847. Chalmers upheld the principles of orthodox political economy, but argued that in the case of a 'local' not 'general' famine, such as that afflicting 'our people' in Ireland and the Scottish Highlands, 'national honour' required that all public and private exertions be made to alleviate it:

> Providence has … laid the full weight of [famine] upon the distant extremities of the United Kingdom; and left the task of equalisation – if there be enough of wisdom and mercy below for the accomplishment of the task – to the ordering of man.

Opposed to any extension of the Poor Law in Ireland and calling for emergency aid in its place, Chalmers nevertheless concluded by warning the Irish landowners that 'patriotic cooperation' was required from them if any British initiative was to succeed.[23]

The language of commonalty between Britain and Ireland appeared in the spring of 1847 in British charity sermons, newspaper articles and pamphlets, but it was to prove ephemeral, and a more particularist reading of Ireland's sufferings was to replace it in the ensuing months, as public opinion was turning against the idea of the 'equalisation' of the burden throughout the United Kingdom by public policy and private philanthropy. An element of conditionality had always been latent in responses to the charitable campaign, and a strong reaction set in as the year progressed and expectations of Irish 'gratitude' were not realised. A second national collection in October 1847 proved a damp squib, and was associated with public denunciations of the 'indolent Irish' and the degradation of its people 'into "contentment" with subsistence upon charity'.[24]

The charitable surge of early 1847 had prepared public opinion for the government's major shift of policy – the decision to abandon public works relief and break the strict rules of political economy by feeding the destitute directly from local soup kitchens funded by a mixture of Treasury grants and loans. This was defended as an exceptional response to an extraordinary (and thus strictly temporary) situation – the parallel in public policy to the private philanthropy of the Queen's letter and British Association collections. Although belatedly introduced, and freighted with excessive bureaucracy, the soup kitchens were the one relief initiative that appears to have made a significant difference to mortality rates in the period of operation, in May to August 1847.

However, the shifting public mood had implications for public policy, especially at a time when industrial recession in Britain refocused charity on 'our own poor'. This was encapsulated by the title of one 1847 pamphlet published by a former MP – *Irish Improvidence Encouraged by English Bounty* – which warned of the 'lavish waste of public money … to the performance of a duty which ought to be performed by the Irish, and Irish only'.[25] Already in the spring of 1847 public discourse in Britain had been coalescing around a 'permanent' solution for Irish distress, to come into operation once the 'extraordinary' conditions of the 1846 to 1847 season were deemed to have passed. This took the shape of the Irish Poor Law Amendment Act, passed in June and implemented in September 1847, based on the explicit principle that 'Irish property should pay for Irish poverty' through the transfer of relief costs to locally levied and away from national grants and loans.[26]

Deeming the famine to be substantially over in the wake of the good UK harvest of 1847, this policy was implemented, and Treasury aid to the designated 'distressed' Unions of the Irish west reduced to minimal transfers augmented by the rapidly contracting remnants of the charitable funds of 1847. Once adopted, Treasury officials and 'moralist' ministers insisted that the imposition of relief costs upon Ireland (and, more specifically, upon the Irish localities through the raising of poor rates) be strictly adhered to: 'The popular members say the Poor Law is right and keeps the people', warned the Chancellor the Exchequer Charles Wood in 1848:

> the landlords wish to shift the burthen on to British shoulders – and the British people have made up their minds to pay no more for Irish landlords. How this square is to be broken through I don't see.... You must not suppose that I am at all insensible of what you urge on behalf of the Irish proprietors, whom it is desirable to keep well attached to the Government; but we can judge better of the feeling here; and there is the very strongest determination not to pursue the old system of buying the landlords to keep down the people ... people here will not interpose their money between the Irish landlords and their losses.[27]

With growing distress in Britain, and Irish 'ingratitude' towards what one Westminster insider described as 'our superhuman exertions in the famine' brought vividly before the public by the revival of both agrarian and nationalist agitations in Ireland in late 1847, there appeared to be little sympathy for continued aid.[28] Indeed, British outrage at the highly vociferous (if politically marginal) activities of the Young Ireland activists leading up to the abortive rising of July 1848, and highly publicised incidents such as the assassination of the evicting landlord Denis Mahon in November 1847 tended to crowd out any sympathetic coverage of the continuing famine crisis in Ireland. The political diarist Charles Greville shared the prevalent sense of 'disgust ... here at the state of Ireland and the incurable madness of the people'. Mass starvation was now, he believed, inevitable:

> the Irish will look in vain to England, for no subscription or parliamentary grants or aid of any sort, public or private, will they get; the sources of charity and benevolence are dried up; the current which flowed last year has been effectually choked by the brutality and ingratitude of the people, and the rancorous fury and hatred with which they have met our exertions to serve them. The prospect, neither more nor less than that of civil war and famine, is dreadful, but it is unavoidable.[29]

To *The Times*, the renewed potato blight in the summer of 1848 was a further judgment of God, but of a different order to that of 1846. The continuing availability of cheap imported Indian corn now made the famine 'partial' even within the island, and Ireland's aggregate wages fund would, it was asserted, be sufficient to support the western destitute. 'John Bull' had learned from the mistaken policy of seeking to conciliate 'Paddy', and would now insist upon the imposition of strict moral and physical discipline for all classes.[30] The newspaper's editor J.T. Delane was at one with his correspondent Charles Wood in thinking that the habitual 'perversion' of British aid would render all but a minimalist policy unacceptable in future.[31]

In the latter stages of the famine crisis, public rhetoric was dominated by the trope of 'natural causes' stressing the unavoidable suffering that Ireland must now face in the process of moral reconstruction and for which Britain was no longer responsible. Alarmed at the continuing crisis in Ireland, Prime Minister Russell despairingly pointed out that it was less the 'crude Trevelyanism' of the government moralists than feelings lying 'deep in the breasts of the British people' that now made any further substantive intervention politically impracticable.[32] The continuation of localised distress appeared to British moralists to be self-inflicted, and at the same time necessary for the 'working of a gigantic remedy' that would lead to a 'social revolution' in the Irish countryside. In 1849 Trevelyan continued to reject further central state intervention in the western counties, using the medical metaphor employed so frequently about Ireland during this period:

> what the patient now requires is rest and quiet and time for the remedies which have been given to operate. Continual dosing and dependence upon physicians is not good either for the body politic or corporate.[33]

The one exception to the rule of non-intervention (except to ensure the rigorous application of the Poor Law through the inspection and surveillance regime) was the Rate in Aid scheme, itself revealing of the reduction of Ireland to peripheral status in British thinking. In the spring of 1849, in the teeth of strong hostility in Parliament, the government proposed a (relatively modest) additional relief loan of £50,000 for the distressed and bankrupt western unions. The political price was that repayment would not fall on national taxation, but on the recovering Irish unions of the north and east through a rate-in-aid – an additional levy on the local property rates in Ireland only.[34] The political significance of this taxation of the national periphery (Ireland) to pay for the continuing relief of its own periphery (the western unions) was not lost on Irish observers. Many in the north used similar language to British observers to denounce the moral and social degeneracy of the Catholic and Celtic west.[35] However, for Isaac Butt, who penned a pamphlet denouncing the initiative, it was a further denial of true meaning of the British–Irish union to thus treat Ireland explicitly as 'a separate state'. He concluded that:

> the imposition of this tax is, in truth, to declare the Union a nullity. The moment you declare that you must make up the deficiency of the bankrupt

> unions from some source external to themselves, that moment you admit the purpose to be one to be supplied from the revenues of the state or the nation What state? – what nation? If the imposition of your tax answers – Ireland! then you have no answer to the demand that the Irish state and nation should have her separate legislature, and her own exchequer.[36]

He appealed to northerners not to separate themselves mentally from their country, but to recognise that British policy had created a new dispensation:

> let acts of parliament declare what they will, Antrim and Cork are parts of the same nation – Mayo and Kent are not. The individuality of countries cannot, perhaps, be destroyed by the ordinances that consolidate their legislatures. In our case, it is certain that it has not been so, and after half a century's experience of the Union, we still feel that Ireland is a separate country. Those who have spoken of the English exchequer, and proposed an Irish national rate in aid, have unequivocally proclaimed their conviction that it is so.[37]

In conclusion, although the political meaning which Butt extracted from the rate-in-aid (coming on top of his 1847 tirade in the *Dublin University Magazine*) reflected his own reluctant intellectual journey towards nationalism, his critique was in part shared by others. Tellingly, two of these were senior administrators of the Irish poor law system. Edward Twisleton, who resigned as chief commissioner over the rate-in-aid issue, denounced a policy he believed meant that 'those people should be left to die … [while] their brothers in the rest of the empire are to look on and let them die'.[38] For his part the Catholic liberal John Ball argued that Irish resources had already been stretched beyond breaking point by the imposition of the relief burden and that a policy which denied Treasury assistance was the 'grossest infraction of justice and the most insane defiance of common sense'. Irish nationalists and English xenophobes were to him equally at fault for the alienation of common sympathies:

> When the history of the time is fairly written, the same stern condemnation which awaits those who, forgetful of recent benefits, could only seek to excite in Ireland a blind hostility against England, will not less surely be awarded to those who contributed to the same object by embittering the feelings of Englishmen towards Ireland, and by making the very benefits conferred by them wear the garb of injuries.[39]

The government belatedly recognised the political damage wrought by treating Ireland as peripheral to the national interest and dispatched the Queen (on her first of four visits to Ireland) to the country in August 1849, both to work the political magic of monarchy and to symbolically mark the end of the famine. However, the damage was done, and two contradictory narratives (of Irish victimisation by a heartless or malevolent British state; and of British benevolence frustrated by Irish ingratitude and backwardness) were soon inscribed in rival historiographies. There would be no 'Great British Famine' in the public memories of what became in the early twentieth century different countries. In retrospect, what is perhaps more surprising is not the peripheralisation of Ireland during the famine in the British public and official mind, nor the fact that this was contested by Irish elites, but that during a certain moment in the crisis an alternative (if always somewhat ambivalent) imagining of Ireland as sharing a common Britishness took hold, however briefly and conditionally.

Notes

1 James S. Donnelly, 'The Construction of the Memory of the Famine in Ireland and the Irish Diaspora, 1850–1900', *Eire-Ireland* 31 (1996), 26–61.
2 William J. Smyth, 'The *longue durée:* Imperial Britain and Colonial Ireland', in *Atlas of the Great Irish Famine*, ed. John Crowley, William J. Smyth and Mike Murphy (Cork: Cork University Press, 2012), 46.
3 For the case that Ireland was a welfare periphery within the UK, see Virginia Crossman, 'Welfare and Nationality: The Poor Laws in Nineteenth-century Ireland', in *Welfare Peripheries: the Development of Welfare States in Nineteenth and Twentieth-century Europe*, ed. Steven King and John Stewart (Bern: Peter Lang, 2007), 67–124.
4 Thomas M. Devine, *The Great Highland Famine: Hunger, Emigration and the Scottish Highlands in the Nineteenth Century* (Edinburgh: John Donald, 1988); Frank Neal, *Black '47: Britain and the Famine Irish* (London: Palgrave Macmillan, 1997).
5 Cormac Ó Gráda, *Famine: A Short History* (Princeton, NJ: Princeton University Press, 2009), 235–241.
6 Peter Gray, 'The Great Famine in British and Irish Historiographies, c.1860–1914', in *Global Legacies of the Great Irish Famine: Transnational and Interdisciplinary Perspectives*, ed. Marguérite Corporaal, Christopher Cusack, Lindsay Janssen and Ruud van den Beuken (Bern: Peter Lang, 2014), 39–60.
7 Isaac Butt, 'The Famine in the Land: What has been Done, and What is to be Done?', *Dublin University Magazine* 29 (April 1847), 514.
8 Alan O'Day, 'Butt, Isaac (1813–1879)', *Oxford Dictionary of National Biography.* Available online at http://dx.doi.org/10.1093/ref:odnb/4222 (accessed 1 July 2014).
9 For example, Thomas Campbell Foster, 'The Condition of the People of Ireland', *The Times*, August 1845 to January 1846; John Stuart Mill, 'The Condition of Ireland', *Morning Chronicle*, October 1846 to January 1847.
10 Peter Gray, *Famine, Land and Politics: British Government and Irish Society, 1843–50* (Dublin: Irish Academic Press, 1999), 80–81.
11 Gray, *Famine, Land and Politics*, 117.
12 British Library, Peel Papers, Add. MSS 40,452, fol. 90 (Graham to Peel, 31 December 1845).
13 *Hansard*, 3rd series, 87, cols 423–424 (12 June 1846).
14 *Punch*, 13 December 1845.
15 *The Times*, 10 October 1845, 22 September 1846.
16 *The Times*, 2 Apri 1846; *Illustrated London News*, 4 Apri 1846.
17 *Hansard*, 3rd series, 88, cols 772–778 (17 August 1846).
18 National Library of Ireland, Monteagle Papers, MS 13,397/11 (Trevelyan to Monteagle, 9 October 1846).
19 The British National Archives, Russell Papers, PRO 30/22/5D, fols 84–87 (Russell to Bessborough, 4 October 1846).
20 *Examiner*, 9 January 1847.

21 Peter Gray, 'National Humiliation and the Great Hunger: Fast and Famine in 1847', *Irish Historical Studies* 32 (2000), 193–216.
22 *Illustrated London News*, 17 March 1847.
23 Thomas Chalmers, 'Political Economy of a Famine', in *North British Review* 7 (May 1847), 247–290.
24 *The Times*, 13 October 1847; Gray, 'National Humiliation'.
25 *Irish Improvidence Encouraged by English Bounty: being a Remonstrance against the Government Projects for Irish Relief… by an Ex-Member of the British Parliament* (London, n.d. [1847]).
26 James S. Donnelly, '"Irish property must pay for Irish poverty": British Public Opinion and the Great Irish Famine', in *Fearful Realities: New Perspectives on the Famine*, ed. Chris Morash and Richard Hayes (Dublin: Irish Academic Press, 1996), 60–76.
27 Cambridge University Library, Hickleton Papers, A4/185/2 (microfilm) (Wood to Clarendon, 3 April 1848).
28 Charles C.E. Greville, *A Journal of the Reigns of King George IV, King William IV and Queen Victoria* (Cambridge: Cambridge University Press, 2011 edn), iii (2 April 1848), 159–160.
29 Greville, *Journal* iii (21 July 1848), 207–208.
30 *The Times*, 28 August, 4 October 1848.
31 Wood to Delane, 13 September 1848. Printed in Arthur I. Dasent, *John Thadeus Delane, Editor of 'The Times': His Life and Correspondence* (2 vols, London: Murray, 1908), i, 82–84.
32 Bodleian Library, Univesity of Oxford, Clarendon Papers, Clar. Dep. Ir., Box 43 (Russell to Clarendon, 8 December 1848); Clar. Dep. Ir., Box 26 (Russell to Clarendon, 24 February 1849).
33 Cambridge University Library, Hickleton Papers, A4/59/2 (Trevelyan to Wood, 16 September, 20 October 1849).
34 Gray, *Famine, Land and Politics*, 311–314.
35 James Grant, 'The Great Famine and the Poor Law in Ulster: The Rate-in-aid Issue of 1849', *Irish Historical Studies* 27 (1990), 30–47.
36 Isaac Butt, *The Rate in Aid: A Letter to the Rt. Hon. the Earl of Roden* (Dublin: J. McGlashan, 1849), 27.
37 Butt, *Rate in Aid*, 67.
38 *Fourth Report from the Select Committee on Poor Laws (Ireland)*, HC 1849 (170), xv, 299.
39 John Ball, *What is to be Done for Ireland?* (2nd edn) (London: James Ridgeway, 1849), 26.

Part II

Finnish Famine [*Suuret Nälkävuodet*], 1867 to 1868

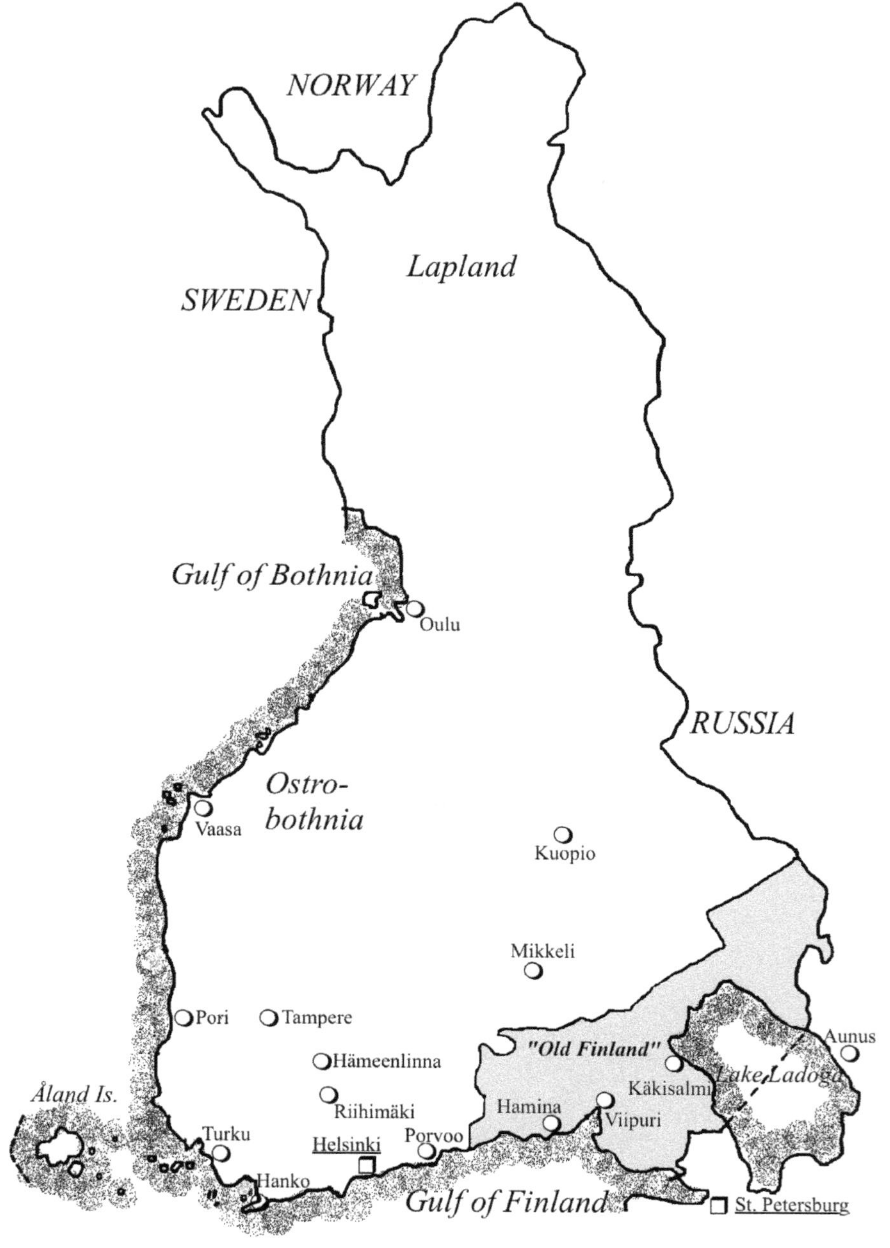

Map PII.1 Map of Finland.

4 Finland's famine years of the 1860s

A nineteenth-century perspective

Antti Häkkinen and Henrik Forsberg

Introduction

The period of hunger and destitution experienced in Finland during the 1860s, which formed one of the most devastating catastrophes in the nation's history, is generally remembered as the 'Hunger Years', or the 'Years of Crop Failure'.[1] Kari Pitkänen has described the period as a 'decade of misery', demonstrating how the most notorious year, 1868, represented merely the culmination of a much longer crisis.[2] In global and historical contexts, 1868 has been noted as exceptionally disastrous, not necessarily due to the total number of excess deaths, but rather because of the high *percentage* death rate.[3] In a short time period (1866–1868), 270,000 people died out of a population of fewer than two million, of which approximately 150,000 were 'excess' deaths. In the worst year, 1868, 137,702 people perished, representing 8 per cent of the population.[4] This overview will open with a brief examination of Finland's pre-1860s constitutional position, and its shift from a Swedish province to a Russian Grand Duchy, with a relatively autonomous position and developing sense of nationhood. It will then describe the pre-famine economic and social development of Finland, including landholding and demographic issues. Subsequently, it will outline the climatic factors which prompted the crisis of the 1860s, and how this affected Finnish society in terms of mortality, relief and (e)migration. A recurring theme is that, despite Finland's ostensibly homogeneous society (and the promotion of this homogeneity by the nation's 'fathers' and in subsequent historiography), the economic difficulties of the famine years underlined and accentuated various divisions in Finnish society.

Finland's constitutional and political situation before the 1860s

Situated at the northeastern corner of Europe, between Scandinavia and Russia, Finland's boundaries fluctuated considerably during its time under Swedish rule, from the thirteenth century to 1809.[5] Sweden's position as a great northern power had declined from the early eighteenth century, and the turmoil of the Napoleonic Wars precipitated a further humiliation. After their unsuccessful 'Finnish War' against Russia, the Treaty of Hamina in September 1809 was catastrophic for Sweden. The Swedes lost a considerable amount of territory to the Russians – not only their Finnish-speaking provinces, but also the Åland Islands and a part of Western Lapland. Thus, after nearly seven centuries as a poor eastern province of Sweden (during which time it has been noted that 'the absence of any special Finnishness' was 'striking'),[6] Finland became a relatively autonomous Grand Duchy of the Russian Empire, with the Tsar taking the position in Finland as Grand Duke.[7] Tsar Alexander I convened the four Estates – representatives of the peasantry, clergy, burghers and nobility – to the Diet of Porvoo in 1809, at which his sovereignty was confirmed.[8] Alexander concluded the Diet with the enigmatic statement that Finland could now join 'the rank of nations, governed by its own laws'.[9] His tactical aim was to convert those who had wished to retain Swedish rule, to weaken Swedish cultural and economic influence, and to consolidate his authority over his new territory. In principle the Diet had power over legislation, under the ultimate authority of the Tsar. The Tsar could make decisions over the Finnish economy, with the technical proviso that revenues raised within Finland were to be put to Finland's benefit.[10] After 1816, a Senate in Helsinki, under the control of a Governor General, managed Finland's economic and legal matters, and as Finland did not make any financial claims on the Russian imperial Treasury, it was not in the Tsar's interests to limit this autonomy.[11] In practice, however, the Diet was not reconvened until 1863, by which time practical power in the country had shifted to the civil servants, working under the Senate's control.

Tsar Alexander II succeeded his father in 1855, with Russia's geopolitical position weakened by the Crimean War. A liberal-minded, western-oriented Tsar, Alexander II enacted progressive reforms throughout his empire, covering the economy, social rights, local government, jurisdiction and the army.[12] The Finns' internal autonomy came under some scrutiny in St Petersburg in the early 1860s, especially following the proclamation in April 1861 summoning the Estates to prepare for an Imperial Diet in 1863.[13] Commentary in Russia was divided over the Finnish Question, but the semi-official *Russkii Invalid* seemed to accept Finland's unusual constitutional status, while also expressing a hope that the free decisions of the Finnish Diet would 'still more frankly and closely join the common circle of the great Russian family'.[14] After 1863 the Diet convened every fifth year, and Finland's national political life became increasingly active as the century progressed. However, it was difficult to reconcile the competing ambitions of Russian nationalists on the one hand, and Finnish nationalists on the other.[15] For the Finns, the reforms needed to be taken further; for the Russians, they were already far too extensive. At the end of the nineteenth century this clash of understanding led to a marked escalation of tension, the period of Finland's 'Russification'.[16]

Finnish economic development prior to the 1860s

Agriculture

It has been argued that Finland's economic and political relationship with Sweden had resembled that of a colony, and certainly Finnish agriculture developed in a manner dictated by Sweden prior to 1809.[17] Irrespective of its political or constitutional status, Finland's geography and climate have had a considerable impact upon its economic potential: a boreal zone with short growing seasons but with long summer days for ripening crops. Thick forests abound, which provide economic possibilities but also (alongside Finland's consistently low population density) logistical challenges. The Gulf Stream provides the possibility for cultivation unseen at other, similar latitudes.[18] Some progress towards agricultural 'improvement' had been made in the second half of the eighteenth century, however. In 1757, the Swedish Crown had introduced land enclosure in the hope of developing farmland.[19] Towards the end of the eighteenth century, the Swedish 'Royal Patriotic Society' had made grants in south-western Finland to reward 'enterprising husbandmen', and the foundation in 1797 of the Finnish Economic Society seemed to indicate that mainstream European ideas were starting to be implemented.[20] Although industrial production was limited, agricultural capacity had developed positively in the latter part of the eighteenth century. Despite steady population growth during the eighteenth century, which was particularly pronounced in rural areas and the interior, Finland remained practically self-sufficient in food production during normal harvest years.[21]

In the nineteenth century the agrarian economy came under considerable pressure, and the first part of the century was, at best, a period of slow economic and social progress. The main problem was that the primitive methods of cultivation with undeveloped technology, and inefficient landholding systems, were no longer able to respond to the demand for food, increasing in line with consistent population growth. Finland became more and more dependent on imported grain and other foodstuffs.[22]

Unlike Ireland, Finland's agricultural economy was not affected by the presence of a landowning gentry or aristocracy. The development in the Swedish kingdom of a 'free peasantry' also had an impact on Finland (where this class of peasant proprietors were known as *talolliset* or *talonpojat*).[23] Alongside the free peasantry's economic role in Finland, the concept also played a part in the development of Finland's national auto-stereotype: contrasting its own Scandinavian heritage in this regard with Russian serfdom during the nineteenth century. The absence of an ancillary occupation in many cases also created a cohort of landless peasants. The landless population increased during the nineteenth century, and, owing to the practice of *talolliset* leasing out small amounts of land, creating partial farm leases, a crofter population developed: by the 1860s, there were approximately 62,000 crofters (*torpparit*) and 82,000 independent farmers in Finland.[24] Landless cottiers, the *mäkitupalaiset*, formed a notable subclass. *Mäkitupalaiset* worked as hired labourers for larger farmers or spent winters working the forests.[25]

Although Finland's national coherence increased during the nineteenth century, there remained considerable regional variations which reflected historical differences in agricultural practice. Slash-and-burn techniques had been practised widely, particularly in the east of Finland. In the west, field husbandry had started to grow in importance from the middle ages. The raising of cattle for dairy, meat and manure also developed, especially in the south.[26] Agricultural production gradually commercialised in the nineteenth century, given extra impetus by the reintegration of 'Old Finland' – which had been part of Russia rather than Sweden from 1721 to 1809 and was an important source of agricultural production for St Petersburg – into the new Grand Duchy. This commercialisation altered Finland's susceptibility to agrarian crises: in addition to the climatic difficulties of a subsistence economy, international economics now had an impact. These fluctuations resulted from the importation of cheap grain and foodstuffs from Australia and America to Europe, and from Russia to Finland, making market-oriented grain production unprofitable.[27] A change in the line of production (a gradual change from grain production to meat and dairy) was the answer to this new challenge. The commercialisation of agriculture had other important repercussions. In the markets the food price variations increased, and in times of famine the value of grain multiplied. The labour markets also changed. Employment became dependent on economic fluctuations both in the markets of primary (agriculture, etc.) and secondary (industrial work, etc.) sectors. In the 1860s, when poor harvests were accompanied by negative market trends, this combination had dire consequences.

Finance and the growth of industry

By the start of the 1860s, only 6 per cent of the Finnish population lived in towns, and 85 per cent depended for their livelihoods on either agriculture or forestry, or a combination of both.[28] Nevertheless, industry had started to take hold in some parts of the country in the previous half-century.[29] Finland was one of the most important producers of tar in the world and this labour-intensive production, along with plank sawing, constituted the main part of its export.[30] The export structure was typical for a country that traded almost exclusively in raw materials. The few small coastal towns flourished by exporting these materials, and by importing salt, iron, clothes, wines and spices. Some plants in western Finland processed Swedish iron ore.[31]

Under the terms of the Treaty of Hamina, Finns were granted some autonomy in foreign trade matters, and the trade relationship with Sweden was not immediately broken, with a view to easing economic transition.[32] Although the process of industrialisation in Finland is often presented as commencing in the 1850s or 1860s, it is possible to argue that some of the preconditions for economic growth had been put in place in the first decades of Russian rule. One of the results of the power change was that the Russian Empire opened up large commercial markets for the Finnish export industry, and the favourable customs policy fed the Finnish textile and metal industries. New towns were founded in the interior. The Scotsman James Finlayson established a mill at Tampere, which came to stimulate a cluster of industry in the city, as well as encouraging other projects such as John Barker's mill in Turku in the 1840s.[33] Intrinsic to the success of the latter project was the position of the Bank of Finland, which had been founded in 1811 as an issuer of low-value notes, but which bolstered Finland's relative independence in financial and economic policy.[34] The first half of the century also saw the foundation of the Finnish merchant navy, an institution that soon reached a prominent position in international commercial shipping.[35] Some important infrastructural projects were carried out during this period, most notably the construction of the Saimaa Canal, which connected the eastern parts of country to the Gulf of Finland. Similar projects were realised all over the country, with several new roads built both in Ostrobothnia and in the eastern provinces.[36] Finnish railways became something of a microcosm of the dichotomy between autonomy and empire, with some Finnish nationalists prioritising an inland track as a means of boosting Finland's own economy, and others highlighting the importance of a line between Helsinki and St Petersburg as a means of strengthening the economic and political ties with Russia.[37] The inland track between Helsinki and Hämeenlinna eventually opened in 1862, whereas the extension from Riihimäki to St Petersburg (which would connect the Finnish and Russian capitals) started to be built in the winter of 1868, and was opened in 1870.[38] As noted below, these infrastructure projects also played a part in emergency relief programmes during the famine times, as relief was given in return for work tasks.

The industrialisation process accelerated in the mid-nineteenth century, stimulated in part by international trade. Britain, Germany, France, the United States and even Sweden experienced rapid economic growth, which provided destinations for Finnish exports. The increasing international demand for lumber, pulp and paper also attracted foreign capital to forest-rich countries like Finland.[39] The metal industry also benefited when export to the Russian markets was improved by the new customs policies.

Finland's position within the Russian Empire had broader international implications, and both its economy and its society were affected by the war in the Baltic in 1854 to 1855.[40] In the short term, the British fleet's bombardment of the Finnish west coast, and destruction of grain stores, has been presented as one of the main triggers of famine during the 1850s and 1860s.[41] It is also clear that Russia's economic instability after the Crimean War, and reforms prompted by the humiliation of defeat, had a significant influence on Finland's position in relation to St Petersburg. Although Tsar Alexander II's visit to Helsinki in March 1856 has perhaps been given too much credit for Finland's 'liberalisation', the 'five vague points' he put to the Senate would have important ramifications.[42] He invited the Senate to propose measures which could repair the damage caused by the war, boost Finland's industrial base, and improve education and the communications infrastructure. Under an imperial umbrella, therefore, Finland's Senate began to embark upon a programme of national legislation: on the construction of railways (1857); the use of steam-powered sawmills (1857); countryside commerce (1859); and joint-stock companies (1864). Moreover, a national school system was introduced, and vocational education extended.[43] The fiscal autonomy that came from the 1809 settlement was also being developed. Monetary reform was especially important for the development of the national economy, and the *markka*, Finland's own national currency, was introduced in 1860. Despite these innovations, industrial development remained sluggish, and by the end of the nineteenth century over two-thirds of the population were still making their living from agriculture.[44]

Pre-famine society and demographics

At the time of the Treaty of Hamina, Finland's GDP per capita was one of the lowest in Europe (calculated in 1820 to have been 781 International Geary-Khamis Dollars (Int. GK$)), approximately half of the average in Europe at the time), and almost 90 per cent of all employment came from the primary sector, mostly from agriculture.[45] Finland's population increased considerably throughout the nineteenth century, from 830,000 in 1800 to 2,700,000 in 1900.[46] The economic autonomy that had been granted to the Senate in Helsinki needed to formulate medium- to long-term plans to address this population growth.[47]

The supposed homogeneity of this expanding population has been given as one of the factors behind the standard Finnish narrative of an economy that developed during the twentieth century from poverty to prosperity.[48] However, this homogeneity thesis cannot go unchallenged, as several lines of societal cleavage existed in nineteenth-century Finland, which endured (and even increased). The traditional regional divisions based on socio-economic structure, dialect, mentality or ethnic background were not simply erased by a national master-narrative emanating from an elite in Helsinki. Although the nationalist movement (the Fennomen) emphasised the unity of the nation, and although coherent trans-regional or 'national' movements emerged (often influenced by

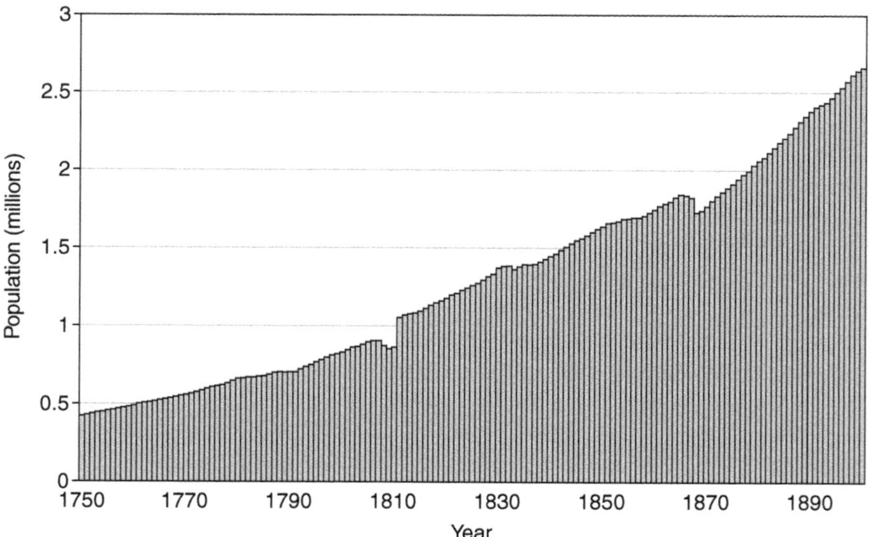

Figure 4.1 Population of Finland, 1750 to 1900.

and allied with international organisations, such as the temperance movement, women's movement, and so on), other fissures developed. These included divergence between government and citizens, between different regions within the country, between urban and rural areas, and, most notably, between different social classes.[49] This final point is especially important when looking at the 1860s, because as is often emphasised in global famine research, the distribution of foodstuffs has never been only a question of quantitative amounts of grain per capita, but necessarily deals with societal power relations.[50]

Three key problems continued from the late eighteenth century: (1) the rapidly increasing proportion of landless agricultural labourers; (2) the slow improvement in the poor's standard of living, hampered by several famines and other crises during the period; and (3) a widening gap developing between the landowning and the landless population in regard to the standard of living and civil rights.[51] In Figure 4.2, the number of households of three main social groups in the Finnish countryside is presented at four points between 1784 and 1901, highlighting the increasing number and proportion of landless labourers.

Finland's emerging nationhood in the nineteenth century was intimately connected with Lutheranism, which gave the Grand Duchy a cultural and social distinctiveness within the Russian Empire, and connected it back to a Scandinavian history.[52] The Lutheran church held a central position in teaching and controlling the lives and ideology of people. The parish system underpinned the Finnish Poor Law, and Lutheranism was an essential component of a national identity that promoted hard work and self-sufficiency. By 1900, Finland was almost uniformly (98.1 per cent of the population) Lutheran, with only a small minority

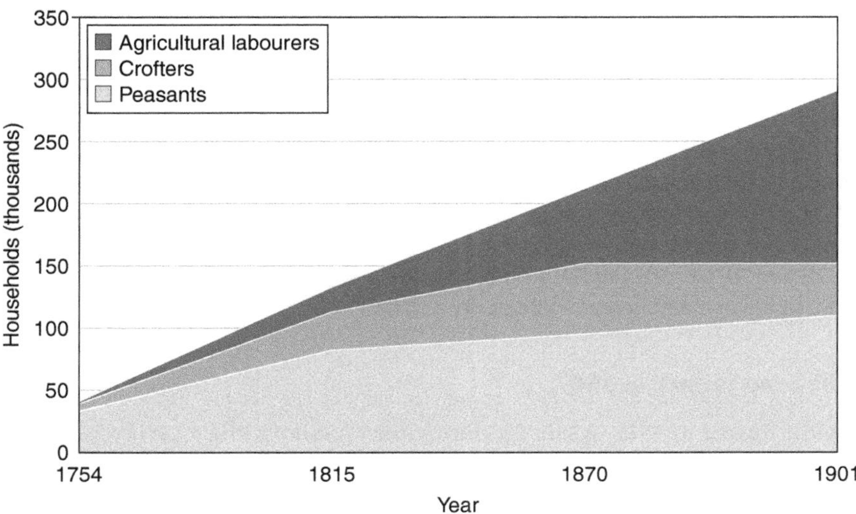

Figure 4.2 The number of agrarian population of Finland by social group and year (1,000 households).

(1.7%) adhering to the Orthodox Church.[53] And yet, while Lutheranism contributed hugely to a sense of ethnic 'Finnishness', and the idea of a homogeneous people – in many ways adopting the role of 'bearer of the nation' – its patriarchal attitudes also legitimised the increasing class divisions in society.[54] Contemporaries recognised these social trends. Concern over poverty and the quick growth of the number of the landless population, particularly in the eastern and northern parts of the country, was already a regular subject of newspaper debate in the 1840s.[55] Subsequently, these worries were also articulated in governors' reports, provincial doctors' accounts and in the sermons of the clergy.[56] Such concerns seemed to be borne out by statistics, although the figures also highlighted the increasing regional inequalities within the supposedly homogeneous nation: southern Ostrobothnia and central Finland saw a fourfold increase in the number of landless people during the nineteenth century; in eastern Finland the figure tripled; and even in southern Finland the figure grew by two and a half times over the course of the century. On a national scale, the landowner–landless ratio changed from 3:1 in 1825, to 1:1 in 1875, and was exacerbated in times of harvest failure.[57]

The most evident mark of social injustice during the famine period is that mortality was strongly dependent on social background. Attitudes towards this 'underclass', particularly from local elites or those in the capital, were similar in tone to much of the rhetoric which Irish nationalist accounts have remembered emanating from the decision makers in London during the 1840s. And yet, the overarching narrative of national cohesion has meant that these attitudes have not been prominent in the Finnish historiography. During the post-Crimean crisis, for example, a correspondent from 'desolate Carelia' wrote in one Helsinki newspaper about local conditions and the destitution of the 'lesser classes', and how state poor relief upheld their intrinsic laziness. Government subsidies were claimed to be a source of local corruption and abuse. This correspondent proposed the introduction of workhouses where food would be provided in return for labour.[58] In a European context Finland remained economically underdeveloped at the dawn of the twentieth century. Using its GDP per capita measurement, by the last year of the century it had little more than doubled from its 1820 level (to 1688 Int. GK$), and remained one of the lowest in Europe. The number of people surviving on temporary work increased considerably between 1870 and 1910, precipitating both internal migration and transatlantic emigration, but also creating a new urban proletariat.[59]

The crop failure in 1867

Unlike Ireland in 1845, where the *phytopthera infestans* blight had been hitherto unknown, the basic cause of crop failure in Finland in 1867 to 1868 was a familiar long-standing foe – namely frost. Food shortages resulting from frost-induced crop failures were relatively common in pre-modern Finland, and the capricious nature of summer frosts was a common cause: 'summer frosts leap all over the place like grasshoppers' is a colourful phrase attributed to a contemporary

Finnish farmer.[60] Agriculturally and meteorologically, it was difficult to predict where the frosts might strike. Nevertheless, the harsh winter of 1866/1867 had meant that crops were sown relatively late that spring, which had allowed little margin for any interruptions to the ripening season. Ploughing had only commenced in early June, and a warm summer lasting through to mid-September would have been necessary to secure the crop. However, frost returned in early September and the combination of a failed crop and depleted reserves ensured that a catastrophe was triggered.[61]

The climatic conditions that precipitated the harvest failure initially hit the northern provinces of Kuopio, Vaasa and Oulu, as well as the northern parts of Turku and Pori.[62] News of the desperate conditions in the north only very slowly reached the southern newspapers, and these regional variations came into stark focus in 1867, when the Finnish government dispatched two senators – Norrmén and Antell – from Helsinki into the provinces with a view to assessing the economic and social situation.[63] It is clear from their report that there were large variations in how local authorities responded to the crisis.[64] In the last resort, the Tsar would have been in a position of decisive power, but in practical terms the Senate was responsible for the most crucial decisions.[65] Head of Office for State Finances in the Finnish Senate during this period was Johan Vilhelm Snellman, a philosopher and journalist who is remembered as one of the key figures in Finland's national development.[66] Snellman believed that economic independence was an essential component of political state independence, and accordingly his policies during the famine period may be seen as prioritising the longer term development of the nation before individuals or regions.[67] In any event, the Russian imperial finances were in poor shape during this period and thus St Petersburg was more than prepared to humour the Finnish preoccupation with self-sufficiency.[68]

To support the new currency, the Bank of Finland restricted business loans and maintained a low circulation of money, meaning that interest rates grew. Moreover, when the *markka* was pegged to the silver standard in 1865, it was revalued by 20 per cent.[69] In taking this course of action, it has been argued that Snellman worsened the economic situation in many Finnish regions during the famine period.[70] The tight fiscal controls and decrease in prices meant that businessmen were not in a position to give loans, or undertake large-scale grain imports. The longer term economic malaise in Finland meant that bankruptcies were already increasing well before the worst months of 1867/1868. Therefore, the infamous night frost of 3–4 September 1867 may have been perceived as the trigger for crop failure, but given the late sowing it was always possible that frost could destroy the autumn harvest. This places culpability back on to the Snellman administration for a failure to prepare for, or respond to, a likely shortage.

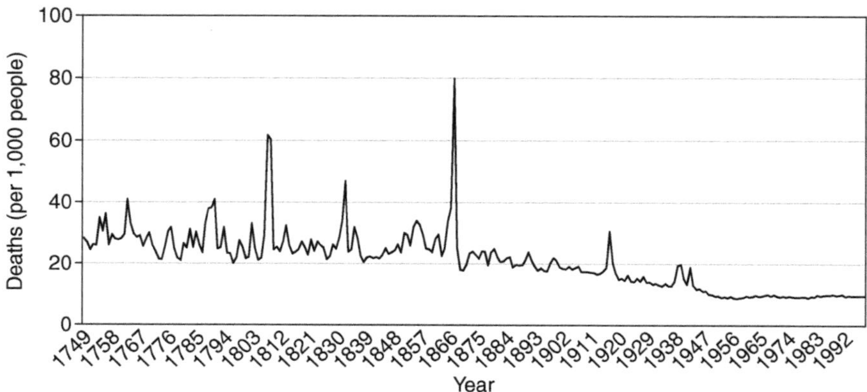

Figure 4.3 Annual deaths per 1,000 in Finland, 1749 to 2000.

Famine mortality

Social institutions were unprepared for the depth of the 1860s crisis, and after the failed harvest in 1867, economic and social problems escalated. The price of grain rose by almost 10 per cent each month. The government sought to import relief grain from abroad, but the early onset of winter hindered efficient distribution. At the beginning of autumn, the number of thefts began to grow. From November, deaths began to increase, at first uniformly, but then at an accelerating rate. The poor population began to move *en masse* out of the areas affected most by crop failure towards the coast, the south, and Russia. Measures were introduced which sought to limit or discourage this vagrancy, underpinned largely by a fear of a nationwide spread of contagious disease. Workrooms were opened by parishes to give beggars from their own areas work in return for a 'food wage'. However, the spread of the epidemics seems to have become unmanageable in late February 1868.[71] In an attempt to control the situation, additional hospitals and temporary huts were introduced. The death rates in these confined spaces grew rapidly.

According to Oiva Turpeinen's calculations, almost one-third of the population contracted typhus.[72] Statistics show that approximately one in ten sick passed away, but in reality the proportion was probably much higher. It is difficult to prove the direct link between the three problems of hunger, disease and mortality, but it may be shown that mortality was strongly linked to social groupings, with lower social classes suffering an increased chance of death.[73] The risk may be compared to pre-famine 'normal mortality' times. Accordingly, for a peasant farmer (*talollinen*) the risk of death nearly doubled. For a crofter (*torppari*) it quadrupled, and for labourers the risk increased fivefold. The worst peaks of typhus mortality were, to within a few weeks, the same across different parts of the land. Mortality from the epidemic began to increase significantly in the third week of February and peaked in April/May. Measured by mortality, the peak of the crisis was in May 1868, when 25,300 died, at least half from 'typhus', a general term which covered typhus, typhoid, relapsing fever and other diseases. It also seems clear that mortality from communicable disease was exacerbated by the congregation of the sick and diseased in workhouses and hospitals. Other causes of death were dysentery and other intestinal diseases, frostbite, poisoning and various types of accidents.[74] Large numbers also died of outright starvation, either directly or because of complications caused by a lack of nutrition.[75]

Nutrition and food surrogates

The Finnish rural diet still consisted predominantly of cereals in the 1800s, though root crops, peas and beans were also consumed. The potato was increasing in popularity, and dairy products were used.[76] Meat was eaten from time to time, as was fish. However, the core diet consisted of cereal products – especially rye, barley and some oats and wheat – which meant annual dependence upon the harvest. Food surrogates were also well known: *pettu* (the traditional bark-bread which incorporated ground phloem) and *vehka* (bog arum, the roots of which had long been used to provide surrogate nutrition) were used extensively even in normal harvest years.[77] In 1867, the rye crop was destroyed, along with almost the entire barley crop, and other plants were severely affected. The area which needed the most supplementary food aid coincided almost exactly with the area in which mortality rates rose most. It comprised a zone (see Map 4.1) starting from southwestern Finland, through the midland lake district, the southern parts of Lapland and round to northern Karelia, covering approximately a quarter of the country.[78] In coastal areas, Åland and the south of the country the harvest was almost normal, but even within regions there could be considerable differences on the parish level.[79] County (*lääni*) magazines stored grain for military requirements and, where necessary, this was distributed as a loan or given as emergency relief. Parish magazines stored grain mainly for planting. These stores had been almost entirely depleted during the 1860s owing to earlier harvest failures, and this contributed to the catastrophe of 1867/1868. There is a lack of data on private stores, but these can be expected to have been as low as the public stocks. For the landless, of course, there were no supplies.[80] With this lack of stored grain arose the question of how best to import supplies from abroad while preserving the credibility of the national economy. Because of differences in regional requirements, there also needed to be an efficient system of grain transport and distribution. In both of these areas efforts failed. About one-third of the necessary grain was purchased with the help of the banker von Rothschild, although financial support also came from other foreign diplomatic and philanthropic channels.[81]

The investigations of local doctors and landlords concluded that the feeding of the sick was organised very poorly, and that often the starving were offered bread or gruel made from lichen. The care and nutrition available in the workhouses or hospitals was so weak that mortality increased as a result.

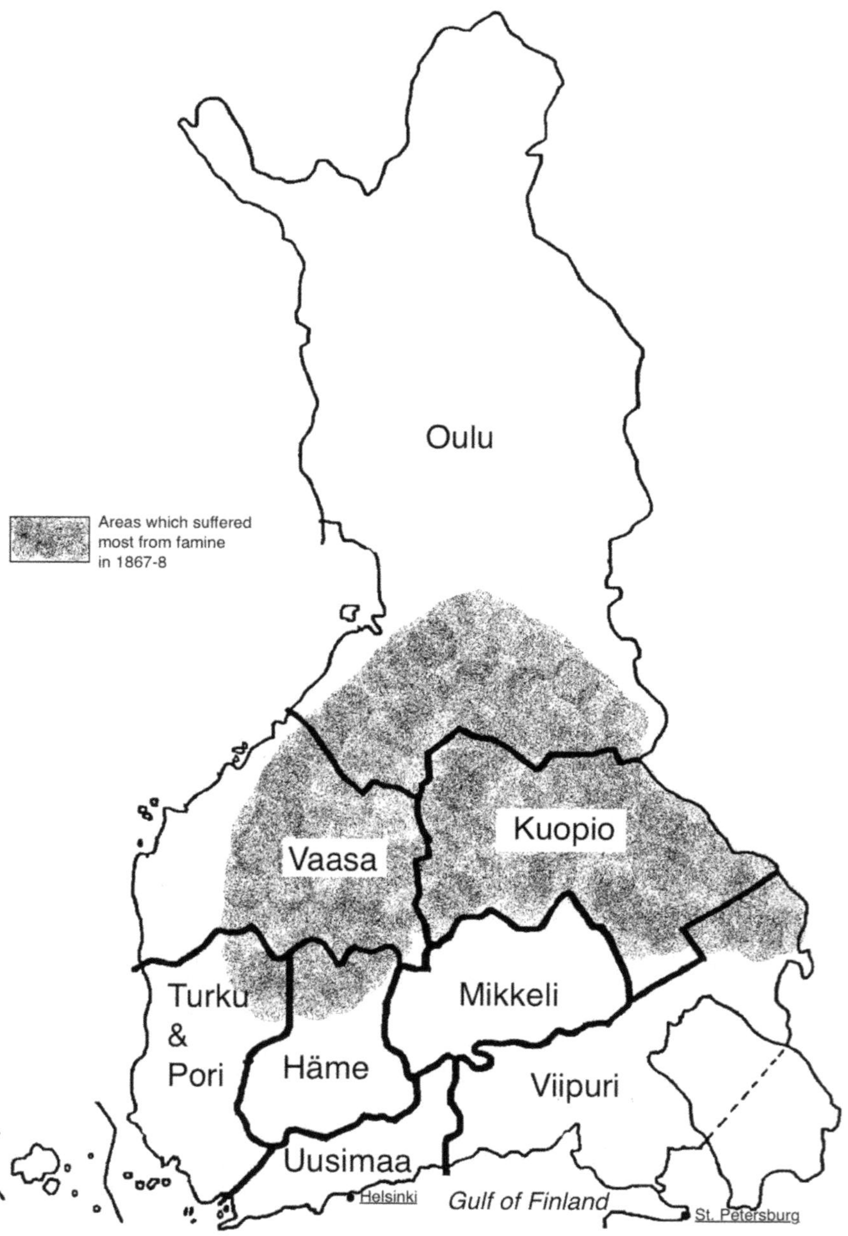

Map 4.1 The Grand Duchy of Finland in 1867 and the areas that suffered most from the famine (source: map credit Andrew G. Newby).

Relief efforts

The Poor Law in Finland was intimately linked to the Lutheran church, and had since the Reformation been a locally funded system based on Lutheran parish structures. The relief of certain groups, such as the 'incurable sick' and the able-bodied poor, was overseen by the state, which also controlled migration and punished vagrancy.[82] The early decades of the nascent Finnish state also saw the encouragement of philanthropy, particularly in the areas of child welfare and education.[83] The increase of population in the nineteenth century, and particularly the increase of landless labourers, threw into chaos a system based on patriarchal legal protection. After a decade-long process of deliberation, the Senate enacted a new Poor Law in 1852, which established compulsory local boards, and accompanying taxation, for relief. Alongside this act, however, was the Act on Forced Labour and Vagrancy (1852), which reintroduced the idea of the poor being given relief in return for work.[84] The re-establishment of these paternalistic control measures did not settle the question of how best to deal with 'excess population', and indeed Pirjo Markkola has argued that the 1852 Poor Law was 'immediately obsolete'.[85]

One of the Senate's main national reforms of the 1860s oversaw a fundamental change in municipal government, which separated the responsibilities of municipalities and parishes. Most of the duties carried out earlier by the church now became the responsibility of civil government, but change came slowly and a variety of systems were in use when the famine struck. The rather anarchic state of local government, in the context of a state already in turmoil following years of harvest shortages and attendant social dislocation, was one of the factors that prevented an effective and organised reaction in 1867/1868.[86]

Aid distribution was hindered on a national level by a slow and bureaucratic system. Furthermore, parishes and municipalities received finance only as repayable loans, although later on they also got interest-free aid.[87] In 1862 many donations from Finland and abroad, and especially from Russia, had made it possible to organise local work programmes, for example, by digging ditches, which meant that people remained in their home municipalities and did not put pressure on their neighbouring communities' equally fragile economies through begging, stealing or spreading disease. This was only a temporary expedient, and by 1866 the local management of relief was beginning to collapse under the strain of widespread poverty. By 1867, impoverished and indebted municipalities were not willing to take out extra loans. The state was forced into a more active role, and so larger national work schemes were set in motion in the form of road and bridge construction, dredging rivers, canal building and the expansion of the railway network.[88] Aid was not given directly to the needy unless it was connected to a work obligation. The system could produce inhumane results, with starving men, women and children undertaking these labour tasks, sometimes in temperatures of minus 25 degrees. However, there were places where centralised relief works or workhouses were replaced by direct aid in people's homes. The poor were also placed in private homes. This occurred in regions where the losses of the harvest were fewer, and mortality rates less severe, although the system itself was clearly more expensive. The idea of the aid policy was to avoid undue concentration of the 'redundant population' in one place.[89] This succeeded at least to the extent of minimising disease, and possibly also allowing for a greater amount and better quality of food aid.[90]

'Families driven from their northern homes': migration and emigration

> One cannot wonder but that many now reverse the dear old adage and think: 'it is good to be at home, but best to be away'![91]

Migration within Finland

The crisis years left the poor and the vulnerable with two avenues of survival.[92] They could stay within the sphere of the local community and trust the shelter provided by the poor relief system, or they could move out in search of bread and work. The former option represented sticking to the sphere of social relationships and institutions of the system of legal protection. Leaving meant casting oneself at the mercy of unknown circumstances, and defying the statutes concerning migration. Nevertheless, numerous people took up this option. The largest number of migrants came from those areas – the provinces of Kuopio, Vaasa and Oulu – that had been suffering the worst harvest shortages during the 1860s. Data suggest that interprovincial migration was not a priority from southern coastal regions, nor certain parts of Turku, Pori, Häme or Mikkeli, but in assessing these data Kari Pitkänen warns of the possibility that the distressed people of these areas may nevertheless have 'circulated in their home parishes, or even in neighbouring areas'.[93]

Claims of what Orta has characterised as 'the planless drifting of an apathetic mass'[94] were prominent in international reports of the period, with tropes familiar from many other famine crises:

> [N]o words of mine can describe the misery, suffering and sickness at present prevailing from one end of this unhappy famine-stricken country to the other. Iceland moss, pine bark, and pease straw, ground up with a little flour, is the only food wherewith the mother can now feed her child, and the only food upon which thousands will be dependent for many months to come … believe me, it is truly heartbreaking to see whole families driven from their northern homes by famine and despair, wandering from place to place, half dead with cold, in search of food and work, but finding neither. Such is Finland's present state.[95]

In general terms, Pitkänen identifies three main migratory trends during the 1860s: (1) most of the internal migration saw people move from the north to south, particularly the southeast, often towards Helsinki or Viipuri, or on towards

St Petersburg or other parts of Russia; (2) the northernmost migrants travelled the longest distances, whereas those in the south tended to gravitate towards the nearest urban settlements; and (3) rural areas which hosted large-scale public works or construction projects attracted huge numbers.[96] The vast migrant population had an impact on local systems of social relationships. In the poor regions entire villages lost their inhabitants, farms went uncultivated, and the consequences of the crisis were felt long into the future. However, the migration from the poor regions created new life patterns and opportunities for survivors. The migration hastened the process of urbanisation and facilitated emigration in the decades following the famine years.

While the population displacement caused by the crisis was considerable, transatlantic emigration was not yet considered a realistic option for most Finns. The vast majority of migration took place within the bounds of the Grand Duchy. If people moved further afield it was generally to the fishing and mining communities of the Norwegian coast, or eastward to destinations within the Russian Empire.[97] Indeed, Kari Pitkänen argues, specifically in contrast with post-famine emigration in Ireland, as distinct from temporary migration, 'permanent, or registered migration does not show any significant changes during the 1860s'.[98] The extent to which certain historiographical themes around the Finnish famine have been influenced by the Irish case is not quite clear, but there have been attempts to link the crisis of 1867/1868 with transatlantic emigration from Finland. Fred Singleton's *Short History of Finland*, for example, makes an explicit comparison: 'the whole decade was known as the "Hungry Sixties" and, as in Ireland during the "Hungry Forties", large numbers of poor farmers and landless peasants emigrated in order to escape from the misery which followed the failure of crops.'[99] The 'American Fever', however, began in earnest well over a decade after the calamitous year of 1868, not least because of lack of transport opportunities between Finland and the New World.[100]

Emigration from Finland

The internal core–periphery dynamic had shifted within Finland from west to south after 1809, and particularly after Helsinki had become the Grand Duchy's capital in 1812.[101] The economic problems of the west coast had grown from the early nineteenth century, and were aggravated by the concerted bombing attacks by the British navy during the Crimean War. Further problems were caused by the slump in the price of tar following the American Civil War. Tar burning had helped to sustain the economy of the Oulu and Vaasa regions, but had also damaged forests to such an extent that new opportunities elsewhere in Finland based around the exploitation of forests were not possible in the Bothnia region.[102] As noted above, this led to internal migration, but it also meant that emigration agents began to see western Finland as potentially fruitful ground.[103] Patterns of landholding also led to intolerable pressure on the population in some regions, with the subdivision of individual farmlands leading to a situation where holdings were of insufficient size to support their tenants.[104] In the 1860s, therefore, localised economic crises began to force consideration of the opportunities available on the other side of the Atlantic, in a context of wider discussions of migration.

North Norway

The opportunities in the north of Norway – fishing and mining – were taken by many Finns. This also provided a stimulus for eventual transatlantic migration, as transport opportunities and a more general discussion around American emigration existed in Norway. Migration to *Ruija* from Finland's northern provinces pre-dated the 1860s famine years – indeed, there are records of such migration from at least the early eighteenth century, when a Finnish settlement developed at Alta.[105] This movement accelerated during the nineteenth century, and although the reasons for it were more complex than merely the economic push factors, the economic troubles of the 1860s stimulated increased migration from the Bothnian provinces of Oulu and Vaasa.[106] When emigration agents increased their operations in Scandinavia, Finns in northern Norway were among those who took a chance on crossing the Atlantic. Moreover, the experience gained by some in the copper mines of Alta and Kaafjord made them desirable workers in the American Midwest.[107] Compared with Ireland, and indeed with Norway as a whole, the number of Finns emigrating to America from Finnmark remained small, probably fewer than 1,000 individuals.[108]

Kola, Karelia, Ingria and St Petersburg

The eastern border of the Finnish state was only formalised in 1617 under the terms of the (Russian–Swedish) Treaty of Stolbovo, but was subject to fluctuation, and indeed some parts of the state were named 'Old Finland', as this area had remained a part of the Russian Empire even prior to 1809. To this extent, in terms of the Finns' mental geography, economic migration to Ingria, Karelian towns such as Olonets (Aunus), and even the imperial capital, St Petersburg, may be considered as an extension of internal migration rather than as an aspect of 'international' emigration. Oulu Province also provided the majority of emigrants from Finland to the Murman Coast, which started during the famine years of the 1860s but which, like the migrations to Finnmark, developed from the well-established Arctic fishing expeditions. Again, though, only relatively small numbers took advantage of this economic migration, and when in 1870 they were visited by a Finnish priest there were reckoned to be 361 colonists strung out between Kola Bay and the Fisherman's Peninsula. As with localised movements from Finland to northern Norway, migration from the east of Finland to Aunus had been a part of life for generations, either as an end in itself or as part of a step migration to the metropolis of St Petersburg. This type of migration was relatively short and was largely the preserve of Finland's rural proletariat.[109]

The Russian Empire

Longer distance and longer term migration from Finland during the 1860s lay less in America than in the eastern part of the Russian Empire, particularly in the newly colonised province of Amur.[110] Although the economic malaise in Finland helped to create conditions conducive for this emigration, the Russian context was also important, with state and private companies offering inducements to would-be colonists.[111] Although the influential Helsinki newspaper *Hufvudstadsbladet* decried Finnish 'Emigration Fever' in 1868, this referred to Russian imperial emigration rather than to any large-scale movement to America.[112]

Transatlantic

Although Finns had been present in Swedish North American colonies since the seventeenth century, it was the nineteenth century when, in common with many other European regions, the great movement of Finns across the Atlantic began.[113] The 1850s had seen some limited settlement by Finns in the United States, as a result of naval desertions and the attraction of the Gold Rush.[114] However, in comparison with Ireland, and even neighbouring Norway and Sweden, Finnish transatlantic emigration began very late – accelerating through the 1870s to reach a peak in the 1890s. In the 1860s, this phenomenon started from areas that had experienced economic crisis, notably Ostrobothnia and Northern Satakunta. Emigration agents did play on the economic woes, but there were also pull factors, such as the idea that life in America was freer than in Finland, and that it would be possible to build communities with idealised 'Finnish' qualities on the other side of the Atlantic.[115] However, while emigration to America was an option for those who had first settled in northern Norway, or who had been approached by agents, the transatlantic routes were not generally accessible or obvious for most people in southern Finland. Only after the establishment of regular boat services between Hanko and the English port of Hull in the 1880s did emigration really reach 'epidemic' proportions on a national scale.[116]

Consequences

Unlike Ireland, the demographic consequences of the 1860s famine years were relatively short-lived, as may be seen in Figure 4.1. Similarly, the link between these crisis years and transatlantic emigration is tenuous, and indeed emigration in Finland was narrated as a longer term response to general economic restructuring.[117] In considering social consequences, it has been asserted that the 1860s witnessed the birth of modernity in Finland.[118] Vuolle's description of 'the creation of the Finnish welfare state after the famine in the 1860s' is typical of this teleological approach, and implies a far greater degree of planning and forethought than was ever the case.[119] It is more realistic to argue *at most* that processes in train before the years of hunger survived considerable economic and social disruption and came to fruition in subsequent decades.[120] There were so many different changes taking place in Finnish society – fiscal reform, educational reform, local government reform, questions over poor relief – that it was difficult subsequently to discern what processes were accelerated and what may have been hindered by the 1860s famine years. Although the memory of famine may have provided a mental turning point for later generations, it seems likely that without the crisis of 1867/1868, these reforms could have happened more quickly.

The theme of self-sufficiency as a cornerstone of personal and national identity was stressed repeatedly. In the 1860s some peripheral areas of Finland, especially in the north, were perceived by the core elite in Helsinki as chronically poor, and a belief grew that the peasants had to be made thriftier, less lazy, more self-sustained and less dependent on the Emperor's feeding hand.[121] Agathon Meurman commented 25 years later that 'every effort to aid a population is useless as long as that same population is incapable of helping itself'.[122] This *Zeitgeist* contextualised the reform of the Finnish Poor Law in 1879, which put the onus on those individuals who earned a living through work, but was also arranged on a municipal level to assist those denied the possibility of achieving this ideal (such as infirmity, or a general crop failure).

On the economic level the 1860s saw a severe setback for economic progress. The crisis delayed the development of agriculture, industrial production and trade. The farming industry in particular suffered from continual poor harvests, as technological innovations and cultivation improvements were delayed. In terms of economic development it is easy to distinguish a growth trend following the nadir of the spring of 1868. Besides the expansion of the railway network, export-oriented industry of wood products such as timber, pulp and paper grew, as well as the export of dairy products. The Grand Duchy's national production became much more diverse, although this hardly made Finland more self-sufficient in any meaningful way; on the contrary, it tied Finland's economy more tightly to the international economy.

In respect of national administration, new arrangements were made to better provide for future crop failures. A nationwide network of granaries was built and a centralised poor relief committee system was organised to systematise the supply of relief food in hard times. These improvements were, together with an improved national infrastructure, effective enough to prevent a disaster in the crop failures of 1893, 1902 and 1923.[123] This statist, centralised and bureaucratic poor relief system was employed later in other emergencies. During both World Wars, for example, the production and consumption of the most important consumer goods were regulated within a similar framework, with a powerful central organisation with a network of effective local committees. On an ideological level, however, it is difficult to see any connections between the great famine years in 1860s Finland and the twentieth-century welfare state system.

The 1860s may also be seen as an exemplar of the uneven impact of famine on a society: the increase in mortality occurred particularly in the countryside, in Finland's eastern and central regions, and hit infants and old people, mainly of the labouring population, especially hard.[124] Finland was a poor agrarian country in Europe at that time,[125] but what makes the course of events astonishing is that it came during the so-called *Pax Russica*. It was a century of slow but stable economic progress, profound liberal social and political reforms, without any remarkable military conflicts, excluding the Finnish War in 1808 to 1809 and the Crimean War, which affected the region in 1854 to 1856. All this happened in a Grand Duchy, at the western modernised part of the Russian Empire with relatively strong central government machinery,[126] with workable telegraph networks[127] located in the economic orbit of St Petersburg, one of Europe's largest metropoles. An old agrarian 'crop failure famine model'[128] does not match well with the subsequent population crisis. As demonstrated by Sen, questions of power relations, unequal distribution of food and the market mechanism have to be asked in order to comprehend the disaster.[129]

Conclusion

The Great Hunger Years of the 1860s have not had remotely the same place in Finnish history as *An Gorta Mór* or the *Holodomor* have had in Ireland or Ukraine respectively. The 'Home Rule' administration in Helsinki was largely responsible for the response to the crisis, and it was therefore inappropriate to apportion blame to the Russian imperial authorities. These years have created a powerful collective memory of the mendicant hordes, who passed hopelessly from house to house, without any real purpose other than survival. When the bread ran out, the only real hope was to grab the 'begging stick'. Key issues came to the fore: charity, hospitality, community and moral responsibility. Here we find contradictory images, and memories and reminiscences tell two different stories. On the one hand, we hear that poverty was equally divided between affluent and poor. On the other hand, it is said that the rest of the population reacted in a hard-hearted fashion to the suffering. A clear distinction was made between the poor of one's own parish and those who came in from outside. One's own were looked after – but outsiders were expelled or moved on to the next house.[130]

Various key issues therefore arise from this overview of Finland's famine years. First, there was a grave lack of awareness, even wilful ignorance, about how precarious the situation was, which hindered the relief process from Helsinki. There are of course numerous explanatory factors behind this procedure, but the outcome was disastrous. Second, Finland was a poor country, with outmoded agricultural processes, and industrialising only gradually. There were few resources that could be moved from one sector to another. Repeated famines and general economic stagnation formed a fatal combination. Third, a process of impoverishment was taking place, featuring an increasingly negative ratio between the landowning and the landless population, which made society vulnerable to social crises. Furthermore, ever more people had become dependent upon labour markets, and lacked protection in the event of crop failures or economic stagnation. Fourth, the local governing system was a relic of a patriarchal society, being reformed slowly and in a piecemeal manner, which hindered effective relief measures. There is no single reason to explain the catastrophe satisfactorily. There was a chain of unfavourable conditions, supplemented by negative external factors, and exacerbated by ineffective relief measures on both central and local levels.

Notes

1 'Hunger Years' is expressed as *Nälkävuodet* in Finnish, *Hungeråren* in Swedish. 'Years of dearth' is the closest translation for the terms *Katovuodet* (Finnish) or *Missväxtåren* (Swedish). The general terms for famine, *Nälänhätä* (Finnish) or *Hungersnöden* (Swedish), translate literally as 'hunger emergency'.
2 Kari J. Pitkänen, *Deprivation and Disease: Mortality During the Great Finnish Famine of the 1860s* (Helsinki: Finnish Demographic Society, 1993), 51.
3 Cormac Ó Gráda, *Famine: A Short History* (Princeton, NJ: Princeton University Press, 2009), 23–24.
4 Antti Häkkinen, 'Suomen 1860-luvun Nälkäkatastrofi – Syitä ja Seurauksia', *Duodecim* 128 (2012), 2425.
5 Kirby's *Concise History* contains a useful map outlining the various boundary changes during this period. David Kirby, *A Concise History of Finland* (Cambridge: Cambridge University Press, 2006), 32. See also Ismo Björn, 'Life in the Borderland Forests: The Takeover of Nature and its Social Organisation in North Karelia', in *Encountering the Past in Nature: Essays in Environmental History*, ed. Timo Myllyntaus and Mikko Saikku (Athens: Ohio University Press, 1999), 56–57.
6 Matti Klinge, 'Finland: From Napoleonic Legacy to Nordic Cooperation', in *The National Question in Europe in Historical Context*, ed. Mikuláš Teich and Roy Porter (Cambridge: Cambridge University Press, 1993), 321.
7 Henrik Meinander, *A History of Finland* (London: Hurst & Company, 2011), 75; Nils Erik Villstrand, *Valtakunnanosa: Suurvalta ja Valtakunnan Hajoaminen 1560–1812, Suomen Ruotsalainen Historia 2* (Helsinki: SLS, 2012), 361–362.
8 Meinander, *History of Finland*, 76; Henrika Tandefelt, *Borgå 1809: Ceremoni och Fest* (Helsingfors: SLS, 2009), 80–82.
9 Fred Singleton, *A Short History of Finland* (2nd edn (rev. A. Upton), Cambridge: Cambridge University Press, 1998), 63. This sentence has been interpreted in different ways. Jorma Ahvenainen has written that the empire presented Finland as a united state, having been previously only a group of Swedish provinces. See Pentti Virrankoski, *Suomen Historia: Maa ja Kansa Kautta Aikoja* (Helsinki: SKS, 2012), 161.
10 Erkki Pihkala, 'The Finnish Economy and Russia, 1809–1917', *Finland and Poland in the Russian Empire: A Comparative Study*, ed. Michael Branch, Janet Hartley and Antoni Mączak (London, SEESS, 1995), 153.
11 Pihkala, 'Finnish Economy and Russia', 153.
12 Virrankoski, *Suomen Historia*, 203.
13 Keijo Korhonen, *Autonomous Finland in the Political Thought of Nineteenth Century Russia* (Turku: Turun Yliopisto, 1967), 49.
14 Korhonen, *Autonomous Finland*, 56–58. Note also the countering claims of Russian Nationalists such as Mikhail Katkov, who countered the rhetoric of *Helsingfors Dagblad* by claiming that all Finland's 'great privileges she had obtained by the grace of Russia.... As Finland did not enjoy the position of a state during the Swedish connection, she did not enjoy it now.'
15 Pauli Kurkinen (ed.), *Venäläiset Suomessa 1809–1917* (Helsinki: SHS, 1983).
16 Meinander, *History of Finland*, 108–123; Kirby, *A Concise History of Finland*, 105–149.

17 Jari Ojala and Ilkka Nummela, 'Feeding Economic Growth: Agriculture', in *The Road to Prosperity: An Economic History of Finland*, ed. Jari Ojala, Jari Eloranta and Jukka Jalava (Helsinki: SKS, 2006), 67–69; Kirby, *Concise History of Finland*, 46–47; Michael C. Coleman, '"You Might All Be Speaking Swedish Today": Language Change in 19th Century Finland and Ireland', *Scandinavian Journal of History* 35 (2010), 46.
18 Ojala and Nummela, 'Feeding Economic Growth', 69–70.
19 Kirby, *Concise History of Finland*, 55–56.
20 W.R. Mead, *An Historical Geography of Scandinavia* (London: Academic Press, 1981), 158; Jani Marjanen, 'Between "Public" and "Private" Economy: The Finnish Economic Society and the Decline of Economic Patriotism, 1797–1833', in *The Rise of Economic Societies in the Eighteenth Century*, ed. Koen Stapelbroek and Jani Marjanen (Basingstoke: Palgrave, 2012), 314, 318–319.
21 Kirby, *Concise History of Finland*, 55–56. For Finland's population growth in relation to other states (1800–1910), see Oiva Turpeinen, *Näläntorjunta ja Hyvinvointivaltion Perusteet* (Helsinki: VAPK Kustannus, 1991), 4.
22 Arvo M. Soininen, *Vanha Maataloutemme. Maatalous ja Maatalousväestö Suomessa Perinteisen Maatalouden Loppukaudella 1720-luvulta 1870-luvulle* (Helsinki: SHS, 1974), 186–199, 382–394.
23 Johannes Kananen, *The Nordic Welfare State In Three Eras: From Emancipation to Discipline* (Farnham: Ashgate, 2014), 59.
24 Viljo Rasila, 'Agrarian Problems', in *Finland and Poland in the Russian Empire: A Comparative Study*, ed. Michael Branch, Janet Hartley and Antoni Mączak (London: SEESS, 1995), 167–168; Kirby, *Concise History of Finland*, 55–56.
25 Singleton, *Short History of Finland*, 87–88. Other than in the area of 'Old Finland' serfdom was not an issue in Finland.
26 Ojala and Nummela, 'Feeding Economic Growth', 70.
27 Osmo Jussila, Seppo Hentilä and Jukka Nevakivi, *From Grand Duchy to Modern State: A Political History of Finland since 1809* (London: Hurst & Company, 1995), 2, 6; Soininen, *Vanha Maataloutemme*, 186–199.
28 Erkki Pihkala, 'The Finnish Economy and Russia, 1809–1917', in *Finland and Poland in the Russian Empire: A Comparative Study*, ed. Michael Branch, Janet Hartley and Antoni Mączak (London: SEESS, 1995), 153.
29 Jari Ojala and Petri Karonen, 'Business: Rooted in Social Capital over the Centuries', in *The Road to Prosperity: An Economic History of Finland*, ed. Jari Ojala, Jari Eloranta and Jukka Jalava (Helsinki: SKS, 2006), 101–110.
30 Yrjö Kaukiainen, 'Foreign Trade and Transport', in *The Road to Prosperity: An Economic History of Finland*, ed. Jari Ojala, Jari Eloranta and Jukka Jalava (Helsinki: SKS, 2006), 133.
31 Riitta Hjerppe and Jukka Jalava, 'Economic Growth and Structural Change: A Century and a Half of Catching Up', in *The Road to Prosperity: An Economic History of Finland*, ed. Jari Ojala, Jari Eloranta and Jukka Jalava (Helsinki: SKS, 2006), 35.
32 Pihkala, 'Finnish Economy and Russia', 154–155.
33 Mead, *Historical Geography of Scandinavia*, 168.
34 Pihkala, 'Finnish Economy and Russia', 159.
35 Virrankoski, *Suomen Historia*, 171–172; Yrjö Kaukiainen, *Sailing into Twilight: Finnish Shipping in an Age of Transport Revolution, 1860–1914* (Helsinki: Suomen Historiallinen Seura, 1991).
36 Jussila *et al.*, *Grand Duchy to Modern State*, 32–33.
37 Kari Pitkänen, 'The Road to Survival or Death? Temporary Migration During the Great Finnish Famine in the 1860s', in *Just a Sack of Potatoes? Crisis Experiences in European Societies, Past and Present*, ed. Antti Häkkinen (Helsinki: SHS, 1992), 93.

38 Timo Myllyntaus, 'Summer Frost: A Natural Hazard with Fatal Consequences in Pre-Industrial Finland', in *Natural Disasters, Cultural Responses: Case Studies Toward a Global Environmental History*, ed. Christof Mauch and Christian Pfister (Lanham, MD: Lexington Books, 2009), 85.

39 Kananen, *Nordic Welfare State*, 58.

40 This is considered in Britain to be a regional/Baltic front of the Crimean War, but known in Finland specifically as the Åland War.

41 William. R. Mead, 'The Conquest of Finland', *The Norseman* 9 (1951), 14–15; Myllyntaus, 'Summer Frost', 84–85.

42 Jussila *et al.*, *Grand Duchy to Modern State*, 48.

43 Pihkala, 'Finnish Economy and Russia', 155.

44 Ojala and Nummela, 'Feeding Economic Growth', 68.

45 Available at: www.ggdc.net/maddison/Maddison.htm (accessed 22 December 2012). By way of comparison, using the same dataset, the figure for Ireland in 1820 was higher than for Finland (Int.GK$877) but still well below the European average. See also Ojala and Nummela, 'Feeding Economic Growth', 66.

46 Pitkänen, *Deprivation and Disease*, 63; Antti Kujala, 'Finland in 1905: The Political and Social History of the Revolution', in *The Russian Revolution of 1905: Centenary Perspectives*, ed. Jonathan D. Smele and Anthony J. Heywood (London and New York: Routledge, 2005), 80.

47 Pihkala, 'Finnish Economy and Russia', 153.

48 Jari Eloranta, Concepción García-Inglesias, Jari Ojala and Jukka Jalava, 'On the Road to Propserity: An Introduction', in *The Road to Prosperity: An Economic History of Finland*, ed. Jari Ojala, Jari Eloranta and Jukka Jalava (Helsinki: SKS, 2006), 22.

49 Antti Häkkinen and Miika Tervonen, 'Ethnicity, Marginalization and Poverty in 20th-Century Finland', in *Welfare Society at Risk: Inequality, Social Exclusion and Ethnic Relations in Finland in the 1990s*, ed. Vesa Puuronen, Antti Häkkinen, Anu Pylkkänen, Tom Sandlund and Reetta Toivanen (Joensuu: Publications of Karelian Institute, 2004), 22–39.

50 Pitkänen, *Deprivation and Disease*, 63.

51 Eino Jutikkala, *Bonden i Finland Genom Tiderna* (Helsingfors: Holger Schildts Förlag, 1963), 372.

52 Pertti Anttonen, 'Oral Traditions and the Making of the Finnish Nation', in *Folklore and Nationalism in Europe during the Long Nineteenth Century*, ed. Timothy Baycroft and David Hopkin (Leiden: Brill, 2012), 340.

53 Statistics Finland, Population Structure Statistics. Available at: www.stat.fi/tup/suoluk/suoluk_vaesto_en.html#structure (accessed 1 June 2014).

54 Ainur Elmgren, 'The Jesuit Stereotype: An Image of the Universal Enemy in Finnish Nationalism', in *European Anti-Catholicism in a Comparative and Transnational Context*, ed. Yvonne Maria Werner and Jonas Harvard (Amsterdam: Rodopi, 2013), 197.

55 *Saima*, 2 December 1846; 'Köyhiä Suomessa', *Suometar*, 8 January 1850.

56 *Helsingfors Morgonblad*, 13 July 1832; *Oulun Wiikko-Sanomia*, 1 September 1832, 15 December 1832, 27 September 1834; *Helsingfors Tidningar*, 10 April 1833, 6 August 1834; *Åbo Tidningar*, 4 April 1840, 23 May 1840; *Saima*, 20 February 1845; *Morgonbladet*, 10 February 1845; *Borgå Tidning*, 16 October 1841, 15 March 1845; *Suometar*, 22 December 1848; Pekka Haatanen, *Suomen Maalaisköyhälistö Tutkimusten ja Kaunokirjallisuuden Valossa* (Helsinki: W. Söderström, 1968), 54–59. In the Swedish-language newspapers the term 'poor' (*fattig*) was already common in the 1810s. However, the equivalent phrase (*köyhä*) only appeared in the Finnish-language newspapers as late as the 1850s. Jari Heinonen, *Pienviljelijäprojektista Sosiaalivaltioon: Näkökulma Suomalaisen Sosiaalipolitiikan Syntyyn, Kehitykseen ja Murroksiin 1800-luvulta Nykypäivään* (Tampere: Acta Universitatis Tamperensis, 1990), 302 (fn. 57).

57 Soininen, *Vanha Maataloutemme*, 43 (Table 8); Antti Häkkinen, Vappu Ikonen, Kari Pitkänen and Hannu Soikkanen, *1860-luvun Suuret Nälkävuodet. Tutkimus eri Väestöryhmien Mielialoista ja Toimintamalleista. Loppuraportti.* (Helsinki: Helsingin Yliopiston Talous- ja Sosiaalihistorian Laitoksen Tiedonantoja, 21/1989), 41.

58 *Finlands Allmänna Tidning*, 9 April 1857.

59 Viljo Rasila, 'Väestönkehitys ja Sosiaaliset Ongelmat', in *Suomen Taloushistoria 2: Teollistuva Suomi*, ed. Jorma Ahvenainen, Erkki Pihkala and Viljo Rasila (Helsinki: Tammi, 1982), 136; Reino Kero, *Migration from Finland to North America in the Years between the United States Civil War and the First World War* (Turku: Turun Yliopisto, 1974), 13 and Table 9; Kaarina Vattula and Sinikka Lampivuo, *Suomen Taloushistoria 3* (Helsinki: Tammi, 1983), Tables 1.5 and 1.15; Heikki Waris, *Työläisyhteiskunnan Syntyminen Helsingin Pitkänsillan Pohjoispuolelle* (Helsinki: SHS), 1932 to 1934.

60 Quoted in William R. Mead, *Land Use in Early Nineteenth Century Finland* (Turku: Turun Yliopisto, 1953), 13–16.

61 Myllyntaus, 'Summer Frost', 78–79.

62 Matti Klinge, *Keisarin Suomi* (Espoo: Schildt, 1997), 237–243. For a recent discussion on the relationship between climate and agricultural conditions in Finland, see Reijo Solantie, *Ilmasto ja sen Määräämät Luonnonolot Suomen Asutuksen ja Maatalouden Historiassa* (Jyväskyla: Jyväskylän Yliopisto, 2012).

63 *Wiborgs Tidning*, 11 January 1868; Antti Häkkinen, 'On Attitudes and Living Strategies in the Finnish Countryside in the Years of Famine 1867–68', in *Just a Sack of Potatoes? Crisis Experiences in European Societies, Past and Present*, ed. Antti Häkkinen (Helsinki: SHS, 1992), 153–154.

64 Häkkinen, 'Attitudes and Living Strategies', 158–159.

65 Jussila *et al.*, *Grand Duchy to Modern State*, 32–33; David Kirby, *Finland in the Twentieth Century: A History and an Interpretation* (London: Hurst & Company, 1979), 15.

66 Mika Arola, *Foreign Capital and Finland: Central Government's First Period of Reliance on International Financial Markets, 1862–1938* (Helsinki: Bank of Finland, 2006), 73–74; Sakari Heikkinen, Visa Heinonen, Antti Kuusterä and Jukka Pekkarinen (eds), *The History of Finnish Economic Thought 1809–1917* (Tammisaari – Ekenäs: Societas Scientarum Fennica, 2001), 69–72.

67 Heikkinen *et al.*, *The History of Finnish Economic Thought*, 81.

68 Oiva Turpeinen, *Nälkä vai Tauti Tappoi? Kauhunvuodet 1866–1868* (Helsinki: Societas Historica Finlandiae, 1986), 149.

69 Myllyntaus, 'Summer Frost', 91.

70 Antti Kuusterä, '1860-luvun epäonnistunut talouspolitiikka', in *Nälkä, Talous, Kontrolli: Näkökulmia Kriisien ja Konfliktien Syntyyn, Merkitykseen ja Kontrolliin*, ed. Kari Pitkänen (Helsinki: University of Helsinki, 1987), 43–57.

71 Turpeinen, *Nälkä vai Tauti Tappoi*, 111–122.

72 Turpeinen, *Nälkä vai Tauti Tappoi*, 77–88.

73 Häkkinen, 'Suomen 1860-luvun Nälkäkatastrofi', 2429; Häkkinen *et al.*, *1860-luvun Suuret Nälkävuodet*, 38.

74 By way of comparison, see the overview by Laurence Geary, 'Epidemic Diseases of the Great Irish Famine', *History Ireland* iv (spring 1996), 27–32.

75 Häkkinen, 'Suomen 1860-luvun Nälkäkatastrofi', 2427.

76 Asko O. Hannukkala, 'History and Consequences of Migrations, Changes in Epidemiology and Population Structure of Potato Late Blight, *Phytophthora Infestans*, in Finland from 1845–2011', *MTT Science* 18 (2012), 43–44.

77 Turpeinen, *Nälkä vai Tauti Tappoi*, 162–166; Eino Jutikkala (ed.), *Suomen Historian Kartasto/Atlas of Finnish History* (Helsinki: WSOY, 1959), 54 (Map 48: 'Rural Economic Conditions in the 1830s').

78 Häkkinen, 'Attitudes and Living Strategies', 151 (Figure 1).

79 Kuopio county was estimated to have had a rye harvest only 22 per cent of normal, 23 per cent of barley and 15 per cent of oats. In Oulu the corresponding figures were 25 per cent, 38 per cent and 16 per cent, and Mikkeli 45 per cent, 33 per cent and 22 per cent. In Häme the situation was considered to be quite good, but in Turku and northern Pori, as well as in Vaasa, the losses were considerable. All figures here are from the report by Antell and Normén. The report by Senator Antell is about his expedition to the provinces of Mikkeli, Kuopio and Oulu at the end of 1867 and at the beginning of 1868. Turun Maakunta Arkisto (Archives of Turku Province), Juhani Rinteen Kokoelma (Juhani Rinne Collection), Suurten Nälkävuosien Asiakirjojen Kokoelma (Collection of Great Famine Years Documents), 1867–1868.

80 Häkkinen, 'Suomen 1860-luvun Nälkäkatastrofi', 2427.

81 Pitkänen, *Deprivation and Disease*, 62; Turpeinen, *Nälkä vai Tauti Tappoi*, 216–217. See also Andrew G. Newby, '"Rather Peculiar Claims Upon Our Sympathies": Britain and Famine in Finland, 1856–68', in *Global Legacies of the Great Irish Famine: Transnational and Interdisciplinary Perspectives*, ed. Marguérite Corporaal, Christopher Cusack, Lindsay Janssen and Ruud van den Beuken (Bern: Peter Lang, 2014), 61–80.

82 Pirjo Markkola, 'Changing Patterns of Welfare: Finland in the Nineteenth and Early Twentieth Centuries', in *Welfare Peripheries: the Development of Welfare States in Nineteenth and Twentieth-century Europe*, ed. Steven King and John Stewart (Bern: Peter Lang, 2007), 211.

83 Markkola, 'Changing Patterns of Welfare', 213.

84 Panu Pulma, 'Maatalousyhteiskunta Ajautuu Kriisiin', in *Armeliaisuus, Yhteisöapu, Sosiaaliturva: Suomalaisen Sosiaalisen Turvan Historia*, ed. Jouko Jaakkola, Panu Pulma, Mirja Satka and Kyösti Urponen (Helsinki: Sosiaaliturvan Keskusliitto, 1994), 59–61; Soininen, *Vanha Maataloutemme*, 382–415; Reino Kallio, *Pohjanmaan Suomenkielisten Kylien Oltermannihallinto* (Jyväskylä: Studia Historica Jyväskyläensia, 1982), 147–159, 277–285; Antti Häkkinen, 'Rikos, Rikollinen ja Oikeus 1800-luvun Suomessa', Licentiate Thesis, Department of Sociology, University of Helsinki, 1989.

85 Markkola, 'Changing Patterns of Welfare', 215; Kananen, *Nordic Welfare State*, 59.

86 Häkkinen, 'Suomen 1860-luvun Nälkäkatastrofi', 2428–2429.

87 Turpeinen, *Nälkä vai Tauti Tappoi*, 216.

88 'Report of Mr. Consul Herman Lorentz on the Trade and Commerce of Wiborg for the Year 1867', in *Commercial Reports Received at the Foreign Office from Her Majesty's Consuls in 1868* (London: Harrison and Sons, 1868), 420–424.

89 Turpeinen, *Nälkä vai Tauti Tappoi*, 303–304.

90 Häkkinen, 'Suomen 1860-luvun Nälkäkatastrofi', 2428–2429.

91 *Åbo Underättelser*, 5 October 1867.

92 Pihkala, 'Kehitysmaasta Hyvinvointivaltioksi', in *Suomen Taloushistoria 2*, ed. Jorma Ahvenainen, Erkki Pihkala and Viljo Rasila (Helsinki: Tammi, 1982), 528.

93 Pitkänen, 'Road to Survival or Death', 98.

94 Timo Orta, 'Finnish Emigration Prior to 1893: Economic, Demographic and Social Backgrounds', in *The Finnish Experience in the Western Great Lakes Region: New Perspectives*, ed. M.G. Karni, M.E. Kaupps and D.J. Ollila (Vammala: Institute of Migration, 1975), 30.

95 'Report of the British Consul General, Helsingfors'. Reprinted in *Manchester Guardian*, 24 March 1868.

96 Pitkänen, 'Road to Survival or Death', 99–100.

97 For an account of Finnish famine emigration in a comparative context, see Andrew G. Newby, '"Neither do these Tenants or their Children Emigrate": Famine and Transatlantic Emigration from Finland in the Nineteenth Century', *Atlantic Studies* 11 (2014), 383–402.

98 Pitkänen, 'Road to Survival or Death', 98.

99 Singleton, *Short History of Finland*, 86.
100 Reino Kero, 'The Background of Finnish Emigration', in *The Finns in North America: A Social Symposium*, ed. Ralph J. Jalkanen (Hancock: Michigan State University Press, 1969), 56.
101 Risto Alapuro, *Finland: An Interface Periphery* (Helsinki: University of Helsinki, 1980), 20–54.
102 Anna-Leena Toivonen, *Etelä-Pohjanmaan Valtamerentakainen Siirtolaisuus 1867–1930* (Helsinki: SHS, 1963), 20–21; Kero, 'Background of Finnish Emigration', 56–57.
103 Kero, 'Background of Finnish Emigration', 58–59.
104 Jouni Korkiasaari, *Suomalaiset Maailmalla* (Turku: Siirtolaisuusinstituutti, 1989), 20; John I. Kolehmainen and George W. Hill, *Haven in the Woods: The Story of the Finns in Wisconsin* (Madison: State Historical Society of Wisconsin, 1951), 18–19.
105 J.I. Kolehmainen, 'Finnish Overseas Emigration from Arctic Norway and Russia', *Agricultural History* 19 (1945), 225.
106 Arthur E. Puotinen, *Finnish Radicals and Religion in Mid-Western Mining Towns, 1865–1914* (New York: Arno Press, 1979), 44.
107 Puotinen, *Finnish Radicals*, 92–96.
108 Kolehmainen, 'Finnish Overseas Emigration', 224–232.
109 Max Engman, 'Migration from Finland to Russia during the Nineteenth Century', *Scandinavian Journal of History* 3 (1978), 155–177.
110 Korkiasaari, *Suomalaiset Maailmalla*, 54.
111 *Wiborgs Tidning*, 15 January 1868; *Åbo Underrättelser*, 9 June 1868; *Björneborg*, 13 June 1868; *Borgåbladet*, 19 September 1868.
112 *Hufvudstadsbladet*, 11 May 1868.
113 Newby, 'Neither do these Tenants or their Children Emigrate', 389.
114 Kero, *Migration from Finland*, 16.
115 Singleton, *Short History of Finland*, 86.
116 Walter T.K. Nugent, *Crossings: The Great Transatlantic Migrations 1870–1914* (Bloomington: Indiana University Press, 1992), 59.
117 Newby, 'Neither do these Tenants or their Children Emigrate', 390.
118 Vesa Saarikoski, 'Yhteiskunnan Modernisoituminen', in *Suomalaisen Yhteiskunnan Poliittinen Historia*, ed. Ville Pernaa and Mari K. Niemi (Helsinki: Edita, 2005), 115–116; Kananen, *Nordic Welfare State*, 58.
119 Tuula Vuolle, *Paikallisesta Hyväntekeväisyydestä Valtion Asiaksi* (Jyväskyla: Jyväskylän Yliopisto, 1993), 5.
120 Turpeinen, *Nalantorjunta*, 171–172.
121 Klinge, *Keisarin Suomi*, 237–243.
122 Agaton Meurman, *Nälkäwuodet 1860-luwulla* (Helsinki: Kansanvalistusseura, 1892), 7–11; see also Yrjö Sakari Yrjö Koskinen, *Oppikirja Suomen Kansan Historiasta* (Helsinki: Tekijä, 1869), 561–563.
123 Myllyntaus, 'Summer Frost', 85; *Kertomus Vuoden 1902 Kadosta ja sen Aiheuttamista Hätäaputoimista* (Helsinki: Keisarillisen Senaatin Kirjapaino, 1904).
124 Pitkänen, *Deprivation and Disease*, 88–89, 116 (Figures 6.1 and 6.2); Pitkänen, 'Patterns of Mortality', 94–97.
125 Hjerppe and Jalava, 'Economic Growth and Structural Change', 34.
126 Eloranta *et al.*, 'On the Road to Prosperity', 22–23.
127 Einar Risberg, *Suomen Lennätinlaitoksen Historia 1855–1955* (Helsinki: Posti- ja Lennätinhallitus, 1959), 188.
128 See e,g. John W. Mellor and Sarah Gavian, 'Famine, Causes, Prevention, and Relief', *Science* 235 (1987), 539.
129 Amartya Sen, *Poverty and Famines. An Essay on Entitlement and Deprivation* (Oxford: Clarendon Press, 1981), 39–44.
130 Häkkinen, 'Suomen 1860-luvun Nälkäkatastrofi', 2430.

5 Feeding the famine

Social vulnerability and dislocation during the Finnish famine of the 1860s

Miikka Voutilainen

Introduction

In recent years, it has been standard practice for accounts of the regular famines that occurred in pre-modern Finland to make a strong causal link between early autumn frosts with subsequent increases in mortality. A recent example is provided by Timo Myllyntaus, who in a 2009 article on the role of the natural hazard of summer frosts in pre-industrial Finland pondered why crop failures could 'so easily cause a crisis in agrarian Finnish society'.[1] This apparent and logical causal explanation has left Finnish famine history – and particularly the study of the 1860s famine period – centring largely around the themes of imminent mortality causation and coping strategies, and therefore lacking closer scrutiny of quantitative structural analysis and use of closed form economic theory and econometric modelling. Although this chapter does not seek to deny that repeated harvest failures were vital triggers, it argues that the Great Finnish Famine unfolded in considerable part because of the disintegration of societal structures and social institutions in response to those recurrent failures.

Regardless of the 'disease versus hunger' debate surrounding the bulk of research into famine mortality, the close connection between harvest failures and mortality increase has long been observed. For example, Fernand Braudel underlined in the 1960s that it required at least two consecutive bad harvests to spell disaster in a peasant society.[2] This stance is largely supported by the Irish economist Cormac Ó Gráda, who stresses that while famine-causing successive crop failures were rare, in the event that they did occur they often turned out to be lethal.[3] The tradition and basis of the Finnish debate have mainly been influenced by Eino Jutikkala's and Oiva Turpeinen's representation of famine mortality as an epidemiological phenomenon.[4] This has meant an emphasis on the peculiar punctuated nature of past food crises, prompting the conclusion that the 1866 to 1868 famine was effectively a coincidental occurrence – a disease outbreak in the wake of a random harvest failure.[5]

The past 20 years have brought a considerably more nuanced view of the Finnish crisis. Antti Häkkinen has emphasised the role of insufficient or misplaced poor relief.[6] Kari Pitkänen has demonstrated the extent of social dislocation and the interactive relationship between malnutrition and deadly infections.[7] Antti Kuusterä's research has stressed the role of the prevalent economic policy environment in explaining the government's lack of action in relieving the famine.[8] Even within this context, two background factors have maintained a prominent position in this historiography: Arvo Soininen's conceptions about old 'traditional' Finnish agriculture and its inability to cope with recurrent crop failures, and the long-term growth of inequality between the landless and the landowning agricultural population.[9]

The Great Finnish Famine of the 1860s was characterised by high mortality, even in comparison with several continental famines during the eighteenth and nineteenth centuries.[10] War-related mortality peaks aside, from the beginning of the sixteenth century Finland experienced a handful of severe crises: the most significant ones occurred in 1542 to 1545; 'The Straw Years' at the beginning of the seventeenth century; the Great Famine of the 1690s; and the famines at the beginning of the 1740s and during the 1830s. In this context, the famine of the 1860s is typically seen as a blow at the last possible stage before modernisation, either because it stimulated a transition from unproductive and inefficient agriculture to a more modern and industrialised society, or because Finland was later wealthier and vastly better equipped to counter such a natural calamity.

In general famine studies, the idea has become more accepted over the past two decades that a famine should be understood as an outcome of a long-term socio-economic process which accelerates the destitution among some groups in society to the point where their livelihood systems become untenable.[11] In the specific Finnish case, this of course begs the question as to whether 1860s Finland was a society in which frequent subsistence shocks inevitably led to a full-blown demographic cataclysm. Although Turpeinen has challenged the 'deterministic' chronology of Finnish famine on a number of occasions, this chapter argues that the apparent 'certainty' of the famine has to be understood in the context of the society in which such catastrophic mortality was possible in the first place. It is often considered that social structures of common help, lending and of occasional governmental aid provided Finnish farmers and their labourers with shelter through short-lived agricultural downturns. Pitkänen has stated that rural labourers (who were often the first to face the harsh conditions of an economic crisis) may not have fallen into immediate risk due to crop failures, provided that the landowners themselves were relatively well-off.[12] This emphasises the paternalistic side of a moral economy largely relevant during crop failures that were deemed 'normal'. According to Eric Vanhaute, famines triggered by harvest failures only occurred when societal institutions failed and the moral economy ceased to function.[13] This research therefore seeks to study *social vulnerability*: those social and economic structures that were at risk of disintegration after protracted stress, worsening the social status of the affected people, and subsequently contributing to famine-related excess mortality.

The chapter is structured as follows. First, it outlines the theoretical framework of vulnerability and presents the debate over its measurement. The subsequent section uses novel data to estimate some aspects of the prevailing social structure before the outbreak of the famine and links this structure to the unfolding process. These findings are then summarised in the conclusion.

Understanding the unfolding of famine: the role of vulnerability and social dislocation

When the passenger liner *RMS Titanic* sank after colliding with an iceberg in April 1912, the resulting mortality was distributed extremely unequally among sexes and three passenger classes. A third-class male passenger faced a mortality risk almost 30 times greater than a female travelling in first class. It would be absurd, of course, to claim that third-class men were somehow more biologically prone to drown than first-class women, but rather the latter group were socially favoured in terms of leaving the ship in lifeboats, and hence were less likely to find themselves in life-threatening conditions of icy sea water.[14]

While the sinking of a ship is ultimately about water and famine is essentially about food, and while a crisis develops through an aggregation of individual fates, the unfolding of the disaster in terms of loss of lives is determined beyond the mere subjective variables such as bundles of available resources or individual capacities.[15] In the event of a disaster, if an individual loses the possibility of retaining the means of staying alive, the odds of getting them replaced (a place in a lifeboat, or food aid) is determined within the surrounding social context according to existing valuations. In order to gain analytical insight, we have to understand which segments of people are at the greatest risk to the particular set of environmental changes. At a very general level, this is captured in the concept of *vulnerability*. Because the possibilities, risks and resources assigned to an individual's societal position are determined by larger conventions of social and institutional organisation, it is reasonable to talk about *social vulnerability* associated with disasters.

This chapter adopts the stance of 'livelihood literature' in defining famine as an event where numerous people's livelihoods simultaneously cease to produce sufficient nutrition, either directly or indirectly.[16] Furthermore, we propose that in the event of livelihood stress, social vulnerability refers to *the measure of an individual inability to maintain, re-establish or substitute a (lost) livelihood and in due process to avoid exposure to potentially hazardous socio-environmental conditions.*

This definition is not only practicable but also clarifies previous plural definitions and their inconsistent use.[17] First of all, this definition treats not only the disaster itself but also the vulnerability as dynamic and importantly as an evolving phenomenon affecting different individuals in various ways at different stages of the crisis. Second, this definition incorporates the concept of sustainability of livelihood, which in the Finnish context is naturally seen through the monoculture of grain production, resulting in high connectivity to an under-diversified ecosystem, often seen as a risk factor.[18] Third, the definition includes social disintegration and allows it to increase the mortality risk of people trying to re-establish their food consumption, not only through increased risk of infections, but also through other factors such as the increased threat of physical violence. From the perspective of an individual, the crisis chronology thus follows a path where it is initially impossible to maintain an existing livelihood (subsistence shock); it is subsequently not possible to re-establish that livelihood; and eventually it remains impossible to substitute for it (i.e. from an absence of or shortfall in aid). Transition from one phase to another coincides with a deterioration of the socio-economic environment.

It is widely supposed that malnutrition associated with deep structural poverty persistent in many historical peasant populations, even in times of relative plenty, helped swell the heavy death-tolls when crop failures struck.[19] There are reasons to believe that in pre-industrial societies there was always some proportion of people living under the poverty line and hence suffering from (at least) seasonal hunger, though a subsistence economy does not imply starvation per se.[20] In this setting, it is important to acknowledge that although vulnerability and poverty are closely associated, they are far from being identical: the poor may be vulnerable but the vulnerable do not have to be poor. Karl Marx made the quip that the Irish famine of the 1840s killed 'poor devils only', reflected in the long-standing analogy that famines are like ripples in water, and those with noses closest to the surface drown first.[21] While famine necessarily requires starvation to occur, the opposite may not be true: starvation can only occur in prevalence of poverty, but poverty may not necessarily lead to starvation.[22] In this regard, Joel Mokyr has warned that circular reasoning ('a land starves due to its poverty and is poor because it starves') can underpin assessments of famines, economic development and prevailing deprivation.[23]

While poverty forms a problematic independent variable in explaining food crises, it also presents a conceptual challenge when applied to historical events. In a situation where a lack of health care, social security and welfare commodities created significant upward mortality risk for anyone losing the access to their livelihood, using the concept of poverty (as it is understood today) is clearly ambiguous.[24] To elaborate on this, although mortality rates may vary among social classes, conditional mortality rates (conditioned with disease or disability of some kind) may not. Thus, what should be emphasised is the risk of being 'conditioned' and the consequent risk of facing possible outcomes (such as death) due to this condition. Social class differences in famine mortality may be interpreted to reflect this conditioning tendency. Of empirical studies focusing explicitly on mortality differences, Kari Pitkänen has provided evidence from the 1860s Finnish famine which demonstrates that, regardless of whether the region under investigation was devastated by crop failure, rural workers faced a substantially larger increase in mortality when compared with land-cultivating farmers. Social differences in famine deprivation can also have long-term health effects. According to results by Klemp and Weisdorf from 1720s England, only individuals born during the famine to families of a lower socio-economic rank suffered a substantially increased long-term death risk in comparison to the post-famine control group.[25] Lindeboom et al. present similar evidence from the

1840s Holland. Using Malian data, Allan G. Hill reports above-average mortality rates among those groups engaging in migration to urban areas.[26] Furthermore, evidence gathered from Darfur's 1984/1985 famine led Alex de Waal to conclude that 'it is not the undernutrition caused by the famine but the social disruption caused by it that is critical in causing excess deaths'.[27]

In order to gain a more coherent picture, it is necessary to highlight de Waal's suggestion that we should ultimately abandon the concept of famine as necessarily involving mass starvation until death, and instead consider famines as a virulent form of poverty. In this construction, famines are not *caused by* groups of individuals falling to poverty; rather, famines *are* situations marked by widespread acute poverty.[28] Allan G. Hill's findings are worthy of consideration here. According to Hill, the prevailing high baseline mortality of a social group is a symptom of low-income social status. In this reasoning, famine is a situation where noticeable proportions of people with higher social status succumb among the poor and subsequently face a higher mortality risk, translating to an increase in death-tolls on the macro level.[29] This process is what is generally considered as social dislocation: *people move from a pre-crisis social position to one where they are at a higher mortality risk.* In the case of Finland, Pitkänen has estimated that social dislocation (as manifested through migration from regions experiencing crop failure) could account for up to 70 per cent of excess mortality during the crisis.[30] Turpeinen emphasises the same phenomenon, with the juxtaposition of disease and deprivation explanations.[31] We perceive vulnerability and social dislocation as being causally entwined: social dislocation should a priori work its way through the socio-economic structure in the order of social group vulnerability. The first group affected is the one at immediate risk due to the occurrence of a hazardous event (such as crop failure), the following groups either due to prolonged economic depression or through social turmoil resulting from other groups losing ground. This brings the focus of research to the very moment when social disruption becomes a social collapse; that is, when coping strategies break down, and the possibility of preserving (at least the main features of) a previous way of life vanishes.[32]

The identification of social dislocation as a critical background factor of famine mortality is only a small proportion of the story, and often a trivial task; the larger dilemma is identifying the pre-famine vulnerable groups. The definitional plurality of the vulnerability concept has in turn led to diverse methods of its measurement, obfuscating the task of identification.[33] The generic methodological solution is reliance on a more or less explicit assumption that statistically constructed composite indicators and the actual underlying vulnerability structure correlate positively; the higher the score of the indicator, the more of a certain type of vulnerability it measures. Deducing vulnerability from this kind of reasoning is straightforward enough, but entails a crucial yet simple assumption: in order to have a crisis, an outbreak must take place along these a priori social fault lines. In a historical situation it is relatively easy to come up with various rationales that, for example, economic inequality may make an equivocal contribution to famine vulnerability; under certain conditions inequality may be beneficial (not everybody in a community need be affected by a catastrophe, and so the sufferers may have someone to call on for help), while under others it may yield devastating results (those unaffected refuse to help). The question of effect dominance rises, possibly in an unresolvable manner, displaying the inherent non-linearity in socio-economic settings: similar conditions may not cause social cataclysm in the absence of certain crucial catalysts or other interactive variables. We may have found some aggregation of variables which yet may not necessarily qualify as measures of vulnerability, or even contextually defined poverty.

The methodological solution put forward here is to search for societal constraints and to study the unfolding of the crisis with respect to spatially defined socio-economic environments. Only then should we be able to deduce something about the genuine vulnerability structure prevalent prior to the catastrophe.[34] This is close to the so-called 'vulnerability of places' approach, which emphasises the interplay between the prevalent (contextually independent) socio-economic environment and vulnerability's time- and place-specific characteristics, taken here a step further to reveal disparities in the outcome of the crisis.[35] At this stage, it is worthwhile highlighting that Alwang, Siegel and Jorgensen stress that *ex-post* welfare losses are neither necessary nor sufficient for the existence of *ex-ante* vulnerability.[36] While this is unquestionably true, to avoid the historio-philosophical bog of counter-factuality, it does seem reasonable to focus on past cases where vulnerability did become measurable, i.e. visible.[37] Credible, historically based famine analysis must be built upon theoretical knowledge of the socio-economic mechanisms leading to starvation, but it ultimately rests in an understanding of the different variables playing an important role in the society and famine in question.

Empirical findings

The cataclysmic mortality surge of the winter of 1867/1868 had been a long time coming. Gradual economic growth in Finland from the end of the 1830s until the early 1850s was cut short by the Crimean War and by a smaller scale famine in 1856/1857. Instead of returning to a path of shaky growth, economic conditions gradually deteriorated, culminating in four bad harvests during the 1860s: of the crop failures in 1862, 1865, 1866 and 1867, only the one in 1866 was regionally confined (to western parts of the country); all the others effected the whole of Finland.[38] In the absence of economic growth, better individual harvest years in between could not correct the structural basis of the deteriorating poverty: by the spring of 1866 the demographic responses to the economic downturn were clearly visible.[39]

Previous literature provides a good primer for theorising the nature of the prevalent structures, and displays the potential a priori vulnerable groups. The crucial ingredient in the famine threat prior to the actual outbreak of the crisis in 1867/1868 was tied to widespread dependence on grain production, the extent of which greatly influenced the subsequent social group-specific mortality: through either crude food unavailability or from the effects of social stratification and from the malfunctions in moral economy. These differences are duly reflected in the famine chronology: how far had the famine to develop in order to force yet another group to succumb, and how long could social structures remain intact in these circumstances? According to Pekka Haatanen's classic inquiry into mid-1800s rural Finnish poverty, the group of major concern was the large landless population with low living standards, characterised by persistent and intergenerational poverty.[40] Furthermore, this high-risk group was supplemented by the sick and disabled, and those already living in destitution and using poor relief in normal harvest years, severely affected by further decreases in their food intake. The second of the risky groups comprised those facing an exogenously sustained livelihood. These consisted of small-scale (subsistence) farmers and seasonal agricultural labourers, their labour supply unrequired if there should be no crops to harvest. The third group comprised a variety of rural labourers, such as artisans, servants, etc., whose employment opportunities closely followed the availability of disposable income in the upper social strata. Then there were, of course, the groups resorting to market purchases of staple food affected by high inflation of food prices during the crisis. The actual importance of this group is somewhat unclear: the pre-industrial markets were far from complete, and the vast majority of grain was never supplied to markets, thus causing market price variation to reflect poorly the actual extent of the variance of purchasing possibilities.[41]

For the purpose of this study, information concerning various kinds of explanatory variables was collected: income level, income inequality, and several social variables. The statistical unit used here is a township (*pitäjä*), of which there are 251 in the area of research. The whole country is included in the analysis, excluding only the province of Viipuri in the southeast and the district of Lapland due to a lack of data. Income data were compiled using information obtained from income taxes (*suostuntavero)* collected in 1865. The classification of taxpayers into different income groups allows us to use these data also to calculate prevailing income inequality.[42] Due to the structure of society and women's position in the labour markets, technically only men were responsible for paying income tax and hence it is households that should be considered as the unit of taxation. This allows us to calculate household-level income, which is clearly a better measure of social entitlement than individual income.[43] Household counts, tax exemptions and population information may be obtained from poll tax registers (*henkikirja*). These registers were originally composed to track and list taxpayers, but they provide valuable information concerning economic and societal conditions.[44] Turpeinen has published parish-level mortality rates and population counts, which are used in subsequent analyses.[45]

Factor and principal component analysis have remained the most frequently applied methods for extracting vulnerability estimates in a multivariate setting.[46] We applied the latter, yielding two components together counting a high 84.2 per cent of variable variance, but encountering the interpretation problem noted previously: both ends of both components a priori correlate positively with

Table 5.1 Township-level variables of interest

Variable	*Mean*	*Standard deviation*	*Min.*	*Max.*	*N*
Exemption from household flat tax (rate) (1865)	0.26	0.16	0.01	0.69	251
Households per capita (1865)	0.17	0.04	0.08	0.25	251
Exemption from poll tax (persons, rate) (1865)	0.07	0.06	*c.*0.00	0.50	251
Income per household (1865)	500.33	158.86	276.70	1,228.70	251
Gini coefficient (1865)	0.58	0.12	0.19	0.84	251
Income-taxed households (rate) (1865)	0.25	0.15	0.03	0.71	251
Township population (1865)	5,328.9	3,996.2	168	27,529	251
Sum of township population (1866–1868)	16,684.2	12,647.2	519	93,142	243
Excess mortality (1866–1868)	476.6	4,484	13	3,325	243
Pre-famine average yearly mortality (1861–1865)	139.2	110.0	5.2	777.4	243

Sources: Poll tax registers (1865); SVT IV (1875); O. Turpeinen, *Nälkä vai Tauti Tappoi? Kauhunvuodet 1866–1868* (Helsinki: Societas Historica Finlandiae, 1986), 149.

Note
Year(s) of coverage in parentheses. Statistical unit: township.

underlying vulnerability. In the first component, positive scores reflected large households able to pay the taxes levied, but simultaneously characterised the eastern part of the country and an area of scattered land ownership, associated with large numbers of agricultural labourers and landless people. The negative scores demonstrated the western pattern of high numbers of unviable farms and relatively low income per household. The second component, displaying the patterns of inequality within and between households, produced similar ambivalence in interpretation: inequality and vulnerability are difficult to link to one another in a linear fashion.[47]

Because of these hindrances, we proceeded with cluster analysis. Sharma and Patwardhan have advocated the use of cluster analysis in vulnerability studies on the basis that it provides nominal instead of continuous information. They state that there is actually no direct means of interpreting the differences between two statistical units with respect to continuous measures.[48] While these two can be ordered (i.e. a measure that is quantitatively larger than the other one), there is however no indication that this *ex-ante* difference actually means any divergent behaviour in a hazardous event. On the contrary, the proposed clustering can reveal qualitative differences in the regional social structure and hence pinpoint geographical patterns in the extent and nature of vulnerability.[49]

There is a wide range of methods suitable for this kind of task, but due to several well-known shortcomings in generally used clustering algorithms, and because of the sizeable sample of statistical units, we applied the so-called 'two-step' clustering to categorise cases to subgroups.[50] This cluster procedure, as implied by its name, consists of two stages. In the first stage, cases are pre-clustered into several small groups, then in the second stage a hierarchical procedure is conducted in order to form a large cluster from these small ones.[51] Of the two available distance measures, namely Euclidian and log-likelihood, the latter was applied to ensure a probability-based estimation. Unlike several clustering methods, which rely on researchers' opinion concerning the number of clusters, the two-step procedure produces statistically defined 'optimal' numbers based on information criteria. Three clusters were obtained using Bayesian information criterion (BIC), while Akaike's information criterion produced no qualitative difference to the results obtained.

Table 5.2 reports clusters extracted with two-step analysis using pre-famine data from 1865. All variables of interest loaded significantly at least to two of the clusters. The first cluster consists of 125 townships (49.8%), shown in Map 5.1. As reported in Table 5.2, a cluster is characterised with an above-average number of households per capita ($p<0.001$), and simultaneously significantly a higher number of households exempted from flat tax ($p<0.001$). The average share of households paying income tax is less than in the whole country ($p<0.001$), and the income distribution is more skewed than in general ($p<0.001$). This is mainly due to the relatively thicker right-hand tail of the income distribution. Regionally, townships allocated to this cluster prevail in southern Finland, in western Uusimaa and southern Häme, in Finland Proper, and in northern Ostrobothnia and Kainuu.

Table 5.2 Estimated two-step clusters

	(1)	*(2)*	*(3)*	*Whole country*
Households per capita	0.20 (0.024)***	0.17 (0.027)	0.11 (0.020)***	0.17 (0.041)
Exemption from household flat tax	0.37 (0.135)***	0.17 (0.083)***	0.11 (0.095)***	0.26 (0.163)
Gini coefficient	0.64 (0.077)***	0.44 (0.088)***	0.60 (0.092)	0.58 (0.116)
Income per household	472.06 (88.31)***	377.92 (53.66)***	683.67 (181.87)***	500.33 (158.86)
Income-taxed households	0.22 (0.100)***	0.15 (0.087) ***	0.43 (0.128)***	0.25 (0.148)
Number of townships	125	64	62	251
Population in 1865	531388	393152	413008	1337548

Notes

Estimated cluster means reported, standard deviations in parentheses. T-test is used to measure the significance between the differences of cluster and population mean. *** – denotes significance at 1% level.

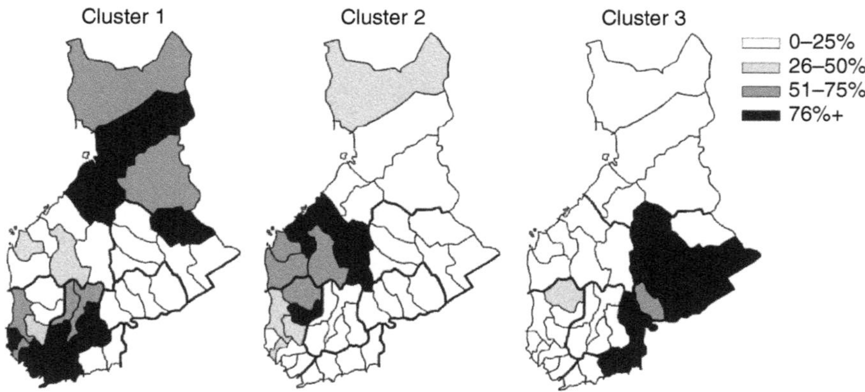

Map 5.1 Spatial distribution of clusters: townships in administrational districts (%).

The second cluster includes 64 townships (25.5%), mainly from Middle Finland, Middle Ostrobothnia and from the region of Satakunta. This cluster features below-average Gini coefficient ($p<0.001$) and below-average household income ($p<0.001$). The vast majority of households were exempted from income tax ($p<0.001$), but more often than on average paid the household-specific tax ($p<0.001$). Townships in this cluster are categorised as being evenly poor.

The third cluster prevails in eastern Finland, in the provinces of Kuopio and Mikkeli, but also in eastern Uusimaa. This cluster is made up of 62 townships (24.7%), which are characterised by a high rate of income ($p<0.001$) and flat-taxed ($p<0.001$) households. Townships feature below-average household per capita ratio ($p<0.001$); that is, households are of larger size and with above-average income per household ($p<0.001$). This does not, however, imply that eastern households are large and wealthy. The social structure prevailing in eastern Finland only displays another form of social stratification: in western Finland the inequality is mainly *between* households and is thus *horizontal*, whereas in eastern Finland the inequality is located also *within* the household, and is thus more of a *vertical* type. Population pressure levied on households is higher in the third cluster than in the two previous ones, signifying the apparent feature of inequality in decision power concerning agricultural output and inequality in its intra-household distribution.

We also compared these results to those obtained with K-means clustering, using standardised values of the variables and setting the cluster number to three as indicated by the two-step algorithm. This provided no qualitative difference in the results obtained: cross-tabulation of the clustering solutions had 90.4 per cent of its elements in the diagonal with agreement measuring kappa-coefficient a high 0.851 ($p<0.001$). The K-means cluster solution provided higher entropy relation ($H/H_{max}=0.976$) than the two-step procedure ($H/H_{max}=0.948$), which is expected, since K-means clustering tends to produce cluster closer in size.

Sharma and Patwardhan use vulnerability impacts (cumulative death-toll) in the clustering sequence. We contend that response should not be included in the clustering phase: cluster analysis cannot be used in causal inference, i.e. due to missing variable bias, certain clusters may erroneously be interpreted as displaying an underlying relation between pre-crisis and manifested variables. If clusters represent different aspects of spatial social structure, we propose the use of the clustering solutions as sub-samples to reveal disparities between relations of independent and dependent variables. On the basis of the vulnerability framework, we should detect empirical evidence favouring the following two hypotheses: (1) the relationship between famine mortality and independent variables should differ between clusters; and (2) explanatory variables with statistically significant loadings should reflect the cluster-specific vulnerability structure: famine cannot happen without certain catalytic conditions embedded in the fabric of society. In other words, subsistence crises reinforce social patterns that already exist.[52]

Violetta Hionidou has suggested that a disease-prone environment coupled with social disintegration creates epidemic-driven famine mortality like that observed in 1860s Finland.[53] A key feature of the famine period in Finland was the out-migration of destitute people from regions ravaged by the crop failures.[54] Methodologically, this suggests that we should seek to understand the factors behind large numbers of people *simultaneously* abandoning their places of residence. Furthermore, it indicates that the severity of the famine is ultimately dictated by the extent of social breakdown; not in relative terms, but in individuals spreading deprivation in their wake (thus highlighting the 'virulence of poverty' idea embedded in the works of de Waal and Hill). A logical way to implement this is to study the famine mortality using count instead of proportional data. Use of relative proportions (mortality rates) implicitly incorporates the idea that famine escalation follows a linear and continuous process, when actually an estimated average increase in regional mortality rates due to a unit increase in dependent variable could effectively result in a highly heterogeneous response in mortality counts and miss the relationships important for famine escalation on a larger scale. This is enforced by the rationale that high mortality rates in regions with only a handful of inhabitants could scarcely spread the crisis to neighbouring regions, whereas extensive harvest failures even if manifested in low mortality rates in populous regions could easily produce a mass out-migration and hasten the deterioration of living conditions also in the surrounding areas.

From the technical side, according to Osgood, applying OLS regression (or its variants) to incidence rate data should frame the population of comparison as large relative to the number of events. If this is not the case, the discrete nature of events cannot be ignored, because for a population of a few thousand even the addition of a single event corresponds to a substantial increase in the rate.[55] A count data approach has been applied in recent famine studies but without any explicit theoretical rationale.[56]

A useful property of Finnish mortality statistics is that they assist in tracking the regional social risk: in principle, deaths had to be reported to the parish of residence. Although it is obvious that registration of the deceased most likely deteriorated during the crisis, this convention still provides us with an explanatory variable of location-specific mortality and through statistical analysis an insight into the question about the local structures subjecting people to out-migrate, giving rise to the *mass* mortality observed.

When we inspect the spatial distribution of famine mortality during the 1860s (Map 5.2), it becomes abundantly clear that death took its toll well beyond the peripheries of northeast Finland. Mortality levels show significant surges in Satakunta, southern Ostrobothnia, Häme and western Uusimaa, and yet for a long time no apparent increases in eastern Finland. According to regression results conducted by Pitkänen, variables indicating the importance of social structure had no significant explanatory value in analysing regional excess mortality, while income and price variables and grain dependence did contribute to an explanation of excess mortality rates.[57] Count regression model results fitted to township-level data are reported in Table 5.3, where the dependent variable is the total excess mortality for the famine period (1866–1868) in each township.[58] As the variance of the dependent variable exceeded its mean, we applied negative binomial regression design to handle over-dispersion, instead of the generic Poisson regression. The choice is verified in all four models reported, with highly significant likelihood test ratios. Furthermore, because all of the observations of the dependent variable are positive, we apply a zero-truncated model. As there is reason to believe that a larger base population could result in a higher number of famine victims, we use the sum of township population as an exposure variable. We run four separate models, each with a different sample: the first included every township, the last three townships were assigned to each cluster.[59] We did not observe any significant spatial clustering of residuals, implying that the impact of potential spatial autocorrelation should not cause a serious bias in the results.

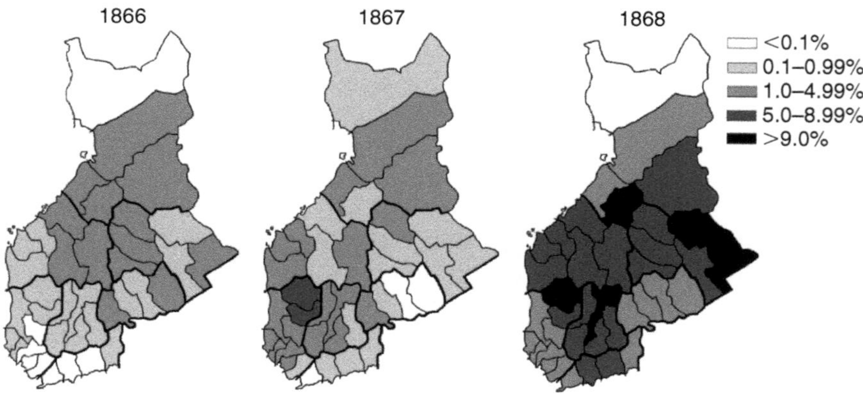

Map 5.2 Excess mortality in administrational districts: crude mortality in comparison to average of 1861 to 1865.

Table 5.3 Zero-truncated negative binomial regression results for township-level excess mortality

Model	*(1)*	*(2)*	*(3)*	*(4)*
Constant	–3.939 (<0.001)***	–3.203 (<0.001)***	–1.842 (0.257)	–8.247 (<0.001)***
Households per capita	–3.387 (0.005)***	–4.966 (0.014)**	–8.234 (0.009)***	–1.609 (0.567)
Exemption from poll tax (rate)	0.921 (0.091)*	2.256 (0.144)	6.392 (0.009)***	0.605 (0.155)
Exemption from household flat tax (rate)	0.916 (0.004)***	0.869 (0.023)**	0.151 (0.921)	–0.198 (0.738)
Proportion of children under 16 years (rate)	1.629 (0.176)	–2.267 (0.203)	0.918 (0.657)	11.211 (<0.001)***
Average income per household	0.00001 (0.981)	0.0004 (0.705)	–0.003 (0.646)	–0.001 (0.143)
Income-taxed households	–0.488 (0.193)	0.017 (0.980)	0.277 (0.904)	0.240 (0.707)
Gini coefficient	–0.596 (0.196)	0.981 (0.985)	0.478 (0.844)	1.772 (0.039)**
Crop failure in 1865 (dummy)	0.204 (0.012)**	0.396 (0.001)***	–0.107 (0.518)	–0.127 (0.291)
Crop failure in 1866 (dummy)	0.378 (<0.001)***	0.216 (0.049)**	0.408 (0.009)***	–0.001 (0.996)
Crop failure in 1867 (dummy)	0.377 (<0.001)***	0.535 (<0.001)***	–0.262 (0.389)	0.226 (0.058)*
Sample	All	Cluster one	Cluster two	Cluster three
N	243	120	62	61
Log-likelihood	–1567.79	–727.95	–419.80	–380.97
P-value for likelihood ratio test, $\beta_i=0, \forall i$	<0.001	<0.001	0.0045	<0.001
P-value for likelihood ratio test $\alpha=0$	<0.001	<0.001	<0.001	<0.001
Pseudo R^2	0.0242	0.0374	0.0295	0.0611

Notes
Dispersion: mean. Dependent variable: township-level excess mortality, count. Exposure variable: sum of township-level population 1866–1868, count.
Zero-truncated negative binomial regression, coefficients reported in incidence rate-ratios. *** – denotes statistical significance at 1%, ** – at 5%, * – at 10% level.
P-values in parenthesis.

The first model reports the findings based on the whole country sample of 243 rural townships. Three social variables have a statistically significant effect to excess mortality. Increase in the number of households corresponds to decrease in famine excess mortality. We do not report the result from inverse measure (mean household size) as households per capita is a convenient way of interpreting the distribution of food entitlement in the population: even small-scale farmers were relatively better-off than seasonal workers and farm-hands. The positive mortality impact of exemption from household flat tax brings the other side of subsistence farming to the fore: regions where farms were unable to pay this household-level tax were subject to higher excess mortality. Farming-based food entitlements thus include a qualitative difference: to ensure subsistence, farms had to be sufficiently productive. As is evident from model (2), households exempted from this tax were only associated positively in the first cluster, where the number of households per capita was the highest. This implies that the average increased ability to establish one's own household resulted in a larger variation in average household viability. Because the Finnish government did not provide extensive aid, township-level incomes may be considered as proxies for local possibilities for famine relief. The lack of statistical significance of income-level variables in explaining mortality patterns may be interpreted as emphasising the household-level entitlements, enforcing the connection between viability of agriculture and its sustainability.[60]

A higher exemption rate from poll tax is also associated with higher mortality levels. The whole country sample features significance at 10 per cent level, resulting from a highly significant relationship in the second cluster ($p=0.009$). According to Tukey HSD post-hoc comparison, the first and the second cluster do not differ statistically in terms of the poll tax exemption rate ($p=0.980$), yet the rate is significantly higher in the third cluster than in the other two ($p<0.001$). Why then is the contribution positive only in the second cluster? As was evident from Table 5.2, the second cluster was characterised by above-average equality but among low-income households. Those exempted from the poll tax were often poor, sick and deprived even in normal harvest years and the lack of communal resources could have turned into an inability to provide people with shelter for the whole course of protracted livelihood stress; i.e. the few resources available were hastily dispensed, forcing people to re-migrate and prolong the exposure to hazardous conditions. These results back up the previous accounts of the famine-induced migration from regions suffering from earlier crop failures, especially the northern parts of southwest Finland (i.e. Satakunta) and the western coastal area of Ostrobothnia.[61]

Inequality-measuring Gini coefficients associate positively with excess mortality in the third cluster, as does the proportion of children under the age of 16. The fact that the Gini coefficient is not joined with a statistically significant increase in mortality in other clusters suits the vulnerability interpretation: high inequality translates to a high concentration of labour demand. When the crisis then escalated to the point where farms had to lay off their seasonal labourers, it most likely happened simultaneously throughout the farming sector within the third cluster, leading to an abrupt increase in unemployment and radically diminishing opportunities for re-employment. From the perspective of survival, these kinds of conditions furthermore translated to decreased possibilities of finding even a temporary place of shelter or food aid: when farm labourers were laid off, they consequently became socially dislocated.

The positive effect of the proportion of children suggests furthermore that instead of laying off only a handful of people, farm owners deported whole families. If the positive association of the children's proportion would only capture their higher risk of death due to infectious diseases the variable should also show a positive association with excess mortality in other clusters. As it does not, we propose that the hazardous socio-environmental factors dominated in the third cluster of eastern Finland, whereas a mere inability to re-establish a lost livelihood prevailed in the first two clusters. These also hint that the crisis escalated abruptly in the east, forcing large numbers of people simultaneously to seek relief, leaving children especially vulnerable, in contrast to the more steadfast process in the western parts of the country. This interpretation is also in line with regional and inter-temporal patterns of excess mortality displayed in Map 5.2.

Conclusion

This chapter has attempted to estimate the extent and nature of social vulnerability prior to the famine outbreak and its association with regional excess mortality rates. According to the results presented here, we assert that the prevalent pre-famine vulnerability was multidimensional and led to sequential, even nonlinear famine escalation as opposed to linearly worsening living conditions of the landless rural poor. The collapse of one population segment's livelihood increased stress in others, enforcing the positive feedback, ultimately leading to a mortality catastrophe during the winter of 1867/1868.

Country-level excess mortality remained fairly low until the autumn of 1867, when the subsistence crisis intensified to a full-blown famine.[62] This has led previous literature to emphasise the impact of the near-complete harvest failure of 1867 as the obvious culprit. And yet, objections remain. The regression results reported above do indicate that while crop failures contributed to regional patterns of excess mortality, in isolation they really do not provide a thorough understanding of how the famine unfolded within different parts of the country and with what kinds of qualitative characteristics. There are also results available based on cohort-specific life expectancy suggesting that even the longer definition of the famine period (1866–1868) could be considered too short, not supporting a clear-cut punctuation of crop failure-induced mortality increases.[63]

While we operate on aggregate scale, we contend that there existed at least three different population groups that were severely vulnerable not only to crop failures per se but also to long-term economic deterioration and subsequent social upheaval. Population segments suffering from chronic poverty were the first to face catastrophe, followed by agricultural labourers and subsistence and small-scale farmers. The groups facing social dislocation in later phases of the crisis could in fact be worse off (i.e. were quicker to face higher mortality risk) than those getting into trouble in the first years of the famine. Not only were the disease conditions much harder at the pinnacle of the famine, but also interregional migration had been exhausting resources for quite some time (for years in some parts of the country) and degrading the moral obligation to help. Häkkinen has stated that during the winter of 1867/1868 the solidarity and humane approach applied at local level turned (at least at face value) distinctly into a more concentrated and 'inhumane' policy driven by governmental requirements. The famine also displayed the inherent risks prevailing in a vastly unequal society: though, with many individual exceptions, the farmers as a group were rather reluctant to organize aid.[64]

What then may be concluded from the famine proneness of Finland in the 1860s? It is worthwhile emphasising that there existed population groups which were vulnerable to even one-off harvest failures on even the smallest scale. This is apparent from the mortality increase of the famine in the 1850s and at the beginning of the 1860s. But the identification of this group is clearly insufficient in describing the mortality patterns of autumn 1867 onward. Pitkänen has advocated using mortality's male bias as a form of yardstick measuring the extent of social collapse associated with the subsistence crisis. According to him, it is only the most extensive and subsistence-related famines where mortality clearly discriminates between sexes, leaving males in a disadvantaged position, as occurred in Finland during the famine of 1866 to 1868.[65] His results back up the interpretation put forward here: social collapse during the famine was a crucial ingredient in the extent of the crisis.

In spite of data deficiencies (i.e. the lack of longitudinal nature on the independent variables), this study backs up previous socially focused interpretations by presenting clear socio-economic determinants of the regional mortality counts. Our findings presented here re-emphasise that the study of 1860s Finland can be fruitful in global historical famine research, particularly due to the availability of extensive data, which allows us to dig deeper into the crisis than what is possible for several other pre-industrial famines. These findings can help us to understand not only the formation of crisis in agricultural economies of the past but also to detect vulnerabilities of modern famine-prone regions, hence furthering the causal investigation of mortality risks inherent in prevailing socio-economic contexts.

Notes

1 Timo Myllyntaus, 'Summer Frost: A Natural Hazard with Fatal Consequences in Pre-Industrial Finland', in *Natural Disasters, Cultural Responses: Case Studies Toward a Global Environmental History*, ed. Christof Mauch and Christian Pfister (Lanham, MD: Lexington Books, 2009), 90.
2 See e.g. Fernand Braudel, *Capitalism and Material Life, 1400–1800* (New York: Harper & Row, 1967), 38.
3 Cormac Ó Gráda, 'Making Famine History', *Journal of Economic Literature* 45 (2007), 7–9.

4 See in particular Oiva Turpeinen, *Nälkä vai Tauti Tappoi? Kauhunvuodet 1866–1868* (Helsinki: Societas Historica Finlandiae, 1986); Eino Jutikkala, *Kuolemalla on Aina Syynsä. Maailman Väestöhistorian Ääriviivoja* (Porvoo: WSOY, 1987); Eino Jutikkala, 'Katovuodet', in *Suomen Maatalouden Historia I. Perinteisen Maatalouden Aika: Esihistoriasta 1870-luvulle*, ed. Viljo Rasila, Eino Jutikkala and Anneli Mäkelä-Alitalo (Helsinki: SKS, 2003), 504–514.

5 That is, crop failures occurred alongside the simultaneous presence of lethal endemic diseases. For this analysis in relation to 1840s Ireland, see Joel Mokyr, *Why Ireland Starved? A Quantitative and Analytical History of the Irish Economy 1800–1850* (London: George Allen & Unwin, 1981), 261–262.

6 Antti Häkkinen, 'Vaikuttivatko Väärät Hätäaputoimet Vuosien 1867–1868 Suureen Kuolleisuuteen?', in *Pane leipään Puolet Petäjäistä – Nälkä ja Pulavuodet Suomen Historiassa*, ed. Petri Karonen (Jyväskylä: Jyväskylän Yliopisto, 1994), 77; Antti Häkkinen and Jarmo Peltola, 'On the Social History of Unemployement and Poverty in Finland, 1860–2000', in *Down From the Heavens, Up From the Ashes: The Finnish Economic Crisis of the 1990s in the Light of Economic and Social Research*, ed. Jorma Kalela, Jaakko Kiander, Ullamaija Kivikuru, Heikki A. Loikkanen and Jussi Simpura (Helsinki: Valtion Taloudellinen Tutkimuskeskus, 2001), 311. This interpretation also surfaces in Cormac Ó Gráda, 'Markets and Famines: Evidence from Nineteenth Century Finland', *Economic Development and Cultural Change* 49 (2001).

7 Kari J. Pitkänen, *Deprivation and Disease. Mortality During the Great Finnish Famine of the 1860s* (Helsinki: Suomen Väestötieteellisen Yhdistyksen Julkaisuja, 1993), 112–113.

8 Antti Kuusterä, '1860-luvun Epäonnistunut Talouspolitiikka', in *Nälkä, Talous ja Kontrolli: Näkökulmia Kriisien ja Konfliktien Syntyyn, Merkitykseen ja Kontrolliin*, ed. Kari J. Pitkänen (Helsinki: Helsingin Yliopisto, 1987), 43–57.

9 Arvo M. Soininen, *Vanha Maataloutemme: Maatalous ja Maatalousväestö Suomessa Perinnäisen Maatalouden Loppukaudella 1720-luvulta 1870-luvulle* (Helsinki: SHS, 1974). See also Häkkinen and Forsberg (Chapter 4, this volume).

10 Paradoxically the Finnish famine is also one of the lesser known famines in the international literature, while the Great Irish Famine, which occurred two decades earlier, is most likely the best known. Joel Mokyr goes on even to state that the Irish famine is 'the last great European natural disaster' and 'the last large-scale natural demographic disaster to strike Europe'. Mokyr, *Why Ireland Starved*, 262, 275.

11 Peter Walker, *Famine Early Warning Systems: Victims and Destitution* (London: Earthscan, 1989), 9.

12 Kari J. Pitkänen, 'The Patterns of Mortality During the Great Finnish Famine in the 1860s', in *Acta Demographica 1992*, ed. G. Buttler, G. Heilig and G. Schmitt-Rink (Heidelberg: Physica-Verlag, 1992), 85.

13 Eric Vanhaute, 'From Famine to Food Crisis: What History can Teach us about Local and Global Subsistence Crises', *Journal of Peasant Studies* 38 (2011), 60.

14 Elinder and Erixson point out that the *Titanic* is actually an exception to the rule: women typically faced higher mortality risk in maritime disasters. See Mikael Elinder and Oscar Erixson, 'Gender, Social Norms, and Survival in Maritime Disasters', *Proceedings of the National Academy of Sciences* 109 (2012), 13220–13224.

15 Martin Ravallion, 'Famines and Economics', *Journal of Economic Literature* 35 (1997), 1205; Ó Gráda, 'Making Famine History', 5.

16 See e.g. Amartya Sen, 'Ingredients of Famine Analysis: Availability and Entitlements', *Quarterly Journal of Economics* 96 (1981), 433–464.

17 Baro and Deubel also point out that 'vulnerability mapping tends to be descriptive. It is important to add an analysis of causality within the framework.' Mamadou Baro and Tara F. Deubel, 'Persistent Hunger: Perspectives on Vulnerability, Famine and Food Security in Sub-Saharan Africa', *Annual Review of Anthropology* 26 (2006), 527.

18 Evan D.G. Fraser, 'Food System Vulnerability: Using Past Famines to Help Understand how Food Systems may Adapt to Climate Change', *Ecological Complexity* 3 (2006), 328–335.

19 Pitkänen, *Deprivation and Disease*, 9; David Arnold, *Famine: Social Crisis and Historical Change* (Oxford and New York: Blackwell, 1988), 54.

20 Gregory Clark, *A Farewell to Alms: A Brief Economic History of the World* (Princeton, NJ: Princeton University Press, 2007), 23.

21 Cormac Ó Gráda, *Black '47 and Beyond: The Great Irish Famine in History, Economy and Memory* (Princeton, NJ: Princeton University Press, 1999), 10.

22 Amartya Sen, *Poverty and Famines. An Essay on Entitlement and Deprivation* (Oxford: Clarendon Press, 1981), 39.

23 Mokyr, *Why Ireland Starved*, 16.

24 Robert Jütte, *Poverty and Deviance in Early Modern Europe: New Approaches to European History* (Cambridge: Cambridge University Press, 1996), 21.

25 Pitkänen, 'Patterns of Mortality', 92–93; Maarten Lindeboom, France Portrait, Gerard J. van den Berg, 'Long-run effects on longevity of a nutritional shock early in life: The Dutch Potato famine of 1846–1847', *Journal of Health Economics* 29 (2010), 617–629; Marc Klemp and Jacob Weisdorf, 'The Lasting Damage to Mortality of Early-life Adversity: Evidence from the English Famine of the 1720s', *European Review of Economic History* 16 (2012), 239–244. Between 1541 and 1871 life expectancy at birth in England varied mainly between 30 and 40 years. In this context, a decrease of 12 years estimated by Klemp and Weisdorf sounds excessively high. For English population development see E.A. Wrigley and R.S. Schofield, *The Population History of England 1541–1871. A Reconstruction* (Cambridge: Cambridge University Press, 1981).

26 Allan G. Hill, 'Demographic Responses to Food Shortages in the Sahel', *Population and Development Review* 15 (1989), 178–179.

27 Alex De Waal, 'A Re-assessment of Entitlement Theory in the Light of the Recent Famines in Africa', *Development and Change* 21 (1990), 481.

28 De Waal, 'A Re-assessment of Entitlement Theory', 484.

29 Hill, 'Demographic Reponses', 178.

30 Kari Pitkänen, 'The Road to Survival or Death? Temporary Migration During the Great Finnish Famine in the 1860s', in *Just a Sack of Potatoes? Crisis Experiences in European Societies, Past and Present*, ed. Antti Häkkinen (Helsinki: SHS, 1992), 87–118; Pitkänen, *Deprivation and Disease*, 113–115.

31 Turpeinen, *Nälka vai Tauti Tappoi?*

32 De Waal, 'A Re-assessment of Entitlement Theory', 484–485.

33 Jeffrey Alwang, Paul B. Siegel and Steen L. Jorensen, 'Vulnerability: A View from Different Disciplines', *SP Discussion Paper* 0115 (2001), 2.

34 The regional and socially specific nature of famine vulnerability is highlighted in Jütte, *Poverty and Deviance*, 32–33.

35 Lisa Rygel, David O'Sullivan and Brent Yarnal, 'A Method for Constructing Social Vulnerability Index: An Application to Hurricane Storm Surges in a Developed Country', *Mitigation and Adaption Strategies for Global Change* 11 (2006), 743–744.

36 Alwang *et al.*, 'Vulnerability', 4. This may, for example, be due to relief and political regime, largely omitted from direct consideration here. The author is grateful to an anonymous referee for highlighting this point.

37 Vanhaute, 'From Famine to Food Crisis', 49.

38 Pitkänen, *Deprivation and Disease*, 54–55.

39 Pitkänen, 'Patterns of Morality', 84–87; Pitkänen, *Deprivation and Disease*, 54–55. For a more detailed description of the famine chronology see e.g. Pitkänen, *Deprivation and Disease*; Ó Gráda, 'Markets and Famines'.

40 Pekka Haatanen, *Suomen Maalaisköyhälistö: Tutkimusten ja Kaunokirjallisuuden Valossa* (Helsinki: WSOY, 1968), 6. Later (p. 40), Haatanen states that 'let it be cottage or piece of land … telling poor from the poorer'.

41 Robert W. Fogel, 'Second Thoughts on the European Escape from Hunger: Famines, Chronic Malnutrition and Mortality Rates', in *Nutrition and Poverty*, ed. S.R. Osmani (Oxford: Clarendon Press, 1992), 243–286. Cormac Ó Gráda concludes from Finnish food market data that a malfunctioning price mechanism did not exacerbate the crisis. See Ó Gráda, 'Markets and Famines'. For a general overview of markets during famines see, *inter alia*, Cormac Ó Gráda, 'Markets and Famines in Pre-Industrial Europe', *Journal of Interdisciplinary History* 36 (2005), 143–166; and Cormac Ó Gráda, *Famine: A Short History* (Princeton, NJ: Princeton University Press, 2009), 129–158. In many cases market functioning is central to a household's ability to access food, and starvation may occur even when food is readily available at local markets if a household lacks the appropriate entitlements. Baro and Deubel, 'Persistent Hunger', 524.

42 Official Statistics of Finland, *Varallisuuden Suhteita. Kertomus Suomenmaan Suostuntaverosta Vuonna 1865* (Helsinki: SVT IV, 1875). Measured here with the Gini coefficient, see e.g. Michael P. Todaro and Stephen C. Smith, *Economic Development* (Harlow: Pearson Education, 2003), 195–220. Only (per annum) incomes exceeding 500 Finnish marks were subject to taxation. In this chapter a simple procedure of estimation is carried out: the taxpayer distribution within every income class is assumed to be uniform and people without any income is calculated from the household-specific flat-tax (*käräjäkappa*) exemption rate.

43 Amartya Sen, 'From Income Inequality to Economic Inequality', *Southern Economic Journal* 64 (1997), 386. In comparison, Stephen Devereux has pointed out that focusing on the household as the principal unit of analysis confounds the entitlement approach, as does its failure to engage with social relations and power inequalities, in this case at the intra-household level. Stephen Devereux, 'Sen's Entitlement Approach: Critiques and Counter-critiques', *Oxford Development Studies* 29 (2001), 250.

44 National Archives of Finland [Digital Archives], *Poll Tax Registers (Henkikirjat) for 1865*; Eljas Orrman, 'Henkikirjat Henkilöhistorian Lähteinä', *Genos* 1(1980), 1–21.

45 Turpeinen, *Nälka vai Tauti Tappoi?*

46 Rygel *et al.*, 'Method for Constructing'; George E. Clark, Susanne C. Moser, Samuel J. Ratick, Kirstin Dow, William B. Meyer, Srinivas Emani, Weigen Jin, Jeanne X. Kasperson, Roger E. Kasperson and Harry E. Schwarz, 'Assessing the Vulnerability of Coastal Communities to Extreme Storms: The Case of Revere, Ma., USA', *Mitigation and Adaptation Strategies for Global Change* 3 (1998), 59–82.

47 For an alternative view see Neil W. Adger, 'Social Vulnerability to Climate Change and Extremes in Coastal Vietnam', *World Development* 27 (1999), 255–256.

48 Upasna Sharma and Anand Patwardhan, 'Methodology for Identifying Vulnerability Hotspots to Tropical Cyclone Hazard in India', *Mitigation and Adaptation Strategies for Global Change* 13 (2008), 713–714.

49 Sharma and Patwardhan, 'Methodology for Identifying', 703–717.

50 Cluster analysis was conducted using IBM SPSS Statistics 20. For the discussion concerning various methods see e.g. Johann Bacher, Knut Wenzig and Melanie Vogler, 'SPSS TwoStep Cluster – A First Evaluation', *Universität Erlangen-Nürnberg: Arbeits- und Diskussionspapiere* 2 (2004); Beth Horn and Wei Huang, *Comparison of Segmentation Approaches* (Decision Analyst Inc., 2009). Generally, cluster analysis aims to produce grouping of the data so that the statistical units in one group are more similar to one another than to those units in other groups. The similarity measures differ between clustering algorithms and variables of interest.

51 Tom Chiu, DongPing Fang, John Chen, Yao Wang and Christopher Jeris, 'A Robust and Scalable Clustering Algorithm for Mixed Type Attributes in Large Database Environment', *Proceedings of the Seventh ACM SIGKDD International Conference on Knowledge Discovery and Data Mining* (San Francisco, CA: ACM, 2001), 263–268.

52 Ó Gráda argues that 'famines have always brought out the best and the worst in human nature'. Ó Gráda, *Famine: A Short History*, 47.

53 Violetta Hionidou, 'Why do People Die in Famines? Evidence from Three Island Populations', *Population Studies* 56 (2002), 75; Pitkänen, *Deprivation and Disease*, 69–80.

54 See in particular Turpeinen, *Nälkä vai Tauti Tappoi*; Pitkänen, *Deprivation and Disease*; and Pitkänen, 'Road to Survival or Death'.

55 D. Wayne Osgood, 'Poisson-based Regression Analysis of Aggregate Crime Rates', *Journal of Quantitative Criminology* 1(16) (2000), 22–23. Technically there is an increased risk of breaking the assumption of homogeneity of error variance and normal error distribution. As depicted in Table 5.1, statistical units (townships) are small in population figures, emphasising this risk.

56 See e.g. Thomas Plümber and Eric Neumayer, 'Famine Mortality, Rational Political Inactivity and International Food Aid', *World Development* 37 (2009), 50–61.

57 Pitkänen, 'Patterns of Mortality', 92–93. For a more detailed description of the famine chronology see e.g. Pitkänen, *Deprivation and Disease*, 51–68.

58 Calculated summing the yearly mortality counts and deducting three times the yearly average mortality of comparison period (1861–1865).

59 Greene gives a good overview of count data models. See William H. Greene, *Econometric Analysis* (Engelwood Cliffs, NJ: Prentice Hall International, 2000), 880–893.

60 Compare to results presented in Pitkänen, 'Patterns of Mortality', 91.

61 See Jütte, *Poverty and Deviance*, 46–50, for a critique of associating poverty and tax exemptions.

62 Pitkänen, 'Patterns of Mortality', 86.

63 Gabriele Doblhammer, Gerard J. van den Berg and L.H. Lumey, 'A Re-analysis of the Long-term Effects on Life Expectancy of the Great Finnish Famine of 1866–68', *Population Studies* 67(3) (2011), 309–322.

64 Antti Häkkinen, 'On Attitudes and Living Strategies in the Finnish Countryside in the Years of Famine 1867–68', in *Just a Sack of Potatoes? Crisis Experiences in European Societies, Past and Present*, ed. Antti Häkkinen (Helsinki: SHS, 1992), 149–166.

65 Kari J. Pitkänen, 'Famine Mortality in Nineteenth Century Finland: Is There a Sex Bias?', in *Famine Demography: Perspectives from the Past and Present*, ed. Tim Dyson and Cormac Ó Gráda (Oxford: Oxford University Press, 2002), 65–92.

6 'The terrible visitation': famine in Finland and Ireland, 1845 to 1868[1]

Towards an agenda for comparative Irish–Finnish famine studies

Andrew G. Newby and Timo Myllyntaus

Ireland and Finland: 'long nineteenth-century' comparisons

Crop failure and famine was a recurrent feature of pre-industrial Europe, persisting well into the late nineteenth century. The Great Irish Famine – during which around one million people (or one-eighth of the population) died, and a further million emigrated – is often seen as a key event in Irish national history, and has had a considerable impact upon Irish identity.[2] Since the 150th anniversary of the Great Famine in the late 1990s, prodigious amounts of academic and popular literature have been published on the subject.[3] From an Irish perspective, the historiography of the Great Finnish Famine, which culminated in 1868, seems somewhat limited. Cormac Ó Gráda, one of the most renowned Irish economic historians, has described the Finnish catastrophe as the 'last great subsistence crisis of the western world', but has also complained that it remains 'unduly neglected', and stressed the potential for comparative studies with Ireland.[4] This period of Finnish history tends to be presented as one of general economic malaise, associated with national 'growing pains' as Finland sought to establish itself as an autonomous country.[5]

It is true that the *Suuret Nälkävuodet* (Great Hunger Years) do not play a large role in general histories of Finland, but it must nevertheless be acknowledged that the events of the 1860s have not been completely 'neglected'.[6] In the decades leading up to Finland's independence in 1917, several Finnish authors discussed the nature and impact of the famine.[7] More recently, since the late 1980s the publications of Antti Häkkinen, Oiva Turpeinen and Kari Pitkänen, in particular, have renewed awareness of the complexities of the period, especially from a socio-economic history perspective. However, these scholars' work has only been made available in a limited way to non-Finnish speakers.[8] Clearly, there is potential for the Finnish historiography to develop in relation to the famine years of the 1860s, and an examination of how the events in 1840s Ireland have been portrayed, analysed and debated provides a good framework for this kind of endeavour. It is also possible that, in exploring some of the important differences in the Finnish case, new light may be cast upon the Great Irish Famine. This chapter presents some early reflections from the Academy of Finland's projects '"The Terrible Visitation": Famine in Finland and Ireland 1845–68', and 'Finnish Harvest Failures and

Famines in the International Context', and is the first general comparative overview of the Finnish and Irish famines to be published, other than Vappu Ikonen's Finnish-language account.[9] Building on Ikonen's largely descriptive overview, this chapter highlights some areas in which comparative work may be fruitfully pursued, either in the famines' causes, the mechanics of relief, or in their subsequent commemoration or politicisation.

As Bill Kissane has observed, the social and historical parallels between nineteenth-century Ireland and Finland are numerous enough to warrant deeper investigation, although there were also considerable structural differences between the two.[10] Narrowing the focus to the nineteenth-century famines produces similarly ambiguous results – the contrasts are just as instructive as the comparisons. Finland passed from Swedish to Russian control following the 'Finnish War' of 1808 to 1809, with the Russian Tsar as head of state. A Governor General, roughly equivalent to the British viceroys in Ireland, ruled on the Tsar's behalf. However, as the nineteenth century progressed, the Senate in Helsinki increasingly took de facto control of Finland's internal affairs, including foreign trade and economic policy. This was an important contrast with the control which London exercised over Ireland, and was crucial in the subsequent memorialisation of the famines in the two countries.

Despite superficially comparable 'long nineteenth-century' timelines between the two countries, this constitutional relationship with the imperial power was the key difference. From an Irish perspective, William Smyth proposes that an 'outstanding feature' of the famine period was the 'exercise of centralised political and administrative control over Ireland and the Irish people, which increased after the passing of the union'.[11] Finland did not conform to this pattern for most of the nineteenth century, although when the Russian authorities sought to increase control over the Grand Duchy as part of their Russificiation policies, especially after 1899, separatist sentiment in Finland grew.[12] The distinctive Finnish position was noted during the Home Rule crises in Ireland, and William Gladstone stressed in 1890 that Finland's 'legislative independence' had provided 'complete satisfaction in Finland, and [had] made Finland most loyally attached to Russia'.[13]

The Russification process which sought to incorporate Finland (and other territories) more closely into the Russian imperial system brought further comment from Irish Nationalists – not least because of Britain's apparently inconsistent support for the rights of 'small nations'.[14] The Great War provided, in Kissane's words, 'the context for growing radicalization' as well as the immediate context for independence and subsequent bitter civil wars.[15] Although the Finnish Civil War (1918) was considerably more bloody than its Irish equivalent (1922–1923), both wars shaped national politics in the respective independent states.

Finland and Ireland before the 'great famines'

> Now that I have seen Ireland, it seems to me that the Lettes, the Esthonians, and the Finlanders, lead a life of comparative comfort; and poor Paddy would feel like a king with their houses, their habiliments, and their daily fare.[16]

So wrote 'Obscure Men of Good Intention' when touring Ireland on the eve of the Great Famine. The very definition of a backhanded compliment to the various nations around the Baltic, the Irish were here constructed as living beyond some previously accepted definition of poverty and squalor, represented by the Finns and their neighbours. In this sense, the impressions of the 'Obscure Men' had not evolved very far in the three centuries since the Italian scholar Cesar Scaliger had bracketed 'Scots and Irish' along with the 'Swedes, Norse, Greenlanders and Goths' as the 'bestial' inhabitants of peripheral corners of Europe.[17] Foreign impressions of these marginal pre-industrial societies often feature racialised generalisations, which masked considerable internal and regional variations in respect of famine vulnerability. In this sense, the Irish and the Finns were seen from 'core' Europe in the early nineteenth century as being part of an 'inferior periphery'.[18]

Both Finland and Ireland endured regular crop failures prior to the calamities that became known as their 'Great' Famines, and indeed both continued to exist under the threat of famine for several decades afterwards.[19] Although not without methodological flaws, William Wilde's inventory of famines in Ireland, undertaken in the early 1850s, recorded more than 80 complete or partial famines taking place in Ireland between 963 and 1850.[20] In Finland, incidences of frost in the summertime increased from the beginning of the seventeenth century onward, linked particularly with the climatic anomaly later characterised as Europe's 'Little Ice Age'.[21] As the Finnish-American historian Armas Holmio observes:

> Histories of Finland tell of numerous bad years, when crops failed. The resultant famines were accompanied by diseases and plagues. The people named the years for the afflictions which characterised them: the Great Cough Year, 1580; the Year of the Great Frost or the Straw Year, 1601–2; the Years of Many Deaths, 1695–97, the Autumn of the Plague, 1710.[22]

Between December 1739 and September 1741, unusual climatic shocks struck across Europe. This period of exceptional weather turned Ireland into an 'Arctic' land, and caused a famine remembered as *Bliain an áir* (the Year of the Slaughter).[23] William Wilde used an extract from *The Groans of Ireland* to describe the scene in 1741, in terms which would be repeated during the Great Famine a century later: 'the most miserable scene of universal distress, that I have ever read of in history: want and misery on every face ... the roads spread with dead and dying; mankind of the colour of the docks and nettles they fed on.'[24] During the mid-eighteenth century, the European climate became gradually warmer and dryer; by the mid-nineteenth century, the 'Little Ice Age' was over in most parts of the continent. Nevertheless, abnormally cold weather continued in Northern Europe – in the Baltic Sea rim especially – until the late 1860s.

Recurrent famines fed into discourse around the nature of the peoples who inhabited these marginal lands, though these constructions could also be highly dependent upon the international political situation. The accessibility and increased popularity of travel accounts also shaped popular perceptions, and tended to organise people in racialised terms.[25] Therefore, despite often being bracketed with the Irish as a somewhat backward and impoverished people, Finns could also be perceived as hardworking, honest and 'improvable' by British observers.[26] This was not only because of the Finns' near-universal adherence to Lutheran Protestantism, but also because British commentators were often keen to undermine the Russian Empire and humiliate the Tsar – bolstering a sense of Finnish national distinctiveness in the international arena was a part of this process. As Häkkinen and Forsberg point out (Chapter 4, this volume), both Ireland and Finland lagged well below the European average GDP per capita in the decades leading up to the Great Famines. Using the Geary-Khamis measurement (Int$) for historical comparison, in 1820 Finland's GDP stood at 781 Int$, whereas Ireland's was a little higher at 877 Int$.[27] Both of these figures were among the lowest in Europe, along with Greece, Sweden and Norway, and stood in contrast to the United Kingdom's 1,706 Int$.[28]

Demographically, there was a gulf in the pre-famine population sizes of these countries (Ireland in 1841 had 8.17 million inhabitants, whereas Finland in 1865 had 1.84 million), although 'congestion' linked to landlessness and underemployment was a common problem in both. Certainly, both societies lacked diversity in agricultural production, which increased vulnerability in the event of climatic shocks (such as the frost which occurred or the advent of the blight). Within this general socio-economic context, however, there were at least two crucial differences between Ireland and Finland in the nineteenth century, which framed the context in which the famines occurred, how they were tackled, and how they were remembered subsequently.

First, although Finland had been subsumed into the Russian Empire in 1809, the landowning patterns in the majority of the country followed the traditions that had developed under Swedish rule in the preceding centuries. Thus, although the population of landless labourers increased during the nineteenth century, agricultural society was underpinned by the existence of a 'free peasantry', owner-occupiers with considerably larger holdings than Irish cottiers. Although some of the same problems occurred in Finland as in Ireland (e.g. overcrowding and subdivision of holdings), there was not the same elite landowning class, and especially no real perception of such an elite being 'foreign' in terms of ethnicity or religion to the majority of the population. As Häkkinen and Forsberg observe, this has perhaps allowed the Finnish historiography to assume that society was rather more egalitarian than was actually the case.

Second, while Ireland's economy in the nineteenth century has been characterised as 'colonial', the Finns were emerging from what had arguably been a colonial relationship with Sweden, into a situation where they were much more able to dictate their own economic policies and international trade relationships.[29] The fact that Finland had its own Senate in Helsinki after 1809, which 'conducted the daily administration of the country in the Emperor's name', highlights an important difference from the Irish case.[30] Moreover, it demonstrates that even a Home Rule government may struggle to prevent a famine in the face of repeated crop failures, particularly when trying to maintain national financial viability. To use an Irish counterfactual example, Liam Kennedy has argued that a Parliament in Dublin would have been less well equipped than Westminster to provide famine relief in the 1840s.[31]

Conversely, in highlighting the 'imperial/colonial dialectic' in the provision of Irish famine relief, William J. Smyth has asserted that 'one could never imagine any Irish Government of whatever hue ... turning their backs and ignoring the "cry of want"'.[32] Finland's action in the 1860s could be instructive here, as it provides a case of an autonomous government that does not wish to involve the imperial power in its economic affairs, despite a looming emergency. Moreover, with famine occurring in other parts of the empire, the St Petersburg authorities were quite prepared to acquiesce to the Finnish desire for self-sufficiency. Thus, a scenario emerged in which an autonomous government, beset by crisis, was forced into decisions that disadvantaged certain regions. Put into an Irish context, this does not necessarily counter Smyth's argument, but it does raise the possibility that a Dublin-based administration may have attempted to maintain international financial stability at the expense of certain regions within Ireland. As will be seen, the extent to which senators in Helsinki 'turned their backs' in the 1860s may be contested, but their actions could not prevent widespread distress.

Core–periphery issues

As a European periphery, and especially in the context of modernisation of the economy, Finland falls into Berend and Ránki's definition of 'eastern Europe, Scandinavia and the Mediterranean (excluding France)'.[33] The lack of a genuine metropolis in Finland in the first half of the nineteenth century has also given rise to the idea of it being an 'interface periphery', situated between the two metropoles of Stockholm and St Petersburg, at this time.[34] In a Russian imperial context, however, while Finland did form the northwestern border of the empire, the notion of core–periphery must be interpreted flexibly. From a Russian perspective, Finland was one end of the 'vast arc' of territory, which, with St Petersburg and Moscow at its core, formed the imperial periphery.[35] If the actual core of the Russian Empire had been geographically in the centre of its territory, then Finland might more easily be accommodated within the usual definition of 'periphery'.[36]

Moreover, some modernisers in St Petersburg were keen to promote Finland as the 'European face' of Russia. These modernisers presented the autonomous position of the Grand Duchy as an emphatic rejoinder to the Russophobic propaganda of the British and others, which condemned Tsarist autocracy. Liberals in Russia were fascinated by the idea of Finland having a separate legislative body, and argued at times for similar structures to be put in place throughout the Empire.[37] Foreshadowing some of the rhetoric of federal Home Rulers in Britain and Ireland in the 1880s, it was hoped that this kind of constitution would strengthen the coherence of the Russian Empire, rather than lead to increasing support for separatism among its constituent parts. In the nineteenth century the Grand Duchy of Finland was, from a Finnish point of view, an autonomous state with its own administrative, financial and cultural centre in Helsinki.[38]

Ireland, similarly, has been treated flexibly when discussing its position as a core or periphery. The most common construction has been as a periphery, particularly in the context of being part of a United Kingdom from 1801. Butterfly and Shepherd make this point explicitly in their book on the politics of starvation:

> [T]here was a core–periphery disparity. The Irish were poor, rural, far from London, and Catholic. They, like their counterparts today in developing countries, were also generally silent in their suffering. During earlier economic difficulties in the 1830s and 1840s … rioting mobs from Lancashire to Glascow [*sic*] and Dunfermline in Scotland quickly got London's attention and aid. The silent starving in Sligo and Skibbereen did not. 'Industrial unrest in England', Young argues, 'was potentially more revolutionary and more disturbing than dispersed unrest in Ireland.'[39]

In her recent account of non-governmental charitable assistance to Ireland, Christine Kinealy contends that 'colonial assistance to the Scottish and Irish poor in the United Kingdom suggested that the Imperial core was not invincible'.[40] And yet, despite the construction of Ireland as 'Britain's oldest colony', which has given rise to very valuable comparative and transnational work with India, for example, there has also been a renewed emphasis in recent years of its place in the British Empire, which reimagines Ireland as much closer to the imperial core.[41] While Ireland faced economic competition from elsewhere in the British Empire, Irish people were well placed to find positions in the imperial administration, another similarity with the Finnish case.[42] In addition to national comparative frameworks, therefore, there is potential for examining Ireland and Finland in imperial comparison, and refining the various ideas of core and periphery associated with both.

Home rule and famine relief

The Great Finnish Famine is usually presented as having occurred in 1868 (the year which saw the worst spike in mortality), or in the hyphenated form of 1867/1868 (which takes into account the autumn frost which triggered a further famine, and subsequent excess mortality). Taking the lead from the Irish case, though without implying that the annual crises taken individually were remotely as dire as in Ireland, the previous chapters on Finland in this volume have adopted the approach that the events of 1867/1868 may only be understood within the context of several years of crop failure. The national poor relief system was in chaos by 1867, infrastructure projects had not been realised, a new currency required nurturing, and the state was low on cash and credit, all of which hampered relief efforts and contributed to a crop failure becoming a famine. Presenting the catastrophe as belonging to a single year arguably adds to the idea that it was a simple nature-induced accident, and consequently abrogates the responsibility of the authorities in Helsinki for tackling the disaster.

The famines in Ireland and Finland were both triggered by natural causes – blight and frost, respectively – but in both cases there were deeper contextual factors that determined the severity of the social impact. It is worth noting that although the British administration in Ireland has received a greater amount of opprobrium for its handling of the Irish crisis than the Helsinki Senate has received in regard to Finland, the natural trigger in the former case (potato late blight, *phytophthora infestans*) was a completely unknown phenomenon when it arrived in Europe in 1845, whereas the Finns had been aware of the potential dangers of late frost for centuries.[43] Nevertheless, various factors – cumulative bad harvests depleting grain stores; a slow reaction to the developing crisis, exacerbated by harsh winter weather hindering the transport of relief grain; lack of governmental experience; and difficulties in protecting a new currency and national economic stability – combined in Finland to create Europe's last major peacetime famine.

Of course, the mere fact that a fungal pathogen was an unknown danger does not change the fact that a society was overly dependent upon a single crop, and had become vulnerable to a natural catastrophe. Similarly, when the early winter of 1867 destroyed that year's harvest in Finland, vulnerability that had developed over the previous decade was brutally exposed. Irish nationalist and republican historiography has generally framed the post-1800 British administration – and particularly Charles Trevelyan, Assistant Secretary to the Treasury 1840 to 1859 – as culpable for the Great Famine. Curiously, the Finns also had cause to curse the British for contributing to the hardship of the 1860s. During the Crimean War (1853–1856), the British had considered Finland, as a Grand Duchy of Russia, to be a legitimate military target, and the years 1854/1855 saw a concerted bombardment of the Finnish coast by the British navy.[44] These attacks, which destroyed non-military targets including grain stores, caused resentment in Finland, but also considerable unease in Great Britain.[45] Part of this unease was provoked by the fear that Britain's international reputation would be damaged, but there was also an awareness that a flourishing trade relationship could be jeopardised.

Having already been involved in a peace mission to the Tsar in an attempt to avert armed conflict, the British Quaker movement was to the fore in providing 'reparations' for the British assault on Finland.[46] There are many parallels between this Quaker intervention in Finland and their activities during the Great Irish Famine. Fact-finding missions were undertaken, money was raised in Britain via subscriptions, and reliable local worthies were found in order to make efficient use of the funds among the distressed communities.[47] Although the aid was not conditional upon the recipient's creed or ethnicity, there was nevertheless a strong sense of self-help implied in Quaker relief efforts. In Finland, a contract was signed that bound the recipient to undertake a 'corresponding amount of work' in improving his farm; otherwise the sum was to be returned to the parish poor-box.[48] Moreover, as in Ireland, funds were set aside for 'improvement' projects, such as drainage, the construction of harbours, or the development of new fishing methods.[49]

The Quakers' work apparently helped to assuage some of the ill will that had been felt towards the British in Finland. The decision to raise money for voluntary war reparations had already been made when their deputation visited Finland in the winter of 1856 and noticed that a crop failure was likely to cause widespread destitution the following year. Thus, the idea of the 'famine relief' effort developed as an adjunct to the original plan; the campaign was not initially a reaction to an anticipated famine. It is, however, interesting to note that the labour task imposed on any recipients of aid – something that had proved controversial in Ireland and in the subsequent Irish historiography – was not considered demeaning in the Finnish case. Indeed, similar policies were adopted in the 1860s by the Finnish government of J.V. Snellman, as it reacted to renewed famine conditions. Ferdinand Granberg, one of the Quaker committee's key contacts in Oulu, stressed that 'gratuitous distribution, which often causes demoralisation, will only be made when absolutely necessary'.[50] The key difference with Ireland here is that the Quakers were strongly opposed to labour tasks that were imposed purely for the sake of giving employment, arguing that the 'moral effects of useless labour' were more deleterious than gratuitous charity.[51] The Quakers again came to the Finns' aid in 1868, as part of a much wider international charitable response. Although the initial permission for the Quaker intervention in 1856/1857 was granted by the Tsar, it seems that the Finnish Senate looked on with interest at their activities.[52] Certainly their methods dovetailed well with Snellman's ideal of *omavaraisuus* (self-sufficiency), which he believed should be a cornerstone of Finnish national identity, and which was intimately connected with Lutheran political theory.[53] The extent to which the Quakers were a direct inspiration for Snellman's own policies in the 1860s is unclear, but there were many echoes in the Finnish government's later famine relief efforts.

Renewed crop failure in 1862, again attributed to frost, caused further misery in Finland. Several factors underline the constitutional differences between Ireland in the 1840s and Finland in the 1860s. Partly as a response to Russian economic difficulties after the Crimean War, the Finns had launched their own currency, the *markka*, in 1860, a degree of financial autonomy that was of course unthinkable in nineteenth-century Ireland. And yet, the financial reforms that were being undertaken, and the Senate's desire to act as independently as possible from St Petersburg, arguably had the effect of swamping the Finnish administration with monetary and social problems.[54] From an Irish perspective, it is worthy of comment that British sources condemned the Russian relief effort for the Finns as being 'scanty and tardy', adding that:

> seeing it fail ... the Imperial Government had recourse to a new method for getting rid of its responsibility in the matter. The semi-official *Invalide Russe* first announced to the public ... that the 'Grand Duchy of Finland'

> was entirely independent of the control of the central government, and that its own administration was alone to be blamed for the insufficiency of proper arrangements for stemming the current of famine.[55]

This was disingenuous, and wilfully misconstrued the relationship between Finland and Russia at this stage. The crisis of 1862 also saw the Finnish Senate raise short-term 'emergency loans' from St Petersburg, prefiguring some larger international loans that were negotiated in the later 1860s as they sought to balance the national accounts.[56] This national-level philosophy was also encouraged on the micro level. The influential Helsinki-based newspaper *Suometar*, for example, used the widespread dearth of 1862 to encourage individual thriftiness and the spirit of self-development.[57] As Häkkinen and Forsberg argue, some parts of Finland 'especially in the north, were by now perceived by the core elite in Helsinki to be chronically poor, and a belief grew that the peasants had to be made thriftier, less lazy, more self-sustained and less dependent on the Emperor's feeding hand' – indeed, some of the rhetoric coming from the elites in Helsinki about their compatriots in the peripheral parts of Finland would not have been out of place in *Punch* articles about Irish tenants.[58]

As Peter Gray notes, however, the events of 1845 to 1850 were never construed as a 'Great British Famine', and the different constitutional context, again, may be seen as the main reason why this similar rhetoric did not lead to similar alienation among the rural Finns as it would among many in Ireland.[59] Moreover, the 1862 emergency – which was perceived as 'even more severe than 1856' – presented an opportunity to underline the coherence of the Finnish nation: *Suometar* argued that Finns working with fellow Finns to prevent individual and national destitution would 'bind together the children of the fatherland with an iron grip'.[60] This combination of political and fiscal autonomy, with energetic nation building which promoted austerity and self-improvement, goes some way towards explaining the vastly different roles played by the Great Famines in the subsequent histories of Finland and Ireland. The Finnish government saw a chance, not only to stand alone, but also to promote national coherence.

After two normal harvests, the summer of 1866 again saw a partial failure, which resulted in further depletion of grain reserves. Worse was yet to come. Snow cover during the winter of 1866/1867 was extraordinarily thick, and the spring of 1867 unusually cold. Frequent blizzards continued into late May, and flooding was widespread, which delayed the sowing season.[61] Before the crops had a chance to ripen, night frosts in early September 1867 destroyed the entire harvest in northern Finland, triggering a much wider famine than anything else seen during the previous decade.[62]

As Finland had economic autonomy, the imperial government in St Petersburg had no obligation to give, or even lend, money to Finland. Within the Grand Duchy, local authorities and landowners remained primarily responsible for poor relief.[63] Moreover, Russia had its own crop failure and economic crisis to address. A special commission was formed in St Petersburg in February 1868 to consider the best ways of relieving the famine-affected areas of the Russian Empire. Finland was included among these areas, but the problems were much more extensive, affecting 13 other Governorates – with a combined population of over ten million people – in the western part of the Empire. From the Russian perspective, this was the context in which relief for Finland had to operate.[64] Nevertheless, the message of a 'unified Finnish people' ruled from Helsinki was not quite getting through to all the inhabitants.[65] A belief prevailed in some eastern regions of Finland that St Petersburg would come to the rescue. This had been the case to a degree in the 1850s, but the idea was based more on the folk memory of 'Jauho Kaisa' – Catherine the Great – who had provided occasional relief during the eighteenth century despite Finland being the responsibility of the King of Sweden.[66]

Following on from their short-term loans in 1862, the Finnish government had taken out two further loans in 1866, totalling over three million marks, from the Finnish Mortgage Society and the Frankfurt-based banker M.A. von Rothschild and Söhne.[67] With state coffers now almost empty, Snellman wrote to the Governor of Oulu province in 1867 that 'the state has no money to give, neither as a gift nor as a loan.... Every penny which from now on is used for emergency help must be borrowed.'[68] That money, again, came from the Rothschilds, who lent Finland 5.4 million Finnish marks for 12 months. This was a considerable undertaking, representing a quarter to one-third of Finland's annual state income during the 1860s.[69] Although the entire amount was transferred to the relief fund in late September 1867, it was too small to contribute substantially to solving the problem of a nationwide famine. The government sought to alleviate the agricultural crisis by supplying edible and seed grain for the three northern provinces. This measure failed for several reasons: the administration had borrowed an insufficient amount of money from international money markets; high grain prices limited acquisitions; Finnish merchants were unwilling to purchase foreign grain on the government's terms; and because an early winter halted shipping and therefore grain distribution.

What occurred in Finland, therefore, provides an example of a 'Home Rule' government attempting, but ultimately failing, to cope with a national-scale calamity. Despite the warning signs provided by the famine conditions of 1856/1857 and 1862, the authorities in Helsinki realised only gradually – from 1865 – the full potential disaster that the Grand Duchy could experience from repeated harvest failures.

Further areas for comparative study

Therefore, while the issues around landholding and governance demonstrate major contrasts in the development of, and responses to, the crises in Finland and Ireland, there are several other related issues that should be scrutinised.

The role of religion

Intrinsically linked to poor relief in the nineteenth century, religion is one of the most notable differences between the two countries, and one of most regularly highlighted contrasts in discussions of Ireland and Finland in the nineteenth century. In Ireland, the population was largely Roman Catholic, which had a certain impact on the way in which the British administration and indeed sections of the British public reacted to the disaster, especially regarding philanthropy. Catholicism 'othered' Ireland within the British Isles, as was made explicit in Edward Wilmot's 1846 pamphlet *Threatened Famine a Divine Judgement for National Unfaithfulness*. Here, Wilmot argued that 'it is difficult to controvert the assertion that, under God, our national eminence is entirely to be attributed to that which has formed the distinctive feature of our national character, viz., our Protestantism'.[70] The idea that Catholic Ireland had to be reformed, and that the Great Famine was an opportunity to realise these reforms, has been a prominent feature of Irish famine discourse. There were of course class and ethnic elements that could be added into the political rhetoric when necessary, but the memories of soup kitchens that forced the hungry to recant their Catholicism have foregrounded the 'Protestant' attitudes of British legislators and charities.[71]

In Finland, the population was almost exclusively Lutheran in most of the country, which meant that there was no religious divide between the landed classes and the landless peasants. However, as Häkkinen and Forsberg note (Chapter 4, this volume), this has also created a historiography – keen to highlight Finland's homogeneity and cultural affinity with Scandinavian customs such as the free peasantry – that has failed to address the role played by Lutheran state religion in acquiescing in, or even deepening, some of the social divisions which existed in nineteenth-century Finland. These divisions, in turn, may have contributed to famine mortality. British Quaker activists who participated in fundraising for the starving Finns used very similar methods and rhetoric to those seen during their work in Ireland. Here the Finns' situation could not be attributed to Catholicism, but the people were perceived to be socially and economically backward, and in need of 'improvement'.[72] The Finnish case demonstrates that although some British attitudes towards Irish poverty conformed to standard anti-Catholic discourse, very similar attitudes could be found in Helsinki towards peripheral parts of Finland, stripped of any obvious religious subtext.[73] In Finland they have been subjected to social, rather than religious or ethnic, critiques.[74]

Emigration

When William Campbell, the British Consul General in Helsinki, wrote in 1870 that famine had not caused Finnish tenants to emigrate, his observation was prompted by the memory of the Great Irish Famine.[75] Whereas the haemorrhaging of population was widely noted by contemporaries in Ireland, and became an important feature of its post-famine political landscape, the same cannot be said of Finland. The Great Irish Famine accelerated emigration and had a clear impact upon the post-famine economic recovery of the island. In the period 1850 to 1913 more than 4.5 million Irish people emigrated.[76] In Finland, emigration during, and after, the famine years occurred at a considerably lower level. The transatlantic emigration of Finns began to increase only in the 1890s, but never reached the same high levels as from the neighbouring Scandinavian countries, or from Ireland.

Finnish migration in the 1860s was primarily internal, or within the Russian Empire, particularly to nearby St Petersburg. Russia's capital was the fifth largest metropolis in Europe at the time, and it is said that in the early nineteenth century, 'more Finns lived in St. Petersburg than in any Finnish city'.[77] As Max Engman notes, these migrants came largely from the ranks of the Finnish rural proletariat, and their decision was generally influenced by economic problems in Finland.[78] In the years after 1868, Finns made up 2.6 per cent of the population of St Petersburg.[79] This is a lower proportion than the equivalent figures for the post-famine Irish in London (in 1841, some 3.9 per cent of London's inhabitants were Irish-born, rising to 4.6 per cent in 1851),[80] but St Petersburg provided a consistent opportunity for migrant Finns.[81]

It was only in the 1880s, following the establishment of a regular service between the southern Finnish port of Hanko, and Hull in England, that 'American Fever' truly took hold in Finland. Also absent in Finland was the more general idea of 'assisted' (or 'forced' emigration), which had long been held up as a solution for Ireland's over-population and economic difficulties, and would again be proposed during and after the *Gorta Beag* ('Little Hunger') of 1879/1880.[82] The Finnish case serves to underline the prevalence of emigration within the general Irish famine narrative – it as also a reminder that famine and transatlantic emigration are not necessarily interlinked. In addition, the small-scale emigration that took place from Finland during the 1860s was again framed by a discourse of general economic depression rather than 'famine'. This movement occurred in the context of a developing national identity that promoted self-sufficiency and self-improvement, meaning that those qualities also came to underpin Finnish-American identity. This, in turn, countered 'the development of a radical Finnish emigrant opposition to the imperial power'.[83]

Language

The Great Famine 'massively escalated' the decline of Irish Gaelic, not least because of the emigration and death which dramatically thinned the population of the strongest Irish-speaking areas.[84] In pre-famine Finland, the territory of the nation was to some extent defined by the vernacular use of Finnish, rather than it being a language that had been pushed to the periphery. Most people in Finland spoke Finnish as their native language in 1800, as they still did in 1900. Moreover, the population of Finland recovered soon after the mortality crisis of 1868. In fact, the 1860s was a decade of justified optimism for the Finnish language. The Language Decree of 1863 stated that within 20 years Finnish was to receive, for the first time in history, official language status alongside Swedish.[85] The 1860s' language decrees were later presented as 'a sort of Magna Carta for the Finnish-speaking part of the nation'.[86] There was enormous enthusiasm to elevate Finnish into a 'language of civilisation', and one consequence of this was that publishing in Finnish soared during the post-famine decades. The output growth of the printing sector was the second fastest of all industries, just after the paper-making industry.[87] The first significant novel written in Finnish (and by a Finnish speaker) was Aleksis Kivi's *Seven Brothers*, published in 1870.[88] Kivi had worked on the book during the famine years, and after its publication it was criticised for its 'crude, uncivilised and unidealistic' portrayal of rural life in Finland.[89] Subsequently, however, it has been argued that the book 'had a major impact on the construction of the Finns' self-image'.[90] The book also made a significant contribution to the growth of Finnish as a literary language. Therefore, while the Great Famine has been closely linked to the acceleration of language decline in Ireland, this was far from the case in Finland. In 1800, Finnish had not been an official language, or language of the upper estates, but by 1900 Finnish had gained official status and the upper strata had switched from speaking Swedish to speaking Finnish.

Memorialising and politicising the famines

In the context of this volume, Finland presents an example of a famine that was not appropriated for nationalist or separatist agendas. The Irish and Ukrainian famines have been politicised, and their categorisation as genocides has been fiercely debated. Tim Pat Coogan's 2012 book on the Great Famine was entitled *The Famine Plot*, promoting the idea that the 'English' government was responsible for a genocide in Ireland.[91] The establishment of memorials demonstrates the centrality of famine to a collective national memory in modern Ireland. There is a National Famine Museum in Strokestown, County Roscommon, and a National Famine Memorial in Murrisk, County Mayo, along with an estimated 140 memorials to the Great Irish Famine worldwide.[92]

The Finnish case presents a strong contrast. There is no national monument, let alone national museum, to victims of Finland's Great Famine. Neither is there any serious acknowledgement of the catastrophe in the National Museum of Finland. These omissions add strength to the idea that the years 1867 and 1868, despite the great spike in mortality, have been contextualised in the *national* consciousness as an element of the economic growing pains of a new nation. Moreover, 'memory studies' in Finland have, understandably, focused less on the nineteenth century and more on the twentieth: the trauma of a Civil War in 1918 that led to the deaths of 30,000 people; the Winter War of 1939/1940; or the Continuation War of 1941 to 1944.[93]

On a local level, matters are rather different, with memorials in various parts of the country, highlighting a variety of tragedies relating to the famine years, such as disease and deaths in railway construction.[94] The Memorial to the Railway Workers, for example, situated in the southern Finnish town of Lahti, commemorates the 1,000 people who died (in a municipality of 7,000) in 1868. Those who perished after migrating to find work in constructing the Riihimäki to St Petersburg line (known colloquially as the *Nälkärata* (Hunger Line) or *Luurata* (Skeleton Line)) could not be accommodated in the parish cemetery, and therefore a new burial site had to be created.[95] The general submersion of the local beneath the national, and certainly the promotion of the national over the imperial, is part of the cementing of the idea of a coherent nation.[96] As noted above in the context of emigration, key concepts of self-sufficiency and self-criticism militated against seeking any perpetrator for Finland's woes beyond its own borders. The contrast is conspicuous, because although in Finland the famine years have been used in the process of national identity building, they have been presented more often as a learning process or a hardship that stimulated and increased the stamina and resourcefulness of the people. In his seminal poem *Saarijärven Paavo* the Finnish national poet Johan Ludvig Runeberg wanted to describe the persistent '*sisu*' of Finns and their optimism that finally made them succeed and reap good harvests.[97] In *Nälkäwuodet 1860-luvulla* (*The Hunger Years of the 1860s*), published in 1892, the nationalist politician and academic writer Agathon Meurman stated that the railway track between Riihimäki and St Petersburg represented the grandest monument and the noblest sacrifice that the starving famine victims had donated to future generations. As a result, there was no need for other monuments.[98]

Conclusion

The immediate trigger for the major famines in nineteenth-century Ireland and Finland was similar – an exceptional natural shock: in Ireland it was potato blight, and in Finland devastating summer frost. Although the crop failures in Finland and Ireland were caused by environmental factors, the famines in both countries were primarily a result of economic, administrative and political failures with marked social and demographic consequences. The Irish and Finnish mode of agricultural production was unable to resist and overcome external shocks and the government's relief measures were insufficient. However, disturbances of these types do not necessarily cause a long-lasting societal calamity.

In terms of depopulation, Finland suffered 100,000 excess deaths and levels of emigration that numbered in the thousands. Both of these statistics are dwarfed by their equivalents in the Irish case. Demographically and economically, Finland recovered much more quickly. In Finland, the acute mortality crises, during three consecutive years, peaked in one catastrophic year, whereas in Ireland above-average death rates continued for more than four years. Although Ireland's 'post-famine adjustment' brought with it a certain amount of 'prosperity and innovation' in the period 1854 to 1876, its population has never returned to the levels seen in 1841.[99] In Finland, however, the economic vigour of the 1870s has seen the famine years being presented as the harbinger of modernity in the country.[100] It is very difficult indeed to separate the reforms of the period into pre- and post-famine categories, something made clear by Häkkinen and Forsberg, but it may be said that the Great Finnish Famine, at worst, did not delay economic progress by any significant amount.[101] Finland's industrialisation accelerated because of exceptionally strong demands on the European market for the country's staple export products: sawn timber, cardboard and paper. The entire national economy experienced a period of strong growth. Therefore, after seven meagre years (1862–1868) Finland experienced seven years of economic expansion (1869–1875).

It has been argued that an 'important difference' between the two cases was the 'autonomous constitutional framework' which allowed Finland to 'fail alone, rather than be saved by Russian intervention'.[102] Cormac Ó Gráda has noted that 'the role of politics and relief seem to loom larger in the historiography of the Irish than of the Finnish famine', and it is true that Finland's constitutional status seems to have created a very different historiography.[103] The Finnish example also demonstrates that such calamities under an imperial system do not necessarily lead to political separatism. John Mitchel's adage that 'The Almighty, indeed, sent the potato blight, but the English created the famine' appears so regularly in famine research that it has become something of a cliché.[104] However, it bears repeating here because the Finnish case demonstrates that even in a less-contested political situation, control over resources and governmental policies can exacerbate natural or climactic shocks. The emphasis on self-sufficiency and unity through adversity, perhaps, discouraged the idea in Finland that 'the Almighty sent the frost, but the politicians in Helsinki created the famine'.

Notes

1 This work was supported by the Academy of Finland under Grants #264940, #257696 and #259881. The authors would like to acknowledge constructive comments from Brian Casey, Michael Coleman, Chris Cusack, Dave Dunne, Lindsay Janssen, and the anonymous referees, in the development of this chapter.

2 Most recently, see Oona Frawley, *Memory Ireland: Volume Three – The Famine and The Troubles* (Syracuse, NY: Syracuse University Press, 2014).

3 For a useful summary of the course of Irish famine historiography, see 'Introduction', in *Atlas of the Great Irish Famine*, ed. John Crowley, William J. Smyth and Mike Murphy (Cork: Cork University Press, 2012), xii–xvi.

4 Cormac Ó Gráda, *Ireland: A New Economic History* (Oxford: Oxford University Press, 1994), 208.

5 A recent economic history of Finland explained almost casually that 'in the late 1860s Finland experienced the last known major peacetime famine, losing one-tenth of its population through starvation' – tackling this catastrophe in a single sentence before moving on to brighter matters. See Jari Ojala, Jari Eloranta and Jukka Jalava (eds), *The Road to Prosperity: An Economic History of Finland* (Helsinki: SKS, 2006), 73.

6 Admittedly, there is a surprising lack of information on the 1860s famine in some general histories. Neither Jutikkala and Pirinen nor Jussila *et al.* mention the famine at all. Osmo Jussila, Seppo Hentilä and Jukka Nevakivi, *From Grand Duchy to a Modern State: A Political History of Finland since 1809* (London: Hurst, 1999); Eino Jutikkala and Kauko Pirinen, *A History of Finland*. (Rev. edn Helsinki: WSOY, 2003). As an example of a general Finnish-language history of the Grand Duchy period, Osmo Jussila's *Suomen Suuriruhtinaskunta: 1809–1917* (Helsinki: WSOY, 2004) has a single brief mention (p. 62) in its 832 pages.

7 These include: Anders Svedberg, *Mitä on Tekeminen Hädän Poistamiseksi, jos Katovuosi Tänäkin Vuonna Kohtaa Maatamme* (Nikolainkaupunki: Waasan Läänin

Maanviljelysseuran Kustannus, 1867); Evert Julius Bonsdorff, *Försök att utreda orsakerna till missväxten i Finland, och de medel, genom hvilka denna kan förekommas lättast uthärdas* (Helsingfors: n.p., 1870); Karl August Tavaststjerna, *Hårda Tider: Berättelse från Finlands Sista Nödår* (Helsingfors: Söderström & Co, 1891); Agaton Meurman, *Nälkäwuodet 1860-luwulla* (Helsinki: Kansanvalistusseura, 1892); Santeri Alkio, *Murtavia Voimia: Kuvauksia Katovuoden 1867 Ajoilta* (Porvoo: Söderström, 1896); J.V. Tallqvist, 'Missväxter på 1860-talet Utövade på den Ekonomiska Företagsamheten i Landet', in *Ekonomiska Samfundets Föredrag och Förhandlingar* (Helsingfors: G.W. Edlund, 1898); Edvard Gylling, 'Nälkävuodet 1867–68: Puolivuosisataismuisto', in *Työväen Kalenteri* XI 1918 (Helsinki: Sosialidemokratinen Puoluetoimikunta, 1917), 110–121. Slightly later, but also notable as a pioneer in Finnish famine studies, was Richard Sievers' account of the famine-related typhus epidemics of the 1860s: Richard Sievers, *Tyfusfarsoterna i Finland under Nödåren pä 1860-talet* (Helsingfors: Mercator, 1930).

8 See e.g. Antti Hakkinen (ed.), *Just a Sack of Potatoes? Crisis Experiences in European Societies, Past and Present* (Helsinki: SHS, 1992); Kari J. Pitkänen, *Deprivation and Disease: Mortality During the Great Finnish Famine of the 1860s* (Helsinki: Finnish Demographic Society, 1993). Oiva Turpeinen's influential work on disease mortality has not been translated into English, although there is a brief English summary in Oiva Turpeinen, *Nälkä vai Tauti Tappoi? Kauhunvuodet 1866–1868* (Helsinki: Societas Historica Finlandiae, 1986), 300–306.

9 Varpu Ikonen, 'Kaksi 1800-luvun nälkäkriisiä – Suomi ja Irlanti', in Antti Häkkinen, Vappu Ikonen, Kari Pitkänen and Hannu Soikkanen (eds), *Kun Halla Nälän Tuskan Toi* (Porvoo: WSOY, 1991), 273–282.

10 Bill Kissane, 'Nineteenth Century Nationalism in Finland and Ireland: A Comparative Analysis', *Nationalism and Ethnic Politics* 6(2), (2000), 25–42.

11 William J. Smyth, 'The *Longue Durée*: Imperial Britain and Colonial Ireland', in *Atlas of the Great Irish Famine*, ed. John Crowley, William J. Smyth and Mike Murphy (Cork: Cork University Press, 2012), 61.

12 Fred Singleton, *A Short History of Finland* (2nd edn, rev. A. Upton), Cambridge: Cambridge University Press, 1998), 76, 91–96.

13 'Mr. Gladstone at Midlothian', *Freeman's Journal*, 28 October 1890.

14 Newby, 'Cold Northern Land of Suomi', 76.

15 Bill Kissane, 'Victory in Defeat? National Identity after Civil War in Finland and Ireland', in *Nationalism and War*, ed. John A. Hall and Siniša Malešević (Cambridge: Cambridge University Press, 2013), 323.

16 'Obscure Men of Good Intention', *Memoranda of Irish Matters* (Dublin: Samuel J. Machen, 1844), 43. Although pseudonymously authored, the 'Obscure Men' are sometimes presented as the Dublin-born anthropologist and poet Hercules Ellis (who appears at several points in the book).

17 Quoted in Joep Leerssen, *National Thought in Europe: A Cultural History* (Amsterdam: Amsterdam University Press, 2006), 56.

18 William A. Douglass, 'Sabino's Sin: Racism and the Founding of Basque Nationalism', in Daniele Conversi, *Ethnonationalism in the Contemporary World: Walker Connor and the Study of Nationalism* (London: Routledge, 2002), 107.

19 In Finland, for example, 'famines' received international attention in 1893 and 1902. In Ireland, the 'Little Famine' (*Górta Beag*) of 1879 caused widespread destitution, especially in the west, and has been seen as a possible trigger for the 'Land War'. See Donald E. Jordan, Jr., *Land and Popular Politics in Ireland: County Mayo from the Plantation to the Land War* (Cambridge: Cambridge University Press, 1994), 204.

20 E. Margaret Crawford (ed.), 'William Wilde's Table of Irish Famines 900–1850', in *Famine: The Irish Experience*, ed. E. Margaret Crawford (Edinburgh: John Donald, 1989), 1–30.

21 Timo Myllyntaus, 'Summer Frost: A Natural Hazard with Fatal Consequences in Pre-Industrial Finland', in *Natural Disasters, Cultural Responses: Case Studies Toward a Global Environmental History*, ed. Christof Mauch and Christian Pfister (Lanham, MD: Lexington Books, 2009), 80.
22 Armas K.E. Holmio, *History of the Finns in Michigan* (Hancock, MI: Great Lakes Books, 2001), 418.
23 David Dickson, *Arctic Ireland: The Extraordinary Story of the Great Frost and Famine of 1740–41* (Belfast: White Row Press, 1997), 11–16; Cormac Ó Gráda, *Famine: A Short History* (Princeton, NJ: Princeton University Press, 2009), 72.
24 Anon., *The Groans of Ireland: In a Letter to a Member of Parliament* (Dublin: George Faulkner, 1741), 3; quoted in Crawford, 'William Wilde's Table', 14.
25 Helen Carr, 'Modernism and Travel (1880–1940)', in *The Cambridge Companion to Travel Writing*, ed. Peter Hulme and Tim Youngs (Cambridge: Cambridge University Press, 2002), 73.
26 Anssi Halmesvirta, *The British Conception of the Finnish Race Nation and Culture, 1760–1918* (Helsinki: SHS, 1990), 143.
27 For these data, collated by the late Professor Angus Maddison, see www.ggdc.net/maddison/Maddison.htm (accessed 10 October 2014).
28 Antti Häkkinen and Henrik Forsberg, 'Finland's famine years of the 1860s: a nineteenth-century perspective' (Chapter 4, this volume).
29 Gerard McCann, *Ireland's Economic History: Crisis and Development in the North and South* (London: Pluto Press, 2011), 5–34.
30 Jason E. Lavery, *The History of Finland* (Westport, CT: Greenwood Press, 2006), 53–54.
31 Liam Kennedy, *Colonialism, Religion and Nationalism in Ireland* (Belfast: QUB Institute of Irish Studies, 1996), 68.
32 Smyth, *The Longue Durée*, 63.
33 Iván T. Berend and György Ránki, *The European Periphery and Industrialisation 1780–1914* (Cambridge: Cambridge University Press, 1982). Berend and Ránki also, however, note the relatively high levels of literacy in Scandinavia and Finland. See Hannu Soikkanen, 'Social Preconditions for the Modernisation of Finnish Society', in *Economic Development in Hungary and Finland, 1860–1939*, ed. Tapani Mauranen (Helsinki: University of Helsinki, 1985), 195.
34 Risto Alapuro, *Finland: An Interface Periphery* (Helsinki: University of Helsinki, 1980), 20–54; Erik Allardt, *Finnish Society: Relationship Between Geopolitical Situation and the Development of Society* (Helsinki: University of Helsinki, 1985), 7–11.
35 Alexander J. Motyl, *Imperial Ends: The Decay, Collapse and Decline of Empires* (New York: Columbia University Press, 2001), 14–15.
36 See Jürgen Kocka, 'Core, Periphery and Civil Society', in *Cores, Peripheries and Globalization: Essays in Honor of Ivan T. Berend*, ed. Peter Hanns Reill and Balázs A. Szelényi (Budapest: Central European University Press, 2011), 97–99.
37 Keijo Korhonen, *Autonomous Finland in the Political Thought of Nineteenth Century Russia* (Turku: Turun Yliopisto, 1967), 49.
38 Risto Alapuro, 'Nineteenth Century Nationalism in Finland: A Comparative Study', *Scandinavian Political Studies* 2(1), (1979), 23–24. For example, in 1860 the per capita income of Finland was 25 per cent higher than that of Russia 'Proper'. See Erkki Pihkala, 'The Finnish Economy and Russia, 1809–1917', in *Finland and Poland in the Russian Empire*, ed. Michael Branch, Janet M. Hartley and Antoni Mączak (London: SSEES, 1995), 153.
39 John R. Butterfly and Jack Shepherd, *Hunger: The Biology and Politics of Starvation* (Dartmouth: Dartmouth College Press, 2010), 50–51.
40 Christine Kinealy, *Charity and the Great Hunger: The Kindness of Strangers* (London: Bloomsbury, 2013), 50.

41 Barry Crosbie, *Irish Imperial Networks: Migration, Social Communication and Exchange in Nineteenth-century India* (Cambridge: Cambridge University Press, 2012), 8; Jill Bender, 'The Imperial Politics of Famine: The 1873–74 Bengal Famine and Irish Parliamentary Nationalism', *Éire-Ireland* 42 (2007), 132–156; Kevin Kenny (ed.), *Ireland and the British Empire* (Oxford: Oxford University Press, 2004).

42 David G. Kirby, *Finland in the Twentieth Century: A History and an Interpretation* (London: Hurst & Co, 1979), 6–7.

43 Peter Gray, *The Irish Famine* (London: Thames and Hudson, 1995), 58; Donnelly, *The Great Irish Potato Famine*, 41–43.

44 Juhani Paasivirta, *Finland and Europe: The Period of Autonomy and the International Crises 1808–1914* (London: Hurst & Co, 1981), 60.

45 Andrew G. Newby, '"Rather Peculiar Claims Upon Our Sympathies": Britain and Famine in Finland, 1856–68', in *Global Legacies of the Great Irish Famine: Transnational and Interdisciplinary Perspectives*, ed. Marguérite Corporaal, Christopher Cusack, Lindsay Janssen and Ruud van den Beuken (Bern: Peter Lang, 2014), 64–65.

46 Oiva Turpeinen, *Oolannin Sota: Itämäinen Sota Suomessa* (Helsinki: Tammi, 2003); Basil Greenhill and Ann Giffard, *The British Assault on Finland 1854–55: A Forgotten Naval War* (London: Naval Institute Press, 1988).

47 William R. Mead, 'The Conquest of Finland', *The Norseman* 9 (1951), 14–22, 98–104.

48 *Report of the Committee for the Relief of Famine in Finland* (London: Richard Barrett, 1858), 19.

49 *Morning Post*, 19 September 1866. See also the detailed earlier report in *Finlands Allmänna Tidning*, 28 December 1864; John Ormerod Greenwood, *Quaker Encounters (1): Friends and Relief* (York: Sessions, 1975), 32.

50 *Report of the Committee for the Relief of Famine in Finland*, 16.

51 'Extracts from William Bennett's Account of his Journey in Ireland', Transactions of the Central Relief Committee of the Society of Friends during the Famine in Ireland in 1846 and 1847 (Dublin: Hodges & Smith, 1852), 161.

52 Newby, 'Rather Peculiar Claims', 68.

53 Teija Tiilikainen, *Europe and Finland: Defining the Political Identity of Finland in Western Europe* (Aldershot: Ashgate, 1998), 73.

54 Häkkinen and Forsberg, Chapter 4, this volume.

55 'Famine in Finland', *The Spectator*, 10 January 1863.

56 Mika Arola, *Foreign Capital and Finland: Central Government's First Period of Reliance on International Financial Markets, 1862–1938* (Helsinki: State Treasury/Bank of Finland, 2006), 134.

57 'Hädästä ja sen Aputoimista', *Suometar*, 19 September 1862.

58 Michael de Nie, *The Eternal Paddy: Irish Identity and the British Press, 1798–1882* (Madison, WI: University of Wisconsin Press, 2004), 11–13, 96–97; Matti Klinge, *Keisarin Suomi* (Helsinki, 1997), 237–243; Helge Pohjola-Pirhonen and Veikko Huttunen, *Kansakunnan Historia 2: Kansakunta Etsii Itseään 1772–1808* (Porvoo, 1970), 121–122.

59 Peter Gray, Chapter 3, this volume. To return to the counter-factual idea of there having been a Parliament in Dublin in the 1840s, it is interesting to consider the extent to which an assembly composed of an urban elite and members of the landowning classes may have reacted towards distress among the cottier tenants of the west.

60 'Hädästä ja sen Aputoimista', *Suometar*, 19 September 1862.

61 K.R. Melander and Gustaf Melander, 'Katovuosista Suomessa', 358.

62 Myllyntaus, 'Summer Frost', 90.

63 Oiva Turpeinen, *Nälkä vai Tauti Tappoi: Kauhunvuodet 1866–68* (Helsinki: SHS, 1985), 3–6.

64 Turpeinen, *Nälka vai Tauti*, 143; *The Cambridge History of Russia: Volume 2: Imperial Russia, 1689–1917*, 258. Discussion of the creation in 1864 of 'zemstvos', which provided a basic societal structure and, for example, famine relief, providing a 'solid foundation for the emergence of modern civil society'. See also R. Robbins, Jr., *Famine in Russia, 1891–92: The Imperial Government Responds to a Crisis* (New York: Columbia University Press, 1975).

65 Maria Lähteenmäki, *The Peoples of Lapland: Boundary Demarcations and Interaction in the North Calotte from 1808 to 1889* (Helsinki: Finnish Academy of Science and Letters, 2005), 179–181.

66 'Jauho Kaisa' translates as 'Flour Cathy', in memory of the meal handouts provided by the Russian government during times of hardship in eastern Finland. Helge Pohjolan-Pirhonen, *Kansakunnan Historia 2: Kansakunta Estii Itseään 1772–1808* (Porvoo: WSOY, 1972), 122; Matti Klinge, *Keisarin Suomi* (Espoo: Schildt, 1997), 237–243. Military granaries were opened by the Russian authorities in 1857. See e.g. *The Times*, 17 February 1857.

67 Mika Arola, *Foreign Capital and Finland: Central Government's First Period of Reliance on International Financial Markets, 1862–1938* (Helsinki: State Treasury/Bank of Finland, 2006), 133.

68 Quoted in Arola, *Foreign Capital and Finland*, 135.

69 Arola, *Foreign Capital and Finland*, 134–135.

70 Edward R.E. Wilmot, *Threatened Famine a Divine Judgement for National Unfaithfulness. A Sermon* (London, 1846), 14.

71 Irene Whelan, 'The Stigma of Souperism', in *The Great Irish Famine*, ed. Cathal Póirtéir (Dublin: RTÉ/Mercier, 1995), 135–154.

72 Newby, 'Rather Peculiar Claims', 71.

73 Häkkinen and Forsberg, Chapter 4, this volume.

74 Tuomas Jussila, 'Nälkävirret: 1860-luvun Nälkävuosien Historiakuva Pietari Päivärinnan, Juho Reijosen ja Teuvo Pakkalan Teoksissa'. Unpublished MA thesis, University of Tampere, 2013; Henrik Forsberg, 'Nälkäkuolema kansallishyveenä? Viimeiset Nälkävuodet Suomalaisessa Kirjallisessa Historiakulttuurissa 1870–1900', *Historiallinen Aikakauskirja* 109 (2011), 267–280. These did, of course, have their equivalents in Ireland. Perhaps the most notable was James Connolly's reformulation of John Mitchel's famous adage: 'England made the famine by a rigid application of the economic principles that lie at the base of capitalist society.' See James Connolly, *Labour in Irish History* (Dublin: Maunsell, 1910), 145.

75 William Campbell, 'Report by Consul Campbell on the Tenure of Land in the Grand Duchy of Finland' , in *Land Tenure (Europe): Accounts and Papers of the House of Commons lxviii* (1870), 255–256.

76 Timothy J. Hatton and Jeffrey G. Williamson, 'After the Famine: Emigration from Ireland, 1850–1913', *Journal of Economic History* 53(3) (1993), 575.

77 Paul Bushkovitch, *A Concise History of Russia* (Cambridge: Cambridge University Press, 2012), 257.

78 Max Engman, 'Migration from Finland to Russia during the Nineteenth Century', *Scandinavian Journal of History* 3 (1978), 159–160.

79 Bushkovitch, *Concise History of Russia*, 164.

80 Graham Davis, 'Little Irelands', in *The Irish in Britain, 1815–1939*, ed. Roger Swift and Sheridan Gilley (London: Rowman & Littlefield, 1989), 106.

81 Marjatta Rahikainen, 'Historical and Present-day Child Labour: Is There a Gap or Bridge Between Them?' *Continuity and Change* 16 (2001), 149; David Kirby, *Finland in the Twentieth Century: A History and an Interpretation* (London: Hurst & Co, 1979), 11.

82 Kerby A. Miller, *Emigrants and Exiles: Ireland and the Irish Exodus to North America* (Oxford: Oxford University Press, 1985), 347; Gerard Moran, '"From Galway to North America": State-Aided Emigration from County Galway in the

1880s', in *Galway: History and Society*, ed. Gerard Moran and Raymond Gillespie (Dublin: Geography Publications, 1996), 487–519.

83 Andrew G. Newby, '"Neither do these Tenants or their Children Emigrate": Famine and Transatlantic Emigration from Finland in the Nineteenth Century', *Atlantic Studies* 11(3) (2014), 395.

84 Michael C. Coleman, '"You Might All Be Speaking Swedish Today!": Language Change in Nineteenth Century Finland and Ireland', *Scandinavian Journal of History* 35(1) (2010), 51; Christine Kinealy, *A Death-dealing Famine: The Great Hunger in Ireland* (London: Pluto Press, 1997), 151; Peter Slomanson, 'Cataclysm as a Catalyst for Language-Shift', in *Global Legacies of the Great Irish Famine: Transnational and Interdisciplinary Perspectives*, ed. Marguérite Corporaal, Christopher Cusack, Lindsay Janssen and Ruud van den Beuken (Bern: Peter Lang, 2014), 81–100.

85 Katherine Schuster, 'Swedish-language Folkhögskolor in Finland: Ethnonationalism, Language, and Adult Education in the Nineteenth Century', in *Language of the Land: Policy, Politics, Identity*, ed. Katherine Schuster and David Witkosky (Charlotte, NC: Information Age Publishing, 2007), 32.

86 Singleton, *Short History of Finland* (2nd edn), 90.

87 Timo Myllyntaus, *The Growth and Structure of Finnish Print Production, 1840–1900* (Helsinki: University of Helsinki, 1984).

88 Aleksis Kivi, *Seitsemän Veljestä* (Helsinki: Simelius, 1870), *Seven Brothers*, trans. Alex Matson (New York: Coward-McCann, 1929).

89 Matti Hyvärinen, 'The Fictional Versions of "Valta" (Power): Reading Aleksis Kivi, Arvid Järnefelt and Juhani Aho Conceptually', *Finnish Yearbook of Political Thought 1998, Vol. 2* (Jyväskylä: Sophi Academic Press, 1998), 209–210. Also quoted in Christopher S. Browning, *Constructivism, Narrative, and Foreign Policy Analysis: A Case Study of Finland* (Bern: Peter Lang, 2008), 85.

90 Browning, *Constructivism, Narrative, and Foreign Policy Analysis*, 85.

91 Tim Pat Coogan, *The Famine Plot: England's Role in Ireland's Greatest Tragedy* (Basingstoke: Palgrave Macmillan, 2012). After the publication of *The Famine Plot*, BBC Northern Ireland's radio show *Sunday Sequence* hosted a debate between Tim Pat Coogan and Liam Kennedy over the use of the term 'genocide' in relation to the Irish Famine. Available at: www.youtube.com/watch?v=7YTOXoyhXvY (accessed 17 July 2014).

92 Emily Mark-FitzGerald, *Commemorating the Irish Famine: Memory and the Monument* (Liverpool: Liverpool University Press, 2013). See also Emily Mark-Fitzgerald's online project, 'Irish Famine Memorials'. Available at: http://irishfaminememorials.com (accessed 10 September 2014).

93 Tuomas Tepora and Aapo Roselius (eds), *The Finnish Civil War 1918: History, Memory, Legacy* (Leiden: Brill, 2014); Hana Worthen and Simo Muir, 'Introduction: Contesting the Silences of History', in *Finland's Holocaust: Silences of History*, ed. Simo Muir and Hana Worthen (Basingstoke: Palgrave Macmillan, 2012), 1–30; Ville Kivimäki, 'Between Defeat and Victory: Finnish Memory Culture of the Second World War', *Scandinavian Journal of History* 37(4) (2012), 482–504. The civil wars and their legacies have also provided fruitful grounds for Irish–Finnish comparative work. See Bill Kissane, 'Victory in Defeat? National Identity After Civil War in Finland and Ireland', in *Nationalism and War*, ed. John A. Hall and Siniša Malešević (Cambridge: Cambridge University Press, 2013), 321–340.

94 According to Antti Häkkinen, there are approximately 50 famine memorials in Finland (personal correspondence with the author, 8 April 2013).

95 For details (in Finnish) and photographs of this memorial site, see www.lahdenseurakuntayhtyma.fi/henkilot_tilat/hautausmaat/radanrakentajien_hautausmaa (accessed 1 October 2014). It is estimated that around 300 victims were buried in this mass grave.

96 Lähteenmäki, *The Peoples of Lapland*, 179–181.
97 Johan Ludvig Runeberg, 'Bonden Paavo', in his anthology of poems *Dikter 1830*, ed. Olaf Homén (Åbo: Förlaget Bro, 1942) [1830)], 'Saarijärven Paavo', *Runoelmia*, translated into Finnish by A. Oksanen in 1845. '*Sisu*' is a concept that translates roughly as an amalgam of determination, bravery and resilience.
98 Meurman, *Nälkäwuodet*, 44, 78.
99 Myllyntaus, 'Summer Frost', 96; Cormac Ó Gráda, *Ireland Before and After the Famine: Explorations in Economic History, 1800–1925* (2nd edn, Manchester: Manchester University Press, 1993), 152.
100 Vesa Saarikoski, 'Yhteiskunnan Modernisoituminen', in *Suomalaisen Yhteiskunnan Poliittinen Historia*, ed. Ville Pernaa and Mari K. Niemi (Helsinki: Edita, 2005), 115–116.
101 Häkkinen and Forsberg, Chapter 4, this volume.
102 Newby, 'Neither do these Tenants or their Children Emigrate', 394.
103 Ó Gráda, *Ireland, A New Economic History*, 208.
104 John Mitchel, *The Last Conquest of Ireland (Perhaps)* (Glasgow: Cameron and Ferguson, 1876), 219.

Part III

Ukrainian Famine [*Holodomor*], 1932 to 1933

Direct famine losses in Ukraine by region (*oblast*), 1932 to 1934

This map was prepared by Kostyantyn Bondarenko and Gennadi Pobereżny as part of the Harvard Ukrainian Research Institute's Holodomor *Atlas Project. It is based on estimates of* Holodomor *losses derived under the 'Estimation of Regional Losses of the 1932 to 1934 Famine in Ukraine' project conducted by Dr Oleh Wolowyna (University of North Carolina at Chapel Hill), and Omelan Rudnytskyi, Nataliia Levchuk, Pavlo Shevchuk and Alla Savchuk (Institute of Demography and Social Studies in Kyiv).*

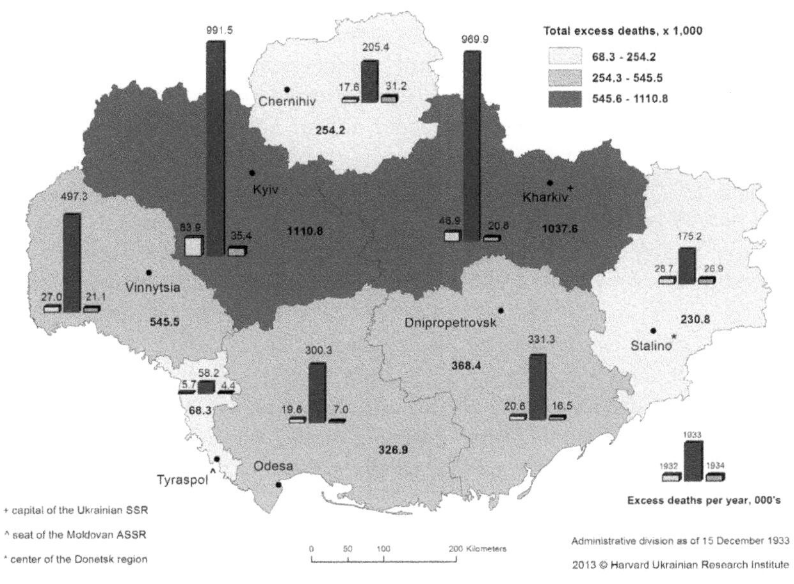

Map PIII.1 Direct famine losses in Ukraine by region, per 1,000 population, 1933.

Estimates of 1932 to 1934 direct (excess deaths) famine losses in Ukraine are based on detailed reconstructions of the population dynamics of the Ukrainian Soviet Socialist Republic by region (*oblast*) and by urban-rural areas in each *oblast*, for the inter-censal period 1926 to 1939, within the borders of the republic as of 6 January 1937. The political-administrative structure during the *Holodomor* years (more precisely as it existed on 15 December 1933) was used to make estimates for seven *oblasts*: Vinnytska (administrative centre – Vinnytsia), Kyivska (Kyiv), Chernihivska (Chernihiv), Kharkivska (Kharkiv), Donetska (Stalino), Dnipropetrovska (Dnipropetrovsk) and Odeska (Odesa) and the Autonomous Republic of Moldova (Tyraspol). Western Ukraine, southern Bessarabia and Crimea are not included as they were not part of Soviet Ukraine in 1932 to 1934.

Actual yearly numbers of deaths, births and net migrants were estimated by single year of age and sex, based on the following data for each of the eight regions: (1) urban and rural populations by age and sex from the 1926 and 1939 censuses; (2) urban and rural populations by sex from the 1937 census; (3) urban population count by age and sex in 1931; (4) yearly births and deaths by sex for urban and rural areas during the 1927 to 1938 period; (5) for all years except 1932, births by sex and age of mother and deaths by sex and age, for urban and rural areas; (6) yearly detailed migration for urban areas; (7) detailed data on forced and voluntary migration for rural areas; (8) urban-rural reclassification. These data were complemented by documents describing the characteristics of the different data collection systems, their quality and shortcomings. The 1926 and 1937 census data were adjusted for undercounts and other problems, while 1939 census data were adjusted to eliminate falsifications implemented to cover up large population losses due to the *Holodomor* and other repressive measures. Yearly registered births and deaths were adjusted for undercounts, especially during famine years when the undercount reached extreme levels. Based on these data, yearly populations were reconstructed by age and sex for the eight regions and by urban-rural areas.

Famine losses are operationally defined as the difference between actual estimated deaths (or births) from 1932 to 1934, and the number of hypothetical deaths (or births) had there been no famine. The difference in deaths is called direct losses or excess deaths; the difference in births is called indirect losses or lost births. The total number of 1932 to 1934 famine losses in Soviet Ukraine is estimated as 4.5 million, with 3.9 million direct losses and 0.6 million indirect losses. Absolute numbers of excess deaths in the seven *oblasts* and the Moldovan Republic are shown on this map. The shading of each region represents the total number of excess deaths during the 1932 to 1934 period, while bars in each region represent yearly excess deaths. Numbers of excess deaths for 1932 to 1934 are divided into three intervals, depicted by three different grey-scale shades, and the number for each region is shown on the map.

The map shows significant regional variations in the number of direct losses during the famine years. Kyivska and Kharkivska *oblasts* experienced the highest number of excess deaths from 1932 to 1934, with 1,110.8 and 1,037.6

thousand, respectively, totalling 54 per cent of all excess deaths. The second group is composed of Vinnytska *oblast* with 545.5 thousand, about half of the highest values, and Dnipropetrovska and Odeska *oblasts*, with 368.4 and 326.9 thousand, respectively. The third group is composed of Chernihivska *oblast* with 254.2 thousand, Donetska *oblast* with 230.8 thousand, and the Moldovan Autonomous Republic a distant third with 68.3 thousand excess deaths.Yearly estimates of direct losses show that in all regions the number of excess deaths in 1933 was vastly larger than the number of excess losses in 1932 and 1934. The total number of direct losses in 1933 was 3,529.2 thousand, while respective numbers in 1932 and 1934 were 250.0 and 163.3 thousand. In relative terms the number of direct losses per 1,000 population for the whole country was between 14 and 21 times larger in 1933 than in 1932 or 1934. Thus the famine had an overwhelming effect in 1933; most of these deaths actually took place during the first half of the year.

It should be pointed out that the absolute number of excess deaths in each region is a function of two factors: the age structure of excess deaths and the size of the population residing in each region. The effect of population size can be controlled by dividing the number of excess deaths by total population, i.e. excess deaths per 1,000 population. Using this indicator and focusing on 1933, Kyivska and Kharkivska *oblasts* had the highest number of relative excess deaths (183.5 and 175.9 excess deaths per 1,000 population, respectively), while Chernihivska and Donetska *oblasts* had the lowest number of relative excess deaths (75.8 and 41.0, respectively).

This is the first time that regional estimates of direct losses have been made for Ukraine, and they suggest questions and hypotheses that require more detailed demographic and historic research. Direct losses at the district (*raion*) level are likely to provide more precise data for testing more specific hypotheses, like the suggestion that the effects of the famine were likely to be less pronounced in border areas. Detailed analysis of historical evidence may provide more substantial explanations for these geopolitical variations.

Text by: Omelian Rudnytskyi,[1] Nataliia Levchuk,[1] Oleh Wolowyna[2] and Pavlo Shevchuk[1]

Notes

1 Ptoukha Institute of Demography and Social Studies at the National Academy of Sciences of Ukraine.
2 University of North Carolina at Chapel Hill.

7 The origins and course of the famine of 1932 to 1933 in Soviet Ukraine

Bohdan Klid

Introduction

In 1932 to 1933, in Soviet Ukraine, which has some of the best farmland in the world, about four million people, mostly Ukrainian peasants, starved to death in a man-made famine.[1] Triggered primarily by unrealistic grain-collection targets and policies adopted by the Soviet leadership to fulfil those plans, the artificial famine in Ukraine was part of a wider, pan-Soviet famine that also affected other regions of the Soviet Union.[2] In Soviet Ukraine, however, the famine was distinguished by its intensity and by the sheer number of deaths. During the famine years, the Soviet leadership paid close attention to Ukraine and made a number of key decisions that either focused on Ukraine or affected it more severely than other Soviet republics.[3] Moreover, the Soviet leadership linked the difficulties associated with fulfilling its grain-procurement targets in Ukraine with Ukrainian nationalism and launched a campaign against so-called Ukrainian nationalists in 1933. These special circumstances warrant a separate study of Soviet Ukraine in the famine years. This chapter will provide a background sketch on the establishment of Soviet rule and Soviet policies in Ukraine, particularly as they affected the peasantry prior to the famine years, and then focus on the famine's origins and on some of the decisions that determined its horrific course of development.

Background and prelude to the famine[4]

Soviet power was not easily established in Ukraine. Although there was support for the Bolshevik Party and the Bolshevik Revolution among the largely Russian and Russified proletariat in Ukraine's cities, Soviet rule was essentially brought to Ukraine from Bolshevik Russia by force of arms. Three attempts were required to establish it.

When the Russian monarchy fell in March 1917, Ukrainian intellectuals and civic leaders established the Central Rada (Council) in Kyiv, which soon developed into a legislative body. In the early summer of 1917 the Rada declared autonomy and established a government, the General Secretariat, headed by Ukrainian socialists. Following the Bolshevik seizure of power in Petrograd, the

Rada issued a declaration of sovereignty and established the Ukrainian People's Republic, briefly maintaining federative ties with a democratic Russia whose government had been overthrown. The Rada finally declared outright independence on 22 January 1918 in response to a military incursion from Bolshevik Russia in support of a rival Bolshevik-installed government in the eastern Ukrainian city of Kharkiv. This contender was established following the failure of Ukraine's Bolsheviks to oust the Central Rada from power in Kyiv. Bolshevik forces did succeed, however, in pushing Ukrainian government forces out of Kyiv in February 1918, which facilitated the Central Rada's decision to ally itself in a subordinate role with the Central Powers. Austro-German forces then provided military assistance to drive the Bolsheviks out of Ukraine and reinstated the Rada.

These developments marked the opening phase of a prolonged period of chaos and armed struggles for power in Ukraine, including foreign interventions (by Austro-German, Polish, French and various Russian forces), a civil war (between Bolshevik Red and White armies), battles between Ukrainian national and Bolshevik forces, and a radical transformation of the countryside, featuring the seizure and distribution of private estates and state properties among the peasants, numerous peasant riots, uprisings and guerrilla warfare.

In Ukraine in 1917, political parties that supported the Central Rada had widespread support in the countryside. In the elections to the Russian Constituent Assembly in November 1917, the pro-Ukrainian parties polled about two-thirds of the vote, which reflected popular sentiment for broad autonomy at the time. Meanwhile, peasant support for Ukrainian state building began to wane when the Rada hesitated to support the immediate distribution of estates, while the Bolshevik slogans of 'factories to the workers' and 'land to the peasants' gained them adherents. Thus, in Ukraine, the battles between supporters of the Central Rada and the Bolsheviks had socio-economic as well as political and national overtones. They also represented a struggle between the city and the countryside for control of the country.

Ukrainian peasants, who comprised the bulk of Ukraine's newly formed national army, proved less reliable than the city-based forces of the rival Bolsheviks. Many had fought in the Great War and were war-weary. They were also prone to return to their villages and families to deal with local matters, including the redistribution of land, which affected them personally. Back in their villages, these peasant soldiers, many of whom kept their arms, resorted at times to uprisings and revolts, and even formed regionally based armed forces supporting their version of the settlement of the land question.

Although most peasants were more interested in local matters – especially the land question – than national affairs, the formation of a national identity among Ukraine's peasantry was enhanced considerably during the brief existence of an autonomous and independent Ukrainian state. The Kuban Cossacks also formed their own Rada, were on friendly terms with Ukraine's government, and supported anti-Bolshevik leaders during the Civil War. This experience also promoted the development of a distinct Kuban Cossack identity.

Ukrainian peasant resistance to the establishment of Bolshevik rule became acute and widespread when the Soviet rulers first decided to promote communal farming in Ukraine as part of their communist programme. That decision was made in early 1919 under the second Soviet government installed in Ukraine, headed by Khristian Rakovsky. His government, which gained control over much of Ukraine following a successful military campaign against the forces of the Ukrainian People's Republic, began establishing state farms on the confiscated estates of large landowners and herding peasants into communal farms. Desperate to feed the industrial centres of the north and the Red Army, the Bolshevik government also sent military units into the countryside to requisition grain from the peasantry. Rakovsky's government collapsed in about seven months, a victim of Anton Denikin's White armies, Ukrainian national forces under Symon Petliura, who emerged as the strongman of the Ukrainian People's Republic, and peasant uprisings headed by local and regional insurgent leaders.

This first attempt to establish large-scale state and communal farms under Bolshevik tutelage thus failed. Ukrainian peasants rose en masse against the Bolsheviks, rejecting communal farming and work on state-run farms. They continued to support instead the partition and distribution of confiscated landowners' estates and state properties among themselves. They also fiercely opposed grain requisitions, which often left them with insufficient grain to feed their families, and treated requisitions as theft of the fruits of their labour.

Following the defeat of the White armies and those of the allied Polish and Ukrainian national forces led by Petliura in 1920, the third Soviet government in Ukraine allowed the peasants to partition and distribute confiscated estates in order to establish small farms but continued its grain requisitions. This again triggered peasant resistance and revolts. In 1921, the central Soviet government led by Lenin, faced with resistance on many fronts, an economy in chaos and ruin, and having only a tenuous grip on power, adopted the New Economic Policy (NEP), which established a fixed tax in place of the hated grain requisitioning. That same year southern Ukraine suffered from drought, which struck the southern Volga region of Russia particularly hard. The result was famine.

The northern regions of Ukraine, however, did not suffer from extreme drought, and enough grain was produced there to feed the hungry in southern Ukraine. All the same, Ukraine, still formally an independent state, was required by Russia to ship grain north to supply the Russian cities, and east to feed the hungry in the famished Volga region. Ukraine also had to feed the almost million-strong contingent of Red Army troops stationed in the country.

When in August 1921 Russia's Soviet government signed an agreement with the American Relief Agency (ARA), the Soviet Ukrainian government was not permitted to do so, and foreign aid was not allowed into the country. Moreover, grain taxes continued to be collected, even in the hungry south. It was only in January 1922, when widespread famine broke out in southern Ukraine, that Rakovsky's government was allowed to sign an agreement to receive aid from the ARA. Thus, although both Ukraine and Russia suffered from drought and famine, the Soviet authorities treated Ukraine differently from Russia. While peasants in the Volga region received aid, Ukrainian peasants suffering from hunger had to pay a grain tax. Moreover, grain was shipped out of the country. Although Ukraine was nominally independent, its authorities had to carry out policies established in Moscow, which aggravated the famine.[5]

Following the long period of warfare and chaos, the famine of 1921 to 1923, the introduction of the NEP, and the completion of the redistribution of confiscated land among the peasantry, agricultural production slowly began to recover. In 1923 the tax in kind was replaced by a money tax. The government in turn purchased grain from the producers, but at prices that it controlled. By the mid-1920s agricultural production had reached pre-war levels, but grain reaching the market and the amount available for export fell short of the quantities required to feed the growing urban population and to finance industrialisation, which was a priority for the Soviet regime.

Unlike the Tsarist government which had received credit abroad, the Bolsheviks, having renounced Tsarist debts, had to rely on internal sources and exports, mainly of raw materials and agricultural products, to finance industrialisation. State policy placed much of the burden of subsidising industrialisation on the shoulders of the peasantry. Stalin admitted in 1928 that, in addition to paying regular taxes, peasants were also being underpaid for agricultural products and were overpaying for manufactured goods. He characterised this as an 'additional tax' that could also be described as 'something in the nature of a "tribute," of a supertax'.[6] Peasants were thus given little incentive to increase production, as the state paid low prices for grain, or to even sell grain to the state, which controlled the market and prices. Artificially high prices on manufactured goods also acted as a disincentive to produce. In the context of industrialisation and migration to the cities, and the disincentive for peasants to produce, the results were grain shortages and a crisis of the regime's own making by 1927.

In late 1927 the Soviet leadership, at Stalin's urging, authorised policies to coerce peasants into giving up their grain, which led to a return to grain requisitioning. At the same time, Stalin began promoting more forcefully, as a way out of the crisis, the idea of transforming agriculture: moving from individual small-scale farming to the establishment of large collective farms 'capable of producing the maximum amount of marketable grain'. The goal, Stalin admitted, was 'to establish a system whereby the collective farms will deliver to the state and co-operative organisations the whole of their marketable grain under penalty of being deprived of state subsidies and credits'.[7] The economic imperative and the need for state control were thus wedded to the communist programme of establishing communal farms as part of building what the authorities represented as socialism.

In the midst of the grain crisis, Ukraine suffered from poor weather in 1927 to 1929, which led to famine in 1928/1929. As a result of the return to grain requisitioning, peasants were stripped not only of any marketable grain they produced but also of reserves held for times of shortages. Moreover, in the famine years of 1927 to 1929, about 20 million poods[8] of grain from Ukraine were exported abroad and 127.7 million sent to internal markets within the Soviet Union. As in the earlier famine of 1921 to 1923, Soviet Ukrainian officials found themselves carrying out directives of the central authorities that deprived their population of agricultural products in the midst of shortages and famine. A certain amount of aid was eventually distributed in Ukraine, but it was insufficient to deal with the scale of the famine or to compensate for the grain extracted from Ukraine's peasants. About 23,000 people died as a direct result of the famine of 1928/1929.[9]

In November 1929, having sidelined the so-called Right Opposition headed by Nikolai Bukharin, which had defended the NEP, the Stalinist leadership approved a policy of wholesale forced collectivisation. This was accompanied by a dekulakisation campaign, aimed ostensibly at eliminating the more prosperous peasants, the traditional village elites and leadership, who were branded as exploiters and class enemies. Any peasant who resisted collectivisation, however, could also be labelled a kulak or sub-kulak, a convenient new term invented to describe less prosperous or poor peasants who were reluctant to join the collectives. The prospect of dekulakisation, which involved the loss of one's possessions and could result in exile and forced labour, was thus a powerful incentive for peasants to 'voluntarily' join the newly established communal farms. The collectivisation decision came several months after the adoption of the first Five-Year Plan, which called for the industrialisation of the Soviet Union at breakneck speed.

Although some of the poorest peasants supported collectivisation, the bulk of the peasantry, who were independent subsistence or small-scale farmers, continued to oppose it. Peasants widely interpreted collectivisation and work on collective farms as a second serfdom. Carrying out this policy turned out to be especially problematic in Soviet Ukraine and in regions such as the Kuban in southern Russia, where individual farming practices were well entrenched and memories of resistance to the Bolsheviks, and even of Cossack traditions, were still strong. Collectivisation was widely resisted.

The heavy-handed, often brutal policy of forcing the peasants into collective farms, as well as the continuation of grain requisitioning, met with fierce opposition in Ukraine, where the number of violent protests and riots exceeded that of other regions in the Soviet Union. Here, resistance sometimes took on national overtones, with peasants calling for the overthrow of the Soviet order and the establishment of an independent Ukraine.[10] The wave of riots and protests, which grew to a crescendo in early 1930, subsided, however, following the appearance of Stalin's article 'Dizziness with Success', published on 2 March 1930 in the central party organ *Pravda*, which blamed local officials for overzealousness in carrying out the party's directives. Shortly after its appearance, the collectivisation drive stalled and was reversed as pressure from the authorities diminished. Many peasants left the collectives to return to individual farming.

Despite the riots and unsettled circumstances, weather conditions were excellent and the grain harvest bountiful in Ukraine in 1930 (about 23.1 million tons). Of that harvest, the Soviet state procured 7.7 million tons, or more than one-third.[11] Following the successful procurement campaign, the collectivisation drive was renewed once again, and in 1931 about two-thirds of all households, farming about the same amount of arable land, were collectivised. The same grain quota was assigned to Ukraine for the 1931 harvest.

The famine begins

Weather conditions were not good, however, in 1931. Agricultural production was also reduced by the enormous waste and chaos associated with the collectivisation drive, mismanagement on the newly established collective farms, the reluctance of peasants to work when much of the grain they produced was taken by the authorities, and peasant resistance. To make matters worse, many farmers slaughtered their livestock rather than give it up to the collective farms, while much of the confiscated livestock was not well cared for or fed adequately. This led to the emaciation and mass deaths of farm animals, including horses, still widely used as draught animals. The 1931 harvest in grain was about 18.3 million tons, almost five million tons less than that of the previous year.[12]

While the grain-procurement quota had been fulfilled in 1930 owing to a bumper crop, the significantly lower harvest in 1931 meant that there was less grain to take from the peasants. Ukraine was thus unable to meet its target,[13] but the top Soviet leadership insisted that the grain-procurement plan be met. Under pressure from the Kremlin, the Politburo of the Communist Party (Bolshevik) of Ukraine [CP(B)U] passed a resolution on 29 December 1931 affirming that 'the complete fulfillment of the grain-procurement plan in Ukraine (510 million poods) is an unconditional necessity and is dictated in the USSR by the entire political and in part international situation'.[14] In the same month that the Ukrainian Politburo called for intensifying grain-collection efforts, famine broke out in Soviet Ukraine, and in the first half of 1932 deaths from starvation and even cannibalism were observed and reported.[15] Large numbers of Ukrainian peasants left or even abandoned their households in search of work and food, heading for the cities and to neighbouring Soviet Russia.[16]

The catastrophic situation caused alarm among Soviet officials in Ukraine. In a letter written no earlier than 23 February 1932, addressed to the Ukrainian Politburo and to the first secretary of the CP(B)U, Stanislav Kosior, Ukraine's head of state, the old Bolshevik Hryhorii Petrovsky, informed Kosior, who was also a member of the All-Union Communist Party (Bolshevik) [AUCP(B)] Politburo in Moscow, of an 'acute shortage of food for the population and feed for animals'. Petrovsky requested that Kosior and the Ukrainian Politburo ask the AUCP(B) Central Committee to stop the grain-procurement campaign and allow free trade in grain. He also proposed that food aid be provided for children and for raions (districts) suffering from food shortages.[17]

Beginning in the second half of April 1932, the Kremlin leadership took steps to provide some – albeit inadequate – relief for Ukraine and other parts of the Soviet Union suffering from famine and food shortages. These measures included ordering the return to port of grain bound for export and authorising the purchase of grain abroad.[18] But no similar steps were taken by the regime in 1933, when famine conditions were full-blown.

It should also be noted that the relief provided came in the midst of the grain-sowing campaign; thus it may be suspected that Stalin and the Soviet leadership were motivated more by the desire to ensure the success of the spring sowing than by humanitarian concerns. However, as aid provided was insufficient and, at the same time, grain exports were not halted, famine continued until the harvest of 1932. Moreover, the overall crisis in agriculture continued and intensified. Signs of impending disaster were evident as fields were left unsown, weeds infested many of those that were sown, and a great many collective farmers and their draught animals were weak and unable to work well, if at all.[19]

On 10 June 1932 two of Ukraine's top leaders – Vlas Chubar, who headed the government, and Petrovsky – wrote letters addressed to Viacheslav Molotov, the Soviet Union's head of state, and to Stalin, the leader of the party. These letters are particularly important in determining the level of the Kremlin leaders' awareness and degree of responsibility for the fateful decisions they were about to make. Both letters described widespread famine conditions and requested relief and the reduction of grain-procurement targets for that year. In his letter, Petrovsky informed Stalin and Molotov of what he himself had seen in the countryside:

> I was in many raion villages and saw a considerable part of the countryside engulfed in famine. There are not many, but there are people swollen from starvation, mainly poor peasants and even middle farmers.... At large meetings in villages, I am cursed furiously; old women cry, and men sometimes do so as well. At times, criticism of the situation created goes very deep: 'Why did they create an artificial famine? After all, we had a harvest. Why did they take away the seed grain? That did not happen even under the old regime. Why should Ukrainians make difficult journeys for grain to non-grain-producing areas? Why is grain not being brought here?'

Petrovsky further informed the Kremlin leaders that mass thefts, mainly of chickens, were occurring because of the famine, and that peasants, in some cases up to two-thirds of all males, had abandoned their villages and headed for Russia and Belarus to get grain.[20]

Chubar informed the two Kremlin leaders that grain, including reserves, had been taken from individual farmers, while 'almost everything of value was confiscated from collective farms'. Thus many farms were left without grain, livestock feed, and food for the disabled and teachers. He further noted that '[i]n March and April there were tens and hundreds of malnourished, starving, and swollen people dying of hunger in every village; children abandoned by their parents and orphans appeared'.[21]

The famine intensifies

Instead of authorising measures to correct or reverse policies that had brought on the disaster and to avert an even greater catastrophe, Stalin reacted with scorn and anger to the Ukrainian leadership's plea for help. It is at this point that we can detect some anti-Ukrainian hostility in Stalin's correspondence with his closest collaborators. In a letter of 15 June to his lieutenant Lazar Kaganovich, he insisted on maintaining the procurement targets, writing: 'Ukraine has been given more than enough.' Moreover, he blamed the unfolding crisis on Ukraine's officials.[22]

Stalin's views on Ukraine, the Ukrainian leadership, and the overall situation in the CP(B)U were expressed most clearly in a letter of 11 August 1932 to Kaganovich. In it Stalin stressed that CP(B)U members and leaders were unreliable, noted the strength of nationalism in the country, including within the party – referring to both 'conscious and unconscious Petliurites'[23] – and twice expressed concern over the possibility of 'losing' Ukraine. Alarmed at the widespread discontent with grain-procurement targets among lower level officials who deemed them unrealistic, Stalin concluded: 'As soon as the situation gets worse, these elements will not hesitate to open a front within (and outside) the Party, *against* the Party.'[24]

This assertion is of crucial importance, as it shows that Stalin expected that the agricultural crisis, which had gripped the Soviet Union and was particularly severe in Ukraine, would intensify.[25] He also anticipated that opposition within the ranks of the CP(B)U would grow, and that this could be dangerous to the integrity of the Soviet state, not to mention his own political survival. Stalin also made known his intention to replace some of Soviet Ukraine's top political leaders and the head of Ukraine's secret police with more reliable figures.

This letter was written about a month after the conclusion of the Third Party Conference of the CP(B)U, which was convened on 6 to 9 July to discuss the agricultural crisis in Ukraine. To counteract discontent and opposition within the ranks of the Ukrainian party to the unrealistic grain-procurement quota, Stalin sent his trusted lieutenants Kaganovich and Molotov to attend the conference in order to enforce central authority and put pressure on Ukraine's party leaders to accept the grain-procurement targets. Although all members of the Ukrainian Politburo initially argued for the reduction of plan targets when they met with the Kremlin envoys on 6 July, Stalin's emissaries succeeded in imposing the Kremlin's will, as conference delegates approved the plan.[26]

While the 1932 grain levy for Ukraine was eventually reduced three times,[27] the revisions were at best symbolic, as they did nothing to reduce the highly unrealistic quota to a level that would prevent mass starvation from breaking out in late 1932. Not only was the 'faminogenic'[28] levy maintained, but in the second half of 1932 Stalin and the Soviet leadership took additional punitive and coercive measures to force Ukrainian peasants into parting with their grain and to terrorise any who resisted into submission. These measures intensified the famine and made things much worse. A particularly severe act was the so-called 'Five Ears of Corn Law', promulgated on 7 August 1932, which declared all collective farm property equivalent to state property and introduced draconian sentences, even death, for the theft of state property. This meant that hungry and starving peasants now faced potential execution for taking grain, even gleaning, on collective farms to feed their families.[29]

To apply additional pressure to Ukrainian party and administrative cadres, on 22 October 1932 Stalin again sent his two lieutenants on a mission: this time Molotov went to Ukraine and Kaganovich to the North Caucasus. Heading up special teams, the two Kremlin enforcers directed republican and local party and government officials to squeeze as much grain as possible from an already exhausted, malnourished peasantry on the brink of mass starvation. To assist in the drive, thousands of communist cadres from Ukrainian and Russian cities were mobilised and dispatched to the countryside to find and remove grain that the peasants had stored or 'hidden' to survive the winter and spring. Procurement teams often took all foodstuffs, not only grain, from peasant homes.[30]

During these expeditions, Stalin's lieutenants pressured the leaders of Ukraine and the North Caucasus into issuing further draconian resolutions and directives authorising the seizure of grain and other food, as well as carrying out repressive and punitive measures against Ukrainian and Kuban Cossack farmers. The CP(B)U resolution of 18 November, drafted under Molotov's direction, which authorised blacklisting and blockading entire villages and banning trade, as well as instituting fines in meat and potatoes for non-fulfilment of the grain quota, is an accurate illustration of the authorisation of such measures against Ukrainian peasants.[31] The judicial system in Ukraine was also directed to intensify punitive measures against those accused of blocking or sabotaging grain procurement. Mobile court sessions were authorised, with summary trials held on the spot.[32]

To ensure that local officials did not waver in carrying out these draconian policies, the Stalinist leadership directed its wrath against those lower ranking government and party officials who protested or spoke out against the grain-procurement plan.[33] Officials and collective farm leaders who stored or hid grain from the collectors and tried to aid the starving peasantry were accused of sabotage and removed from their posts; some were arrested and sentenced to long prison terms or summarily executed.[34] In his communications during this period, Stalin stressed to party subordinates that in most cases 'sabotage' of the grain-procurement campaign was being carried out by local Communist Party members, so he encouraged the repression of officials suspected of it. Showing that he was continuing to pay close attention to Ukraine, and offering an example of how to deal with 'sabotage' at the local level, Stalin went so far as to order the arrest of local officials in the Orikhiv raion of Dnipropetrovsk *oblast* (region) and prescribe five- to ten-year sentences for them.[35]

Loopholes allowing some leeway for collective farms to hold grain reserves that could have been used to feed farmers and their families were closed. Collective farm administrations were forbidden to give in-kind advances in order to pay farmers for workdays. Grain grown on home garden plots of collective farmers was counted as payment for workdays on those collective farms that had not yet met their grain levies.[36] As farmers were paid in kind for their labour, this meant that the grain they were supposed to have received for their work was instead taken to fulfil the grain-procurement plan. In late December, Kaganovich and Pavel Postyshev were sent on a mission to Ukraine to reinforce grain-collection efforts yet again. In the resolution authorising their departure, Ukrainian officials were accused of openly undermining grain-procurement efforts.[37]

Other decisions taken by the central authorities aimed specifically at Ukraine or the Kuban include the crucially important resolution of 14 December, which linked directives and demands pertaining to grain procurement with orders revising Ukrainisation[38] in Ukraine and proscribing it in the Kuban. The resolution ordered Ukrainian officials to fulfil the grain-procurement plan by the end of January 1933 and highlighted the supposed infiltration of 'counterrevolutionary elements', including 'Petliurites, supporters of the Kuban Rada' and 'bourgeois nationalist elements', into party and state bodies, as well as collective farm leadership posts.[39] References to 'Petliurites' and nationalist efforts at sabotaging grain-procurement efforts and at organising insurgencies against Soviet rule became more frequent from the autumn of 1932.

In November, Stalin sent Vsevolod Balytsky, a deputy head of the OGPU and former head of Ukraine's GPU, back to Ukraine armed with plenipotentiary powers to intensify the grain-procurement campaign and ferret out Ukrainian nationalists, a good number of whom, it was alleged, were infiltrating and taking over collective farm leadership and lower level party posts so as to prepare an insurgency.[40] In December 1932 Balytsky began producing reports on the uncovering of alleged counterrevolutionary and anti-Soviet groups in the countryside, including those headed by 'Petliurites'.[41] It should be noted that Stalin responded to Balytsky's memorandum of 23 December with a telegram to Communist Party and secret police officials referring to Balytsky's allegation that Petliurite organisations in Ukraine were sabotaging grain procurement and preparing 'peasant uprisings to separate Ukraine from the USSR and reestablish capitalism'.[42]

On New Year's Day 1933, Stalin sent Ukraine's leaders a telegram containing a resolution of the All-Union Central Committee threatening to apply provisions of the draconian decree of 7 August 1932 to those Ukrainian peasants who were allegedly hiding grain from grain collectors.[43] The Ukrainian historian Stanislav Kulchytskyi emphasises the importance of this resolution and the fact that Stalin himself sent the telegram, which was addressed to all Ukraine's peasants, to the Ukrainian leadership. He concludes that 'Stalin's telegram to Ukrainian peasants signaled the application of massive searches'. If grain was found, peasants were subject to the law of 7 August 1932. In the event that grain was not found, farmers knew that they could still be subject to fines in kind if they or their collective farms failed to meet their grain-procurement quotas.[44]

On 22 January 1933, Stalin and Molotov signed a directive ordering authorities to seal the borders and prevent starving peasants from leaving Ukraine and the Kuban for other areas of the Soviet Union in search of food. The resolution made reference to the previous year's flight of Ukrainian peasants to other parts of the Soviet Union, emphasising that the mass exodus was 'organized by enemies of Soviet rule' for counterrevolutionary purposes.[45] Peasants were thus prevented from travelling or were forced to return to their villages, where they and their families faced starvation.

In addition to the measures taken against Ukrainian peasants and lower level party officials, in late 1932 and early 1933 Stalin began to implement a policy expressed in his correspondence with Kaganovich, augmenting and replacing Ukrainian leaders with more trustworthy and ruthless figures. In September 1932 he appointed a deputy head of the OGPU, I. Akulov, to head the Donetsk *oblast* party organisation. Akulov was soon made a member of the Ukrainian Politburo. In October 1932 he appointed M. Khataevich second secretary of the CP(B)U. Later that month he appointed V. Stroganov, V. Cherniavsky and P. Markitan as secretaries of the Dnipropetrovsk, Vinnytsia and Chernihiv *oblast* organisations of the CP(B)U.[46] These officials worked closely with the Kremlin and its envoys to fulfil the grain-procurement plan.

Stalin's most important personnel changes were given in a resolution of 24 January 1933 adopted by the AUCP(B) Central Committee, in which the CP(B)U was blamed for the grain-procurement failures of 1932. Of particular significance was the appointment of Pavel Postyshev, who effectively became Stalin's plenipotentiary in Ukraine, as secretary of the Kharkiv *oblast* party organisation and second secretary of the CP(B)U.[47] Shortly after assuming control in late January 1933, Postyshev, aided by Balytsky, who took over the Ukrainian GPU in February 1933, commenced a campaign of terror aimed at a large number of Ukraine's cultural figures, intellectuals and communist functionaries, many of whom were accused of nationalism. Speaking at a CC CP(B)U plenum in February 1933, Postyshev indicated the Orikhiv case as an example of local officials interpreting the grain procurements as 'Muscovites taking bread', noting that such nationalist sentiment was common within the ranks of the Ukrainian party.[48]

To complete the task of cleansing the lower level party and state bodies of oppositional and unreliable officials, Postyshev oversaw a thorough purge in 1933. About a quarter of all party members were dismissed as 'class enemies'; 278 new secretaries of raion committees, about 70 per cent of the total, were appointed. The overall number of party functionaries assigned to collective farms also grew substantially, and about half the chairmen and vice-chairmen of the approximately 11,400 collective farms were replaced.[49]

Postyshev also presided over the worst of the famine months and was charged with preparing for and overseeing the sowing, harvesting and grain-procurement campaigns of 1933. On 5 February the campaign to collect the harvest of 1932 was halted. Of the approximately 14.6 million tons of grain harvested, 4.234 million tons were taken to fulfil the grain-procurement plan.[50] On 7 February the first orders were given to begin releasing grain from storage for aid in the form of seed loans, as well as for food, but the total amount released was inadequate to save the millions who were to starve in the coming months.[51] Moreover, the aid was selective, as it was intended mainly to feed those collective farmers capable of working in order to ensure a successful sowing campaign ahead.[52]

Owing to favourable weather conditions, as well as to the work of party officials and others mobilised to aid agricultural efforts, about 22.3 million tons of grain were harvested from the bumper crop of 1933. The amount procured from this crop was about 6.261 million tons.[53] As a result of the bumper crop, the famine, which had raged throughout the winter, spring and early summer months, finally began to subside.

Conclusions

In little more than a decade, Soviet Ukraine suffered through three famines. As the modern state is responsible for the security and well-being of its citizens, it is expected to use its resources to address and alleviate such calamities as food shortages. The Soviet state did not do so. Although natural causes were significant in the early stages of the first two famines in Soviet Ukraine, and bad weather was an important cause of the low grain crop of 1931, in all three famines the decisions of the Soviet authorities aggravated famine conditions.[54] In the famine of 1932/1933, the policies adopted by the highest Soviet authorities had devastating effects.[55]

It is clear that the Soviet regime made little or no effort to organise and offer effective aid to its starving citizens in 1932/1933. In contrast to the famine of 1921 to 1923, no international aid was allowed into the country. Moreover, the famine was not acknowledged officially and was denied by the Soviet authorities until the late 1980s. From the autumn of 1932, foreign journalists were forbidden to travel to the famine-stricken regions, and the ban was not lifted until the famine had run its course. Moreover, while Soviet citizens starved, grain was exported from their country. In Ukraine, peasants were forbidden to travel to areas of Russia where there was grain. There is little dispute today that the famine of 1932/1933 in Ukraine could have been avoided and that the Soviet regime was responsible for it. However, the causes of the famine and the degree of responsibility of the Soviet authorities are not yet settled.

Some scholars point to the decision to industrialise at breakneck speed, as well as the pell-mell pace of collectivisation and the chaos accompanying it, as major causes of the famine of 1932/1933. Such haste notwithstanding, they conclude that the famine was unplanned and undesired, although it could have been anticipated.[56] While one can agree that collectivisation and its consequences led to a severe agricultural crisis, it should be emphasised that the forced collection of grain to fulfil exceedingly high – effectively, unrealistic – grain-procurement quotas was the overriding cause of the outbreak of famine in Soviet Ukraine in December 1931.[57]

While there is no evidence to suggest that the top Soviet leaders planned a famine in late 1931, it is clear that in 1932/1933 they did little or nothing to mitigate or prevent it. Moreover, their key decisions and actions made things much worse. One may conclude that the spike in deaths in Ukraine in the first half of 1933 was largely due to policies approved by Stalin and his close lieutenants Molotov and Kaganovich in the second half of 1932 and early 1933, and to the actions they authorised and encouraged to carry out those policies. Many of those pertained exclusively to Ukraine and the Kuban region of the north Caucasus, or were prompted in whole or in part by developments there.

This conclusion is suggested and supported by key communications and decrees of the top Soviet leaders, especially Stalin, as they pertain to Ukraine during this period. While some of the decisions taken by Stalin and the Soviet leadership in the famine years may be explained by the need to respond to and control a crisis of their own making, and by their resolve, at all costs, to collect as much grain as possible to support rapid industrialisation through grain exports, there were other important goals that should be taken into account when assessing their motives and degree of culpability.

One of these goals was to finally subdue and completely subordinate the Ukrainian peasantry, which had been particularly troublesome, and to ensure that Ukraine's farmers would work as required on the new collective farms. To achieve this goal, beginning in the summer of 1932, Stalin and the Stalinist leadership enacted laws intended to strip individual peasant farms and collective farms of their grain and prevent the storage of grain for the winter and spring months, including seed grain. They also authorised additional repressive measures, ostensibly to fulfil a clearly unrealistic grain-procurement plan. Authorising the seizure of grain and other foods, and imposing punishment by means of fines in kind resulted in starvation, as the Soviet leaders could not have failed to realise. They used famine as a tool to subjugate the Ukrainian peasantry to the party-state.[58]

Subjugation began with the collectivisation campaign. With the peasants herded into collective farms, their economic autonomy and freedom of action were fatally undermined. Collectivisation subordinated Ukraine's independent farmers to the party-state, establishing its control over most agricultural production, and thus potentially allowed the state to squeeze more grain from the peasantry. Although it was touted as fulfilling communist goals, collectivisation also served 'to destroy the social basis of Ukrainian nationalism – individual peasant agriculture'.[59]

Stalin and the Stalinist leadership recognised that Ukrainian peasant opposition to their economic policies, especially forced collectivisation, would provoke interpretations and resistance that could take on national form and content. An unpopular policy ostensibly aimed at a social group could therefore have national ramifications and consequences. The Soviet leaders considered the peasant and national questions to be closely linked, as they showed in commenting on the specific situation in Ukraine in 1932/1933.[60]

In a speech before delegates to the Seventeenth Congress of the AUCP(B) in early 1934, Postyshev stressed that the national and peasant questions intersected in Ukraine, declaring that 'in Ukraine the class enemy masks his activity against socialist construction with the nationalist banner and chauvinist slogans'. He continued: 'The Ukrainian kulak underwent a lengthy schooling in struggle against Soviet power, for in Ukraine the civil war was especially fierce and lengthy, given that political banditry was in control of Ukraine for an especially long period.'[61] By reminding delegates of the protracted struggle waged by Ukrainian peasants against the imposition of Soviet rule, Postyshev also implied that the recent resistance to the collectivisation and grain-procurement campaigns in Ukraine could have developed into a national liberation struggle or taken on national form and substance.[62]

The first secretary of the CP(B)U, Stanislav Kosior, also stressed the interconnectedness of the national and social questions in Ukraine in speeches given in 1933 and 1934. In his report to the CP(B)U plenum of November 1933, Kosior reminded delegates:

> It should never have been forgotten that, especially in Ukraine, the struggle of all types of counter-revolution, in nine cases out of ten, is waged under nationalist slogans, is camouflaged by the nationalist flag, the most treacherous, the most harmful and the most vile flag.[63]

In his speech at the Seventeenth Party Congress of 1934, Kosior claimed that nationalists in the CP(B)U 'played an exceptional role in creating and intensifying the lag in agriculture'. 'In Ukraine,' he continued,

> where the class situation is the most complicated, where the activities of the remnants of the defeated class enemy attain the highest level of acuteness, the national flag plays an exceedingly important role for the class enemy. Moreover, the predominant colouring of the class enemy, with which he masks himself, is above all the national flag, nationalist clothing.[64]

As famine deaths began to peak, party members were reminded that the struggle against 'counterrevolutionary bourgeois-kulak nationalist groups' was being reflected within the party and that party members had been 'underestimating the unbreakable link between the national and peasant questions'.[65]

In his letter of 11 August 1932 to Kaganovich, Stalin implied that Ukraine was a potential centre of resistance to his policies and a separatist threat. As the party's leading expert on nationalities, acutely aware of the overall importance of the Ukrainian republic, Stalin had followed events there closely. In that letter, Stalin established the goal, as he put it, of transforming Ukraine 'into a fortress of the USSR, a real model republic, within the shortest possible time'.[66]

To achieve that goal, he was prepared to go to extreme lengths. As resistance to collectivisation and grain procurement was especially strong in Ukraine, and Ukraine's Communist Party was deemed unreliable, Ukrainians – primarily those accused of nationalism and of sabotaging or resisting grain collection – were subject to repressions and deprived of sustenance. One can therefore pose the question of whether the decisions taken and actions authorised or encouraged by the top Soviet leadership headed by Stalin were intended to punish and destroy, at least in part, a national group. The evidence points in that direction and therefore supports a genocide interpretation of the famine. This interpretation is even better substantiated by the fact that in the early 1930s the Stalinist leadership destroyed much of Ukraine's national intelligentsia and national communist cadres – the cultural and political elites of the nation.[67]

Notes

1 Until the late 1980s, the famine of 1932/1933 was officially denied by Soviet scholars and officials, while outside the Soviet Union it was not thoroughly studied. Relatively little was known about it until the appearance of Robert Conquest's *The Harvest of Sorrow: Soviet Collectivization and the Terror-Famine* (New York: Oxford University Press, 1986).

2 Most severely affected were the north Caucasus region of Russia, which includes the Kuban region, settled mainly by Kuban Cossacks, who were largely ethnic Ukrainians; the middle and lower Volga regions of Russia; and Kazakhstan. For the best treatment of the pan-Soviet famine, see R.W. Davies and Stephen G. Wheatcroft, *The Years of Hunger: Soviet Agriculture, 1931–1933* (New York: Palgrave Macmillan, 2004).

3 In 1932/1933, the AUCP(B) Politburo held 69 meetings at which 270 questions dealt with Ukraine (about four per session), three-quarters of them concerning agricultural matters. See Ruslan Pyrih, 'Peredmova', in *Holodomor 1932–1933 rokiv v Ukraïni: dokumenty i materialy*, ed. Ruslan Pyrih (Kyiv: Vydavnychyi dim 'Kyievo-Mohylians'ka Akademiia', 2007), 7–8. Some decisions that pertained exclusively to Ukraine are given in this essay.

4 For a general history of the Ukrainian peasantry in the 1920s and early 1930s, see the first part of *Istoriia ukraïns'koho selianstva*, vol. 2 (Kyiv: Natsional'na akademiia nauk Ukraïny, Instytut istoriï Ukraïny, 2006). See also Stanislav Kul'chyts'kyi, 'Problema kolektyvizatsiï sil's'koho hospodarstva v stalins'kii "revoliutsiï zverkhu"', in *Problemy istoriï Ukraïny: Fakty, sudzhennia, poshuky. Mizhvidomchyi zbirnyk naukovykh prats'*, vyp. 12, ed. Stanislav Kul'chyts'kyi (Kyiv: Instytut istoriï Ukraïny, 2004). For an interpretive essay on the Bolshevik state and the Soviet peasantry in which the Ukrainian peasantry features prominently, see Andrea Graziosi, 'The Great Soviet Peasant War: Bolsheviks and Peasants, 1917–1933', in his *Stalin, Collectivization and the Great Famine* (Cambridge, MA: Ukrainian Studies Fund, 2009), 5–64.

5 See Kul'chyts'kyi, 'Problema kolektyvizatsiï sil's'koho hospodarstva', pp. 21–22. See also Roman Serbyn, 'The Famine of 1921–1923: A Model for 1932–1933?', in *Famine in Ukraine 1932–1933*, ed. Roman Serbyn and Bohdan Krawchenko (Edmonton: Canadian Institute of Ukrainian Studies, 1986), pp. 147–178. See also O.M. Movchan, 'Holod 1921–1923 rr.: "Heneral'na repetytsiia" 1933-ho', in *Holod 1932–1933 rokiv v Ukraïni: prychyny ta naslidky*, ed. V.M. Lytvyn (Kyiv: Naukova dumka, 2003), 231–233.

6 See Stalin's speech 'Industrialisation and the Grain Problem', in J.V. Stalin, *Works*, vol. 11 (Moscow: Foreign Languages Publishing House, 1954), 167.

7 See his speech of 28 May 1928 'On the Grain Front', ibid., p. 94. Lynne Viola described the end result of collectivisation as 'the transformation of the countryside into an internal colony from which tribute – in the form of grain, taxes, labor, and soldiers – could be extracted to finance the industrialization, modernization, and defense of the country'. See her *Peasant Rebels under Stalin: Collectivization and the Culture of Peasant Resistance* (New York and Oxford: Oxford University Press, 1996), 29.

8 One pood is about 16.38 kilograms, or 36.11 pounds.

9 See Liudmyla Hrynevych, *Ukraïns'kyi holod 1928/29 r. iak naslidok radians'koï polityky tvorennia holodu* = Liudmyla Hrynevych, *Khronika kolektyvizatsiï ta Holodomoru v Ukraïni 1927–1933*, vol. 1, *1927–1929*, bk. 3 (Kyiv: Krytyka, 2012), 5–154. On the 1928/1929 famine, see also Mark Tauger, 'Grain Crisis or Famine? The Ukrainian State Commission for Aid to Crop-failure Victims and the Ukrainian Famine of 1928–29', in *Provincial Landscapes: Local Dimensions of Soviet Power, 1917–1953*, comp. Donald J. Raleigh (Pittsburgh, PA: University of Pittsburgh Press, 2011), 146–170, 360–365. Tauger writes favourably of the Soviet aid programme, for which he is criticised by Hrynevych, who argues that Tauger's interpretation

in essence repeats the interpretation of these events by Stalin himself, who also attempted to justify the ruination and pitiless plunder of the village with noble intentions of overcoming the grain crisis in the country and avoiding the danger of famine in the cities, without making known, however, either [his] refusal of aid offered from abroad (particularly by the well-known benefactor Fridtjof Nansen), or his unwillingness to import the requisite quantity of grain into the USSR, or the continuing export of provisions despite the acute crisis.

(See *Ukraïns'kyi holod*, 11–12)

10 See the report on peasant disturbances and uprisings in the Tulchyn okruh (district), which includes references to Ukrainian peasants voicing national patriotic slogans by Ukraine's GPU chairman V. Balytsky, in *Kollektivizatsiia i krest'ianskoe soprotivlenie na Ukraine (noiabr' 1929–1 marta 1930 gg.)*, ed. Valerii Vasil'ev and Lynne Viola (Vinnytsia: Logos, 1997), pp. 213–214. See also Viola, *Peasant Rebels*, pp. 158–159, and Liudmyla Hrynevych, 'Stalins'ka "revoliutsiia zhory" ta holod 1933 r. iak faktor polityzatsiï ukraïns'koï spil'noty', *Ukrains'kyi istorychnyi zhurnal* 5 (2003), 58–59.

11 The figures are given in Bohdan Krawchenko, *Social Change and National Consciousness in Twentieth-Century Ukraine* (London: Macmillan, 1985), 124. The figure of 7.675 million tons is given in Davies and Wheatcroft, *The Years of Hunger*, 470.

12 See Krawchenko, *Social Change and National Consciousness*, 126.

13 The final figure procured was about 7.253 million tons, which fell short of fulfilling the plan for that year. See Davies and Wheatcroft, *The Years of Hunger*, 470.

14 The resolution makes reference to Molotov's presence at the Ukrainian Politburo meeting, where he read a report admonishing Ukraine's leadership and directed that immediate measures be taken to fulfil the grain-procurement plan. See 'Postanovlenie Politburo TsK KP(b)U "O merakh usileniia khlebozagotovok"', in I. Zelenin *et al.*, *Tragediia sovetskoi derevni. Kollektivizatsiia i raskulachivanie. Dokumenty i materialy*, vol. 3, *Konets 1930–1933* (Moscow: Rosspen, 2001), 227–230.

15 There are many published documents in which high-ranking Soviet officials attest to famine conditions, deaths from famine, and even cannibalism in early 1932. See e.g. Kyiv *oblast* secretary Mykola Demchenko's letter of 6 April 1932 to Stanislav Kosior in *Holodomor 1932–1933 rokiv v Ukraïni*, 114–117. A. Richytsky's letter of 20 May to Kosior (166–168) gives the numbers of deaths from famine in specific villages of Uman raion in Vinnytsia *oblast* and mentions cannibalism.

16 In a letter to the newspaper *Izvestiia* written before 31 March 1932, a member of a village council in central Russia complained about the large number of hungry peasants from Ukraine looking to barter household goods for food. See *The Holodomor Reader: A Sourcebook on the Famine of 1932–1933 in Ukraine*, comp. and ed. Bohdan Klid and Alexander J. Motyl (Edmonton and Toronto: CIUS Press, 2012), 228–229. In a memorandum (ibid., 229) to USSR People's Commissar of Agriculture A. Ya. Yakovlev, his deputy commissar reported that in a south-central raion of Ukraine, Zinovivsk (now Kirovohrad), more than 28,000 out of a population of about 100,000 had left the district, mainly healthy adults, and that 50 per cent of its horses had disappeared. Of those remaining, about half were exhausted and incapable of working.

17 *The Holodomor Reader*, p. 70. See also a letter of 24 March 1932 from Volodymyr Zatonsky to Kosior in which he describes the chaos and ruin in collective farms of the Mariiupol region in southeastern Ukraine (*Holodomor 1932–1933 rokiv v Ukraïni*, 96–97).

18 See the CPC USSR resolutions of 21 May 1932 (*Holodomor 1932–1933 rokiv v Ukraïni*, 172–173) and of 23 May 1932 (178–179), and the AUCP(B) Politburo resolutions of 23 April (127), 16 May (156), 21 May 1932 (173) and 26 May 1932 (189). These decisions also authorised the purchase of grain from Iran. This procurement was authorised by the AUCP(B) Politburo on 29 April 1932 (139).

19 See Davies and Wheatcroft, *The Years of Hunger*, 128–130.

20 See English-language excerpts of Petrovsky's letter in *The Holodomor Reader*, 230. For the full text, see *Holodomor 1932–1933 rokiv v Ukraïni*, 197–199.

21 See English-language excerpts of Chubar's letter in *The Holodomor Reader*, 231. For the full text, see *Holodomor 1932–1933 rokiv v Ukraïni*, 200–205.

22 See English-language excerpt in *The Holodomor Reader*, 232. Stalin also wrote that there was nothing to give; however, if Kaganovich and Molotov insisted, the plan could be reduced, not by 10 to 15 per cent but by 5 to 8 per cent. See *Holodomor 1932–1933 rokiv v. Ukraïni*, 206. There was, however, grain held in reserve, and no further attempts were made to obtain grain or other food products from abroad or to halt further grain exports.

23 Supporters of Ukrainian independence or autonomy were often referred to as 'Petliurites', followers of the Ukrainian independence-era leader Symon Petliura.

24 An English-language excerpt is in *The Holodomor Reader*, 239–240.

25 Intensification of the crisis would occur, one may infer, as a consequence of the continuation and intensification of grain-procurement policies in Ukraine, which would lead to food shortages and famine.

26 Stalin was clearly concerned that the Ukrainian party conference would adopt decisions criticising the grain-procurement quota for Ukraine, or call for its revision, which would be a challenge to central authority. He therefore insisted that Molotov and Kaganovich attend the conference to enforce party discipline. See English-language excerpts of his letter of 2 July 1932 to Kaganovich and Molotov in *The Holodomor Reader*, 234–235. Molotov and Kaganovich notified Stalin about the Ukrainian Politburo's opposition to the plan in their letter of 6 July 1932 (English-language excerpts, 236). David Marples discusses Ukrainian objections to the plan in his 'Ethnic Issues in the Famine of 1932–1933', *Europe-Asia Sudies* 61(3) (May 2009), 505–518. See also Iurii Shapoval, 'III konferentsiia KP(b)U: proloh trahediï holodu', in *Komandyry velykoho holodu. Poïzdky V. Molotova i L. Kahanovycha v Ukraïnu ta na Pivnichnyi Kavkaz, 1932–1933 rr.*, ed. Valerii Vasyl'iev and Iurii Shapoval (Kyiv: Heneza, 2001), 152–164. A Russian-language version of the same article follows on pp. 165–178.

27 With the third reduction, the figure for Ukraine was 4.238 million tons. See Valerii Vasyl'iev, 'Tsina holodnoho khliba. Polityka kerivnytstva SRSR i USRR v 1932–1933 rr.', in *Komandyry velykoho holodu*, 64.

28 The term, meaning 'creating or aiding in the creation of famine', was coined by David Marcus. See his 'Famine Crimes in International Law', *American Journal of International Law* 97(2) (April 2003), 245, n. 9.

29 An English-language excerpt is in *The Holodomor Reader*, 239.

30 Pavel Postyshev, who would soon be appointed Stalin's representative in Ukraine, headed a special team sent to the lower Volga region of Russia in December 1932. An English-language excerpt appears in *The Holodomor Reader*, 241. The entire resolution is in *Holodomor 1932–1933 rokiv v Ukraïni*, 349.

31 See an English-language excerpt of the resolution in *The Holodomor Reader*, 241–243. For the entire resolution, see *Holodomor 1932–1933 rokiv v. Ukraïni*, pp. 388–395. The resolution instituted fines in meat for those collective farms alleged to have abetted the theft of grain. It also authorised the blacklisting of collective farms accused of sabotaging grain procurements. Blacklisting involved the removal of all goods from stores, the suspension of deliveries, and the banning of all trade and credit transactions. In his telegram to Stalin of 20 November 1932, Molotov informed him that he had worked two days on the resolution with the Ukrainian party's Central Committee and noted the reluctance of Kharkiv party members to support the intensification of efforts to procure more grain. See *Holodomor 1932–1933 rokiv v. Ukraïni*, 402.

32 See the resolution of the Politburo of the CP(B)U of 5 November 1932 in *Holodomor 1932–1933 rokiv v. Ukraïni*, 368.

33 In Vinnytsia *oblast*, for example, the province's GPU headquarters reported that in September to October 1932 many local leaders had expressed dissatisfaction with the unrealistically high plan targets and that this dissatisfaction was especially acute among collective farm leaders. At local party plenums, village leaders often declared that trying to meet those targets would lead to unrest and the collapse of the collective farms, and refused to carry out the plans. See V. Vasil'iev, 'Golodovka i golod v Vinnitskoi oblasti: 20–40-e gg. XX stoletiia: popytka sravnitel'nogo analiza', in *Sovremennaia rossiisko-ukrainskaia istoriografiia goloda 1932–1933 gg. V. SSSR*, ed. V.V. Kondrashin (Moscow: Rosspen, 2011), 227.

34 See, for instance, the telegram of 5 November 1932 from M.M. Khataevich (secretary of the CC CP(B)U) and Molotov to the *oblast* party secretaries of the CP(B)U, instructing them to direct the courts and prosecutors to take steps 'to quickly conduct court repressions and [mete out] merciless justice toward criminal elements in the administration of the collective farms' on the basis of the 7 August 'five ears of corn' law. See *Holodomor 1932–1933 rokiv v. Ukraïni*, 371–372.

35 See Stalin's letter of 7 December 1932 to Communist Party leaders and officials in *Orikhivs'ka sprava. 1932. Dokumenty i materialy*, comp. Viktor Tkachenko (Dnipropetrovsk: IMA-pres, 2010), 115–116.

36 See the CP(B)U resolution of 18 November in *The Holodomor Reader*, 241–242. The resolution stated that the fulfilment of the grain-procurement plan was the highest priority, but it did allow the creation of special reserves. However, the resolution also authorised the seizure of reserves held by lagging collective farms if approved by the raion executive committee. At the urging of Kaganovich and M. Chernov, even this loophole was closed, and all reserves held by collective farms were ordered seized to fulfil the plan. See their telegram of 22 December to Stalin (ibid., 248–249), which resulted in the CC CP(B)U issuing two letters, dated 24 and 29 December, ordering the seizure of all grain held by collective farms that had not fulfilled the plan (ibid., 250–251).

37 See 'Postanova TsK VKP(b) ta RNK SRSR pro khlibozahotivli na Ukraïni' (*Holodomor 1932–1933 rokiv v Ukraïni*, 495).

38 Ukrainisation was a policy adopted by the Communist Party in 1923 that facilitated the development and use of the Ukrainian language. For the best treatment of Soviet nationalities policies in the 1920s and 1930s, including Ukrainisation, see Terry Martin, *The Affirmative Action Empire: Nations and Nationalism in the Soviet Union, 1923–1939* (Ithaca, NY, and London: Cornell University Press, 2001).

39 English-language excerpts are in *The Holodomor Reader*, 245–247. See *Holodomor 1932–1933 rokiv v Ukraïni*, 475–477, for the entire document. The beginning of the resolution reads like an ultimatum to the Ukrainian and north Caucasus leaderships to fulfil the grain-procurement plan by the end of January 1933. It directed that severe measures be taken against ostensibly counter-revolutionary elements, including nationalists, in collective farms and local party organisations. The resolution also directed that Ukrainisation in Ukraine be revised and purged of nationalist content, while it was to be proscribed in the Kuban.

40 Balytsky was given plenipotentiary powers in Ukraine and ordered to report to the CC AUCP(B) every 20 days. See 'Postanova Politbiuro TsK VKP(b) "Pro osoblyvoho upovnovazhenoho ODPU na Ukraïni" ', in *Holodomor 1932–1933 rokiv v Ukraïni*, 411. Balytsky was chosen for this special assignment because of his long experience in Soviet Ukraine's secret police service, beginning in 1919, including heading it from September 1923 to June 1931. On Balytsky, see Iurii Shapoval and Vadym Zolotar'ov, *Vsevolod Balyts'kyi: Osoba, chas, otochennia* (Kyiv: Stylos, 2002).

41 See an English-language excerpt of a memorandum from Balytsky to Stalin, dated 23 December 1932, in which he emphasised the threat posed by insurgent nationalist groups in Ukraine (*The Holodomor Reader*, 249). A facsimile of the original is

reproduced in Roman Krutsyk, *Narodna viina: Putivnyk do ekspozytsiï* (Kyiv: Ukraïns'ka vydavnycha spilka, 2011), 230–233. In a sense, Balytsky was merely continuing and intensifying a campaign already begun against 'the c[ounter]-r[evolutionary] leadership and kulak-Petliurite insurgent underground' by Ukraine's then head of the GPU, Stanislav Redens. See his memo of 22 November 1932 to the CC CP(B)U, in *Holodomor 1932–1933 rokiv v Ukraïni*, 409.

42 An excerpt of Stalin's telegram is in *The Holodomor Reader*, 250. A facsimile of the original is reproduced in Krutsyk, *Narodna viina*, 234.

43 See English-language excerpt in *The Holodomor Reader*, 251. See also *Holodomor 1932–1933 rokiv v Ukraïni*, 567.

44 Kulchytsky notes that in-kind fines included not only meat but also potatoes, and that other foodstuffs were also subject to confiscation. See his *Holodomor 1932–1933 rr. iak henotsyd: Trudnoshchi usvidomlennia* (Kyiv: Nash chas, 2008), 300–304.

45 See an English-language excerpt in *The Holodomor Reader*, p. 254; full text in *Holodomor 1932–1933 rokiv v Ukraïni*, 609–610. The Politburo also sent a telegram, dated 16 February 1933, to the Lower Volga Regional Committee instructing it to apply the same measures of 22 January to peasants of the Lower Volga region. See 'Postanovlenie TsK VKP(b) o rasprostranenii na Nizhniuiu Volgu direktivy TsK VKP(b) i SNK SSSR ot 22 ianvaria 1933 g.', in *Tragediia sovetskoi derevni*, 644–645.

46 Valerii Vasyl'iev concludes that these appointments marked the beginning of the implementation of Stalin's plan to replace Ukraine's leadership with figures dedicated to his course of action. See his 'Tsina holodnoho khliba', 34.

47 An English-language excerpt of the resolution authorising the changes is in *The Holodomor Reader*, p. 255. See *Holodomor 1932–1933 rokiv v Ukraïni*, p. 619, for the original. Postyshev replaced R. Terekhov as Kharkiv *oblast* secretary. On 26 May 1964, in *Pravda*, Terekhov wrote that he had informed Stalin personally about famine conditions and requested aid, but was ridiculed and rebuked by him. An English translation of Terekhov's account of his meeting with Stalin appears in Conquest, *The Harvest of Sorrow*, 324–325.

48 Postyshev's remarks are cited in Vasyl'iev, 'Tsina holodnoho khliba', 70.

49 Ibid., 70–71. Vasyl'iev provides a table on p. 71 listing the positions at a typical collective farm and, gives figures and percentages showing changes for each position.

50 The figure of 14.6 million tons for the harvest is taken from Krawchenko, *Social Change and National Consciousness*, 126. The figure for the amount procured is from Davies and Wheatcroft, *The Years of Hunger*, 470. Krawchenko gives a slightly higher figure of 4.7 million tons for the amount procured and estimates that the average amount of grain that remained per peasant household after the end of the requisition campaign was about 80 kg (ibid., 127).

51 Davies and Wheatcroft give a figure of 194,000 tons provided as food aid to Ukraine (*The Years of Hunger*, 440). The Ukrainian historian Stanislav Kulchytsky gives the figure of 176,200 tons and comments that this was less than the amount of grain procured from the Vinnytsia, Kyiv, Kharkiv and Chernihiv *oblasts* alone from November 1932 to January 1933. See his *Holodomor 1932–1933 rr. iak henotsyd*, 338.

52 See e.g. the circular issued by V. Balytsky, chairman of the Ukrainian GPU, on 19 March 1933, in which he issues the following instruction:

> The aid being provided must, first and foremost, assure successful sowing in the raions, villages and collective farms that are experiencing food difficulties, and the first to receive it must be those collective farmers that have fulfilled their obligation to the state, the best brigades, brigade leaders, and collective farms with the largest number of workdays (*trudodni*).

(See the English translation of the document in *Holodomor Studies* 2 (2009), 91, 93, 95. See also Davies and Wheatcroft, *The Years of Hunger*, 221–222)

53 The harvest figure is taken from Krawchenko, *Social Change and National Consciousness*, 126; the amount procured from Davies and Wheatcroft, *The Years of Hunger*, 470.

54 In the early stages of the first two famines, Soviet authorities made decisions that aggravated famine conditions in Ukraine.

55 The well-known scholar Amartya Sen wrote: 'People suffer from hunger when they cannot establish their entitlement over an adequate amount of food.' See his *Development as Freedom* (New York: Knopf, 1999), 162. It is easy to conclude that in 1932/1933 Ukraine's peasants were deliberately deprived of their entitlement to food – food they produced – by the Soviet party-state.

56 Davies and Wheatcroft conclude that the famine was caused by the Soviet leadership's 'wrong-headed policies, but was unexpected and undesirable.... They were formulated by men with little formal education and limited knowledge of agriculture. Above all, they were a consequence of the decision to industrialise this peasant country at breakneck speed' (*Years of Hunger*, 441). Lynne Viola concludes that 'The famine, easily anticipated but hardly planned, was the result of the state's brutal requisitions, the chaos of collectivization, and a political culture in which peasants had little or no value as human beings' (*Peasant Rebels under Stalin*, 209).

57 Krawchenko reaches this conclusion in his *Social Change and National Consciousness*, 126. Furthermore, he points out that the amount of grain harvested from the crop of 1934 was disastrous – only 12.3 million tons. Yet, although this was far less than the amount harvested from the crop of 1932, there was no famine, as Stalin released grain from reserves to feed the populace (ibid., 127).

58 Starvation as a means of teaching the peasants a lesson and changing their attitude was mentioned explicitly by CP(B)U first secretary Stanislav Kosior in a memorandum of 15 March 1933 to the CC AUCP(B). According to him, by that point there was little talk among the peasants that grain had been taken from them. Rather, 'people blame themselves for the poor work, for not safeguarding the grain, for allowing it to be pilfered'. Yet, Kosior noted, this change in attitude towards work on the collective farms was not universal, as 'starvation has not yet knocked sense into the heads of a great many collective farmers' (*The Holodomor Reader*, 262).

59 *Proletars'ka pravda*, 22 January 1930. Cited in James Mace, 'The Man-made Famine of 1933 in the Soviet Ukraine: What Happened and Why?, in *Toward the Understanding and Prevention of Genocide: Proceedings of the International Conference on the Holocaust and Genocide*, ed. Israel W. Charney (Boulder, CO, and London: Westview Press, 1984), 73.

60 Stalin's oft-cited pronouncement of 1925 that 'the peasant question is the basis, the quintessence, of the national question' conveys this understanding well. See J.V. Stalin, 'Concerning the National Question in Yugoslavia. Speech Delivered in the Yugoslav Commission of the E.C.C.I., March 30, 1925', in *Works*, vol. 7 (1954), 71–72. Andrea Graziosi emphasises Stalin's understanding of the close connection between the peasant and national questions. See an excerpt of his article, 'The Soviet 1931–1933 Famines and the Ukrainian Holodomor: Is a New Interpretation Possible, and What Would Its Consequences Be?', in *The Holodomor Reader*, 23–24. Full text in *Harvard Ukrainian Studies* 17(1–4) (2004–2005), 97–109.

61 See *The Holodomor Reader*, 266.

62 Grain-procurement policies were indeed interpreted in national or in nationalistic ways by the Ukrainian peasantry. At the Plenum of the CP(B)U on 12 to 16 March 1928, Kaganovich, then first secretary of the CP(B)U, charged that

> the grain-procurement campaign has caused chauvinism to strengthen. This is a fact. This chauvinism is manifested in that there are conversations about matters such as [our] bread, sugar is being exported to Moscow. And this chauvinism

comes not only from the top but from below. Questions about Moscow, the Soviet Union … are now being sharply raised by the kulak.

(Cited in Hrynevych, Khronika kolektyvizatsiï ta Holodomoru v Ukraïni 1927–1933, vol. 1, bk. 1, 173)

63 See The Holodomor Reader, 263.
64 Stanislav Kosior, speech delivered at the Seventeenth Congress of the All-Union Communist Party (Bolshevik), 30 January 1934, in *XVII S"ezd Vsesoiuznoi Kommunisticheskoi Partii (b), 26 ianvaria–10 fevralia 1934 g. Stenograficheskii otchet* (Moscow: Partizdat, 1934), 199.
65 See 'Vyshe znamia proletarskogo internatsionalizma!' Lead editorial in *Pravda*, 10 March 1933, 1. English-language excerpt in *The Holodomor Reader*, 259–260.
66 See *The Holodomor Reader*, 240.
67 See the introductory essay by Alexander J. Motyl and myself in *The Holodomor Reader*, in which we discuss the destruction of Ukraine's elites and Stalin's views on the national question, pp. xxix–xlv, esp. xxix–xxx, xxxvii–xliv. See also Andrea Graziosi (Chapter 9, this volume).

8 Famine losses in Ukraine in 1932 to 1933 within the context of the Soviet Union

Omelian Rudnytskyi, Nataliia Levchuk, Oleh Wolowyna and Pavlo Shevchuk

Introduction

Although the 1932/1933 famine in the Union of Soviet Socialist Republics (USSR) was one of the largest European catastrophes of the twentieth century, its magnitude is still not widely known.[1] For many years, the Soviet government tried to minimise its scope and blame it on natural causes. The famine's occurrence and its man-made nature are now generally accepted facts. However, one issue still in dispute is the level of population losses due to the famine experienced in different regions of the Soviet Union. This is especially the case for Ukraine, where estimates of excess famine deaths vary between 2.6 and 5.0 million.[2] To illustrate the difficulty of the task, the estimates of one researcher, Maksudov, have varied from one attempt to the next: 4.4 million and then 3.6 million.[3]

One reason for these variations is the earlier limited access to relevant data, forcing researchers to use methods based on assumptions that were difficult to verify. Initial estimates were based on general demographic indicators and historical documents, as well as on the demographic balance method.[4] Once data from the 1926, 1937 and 1939 Soviet censuses and the time series of vital statistics and migration data became fully accessible, researchers were able to apply the more effective population reconstruction method that allows for estimating direct (excess deaths), indirect (lost births) and migration losses by year, sex and age. Full population reconstructions were done by Andreev *et al.* for the Soviet Union as a whole in 1920 to 1959 and the Russian Soviet Federative Socialist Republic in 1927 to 1959, and by Vallin *et al.* and Mesle *et al.* for the Ukrainian Soviet Socialist Republic in 1927 to 1959.[5] Another reason for variation in estimates is the confounding effect of migration. If net migration for a republic or region is measured incorrectly, the population change attributed to excess deaths may be over- or underestimated. A third reason is that many of the official statistics have serious data quality problems, and their use without relevant adjustments is likely to introduce significant biases in the loss estimates.

The 1932/1933 famine affected different regions of the Soviet Union, and previous research on famine losses focused mainly on the Soviet Union as a whole and on specific republics: Russia, Ukraine and Kazakhstan. Up until now no attempt has been made to estimate famine losses in all former Soviet republics and evaluate losses in Ukraine in comparison to the other republics. Our results are based on population reconstructions for all 11 former Soviet republics and the Prydnistrovia (Transdnister) region, after the quality of all data was carefully evaluated and relevant adjustments were made where needed.

Data

All the Soviet republics were analysed within their current international borders and original data were recalculated to conform to these territorial definitions because: (1) during the 1926 to 1939 intercensal period several Soviet republics underwent significant border changes, and borders in 1926 are not consistent with borders in 1939; (2) our reconstruction of Russia is based on the work of Andreev *et al.* and they used Russia within its current borders; (3) this is consistent with common statistical practice, where analysis of data from previous censuses is made consistent with data from the latest census.[6]

Ukraine includes 17 of the current *oblasts* and the Autonomous Republic of Crimea, as well as the seven western *oblasts* and the southwestern part of the Odesa *oblast* that were not part of the Ukrainian Soviet Socialist Republic (UkrSSR) during the 1927 to 1938 period. Also excluded from Ukraine is the region of Prydnistrovia, which belonged to the UkrSSR in 1924 to 1940 and became part of Moldova in 1940. Belarus is analysed within its 17 September 1939 borders; that is, without western Belarus. Russia is defined as it existed within its 1939 borders, excluding Crimea, and all the other republics are analysed within their current borders. In order to simplify the presentation of results for 11 republics and one region, the seven Asian republics are aggregated into two regions: Transcaucasus (Armenia, Georgia and Azerbaijan) and Central Asia (Uzbekistan, Kyrgyzstan, Turkmenistan and Tajikistan), as results for the republics in each of these two regions are fairly similar. Thus, although analyses were performed for each individual republic, the results are presented for the USSR as a whole, and the seven regions of Russia, Ukraine, Prydnistrovia, Belarus, Kazakhstan, Central Asia and Transcaucasus.

One of the challenges for a comprehensive analysis of the USSR and its republics is the unevenness of available demographic data in terms of existence, completeness and quality. A detailed summary of birth, death and migration data availability by country and region is presented in Table 8.1. The Soviet censuses of 1926 and 1939 provide the necessary population information by age, sex and ethnicity, although they require adjustments (see below). Complete annual migration data are available only for the urban populations of all republics. Vital statistics range from very complete for Ukraine to very limited for Kazakhstan and Central Asia. In the case of Ukraine, access was gained to the research manuscripts of the Ukrainian demographer Yurii Korchak-Chepurkivskyi (archives of Korchak-Chepurkivskyi), which allowed us to complete the time series of vital statistics for the 1930 to 1932 period, since the original data were destroyed.[7] In order to take advantage of data that were only available for urban and/or rural areas, all analysis was done by urban-rural areas for each republic and then aggregated on the national level.

Table 8.1 Summary of available Soviet birth, death and migration data, 1926 to 1939

Data	*USSR*	*Belarus*	*Transcaucasus*	*Kazakhstan*	*Russia*	*Central Asia*	*Ukraine*
Births:							
Total	Yearly	Yearly			Yearly		Yearly
Estimated totals			Yearly[1]	1926–1928[3] 1932–1933[4]		Yearly[1] 1926–1928[3] 1932–1933[3]	
By urban-rural	Yearly[1]	Yearly[1]	1936–1939[1]	1936–1940[1]	Yearly[1]	1936–1938[1]	Yearly[1]
By age of mother	1939	1939	1939	1939		1939	Yearly[2]
By nationalities		1926, 1939	1939	1939	1926, 1939	1939	Yearly
By age of mother and nationalities	1939	1939	1939	1939	1939	1939	Yearly[2]
Births by month	1936–1939	Yearly	1936–1939	1936–1939	Yearly	1936–1939	Yearly
By age of mother[4] (indirect estimation)	NA	NA	Yearly	Yearly	NA	Yearly	NA
Deaths:							
Total	Yearly	Yearly			Yearly		Yearly
Estimated totals			Yearly[1]	1926[3] 1928[3] 1932–1933[3]		Yearly[1,3] 1926–1928[3] 1932–1933[3]	
By urban-rural	Yearly[1]	Yearly[1]	1936–1939[1]	1936–1939[1]	Yearly[1]	1936–1939[1]	Yearly
By age and sex	1939	1926, 1939	1926, 1939	1939	1926, 1939	1939	Yearly[2]
By nationalities		1926, 1939	1939	1939	1926, 1939	1939	Yearly
Deaths by month	1936–1939	Yearly	1936–39	1936–39	Yearly	1936–1939	Yearly
Life tables:							
Calculated by authors and different researchers	1926–1927 (Europe part) 1938–1939	1926–1927	1926–1927		1926–1927 (Europe part) 1927–39[6]	1938–1939[5]	1924–1931[7] 1927–1938[8] 1938–1939
Migration:							
Urban migration by origin: destination, age-sex	Yearly	Yearly	Yearly	Yearly	Yearly	Yearly	Yearly
Migration of special groups				Yearly	Yearly		Yearly

Sources: Official vital statistics and migration reports and multiple studies.

Notes
1 Estimates by national statistical offices.
2 All years except 1932.
3 Estimation of vital statistics of rural populations in Central Asia and Kazakhstan, by research expeditions in 1926, 1928 and 1932–1933 (Korchak-Chepurkivskyi, 1947).
4 Derived from age-specific fertility rates estimated from survey data for rural populations in Transcaucasia in 1947, and Central Asia and Kazakhstan in 1960 (Sifman, 1959, 1965, 1966, 1974).
5 Life table for the city of Samarkand (Uzbekistan) for 1938–1939, calculated by Korchak-Chepurkivskyi (archives of Y.O. Korchak-Chepurkivskyi).
6 Andreev *et al.*, 1998;
7 Calculated by Korchak-Chepurkivskyi (archives of Y.O. Korchak-Chepurkivkyi).
8 Calculated by Vallin *et al.* (2002).

Adjustment of census data

The 1926 and 1939 censuses have problems typical of most censuses at that time, and the results of the 1939 census were also affected by deliberate falsifications by the Soviet government, which attempted to hide the effects of the 1932/1933 famine and political repressions in 1937/1938.[8] Detailed adjustments were made to correct these problems.

Adjustments of the 1926 census consisted of: (1) the redistribution of military and border personnel to different republics (to align the de jure 1926 data with the de facto 1939 census data); (2) adjustment for significant undercounting of women aged eight to 27 in republics with large Muslim populations and of children aged 0 to two in all republics; (3) redistribution of persons with unknown age; and (4) application of smoothing techniques to address serious digit preference problems. These modifications increased the overall USSR population by 1.1 per cent, by less than 1.0 per cent for the European republics and between 2.4 and 3.0 per cent for Kazakhstan, Transcaucasus and Central Asia (Table 8.2).

The 1939 census was falsified in three major ways. First, individual records of special populations – armed forces, secret police, prisoners in concentration camps, civilian support populations in the camps – were reassigned during data processing to other republics in order to hide their large concentrations in northern and eastern Russia and Kazakhstan. Second, the number of persons captured in control forms and presumably not registered by the census was artificially inflated. Third, the size of the census undercount was greatly exaggerated. These falsifications are well documented in official documents, which provide information that may be used to adjust the census figures.[9] Andreev *et al.*, Zhiromskaia, and Tolts describe in detail the official communications between the Central Statistical Board and Communist Party General Secretary Joseph Stalin and Soviet Council of Ministers First Deputy Chairman Vyacheslav Molotov, confirming political reasons for these falsifications; they also provide descriptions of irregularities in processing the census data.[10]

Table 8.2 Official and adjusted total populations from the 1926 and 1939 Soviet censuses (in 1,000s): USSR and seven regions

	Official		*Adjusted*		*% adjustment*	
	1926	*1939*	*1926*	*1939*	*1926*	*1939*
USSR	147,027.9	170,557.1	148,583.0	168,870.9	1.1	−1.0
Belarus	4,986.0	5,571.2	4,984.5	5,444.0	0.0	−2.3
Transcaucasus	5,872.2	8,026.6	6,015.5	8,023.2	2.4	0.0
Kazakhstan	6,025.1	6,081.6	6,160.8	5,489.9	2.3	−9.7
Russia	92,734.4	108,262.0	93,493.4	108,027.6	0.8	−0.2
Central Asia	7,653.1	10,542.6	7,885.1	10,634.2	3.0	0.9
Ukraine	29,515.1	31,785.4	29,800.4	30,966.9	1.0	−2.6
Prydnistrovia	242.0	287.7	243.3	285.1	0.5	−0.9

Source: calculations based on the 1926 and 1939 censuses, multiple studies.

Adjustment of the 1939 census was performed in two stages: adjustment of total populations and of age–sex structures. First, taking as the basis the original count of the civilian population, the special subpopulations were added to the original count, and then adjustments were made to reduce the overestimation of control forms, undercounting and the so-called 'unknown difference'. Then the age–sex structure of the civilian population was adjusted to the new totals, taking into account the very different age–sex structure of prisoners and resettled kulaks. The category 'age unknown' was distributed proportionally to the adjusted age–sex structure, and the same methods applied in the 1926 census were used to smooth out age heaping. After all the adjustments were made, the populations in both censuses were shifted to 1 January of the year closest to the census data, to align them for the reconstruction process (a more detailed and technical description of the 1926 and 1939 census adjustments is provided in the appendix).

These adjustments decrease the 1939 census USSR population by 1 per cent. Kazakhstan's population is reduced by close to 10 per cent, and Ukraine's and Belarus' by 2.3 per cent. The population of the Transcaucasus region was unchanged and Central Asia's population increased by almost 1 per cent (Table 8.2).

Reconstruction of natural growth and migration

Reconstructed populations are populations that reflect the actual demographic situation, i.e. they are calculated for a certain period using the demographic balancing equation (1) with adjusted initial population and yearly adjusted numbers of births, deaths and net migrants (difference between in- and out-migrants). The following general steps were used in the population reconstruction process:

- All official statistics were evaluated for errors and falsifications, with appropriate adjustments made.
- The adjusted 1926 and 1939 census populations were used as pillars for the yearly reconstructions during this 12-year period. (The 1937 census population was used only as a standard for the reconstructed total population values for 1937, as data by age at the republic level were not reported in this census.)
- Adjusted (reconstructed) total numbers of births, deaths and net migrants for each country or region for the 1927 to 1939 period were estimated, and these values were disaggregated by year.
- Yearly population balances for the USSR and each republic or region were calculated using the the following demographic balancing equation:

$$P(t+1)=P(t)+B(t,t+1)-D(t,t+1)+\Delta M(t,t+1) \quad (1)$$

where:

$P(t)$ – population at the beginning of year t
$B(t, t+1)$ – number of live births during year t
$D(t, t+1)$ – number of deaths during year t
$\Delta M(t, t+1)$ – number of net migrants during year t.

- Age structures for these births, deaths and net migrants were estimated (detailed below).
- Starting with the adjusted age–sex populations of the 1926 census, yearly reconstructed populations by age and sex were calculated using the demographic balancing equation (1), with each term specified by age and sex.

These reconstructed populations provide the basis for estimating direct and indirect losses during the 1932/1933 famine.

Under-registration of births and deaths is a common characteristic of many vital statistics registration systems. Given the wide variation of vital statistics data availability in the different Soviet republics, it was necessary to develop different adjustment methodologies in each case. The methods used are a combination of results from previous research, empirically validated relationships, demographic models, informed assumptions and use of the demographic balancing equation. Under-registration of births and deaths was particularly severe in 1933, the year when most famine-related deaths occurred. The extraordinary increase in deaths during the first half of 1933 caused severe disruptions in the vital statistics registration system and resulted in very high levels of under-registration. Thus, in most cases two different adjustment methods were used: one for 1933 and another for all the other years (1927–1932 and 1934–1938).

USSR

The estimation of adjusted numbers of births and deaths for the 12-year period was based on estimates derived by Andreev *et al.*[11] Adjustments to these estimates were made to account for the adjusted values of the 1926 and 1937 census populations and a different estimate of net migration: −400,000 instead of the –200,000 estimated by Andreev *et al.* Analysis of available data on migration showed that during the first half of the 1930s, besides the 200,000 migrants from Kazakhstan, there was also emigration from other Central Asian republics: 100,000 from Turkmenistan and 100,000 from Uzbekistan and Tajikistan.[12] According to these researchers, the yearly distribution of these −400,000 net migrants was: −50,000 in 1930, −50,000 in 1931, −100,000 in 1932 and –200,000 in 1933. For the other years, net migration for the USSR was zero.[13]

These census and migration adjustments resulted in 347,800 more births and 29,600 fewer deaths than estimated by Andreev *et al.* for this period, with a total of 74,386,800 reconstructed births and 53,940,400 reconstructed deaths for the 12-year period. The yearly distribution of these totals was done by applying yearly proportions of births and deaths estimated by Andreev *et al.*[14]

Ukraine (and Prydnistrovia)

Adjustment of infant deaths: Infant deaths were adjusted for using the method developed by Arsenii Khomenko, which is based on the following assumptions: (1) under-reporting of infant deaths was concentrated mainly in the first six months of life; (2) adjustment factors may be estimated based on a relationship with a referent country with an infant mortality regime similar to Ukraine's but with better quality statistics, like Hungary; (3) the ratio of infant mortality during the first six months of life in Ukraine and Hungary is equal to the respective ratio of infant mortality during the second half of the first year of life.[15] We adjusted the infant mortality rate for Ukraine during the first six months of life by multiplying the Hungarian infant mortality rate during the first six months of life by the ratio of the Ukrainian infant mortality rate during the sixth to eleventh months of life and the respective infant mortality rates for Hungary. Adjusted rates were calculated for 1926/1927 (30%) and 1938/1939 (10%) and interpolated linearly between these two years, except for 1933.[16] The number of infant deaths for each year (except 1933) was obtained as the product of the number of registered births and the sum of the adjusted infant mortality rates for the first and second half of the year.

For 1933, the number of adjusted infant deaths was obtained as the sum of the registered number of infant deaths and one-half of the difference between the number of adjusted and registered births in 1933.[17] This adjustment factor was derived by comparing the number of births in 1933 to the number of their survivors six years later in the 1939 census. The same method was applied to adjust urban and rural infant deaths.

Adjustment of births: Based on the assumption that the number of under-registered births is equal to the number of under-registered infant deaths, the number of adjusted births was calculated as the number of registered births plus the number of under-registered infant deaths for the first six months. The adjustment factors are 4.4 per cent in 1927 and 1.4 per cent in 1938, and these factors were interpolated linearly for the interim years, except for 1933. For 1933, we extrapolated the previous trend of declining fertility by estimating the number of adjusted births in 1933 as the number of registered births in 1932 times the ratio of adjusted births for 1932 and 1931.[18] The same method was applied to adjust urban and rural births.

Adjustment of deaths aged 1 year or more: Research by the Central Statistical Department of the UkrSSR showed that the under-registration adjustment factor for infant deaths was 2.5 times the under-registration factor for deaths at one year or older.[19] We used this relationship to obtain the adjusted number of deaths at one year or older for all years for a whole country and its urban areas, using the following steps. First, deaths for the whole country and all years except 1933 were estimated using this adjustment factor.[20] Second, for urban deaths the same method was used for all years including 1933.[21] Third, rural deaths were calculated for all years except 1933 as the difference between total and urban deaths. Adjustment of rural deaths in 1933 requires special treatment (described below). The sum of rural and urban deaths in 1933 completes the time series for all deaths.

The number of deaths for 1933 in rural areas was obtained using the demographic balance equation. This requires the estimation of net migration for rural areas for the 12-year period, which is described in the next section. We calculated the adjusted natural growth for 1933 as the total growth for 12 years minus net migration for 12 years and minus the sum of natural growth for 11 years (excluding 1933). Having the adjusted natural growth and adjusted births for 1933, we can calculate the adjusted number of deaths in 1933. For 1933 the adjustment factors for all deaths are 2.18 for the whole country, 2.33 for rural areas and 1.14 for urban areas.

Estimation of net migration: In urban areas net migration (including rural to urban reclassification) for the 12-year period was calculated as the difference between total and natural growth, resulting in 4,995,920 persons, which includes 1,800,000 persons due to reclassification. Of the remaining 3,195,920 net migrants for urban areas, 82 per cent were net migrants from rural areas in Ukraine, and 18 per cent were net migrants from other Soviet republics.[22]

Detailed statistics are available on different migration streams for rural areas: (1) 700,000 voluntary migrants, Gulag prisoners, and those exiled during the 1927 to 1938 period;[23] (2) 300,000 deported kulaks (alleged rich farmers) during 1930 to 1933;[24] (3) 40,000 deported Germans and Poles to Kazakhstan;[25] (4) resettlement of peasants from Russia and Belarus to rural areas in Ukraine depopulated by the 1932/1933 famine: 118,400 in 1933 and 19,100 in 1934.[26] The sum of all internal and external migration streams and the reclassification component resulted in a 5,321,888 net loss for rural areas in Ukraine during the 12-year period, within a net loss of 325,968 migrants for the whole country during the 1927 to 1938 period. According to official statistics, net migration for Ukraine for the 1927 to 1929 period was zero (TSU USRR, 1927–1932). For the other years, annual net migration in rural areas was obtained from the registration system in urban areas (rural to urban migration) and statistics for the different migration streams for rural areas listed above.

Belarus

The methods used for Ukraine were applied to the reconstruction of yearly births and deaths for Belarus with the exception of deaths in 1932 and 1933.[27] The yearly under-registration of deaths before 1932 was estimated at about 25 per cent. Due to lack of data, it was assumed that during the crisis years of 1932 and 1933, registered deaths were underestimated by 50 per cent. Urban births and deaths were also adjusted using the same methods as for Ukraine. Rural births and deaths were obtained as the difference between total and urban values. Net migration for the 1927 to 1938 period for the whole country was calculated as the difference between total and natural growth for this period. Yearly disaggregation of migrants was done by applying yearly proportions of migrants as estimated by Rakov and Maskov.[28] For urban areas, we have yearly estimates of urban net migrants from the registration system, while yearly numbers of net migrants in rural areas is the difference between total and urban net migrants.[29]

Kazakhstan, Transcaucasus and Central Asia

Migration: Net migration was estimated using the ethnodemographic balance (EDB) method, which was successfully applied by several researchers.[30] This approach is based on the assumption that changes in ethnic identification from one census to the next in these Asian republics did not usually cross the European/non-European divide. A self-declared member of one of the European nationalities at the first census was unlikely to choose a non-European nationality at the second census; likewise a member of a non-European nationality would rarely report a European nationality in the second census.[31]

We start by estimating the intercensal natural rates of growth for European and non-European subpopulations in each republic. For the European nationalities, we input the average natural rate of growth of the urban population of the USSR during 1927 to 1938 to each of these three regions, as most people of European nationality resided in the cities. The 1 January 1927 European subpopulation in each region was multiplied by this rate – 9 per 1,000 population – resulting in the expected population on 1 January 1939 had there been zero net migration. The difference between this estimate and the 1939 census of the European subpopulation gives an estimate of its net migration. The yearly disaggregation of this net migration was calculated proportionally to the urban net migration for each of the three regions.[32]

For non-European nationalities, we calculate the rate of change between 1927 and 1938 of the titular ethnic group of each of the republics in these three regions (Kazakhs in Kazakhstan, Uzbeks in Uzbekistan, etc.) and then apply these rates to the respective non-European nationality in the eight republics (the rate of change for Kazakhs in Kazakhstan to Kazakhs in all of the republics, excluding Kazakhstan; the rate of change for Uzbeks in Uzbekistan to Uzbeks in all of the republics, excluding Uzbekistan, etc.). The sum of all of these non-European nationalities in each republic gives us the expected number of non-Europeans in each republic in 1939, assuming zero net migration. The yearly disaggregation of these estimates was done in three steps: (1) we calculated the total number of net urban migrants for these eight republics as the difference of the urban net migrants for the USSR and all the European republics; (2) the total number of intercensal non-European net migrants in each of the eight republics was disaggregated according to the yearly proportions of urban net migrants in these republics as a unit, and (3) we also took into account yearly statistics of forced migrants in these republics.[33]

Births: The number of yearly births for rural populations was estimated by multiplying the age-specific birth rate (estimated by Korchak-Chepurkivskyi and Sifman), and by the number of women in the respective age groups.[34] The yearly number of women at childbearing age for the eight republics was estimated using survivorship ratios based on probabilities of dying interpolated linearly between the 1926 and 1939 values. For urban populations, yearly numbers of births for all eight republics as a unit were calculated as the difference between respective births for the USSR and all the European republics. Official estimates of urban births for each republic are available for 1926 and 1939, and these estimates were adjusted to the totals of the eight republics for these years.[35] The number of births for the intercensal period for each republic was estimated by multiplying the average general fertility rates for urban populations, based on 1926 and 1939 data for each republic, by the average number of women aged 15 to 49. The yearly disaggregation of these births was calculated using yearly proportions of births for the eight republics as a unit.

Deaths: First, the total number of yearly urban deaths for the eight republics as a unit was estimated as the difference of deaths between the USSR and the European republics. The disaggregation of these urban deaths by republic was obtained as the difference between total growth and net migration and births. The yearly numbers of deaths were obtained by applying yearly proportions for the eight republics as a unit; a similar methodology was applied to estimate rural deaths.

Russia

Net migration for the 12-year period was estimated as the difference between net migration for the whole Soviet Union and net migration for all the other regions, resulting in −965,000 net migration, compared to Andreev *et al.*'s +450,000.[36] There is no agreement among researchers on the net migration for Russia during this intercensal period. Andreev *et al.* and Iontsev estimated positive net migration, while Perevedentsev, Rybakovsjkyj, Maksudov and Simchera estimated negative net migration.[37] Our estimate indicates that during this period Russia was a net exporter of population to other republics. Yearly net migration was obtained as the difference between the USSR and all other regions. Net migration for urban areas was obtained from the migration registration statistics.[38] Net migration for rural areas was obtained as the difference between net migrants for all of Russia and in its urban areas.

Our estimate of natural growth for the intercensal period is 15,171,600, while the Andreev *et al.* estimate is 13,840,000.[39] Due to lack of information, the 1,331,600 difference between these two figures was distributed equally between births and deaths: 665,800 were added to births and 665,800 were subtracted from deaths, resulting in 50,061,300 births and 34,889,700 deaths for the 12-year period. Yearly numbers of births and deaths were obtained by applying yearly proportions based on the Andreev *et al.* (1998) estimates of births and deaths. Estimates for urban areas were obtained by applying to official birth and death registrations respective adjustment coefficients for Ukraine's urban population.[40] Yearly numbers of births and deaths in rural areas were obtained by differences between total and urban values.

Some results from the reconstruction

The reconstruction of natural growth and migration allows us to calculate population balances that summarise the population dynamics of each region (Table 8.3). The intercensal yearly natural rate of growth (growth due to births and deaths) for the whole Soviet Union was very low (1.1%), reflecting the effects of the famine and other events during this period. Kazakhstan actually lost population at an average yearly rate of −1.0 per cent. Ukraine had the lowest positive annual rate of growth with 0.4 per cent, followed by Prydnistrovia with 1.1 per cent and Russia with 1.2 per cent. The highest rate of growth was experienced by the Transcaucasus region with 2.0 per cent, followed by Central Asia and Belarus with 1.6 per cent each. Thus, if we exclude Kazakhstan, Ukraine had the lowest rate of population growth among all Soviet republics between 1927 and 1938.

Two patterns of intercensal net migration may be observed among the different regions: European regions experienced negative net migration and Asian regions (with the exception of Kazakhstan) had positive net migration (Table 8.3). Russia had the largest number of negative net migrants with −965,000, followed by Belarus with −593,800 and Ukraine with −326,000. Central Asia gained more than one million net migrants and the Transcaucasus region almost 400,000, while Kazakhstan had zero net migration during the whole period.

An important result from the reconstruction process is the estimation of under-reporting of vital events due to problems in the registration systems in the different republics, especially during the famine years. This under-registration may be measured by comparing registered vital events in republics with functioning registration systems (Russia, Belarus and Ukraine) with their respective reconstructed values. Before the famine, Ukraine had the lowest level of under-registration of births, at about 3 per cent, followed by Belarus at 6 per cent and Russia at 16 per cent; under-registration of deaths was around 9 per cent for Ukraine, 10 per cent for Belarus and 33 per cent for Russia.

Levels of under-registration of both births and deaths experienced increases in 1932 and reached maximum values at the height of the famine in 1933. That year, under-registration of births was 13 per cent in Belarus, 23 per cent in Russia and 35.5 per cent in Ukraine, while under-registration of deaths was 50 per cent in Belarus, 80 per cent in Russia and the number of adjusted deaths was more than twice the number of registered deaths in Ukraine. These high levels of under-registration in 1933 were caused by the disruption of the social fabric in general and the vital registration system in particular due to very high mortality in an extremely short time period, and in many instances the vital statistics bureaucracy was not able to cope with the sudden increase in deaths.

The time series of reconstructed numbers of births and deaths provide an initial view of the regional variations of the impact of the 1932 to 1934 famine in the Soviet Union. Figure 8.1 shows three distinct patterns of yearly births and deaths during the intercensal period. The pattern for Ukraine, with a sudden and extremely high increase in the number of deaths and a decline in the number of

Table 8.3 Population balance for the USSR and seven regions (in 1,000s), 1927 to 1938

Region	*Population on 1 January 1927*	*Births*	*Deaths*	*Net migration*	*Population on 1 January 1939*	*% annual natural rate*
USSR	148,705.8	74,386.8	53,940.4	−400.0	168,752.3	1.1
Belarus	4,988.3	2,177.9	1,132.2	−593.8	5,440.2	1.6
Transcaucasus	6,020.2	3,253.6	1,655.5	399.6	8,017.9	2.0
Kazakhstan	6,162.5	2,466.5	3,143.7	0.0	5,485.3	−1.0
Russia	93,574.1	50,063.5	34,923.1	−759.6	107,954.9	1.2
Central Asia	7,889.6	4,412.3	2,752.3	1,078.7	10,628.3	1.6
Ukraine	29,827.7	11,900.0	10,255.4	−531.4	30,940.9	0.4
Prydnistrovia	243.5	113.0	78.3	6.5	284.7	1.1

Source: authors' calculations.

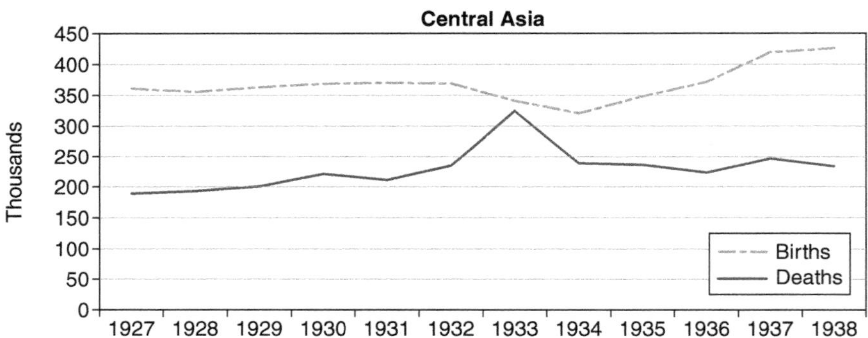

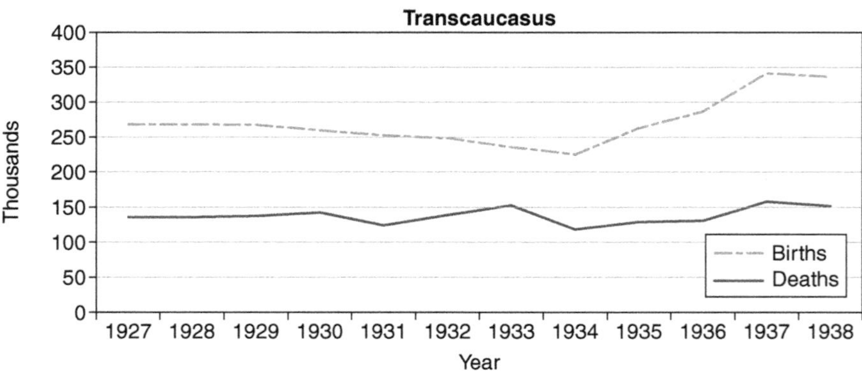

Figure 8.1 Time series of adjusted numbers of births and deaths for Ukraine, Central Asia and Transcaucasus, 1927 to 1938 (source: author's calculations).

births during the famine years, represents similar patterns found in Kazakhstan, Prydnistrovia, and Russia. The pattern for Central Asia – a sudden and more moderate increase in the number of deaths during the famine years – closing the previous significant difference between births and deaths in these republics, as well as demonstrating a moderate decline in the number of births, represents underlying patterns for Tadzhikistan, Turkmenistan, Uzbekistan, Kyrgyzstan and Belarus. The pattern for the Transcaucasus, a very small increase in the number of deaths and a moderate decrease in the number of births, represents underlying patterns for Georgia, Armenia and Azerbaijan. These patterns suggest a categorisation of regions in terms of the impact of the famine. Republics in the first group suffered the most, the second group was less affected, and the third group was least affected. These preliminary results will be validated later with the estimation of direct and indirect famine losses.

Reconstruction of yearly populations by age and sex

Detailed reconstructions were calculated separately for each republic and then aggregated for the Transcaucasus and Central Asia regions. As a first step, complete life tables were constructed for each republic for the base years 1929 and 1939. Life tables for Russia, Ukraine, Belarus and Armenia were constructed using the adjusted age–sex populations from the 1926 and 1939 censuses and registered births and deaths available for these countries and years.[41] Life tables for Georgia and Azerbaijan were constructed using a combination of partial and indirect estimations of vital statistics available for 1926 and 1939 (see Table 8.1). Given the small population size of Prydnistrovia and its similarity to Ukraine, the life table for Ukraine was used for this region.

Since the vital statistics registration system was in its organisational stage during the second half of the 1920s in Kazakhstan and the Central Asian republics, we decided to construct a common model life table for all these republics using the following elements: (1) data collected by expeditions to these countries in 1926, 1928 and 1932/1933 to measure vital statistics; (2) a complete life table for the city of Samarkand constructed by Korchak-Chepurkivskyi, and (3) official registrations of deaths and births in 1938 and 1939.[42]

Starting with the 1 January 1927 population, successive yearly populations are calculated by subtracting from each single age–sex group the respective number of deaths and adding the respective number of net migrants. The first age group was calculated as the number of surviving births plus the number of respective net migrants. This requires the estimation of yearly numbers of deaths and net migrants by age and sex.

Estimation of the number of yearly deaths by age and sex

For Ukraine, Belarus and Prydnistrovia, the number of deaths was estimated by applying to the yearly number of deaths (from the balance) the age structures of registered deaths. For Russia, age-specific mortality rates estima ted by

Andreev *et al.* were multiplied by the respective populations.[43] For Kazakhstan, Transcaucasus and Central Asian republics, we started with age-specific probabilities of dying obtained by linear interpolation between the 1927 and 1939 life tables. These probabilities were transformed into age-specific death rates and then multiplied by the respective populations. This method was used for all these republics and all years except 1933; given the extraordinary effect of the famine in Kazakhstan, the interpolated probability of dying in 1933 was replaced by the respective value for Ukraine. These were initial values used in the first iteration, and they were progressively adjusted in subsequent iterations in order to make them consistent with the adjusted census populations and the yearly balance births, deaths and net migration totals.

Estimation of the number of net migrants by age and sex

Due to lack of information, in most republics we applied the age–sex structure of the total population to the total number of net migrants. In the case of Ukraine and Kazakhstan, we were able to refine these estimates with available data on the age–sex structure of special populations. For prisoners in camps we used data in Kokurin and Petrov, while for special settlers in Kazakhstan and Ukraine we used data from the Russian Academy of Sciences.[44] In each case we subtracted the numbers of the special subpopulations from the total number of migrants, applied the respective age structures, and then added them back to the rest of the migrants.

Reconstruction process

During the first iteration, at each yearly cycle and before moving to the next cycle, the total population in each republic was adjusted to the respective value in the balance. At the end of the first iteration, the projected 1 January 1939 population did not coincide with the census-based population for that date. To assure consistency with the census-based values, the respective age–sex differences were redistributed backward cohort-wise, and during this process the population age–sex structures were adjusted again to the totals in the balance. We then recalculated the yearly age–sex-specific numbers of deaths using the age–sex structures of the adjusted populations. Finally, the total number of deaths was adjusted to coincide with the respective numbers in the balance. Yearly life tables were recalculated for each republic using the final adjusted populations and deaths.

Estimation of famine losses

It is impossible to apply a strict definition of famine losses (i.e. excess deaths and lost births caused by famine), as this requires death statistics by cause of death, and a definition is often problematic even in countries with high-quality vital statistics data on cause of death. The following generally accepted operational definition is used to estimate direct and indirect losses: difference between actual deaths (or births) during the crisis years, and deaths (or births) that would have occurred without the crisis. Thus the operational definition of losses requires two types of populations: actual (also called reconstructed) populations, and hypothetical populations assuming no famine.

In order to estimate numbers of no-crisis deaths and births, we need to define 'normal' mortality and fertility trends during the famine period. This is done by linear interpolation of age-specific death and birth rates using beginning and ending years that were not affected by the crisis. These intervals vary by region, as mortality and fertility trends were affected by different regional socio-economic, historical and epidemiological factors.

Analysis of reconstructed vital events allows us to determine these intervals. Mortality levels started to increase earlier, by 1929, in Central Asia, Kazakhstan and Russia, and later, by 1931, in Ukraine and the Transcaucasus republics (Table 8.4). This is probably due to such factors as epidemics of infectious diseases during the first half of the 1930s in the Central Asian republics,[45] waves of collectivisation of nomad-pastoral peoples in 1929 and 1930 in Kazakhstan,[46] and increased mortality among prisoners in Gulags in Kazakhstan and Russia at the beginning of collectivisation.[47] Fertility trends had a different pattern than mortality trends. As part of a general trend that started in Northern Europe in the late 1800s, the Slavic Soviet republics were experiencing a fertility decline years before the famine period, while this process started later in the Asian regions.[48] For the ending years of the interpolation periods, we selected years not affected by the compensating effects of the famine, that is, a decline in deaths and increase in fertility levels, and these years also vary by region (Table 8.4).

No crisis deaths and births during the famine years were obtained by multiplying the 'normal' age-specific mortality and fertility rates for these years by the respective no-crisis age-specific populations. The estimation of the no-crisis population is problematic due to the fact that it is very difficult to guess the value of net migration without the famine. Assuming that net migration is zero for all years does not solve the problem. Interaction between the age structure of the population with mortality and fertility levels and their age structures can produce 'abnormal' results. For instance, even with lower 'normal' mortality levels we

Table 8.4 Year intervals used for linear interpolations of age-specific mortality and fertility rates to simulate non-crisis mortality and fertility trends

Region	*Mortality*	*Fertility*
Belarus	1931–1935	1931–1935
Transcaucasus	1931–1935	1931–1935
Kazakhstan	1929–1936	1929–1938
Russia	1929–1935	1931–1935
Central Asia	1929–1936	1929–1936
Ukraine	1931–1935	1931–1935
Prydnistrovia	1931–1935	1931–1935

may have higher numbers of no-crisis than crisis deaths, and with higher 'normal' fertility levels we may have lower numbers of no-crisis than crisis births. Given these problems, we decided to use the reconstructed populations to estimate numbers of 'normal' age-specific deaths and births, as this provides a standard that eliminates these structural effects on the number of 'normal' deaths and births.

Two observations should be made about the estimation of famine losses. First, the analysis showed that the effects of the 1932/1933 famine were also felt in 1934, and this is especially the case for lost births.[49] Second, the crisis in Kazakhstan started earlier than in the grain-producing European republics. Increased levels of mortality were observed in Kazakhstan starting in 1929 as a result of forced collectivisation of a society composed largely of herdsmen and nomads.[50] Thus the restriction of our analysis of losses during the 1932 to 1934 period, necessary for a comparative analysis with the other republics, underestimates the losses in Kazakhstan.

Direct losses by region

Direct losses for the Soviet Union are estimated at 8.7 million in 1932 to 1934, with 1.0 million in 1932, 7.1 million in 1933 and 0.6 million in 1934 (Table 8.5). Ukraine had the largest number of direct losses during this period among all republics: 3.9 million, with 3.6 million 1933. Russia had the second largest number of direct losses, with 3.3 million in 1932 to 1934 and 2.6 million in 1933, followed by Kazakhstan, with 1.3 million for the period and 694,000 in 1933. The number of direct losses in 1932 to 1934 for the other regions varied between 401,000 for Transcaucasus and 1,584,000 (are these figures correct?) for Central Asia, and in all cases the number of losses in 1933 was significantly higher than in the other two years.

In order to compare losses among the different regions, it is necessary to control for population size. In relative terms, the Soviet Union experienced 18 excess deaths per 1,000 population during the 1932 to 1934 famine period, with 44 per 1,000 population in 1933. Kazakhstan had the largest relative number of direct losses, with 74 per 1,000 for the whole period and 124 per 1,000 in 1933; Ukraine had 43 per 1,000 direct losses for the whole period and 117 per 1,000 in 1933. Relative losses for Russia were significantly lower, with 11 per 1,000 for the whole period and 26 per 1,000 in 1933, while respective numbers for the other regions were much smaller.

Although the majority of direct losses were concentrated in 1933 in all regions, there are significant differences in the yearly distribution of excess deaths among the regions. Ukraine had the highest percentage of excess deaths in 1933 with 91 per cent of all direct losses, followed by 84 per cent in Prydnistrovia and 80.5 per cent in Belarus. In the other regions, the percentage of excess deaths in 1933 varied between 55 per cent in Kazakhstan to 69 per cent in Central Asia. Kazakhstan has a much more uniform distribution of relative excess deaths than all the other regions. Its numbers of direct losses per 1,000

Table 8.5 Direct losses (excess deaths) in numbers and per 1,000 population

Region	*Thousands*				*Per 1,000 population*			
	1932	*1933*	*1934*	*1932–1934*	*1932*	*1933*	*1934*	*1932–1934*
USSR	1,004.0	7,090.8	637.1	8,731.9	6.1	44.1	4.0	18.1
Belarus	15.6	46.5	5.5	67.6	2.9	8.7	1.0	4.2
Transcaucasus	12.0	22.9	5.2	40.1	1.7	3.2	0.7	1.9
Kazakhstan	399.3	694.0	164.9	1,258.2	63.4	123.7	32.4	74.1
Russia	305.6	2,689.4	269.6	3,264.6	3.0	26.1	2.6	10.6
Central Asia	20.8	109.8	27.8	158.4	2.3	11.8	2.9	5.7
Ukraine	248.5	3,507.1	162.3	3,917.8	7.7	115.7	5.7	43.0
Prydnistrovia	2.2	21.1	1.9	25.2	8.0	80.0	7.3	31.7

Source: authors' calculations.

population in 1932 and 1934 are much higher than in all the other regions. In addition, in all regions except Central Asia, the relative number of excess deaths was higher in 1932 than in 1934.

Indirect losses by region

The number of lost births was significantly lower than the number of excess deaths, and both its regional and temporal patterns were different from patterns of direct losses (Table 8.6). Almost three million famine-related births were lost in the Soviet Union during 1932 to 1934. In absolute terms, Russia had the largest number of lost births, with 1.9 million, followed by Ukraine, with 600,000 and Kazakhstan, with 228,000, while indirect losses in the other three regions varied between 81,000 in Central Asia and 109,000 in Belarus. Contrary to excess deaths, lost births were much more uniformly distributed among the three years, and, with the exception of Kazakhstan and mainly due to the nine-month lag between conception and birth, the number of lost births was significantly higher in 1934 than in 1933.

In relative terms, during the 1932 to 1934 period there were 6.1 lost births per 1,000 population in the Soviet Union. Kazakhstan had the highest ratio, with 13.4 followed by Belarus, with 6.8, Ukraine, with 6.6, Russia, with 5.9 and Prydnistrovia, with 5.6. For the Transcaucasus and Central Asia regions, this ratio was around 3.0 lost births per 1,000 population. With minor exceptions, the ranking of this indicator by year follows closely the ranking for the 1932 to 1934 period. Probably the main exception is that in 1933, the relative number of lost births in Ukraine was higher than in Belarus: 9.0 and 7.7, respectively. Belarus has a slightly higher value than Ukraine for the whole period because in 1932, the number of lost births per 1,000 population was almost twice as high in Belarus than in Ukraine.

Discussion and conclusions

Using the population reconstruction methodology, we have expanded previous research on the 1932/1933 famine losses with a comprehensive analysis of losses in all republics of the former Soviet Union. This methodology allows us to make separate estimates for direct losses (excess deaths) and indirect losses (lost births). We also show that there were famine-related direct and indirect losses in 1934.

Our results document the uneven effect of the famine in different parts of the Soviet Union during the 1932 to 1934 period and allow us to compare Ukraine's *Holodomor* experience with that of other parts of the Soviet Union. In terms of excess deaths, we see a clear pattern of three distinct areas: (1) Kazakhstan, Ukraine, Prydnistrovia and Russia were most impacted, with excess deaths per 1,000 population of 74.1, 42.9, 31.7 and 10.6, respectively; (2) Central Asian republics and Belarus were less affected, with respective indicators per 1,000 population of 5.7 and 4.2 excess deaths; (3) the Transcaucasus republics were the least affected, with 1.9 excess deaths per 1,000 population.

Table 8.6 Indirect losses (lost births) in numbers and per 1,000 population

Region	*Thousands*				*Per 1,000 population*			
	1932	*1933*	*1934*	*1932–1934*	*1932*	*1933*	*1934*	*1932–1934*
USSR	457.8	1,167.4	1,324.2	2,949.4	2.8	7.3	8.4	6.1
Belarus	20.8	41.1	47.2	109.1	3.9	7.7	8.9	6.8
Transcaucasus	8.0	23.0	36.0	67.0	1.1	3.2	4.9	3.1
Kazakhstan	76.8	78.3	72.7	227.8	12.2	14.0	14.3	13.4
Russia	276.3	722.0	861.3	1,859.7	2.7	7.0	8.4	6.0
Central Asia	6.2	26.9	47.8	80.9	0.7	2.9	5.1	2.9
Ukraine	68.8	274.3	257.4	600.5	2.1	9.0	9.0	6.6
Prydnistrovia	0.9	1.8	1.8	4.5	3.2	6.7	7.1	5.6

Source: authors' calculations.

In terms of lost births, the pattern is somewhat different from that of excess deaths. Kazakhstan experienced the highest level, followed by Belarus, Ukraine, Russia and Prednistrovia. As in the case of direct losses, the Trascaucasus and Central Asian regions had the lowest values of lost births per 1,000 population. In general, the variation in the levels of lost births among the different regions was smaller compared to excess deaths. Ukraine was in third place behind Belarus, but with a value very close to that of Belarus, although in 1933 Ukraine had a higher number of relative lost births than Belarus.

In order to evaluate the effects of the 1932 to 1934 famine in Ukraine in relation to the other Soviet republics, it is necessary to point out the special circumstances of Prydnistrovia and Kazakhstan. It is no coincidence that relative direct and indirect famine losses in Prydnistrovia are quite similar to those in Ukraine. This is because Prydnistrovia was part of Soviet Ukraine between 1924 and 1940, and conditions in Prydnistrovia were very similar to those of other regions of Ukraine. Thus, in terms of famine-related losses, one may consider Prydnistrovia as part of Ukraine.

The causes and dynamics of the famine in Kazakhstan, on the other hand, were quite different from the experience in the rest of the Soviet Union. Although the main driving force behind the famine in Kazakhstan was collectivisation, the implementation of this policy was quite different. Kazakhstan was basically a nomadic and semi-nomadic society. Before collectivisation could begin, it was necessary to transform the nomadic population into sedentary farmers. This policy of 'sedentarisation' started in 1929 and resulted in the destruction of a large part of their livestock, their main means of support, and a total disruption of the social fabric of the population. Hunger turned into famine and people started to die of hunger earlier than in other parts of the Soviet Union. Kulakisation, collectivisation and grain confiscation were additional factors that contributed to the worst case of famine in the Soviet Union. There is general consensus among experts that the famine in Kazakhstan had a different dynamic from the famine in the rest of the Soviet Union.[51] If we exclude Kazakhstan and consider Prydnistrovia as part of Ukraine, we are left with losses, Ukraine suffered the most, with Russia a distant second, and the other regions suffered much less. Specifically, for the 1932 to 1934 period the relative number of direct losses in Ukraine was almost four times as high as in Russia and it was even higher in 1933. In terms of lost births, Belarus had a slightly higher number of lost births per 1,000 population than Ukraine, but in 1933 Ukraine's indicator was 17 percent higher than the indicator for Belarus. Russia was in third place, but compared to direct losses the difference with Ukraine was significantly less.

In summary, we have documented that the 1932 to 1934 famine affected all former Soviet republics, but the level of losses varied greatly, from extremely high levels in Kazakhstan to very low levels in the Transcaucasus republics; that is, everybody suffered but not everybody suffered the same (as pointed out above, the famine experience in Kazakhstan is considered different from the 1932 to 1934 famine). In addition, the effect of the famine was significantly larger in Ukraine, especially in terms of direct losses. Belarus had slightly higher relative lost births than Ukraine, and the difference between Ukraine and Russia was relatively small. Thus, overall, the effect of the 1932 to 1934 famine was significantly larger in Ukraine than in Russia. However, the effect of the 1932 to 1934 famine was not uniform across the territory of both countries.

Analyses of direct losses by *oblast* in Ukraine show large regional variations, from very high relative values in the Kyiv and Kharkiv *oblasts* to very low values in the Donetsk *oblast*.[52] In Russia, there is evidence that the northern Caucasus region, with a heavy concentration of ethnic Ukrainians, had losses comparable to Ukraine's, and grain-producing regions like the upper and lower Volga region also experienced heavy famine losses.[53] A more definite answer to the question of whether Russia suffered the same as Ukraine will most likely require the estimation of losses at the regional level in both countries in order to be able to compare regions with similar characteristics.

Appendix: adjustment of census data

1926 census

Military and border personnel were counted separately and registered at their place of service by the 1926 census. In order to align the 1926 census data with the de jure 1939 census data, military personnel were redistributed to the different republics proportionally to the population size of each republic.

Several researchers have pointed out that in republics with large Muslim populations, there were significant undercounts of women aged eight to 27 years due to efforts to hide the consequences of illegal early marriages and of polygamy prevalent in these societies.[54] Based on this research, a total of 135,600 women were added to the populations of these republics, according to the following distribution (in thousands): 37.8 in Uzbekistan, 8.4 in Tajikistan, 8.2 in Kyrgyzstan, 8.1 in Turkmenistan, 27.2 in Azerbaijan, 31.9 in Kazakhstan and 14.0 in northern Caucasus.

Korchak-Chepurkivskyi, Rudnytskyi and Alekseenko have shown that there was also a significant undercount of children aged 0 to two years in this census, especially in Kazakhstan, Central Asia and Transcaucasus, partially to hide the results of polygamy prevalent in these regions.[55] The following adjustment factors were used: 1.10 to 2.42 for age 0, 1.08 to 1.35 for age one, and 1.04 to 1.14 for age two. These factors were derived by a critical examination of the census age structure and estimated fertility and infant mortality trends in each republic, and resulted in adding a total of 1,419,500 children to the USSR population. The final adjustment was the redistribution of persons with unknown age proportionally to the age structure.

The Whipple Index for the different republic populations varied between 125 per cent for men in Ukraine to 333 per cent for women in Azerbaijan, indicating a serious digit preference problem. Different smoothing techniques were used for specified age intervals. For ages 0 to 4, the adjusted figures for 0 to two and reported figures for ages four and five years were used. For ages five to 14, a

3-point running average was used with a weight of 1 for the first and last age and a weight of 3 for the middle age. For ages 15 years or more, the Paievskyi method was used.[56]

1939 census

Adjustment steps of total populations are described in Table A8.1. We started with the original civilian population in each region (col. 1) and added to them the special subpopulations listed in cols 2 to 4. The total number of armed forces in the USSR by sex was redistributed to each republic according to its civilian population size (col. 2). The other subpopulations (cols 3 and 4) were redistributed based on the analysis done by the Russian Academy of Sciences.[57] Totals including these adjustments are presented in col. 5.

Control forms were used for the first time in the 1939 Soviet census in order to minimise undercount of persons not present at their usual place of residence at the time of the census. Out of a total of 4,569,000 registered control forms, the authorities decided to add 1,142,000 (0.68%) persons who were registered in control forms but presumably missed by the census takers. After a careful analysis of the data, Andreev *et al.* decided that this factor was too high and estimated a factor of 0.38 per cent for this adjustment.[58] We used this factor, as well as a factor of 0.3 per cent to adjust for the overall undercount, instead of the official 1 per cent. This undercount factor was also derived by Andreev *et al.* following an analysis of the 1937 census and of the vital statistics time series.[59] Thus, for the whole Soviet Union, 635,800 persons were added due to missed control forms (col. 6) and 503,800 due to undercount (col. 7), compared to the official figures of 1,137,752 and 1,679,523, respectively.

We took as a basis the total USSR population of 168,870,900 (col. 9), as estimated by Andreev *et al.*[60] By applying successively the adjustments for control forms and undercount, we still needed 414,800 (col. 8) to obtain the number in col. 9 (this is the so-called 'unexplained difference'). In order to estimate the total population for Russia in col. 9, we started with the Andreev *et al.* estimate of 107,968,000 and deducted 115,000 persons who at the time of the 1939 census lived in areas belonging to Estonia and Latvia.[61] We then added 89,700 and obtained 107,952,700 as the total population of Russia (col. 9). The 89,700 figure was derived as follows: Andreev *et al.* estimated 669,000 as the number of persons in special populations who were reallocated from Russia to other republics, mainly to Ukraine and Kazakhstan,[62] while an analysis of original sources showed that this number was 758,700.[63] Thus we needed to add the difference (758,700–669,000 = 89,700) to Russia's total population. Adjustments for control forms and undercount for Russia were estimated using the respective proportions of these figures for the Soviet Union.

For the other regions we took the difference between cols 9 and 5 for the USSR and subtracted the respective difference for Russia, which gave us the total adjustments for control forms, undercount and 'unexplained difference' for the other regions. The respective values for each region were obtained by the

Table A8.1 Adjustment steps of 1939 census' total populations (in 1,000s) for the USSR and its seven regions

Regions	*Reported civilian population*	*Special subpopulations*			*1 + 2 + 3 + 4*	*Corrections*			*5 + 6 + 7 + 8*	*Official data*	*% adjustment*
		Army	*Civilian population related to the NKVS*[1]	*Groups A, B, C*[2]		*Correction for control forms*	*Correction for undercount*	*Correction for the 'unknown difference'*			*%[(9/10)–1]*
	1	*2*	*3*	*4*	*5*	*6*	*7*	*8*	*9*	*10*	*11*
USSR	161,434.7	2,100.2	259.8	3,521.8	167,316.5	635.8	503.8	414.8	168,870.9	170,557.1	−1.0
Belarus	5,262.8	68.5	3.3	45.6	5,380.1	26.1	20.7	17.0	5,444.0	5,571.2	−2.3
Transcaucasus	7,762.6	100.9	5.4	60.1	7,929.1	38.5	30.6	25.1	8,023.2	8,026.6	0.0
Kazakhstan	5,157.9	67.1	13.3	187.1	5,425.5	26.4	20.9	17.2	5,489.9	6,081.6	−9.7
Russia	102,690.7	1,336.0	219.5	2,867.2	107,113.3	343.4	272.1	224.0	107,952.7	108,261.9	−0.3
Central Asia	10,210.7	132.9	10.3	155.6	10,509.3	51.0	40.5	33.3	10,634.2	10,542.6	0.9
Ukraine	30,073.7	391.3	8.0	204.6	30,677.4	149.0	118.1	97.2	31,041.7	31,785.4	−2.3
Prydnistrovia	276.3	3.5	0.0	1.6	281.8	1.4	0.9	1.0	285.2	287.8	−0.9

Sources: E. Andreev, L. Darskiy and T. Kharkova, 'Istoriya naseleniya S.S.S.R. 1920–1959 gg.' ['History of the Population of the U.S.S.R. in 1920–1959'], in *Istoriya statistiky* 3–5, 1 (Moscow: Goskomstat U.S.S.R., 1990) (in Russian); E. Andreev, L. Darskiy and T. Kharkova, *Demograficheskaya istoriya Rossiyi: 1927–1959* [Demographic History of Russia: 1927–1959] (Moscow: Informatika, 1998) (in Russian); Iu. A. Poliakov (ed.), *Naseleniye Rossiyi v 1920–1950 gody: chiselnnost, poteri, migratsiyi* [Russia's Population in the 1920–1950s: Numbers, Losses, Migration] (Moscow: Institute of Russian History RAS, 1994) (in Russian); J.B. Simchenko, *Perepis 1939 goda. Dokumentalniye istochniki TSGANH S.S.S.R.* [The 1939 Census. Documentary Sources of the TsGANKh S.S.S.R.], part 1, hh. 18–19 (Moscow, 1990), 24–25 (in Russian); see also authors' calculations.

Notes

1 NKVS: Narodnyi Komisariat Vnutrishnykh Sprav [Peoples Commissariat of Internal Affairs].

2 A = NKVS; B = Prisioners; C = Exiles.

proportions of their populations in col. 5. We then applied to the total adjustment for each region the proportions for each of the three adjustments for the Soviet Union. This completes cols 6, 7, 8 and 9 for the other regions.

Official census populations are given in col. 10, and in col. 11 we have the relative percentage differences between the official census populations and the adjusted values. For the whole Soviet Union, the overestimate was 1 per cent. Kazakhstan had the largest overestimate, with close to 10 per cent, followed by Ukraine and Belarus, with 2.3 per cent each and Russia, with 0.9 per cent. The adjusted population for Transcaucasus was practically the same as the official population, while the estimated population for Central Asia was actually larger than the official population, contrary to expectations. One possible explanation is that the actual residence of armed forces was not proportional to the total population in each region, as was assumed in our calculations, and that perhaps the actual number of soldiers in these Asian republics was somewhat smaller.

The age–sex structure of the civilian population was adjusted to the new totals, taking into account the very different age–sex structure of prisoners and resettled kulaks. Specifically, these subpopulations were subtracted from Ukraine and Kazakhstan and added to Russia, using the fairly detailed age–sex information available. Finally, the category age unknown was distributed proportionally to the adjusted age–sex structure, and age heaping was smoothed using the same methods as for the 1926 census.

Acknowledgements

Work on this chapter was supported by a Fulbright research grant to Oleh Wolowyna and by a grant from the Harvard Ukrainian Research Institute. We are grateful to Mark Tolts, Ward Kingkade and George Liber for helpful comments.

Notes

1 Robert Conquest, *The Harvest of Sorrow: Soviet Collectivization and the Terror-Famine* (New York and Oxford: Oxford University Press, 1986); Massimo Livi-Bacci, 'On the Human Cost of Collectivization in the Soviet Union', *Population and Development Review* 19(4) (1993), 743–766; Anatoliy G. Vishnevsky, *Demograficheskaya modernizatsiya Rossiyi, 1900–2000* [Demographic Modernization in Russia, 1900–2000] (Moscow: Novoe izdatelstvo, 2006) (in Russian); Stanislav Kulchytskyi, *Holodomor 1923–1933 rr. yak henotsyd: trudnoshchi usvidomlennia* [Holodomor 1923–1933 as a Genocide: Difficulties in Perceptions] (Kyiv: Nash Chas, 2007) (in Ukrainian); Andrea Graziosi, *Stalinism, Collectivization and the Great Famine* (Cambridge, MA: Ukrainian Studies Fund, 2009); Norman Naimark, *Stalin's Genocides* (Princeton, NJ: Princeton University Press, 2010); Timothy Snyder, *Bloodlands: Europe Between Hitler and Stalin* (New York: Basic Books, 2010); Steven Rosefielde, *Red Holocaust* (New York: Routledge, 2010).

2 Vallin *et al.* and Conquest provide these contrasting estimates of excess mortality respectively; Jacques Vallin, France Meslé, Sergei Adamets and Serhii Pyrozhkov, 'A New Estimate of Ukrainian Population Losses During the Crises of the 1930s and 1940s', *Population Studies* 56(3) (2002), 249–264; Conquest, *Harvest of Sorrow.*

3 Sergei Maksudov, *Poteri naseleniya S.S.S.R.* [Population Losses of the U.S.S.R.] (Benson, VT: Chelidze Publications, 1989) (in Russian); Sergei Maksudov, 'Nekotorie problemy izucheniya poter naseleniya v gody kollektivizatsiyi' [Some Problems of the Study on Population Losses in the Years of Collectivisation], in *Problemy narodonaseleniya v zerkale istoriyi* [Population Issues in the Mirror of History], ed. V.V. Elizarov and I A. Trozkaya (Moscow: Max Press, 2010), 371–399 (in Russian).

4 For estimates based on demographic indicators and historical documents see: Steven Rosefielde, 'An Assessment of the Sources and Uses of Gulag Forced Labour 1929–56', *Soviet Studies* 33(1) (1981), 51–87; Stephen G. Wheatcroft, 'Famine and Factors Affecting Mortality in the U.S.S.R.: The Demographic Crises of 1914–1922 and 1930–1933', CREES Discussion Papers, SIPS, 1981 (21) (Birmingham: Centre for Russian and East European Studies, University of Birmingham); Barbara Anderson and Brian Silver, 'Demographic Analysis and Population Catastrophes in the U.S.S.R.', *Slavic Review* 44(3) (1985), 517–536; Conquest, *Harvest of Sorrow*; Robert W. Davies and Stephen G. Wheatcroft, *The Years of Hunger* (New York: Palgrave Macmillan, 2004). For estimates constructed using the demographic balance method see: Frank Lorimer, *The Population of the Soviet Union: History and Prospects* (Geneva: League of Nations, 1946); Maksudov, *Poteri naseleniya S.S.S.R.* [Population Losses of the U.S.S.R.]; Sergei Maksudov, 'The Influence of New Data of the 1937 and 1939 Censuses on Calculating the Population Decrease in 1926–1937 and 1939–1945'. *Conference on the USSR's Population in the 1920s to 1930s in Light of Newly Classified Documentary Evidence* (Toronto: University of Toronto, 1995); Maksudov, 'Nekotorie problemy izucheniya poter naseleniya v gody kollektivizatsiyi' ['Some Problems of the Study on Population Losses in the Years of Collectivisation']; Mikhail Denisenko, *Demograficheskoe razvitiye Rossiyi i S.S.S.R. v pervoy polovinye XX veka* [Demographic Development of Russia and the Soviet Union in the First Half of the 20th Century] (Ph.D. dissertation, Moscow State University, 1992) (in Russian); Serhii Pyrozhkov and Arnold Perkovskyi, Ekstremalni sytuatsii i demohrafichni katastrofy v Ukraini (1920–1930) [Extreme Situations and Demographic Catastrophes in Ukraine (1920–1930)], *Pamiat stolit* 5 (1997),103–114 (in Ukrainian); Stephen G. Wheatcroft, 'O demograficheskikh svidetelstvakh tragediyi sovietskoy derevni v 1931–1933 gg.' ['Demographic Evidence of the Tragedy of the Soviet Village during 1931–1933'], in Victor Danilov, Roberta Manning and Lynne Viola (eds), *Tragediya sovietskoi derevni. Kollektivizatsiya i raskulachivaniye. Dokumenty i materialy* [Tragedy of the Soviet Village, Collectivisation and Dekulakisation, Documents and Materials], vol. 3 (Moscow: ROSSPEN, 2001), 866–887 (in Russian).

5 Evgeniy Andreev, Leonid Darskiy and Tatiana Kharkova, 'Istoriya naseleniya S.S.S.R. 1920–1959 gg.' ['History of the Population of the U.S.S.R. in 1920–1959'], in *Istoriya statistiky* 3–5, 1 (Moscow: Goskomstat U.S.S.R., 1990) (in Russian); Evgeniy Andreev, Leonid Darskiy and Tatiana Kharkova, *Demograficheskaya istoriya Rossiyi: 1927–1959* [Demographic History of Russia: 1927–1959] (Moscow: Informatika, 1998) (in Russian); Vallin *et al.*, 'A New Estimate of Ukrainian Population Losses'; France Meslé and Jacques Vallin with Volodymyr Shkolnykov, Serhii Pyrozhkov and Serhii Adamets, *Smertnist ta prychyny smerti v Ukraini u XX stolitti* [Mortality and Causes of Death in Ukraine in the 20th Century]. Kyiv: Stylos, 2008 (in Ukrainian); France Meslé and Jacques Vallin (eds), *Mortality and Causes of Death in 20th Century Ukraine* (New York: Springer, 2012).

6 Andreev *et al.*, *Demograficheskaya istoriya Rossiyi: 1927–1959* [Demographic History of Russia: 1927–1959].

7 Henadii Boriak, 'Population Losses in the Holodomor and the Destruction of Related Archives: New Archival Evidence', in *After the Holodomor: The Enduring Impact of the Great Famine on Ukraine*, ed. Andrea Graziosi, Lubomyr A. Hajda and Halyna Hryn (Cambridge, MA: Harvard University Press, 2014).

8 Conquest, *The Harvest of Sorrow*; Pyrozhkov and Perkovskyi, 'Ekstremalni sytuatsii i demohrafichni katastrofy v Ukraini (1920–1930)' ['Extreme Situations and Demographic Catastrophes in Ukraine (1920–1930)']; Andreev *et al.*, *Demograficheskaya istoriya Rossiyi: 1927–1959* [Demographic History of Russia: 1927–1959].

9 RGAE, Russian State Archive of Economy. Fond 1562, opis 329, delo 16, 19, 20, 21, 22, 23, 26, 49, 56, 58, 83, 107–111, 125, 132, 134, 167, 190, 256, 260, 267, 268 (in Russian).

10 Andreev *et al.*, 'Istoriya naseleniya S.S.S.R. 1920–1959 gg.' ['History of the Population of the U.S.S.R. in 1920–1959']; Valentina Zhiromskaia, *Demograficheskaya istoriya Rossiyi v 1930-e gody: vzgliad v neizvestnoye* [Demographic History of Russia in the 1930s: A Look into the Unknown] (Moscow: ROSSPEN, 2001) (in Russian); Mark Tolts, 'The Soviet Censuses of 1937 and 1939: Some Problems of Data Evaluation'. Paper presented at the Conference on Soviet Population in the 1920s and 1930 (University of Toronto, 27–29 January 1995).

11 Andreev *et al.*, 'Istoriya naseleniya S.S.S.R. 1920–1959 gg.' ['History of the Population of the U.S.S.R. in 1920–1959']; Andreev *et al.*, *Demograficheskaya istoriya Rossiyi: 1927–1959* [Demographic History of Russia: 1927–1959].

12 Marat Durdiev and Shokhrat Kadyrov, *Turkmeny mira (Istoriko-demograficheskiy obzor) [The Turkmen of the world (Historical-demographic Overview)]* (Ashgabat: Kharp, 1991) (in Russian); Vadim Erlichman, *Poteri narodonaseleniya v XX veke* [Population Losses in the 20th Century] (Moscow: Russkaya panorama, 2004) (in Russian).

13 Andreev *et al.*, 'Istoriya naseleniya S.S.S.R. 1920–1959 gg.' ['History of the Population of the U.S.S.R. in 1920–1959']; Maksudov, 'The Influence of New Data of the 1937 and 1939 Censuses on Calculating the Population Decrease in 1926–1937 and 1939–1945'.

14 Andreev *et al.*, 'Istoriya naseleniya S.S.S.R. 1920–1959 gg.' ['History of the Population of the U.S.S.R. in 1920–1959']; Andreev *et al.*, *Demograficheskaya istoriya Rossiyi: 1927–1959* [Demographic History of Russia: 1927–1959].

15 Arsen Khomenko and Rosa Kolner, 'Suchasna smertnist nemovlyat v Ukraini' [Contemporary Infant Mortality in Ukraine] (Kharkiv: Hospodarstvo Ukrainy, 1930) (in Ukrainian).

16 RGAE, Russian State Archive of Economy. Fond 1562, opis 20, delo 20, 29, 30, 34, 38, 41, 42, 48, 61, 73, 75, 86, 126, 143, 147, 153, 155 (in Russian). RGAE, Russian State Archive of Economy. Fond 1562, opis 329, delo 16, 19, 20, 21, 22, 23, 26, 49, 56, 58, 83, 107–111, 125, 132, 134, 167, 190, 256, 260, 267, 268 (in Russian).

17 RGAE, Russian State Archive of Economy. Fond 1562, opis 329, delo 16, 19, 20, 21, 22, 23, 26, 49, 56, 58, 83, 107–111, 125, 132, 134, 167, 190, 256, 260, 267, 268 (in Russian).

18 RGAE, Russian State Archive of Economy. Fond 1562, opis 329, delo 16, 19, 20, 21, 22, 23, 26, 49, 56, 58, 83, 107–111, 125, 132, 134, 167, 190, 256, 260, 267, 268 (in Russian).

19 TsDAVOV [Tsentralnyi derzavnyi arkhiv vyshchyh organiv vlady (Central Government Archives)]. Fond 582, opys 11, sprava 152, 201–202, 274 (in Russian).

20 RGAE, Russian State Archive of Economy. Fond 1562, opis 329, delo 16, 19, 20, 21, 22, 23, 26, 49, 56, 58, 83, 107–111, 125, 132, 134, 167, 190, 256, 260, 267, 268 (in Russian).

21 RGAE, Russian State Archive of Economy. Fond 1562, opis 336, delo 604 (in Russian).

22 RGAE, Russian State Archive of Economy. Fond 1562, opis 20, delo 20, 29, 30, 34, 38, 41, 42, 48, 61, 73, 75, 86, 126, 143, 147, 153, 155 (in Russian).

23 RSA, Russian State Archive. Fond 9414, opis 1, delo 1943, 1944 (in Russian); N.I. Platunov, *Pereselencheskaya politika sovetskogo gosudarstva i yeyo osushchestvleniye v S.S.S.R. (1917–iyun' 1941 gg.)* [Immigration Policy of the Soviet State and its Implementation in the U.S.S.R. (1917 to June 1941)] (Tomsk: TGU, 1976) (in

Russian); Pavel Polian, *Ne po svoyey vole: Istoriya i geografiya prinuditelnykh migratsiyi v S.S.SR* [Against One's Will: History and Geography of Forced Migrations in the U.S.S.R.] (Moscow: O.G.I. – Memorial, 2001) (in Russian); Viktor N. Zemskov, 'Spetsposelentsy (po dokumentatsiyi NKVD–MVD S.S.S.R.)' ['Deportees (According to Documents from NKVD–MVD of the U.S.S.R.)'], *Sotsiologicheskiye issledovaniya* 11 (1990), 3–17 (in Russian); Oleg Mazokhin, 'Statistika repressivnoy deyatelnosti organov bezopasnosti S.S.S.R. (1926–1939)' ['Statistics of the Repressive Activities of the U.S.S.R. (1926–1939)'], 2004. Available at: http://lost-empire.ru/index.php?option=com_content&task=view&id=255&Itemid=9 (accessed 17 June 2011) (in Russian); V. Nikolskyi, *Represyvna diyalnist orhaniv derzhavnoyi bezpeky v Ukraini (kinets 1920-kh–1950-ti rr.). Istoryko-statystychne doslidzhennya* [Repressive Activities of Agencies of State Security in Ukraine (End of the 1920–1950s). Historical and Statistical Studies] (Donetsk: Publishing House of Donetsk National University, 2003) (in Ukrainian).

24 Polian, *Ne po svoyey vole: Istoriya i geografiya prinuditelnykh migratsiyi v S.S.SR.* [Against One's Will]; Zemskov, 'Spetsposelentsy (po dokumentatsiyi NKVD-MVD S.S.S.R.)' ['Deportees (According to Documents from NKVD–MVD of the U.S.S.R.)].

25 Polian, *Ne po svoyey vole: Istoriya i geografiya prinuditelnykh migratsiyi v S.S.SR.* [Against One's Will]; Zemskov, 'Spetsposelentsy (po dokumentatsiyi NKVD-MVD S.S.S.R.)' [Deportees (According to Documents from NKVD–MVD of the U.S.S.R.)].

26 Platunov, *Pereselencheskaya politika sovetskogo gosudarstva i yeyo osushchestvleniye v S.S.S.R. (1917–iyun' 1941 gg.)* [Immigration Policy of the Soviet State and its Implementation in the U.S.S.R.].

27 RGAE, Russian State Archive of Economy. Fond 1562, opis 329, delo 16, 19, 20, 21, 22, 23, 26, 49, 56, 58, 83, 107–111, 125, 132, 134, 167, 190, 256, 260, 267, 268 (in Russian).

28 Adrei Rakov and Lev Maskov, 'Iz demograficheskoy istoriyi Belorussiyi: Demograficheskie izmeneniya v 1914–1941 gg.' ['On the Demographic History of Belarus: Demographic Changes during 1914–1941'], *Problemy narodonaseleniya i trudovykh resursov* 4 (1974), 171–222 (in Russian).

29 RGAE, Russian State Archive of Economy. Fond 1562, opis 20, delo 20, 29, 30, 34, 38, 41, 42, 48, 61, 73, 75, 86, 126, 143, 147, 153, 155 (in Russian).

30 Shokhrat Kadyrov, 'Ob etnodemograficheskom razvitiyi turkmen posle vkhozhdeniya v sostav Rossiyi (konets XIX–nachalo XX veka)' ['On the Ethnic and Demographic Development of the Turkmen after Joining Russia (End of the 19th–early 20th century)'], Izvestiya AN TSSR, *Seriya obshchestvennykh nauk* 3 (1982), 24–32 (in Russian); Kamaldyn Mamedov, *Naselenie Azerbadzhanskoi SSR za 60 let* [The Population of Azerbaijan SSR in the Last 60 Years] (Baku: Azerneshr, 1982) (in Russian); Durdiev and Kadyrov, *Turkmeny mira* [The Turkmen of the World]; Sergei Maksudov, 'Migratsiyi v S.S.S.R. v 1926–1939 godakh' ['Migrations in the U.S.S.R. in 1926–1939'], *Cahiers du Monde Russe* 40(4) (1999), 763–796 (in Russian).

31 Mark Tolts, 'Ethnic Composition of Kazakhstan on the Eve of the Second World War: Re-evaluation of the 1939 Soviet Census Results', *Central Asian Survey* 25(1–2) (2006), 143–148.

32 RGAE, Russian State Archive of Economy. Fond 1562, opis 20, delo 20, 29, 30, 34, 38, 41, 42, 48, 61, 73, 75, 86, 126, 143, 147, 153, 155 (in Russian).

33 Viktor N. Zemskov, 'Spetsposelentsy (po dokumentatsiyi NKVD-MVD S.S.S.R.)' ['Deportees (According to Documents from NKVD–MVD of the U.S.S.R.)']; Viktor N. Zemskov, 'Zakliuchennye, spetsposelentsy, sylnoposelentsy, sylnye i vyslannye (statistiko-geograficheskiy aspekt)' ['Prisoners, Special Settlers, and Exiled (Statistical-geographical Aspects)'], *Istoriia SSSR* 5 (1991), 151–165 (in Russian); Viktor N. Zemskov, 'Spetsposelentsy (1930–1959)' ['Special Settlers (1930–1959)'], in Iu. A. Poliakov (ed.), *Naseleniye Rossiyi v 1920–1950 gody: chiselnnost, poteri,*

migratsiyi [Russia's Population in the 1920–1950s: Numbers, Losses, Migration] (Moscow: Institute of Russian History RAS, 1994), 145–194 (in Russian); Viktor N. Zemskov, 'Zakliuchennye v 30-ie gody (demograficheskiyi aspect)' ['Prisoners in the 1930s (Demographic Aspect)'], *Sotsiologicheskiye issledovaniya* 7 (1996), 3–15 (in Russian); Durdiev and Kadyrov, *Turkmeny mira* [The Turkmen of the World]; Aleksandr N. Alekseenko, 'Naseleniye Kazakhstana v 1926–1939' ['The Population of Kazakhstan in 1926–1939'], in *Kompiutery i istoricheskaya demografiya* [Computers and Historical Demography], ed. V.N. Vladimirova (Barnaul: Altai State University Press, 2000), 9–26 (in Russian); Polian, *Ne po svoyey vole: Istoriya i geografiya prinuditelnykh migratsiyi v S.S.SR.* [Against One's Will]; Mazokhin, 'Statistika repressivnoy deyatelnosti organov bezopasnosti S.S.S.R. (1926–1939)' [Statistics of the Repressive Activities of the U.S.S.R. (1926–1939)].

34 Yurii Korchak-Chepurkivskyi, *Smertnost i prodolzhitelnost zhizni naseleniia g. Samarkanda v 1938–1939* [Mortality and Life Expectancy of the Population of Samarkand in 1938–1939]. Manuscript (Archives of Korchak-Chepurkivskyi, Institute for Demography and Social Studies, National Academy of Sciences of Ukraine, 1947 (in Ukrainian); Rosa Sifman, 'Iz opyta anamnesticheskikh demograficheskikh obsledovaniy v Zakavkaze' ['From the Experience of Retrospective Demographic Surveys in the Caucasus'], in *Problemy demograficheskoy statistiki* [Problems of Demographic Statistics] (Moscow: Gosstatizdat, 1959), 211–228 (in Russian); Rosa Sifman, 'Dinamika rozhdaemosti v srednyeaziatskih respublikakh i metodika ikh izucheniya' ['Dynamics of Fertility in the Central Asian Republics and Methodology of its Research'], in *Trudy vsesoyusnoy mezvusovskoi nauchnoi konferentsiyi po problemam narodonaseleniia Srednei Azii* [Report Presented at the All-Soviet Mezvusovskoy Academic Conference on the Population issues of Central Asia], ed. M.K. Karakhanov (Moscow: Moscow State University, 1965), 297–302 (in Russian).

35 RGAE, Russian State Archive of Economy. Fond 1562, opis 20, delo 20, 29, 30, 34, 38, 41, 42, 48, 61, 73, 75, 86, 126, 143, 147, 153, 155 (in Russian); RGAE, Russian State Archive of Economy. Fond 1562, opis 329, delo 16, 19, 20, 21, 22, 23, 26, 49, 56, 58, 83, 107–111, 125, 132, 134, 167, 190, 256, 260, 267, 268 (in Russian).

36 Andreev *et al.*, *Demograficheskaya istoriya Rossiyi: 1927–1959* [Demographic History of Russia: 1927–1959].

37 Andreev *et al.*, *Demograficheskaya istoriya Rossiyi: 1927–1959* [Demographic History of Russia: 1927–1959]; Vladimir Iontsev, 'Mezhdunarodnaya migratsiya v Rossiyi: 10 let posle Kaira' ['International Migration in Russia: 10 Years after Cairo'], *Narodonaseleniye* 3(25) (2004), 68–103 (in Russian); Viktor Perevedentsev, *Migratsyia naseleniya i trudovye problemy Sibiri* [Population Migration and Labour Issues in Siberia] (Novosibirsk: Nauka, 1966) (in Russian); Leonid Rybakovskyi, 'Migratsionniy obmen naseleniya mezhdu Tsentralnoyi Aziey i Rossiey' ['Migratory Population Exchanges between Central Asia and Russia'], *Sotsiologicheskie issledovaniya* 9 (1995), 89–96 (in Russian); Sergei Maksudov, 'Migratsiyi v S.S.S.R. v 1926–1939 godakh' ['Migrations in the U.S.S.R. in 1926–1939'], *Cahiers du Monde Russe* 40(4) (1999), 763–796 (in Russian); Vasiliy Simchera, *Razvitiye ekonomiki Rossiyi za 100 let: 1900–2000* [Russia: 100 Years of Economic Growth: 1900–2000] (Moscow: Nauka, 2006) (in Russian).

38 RGAE, Russian State Archive of Economy. Fond 1562, opis 20, delo 20, 29, 30, 34, 38, 41, 42, 48, 61, 73, 75, 86, 126, 143, 147, 153, 155 (in Russian).

39 Andreev *et al.*, *Demograficheskaya istoriya Rossiyi: 1927–1959* [Demographic History of Russia: 1927–1959].

40 RGAE, Russian State Archive of Economy. Fond 1562, opis 20, delo 20, 29, 30, 34, 38, 41, 42, 48, 61, 73, 75, 86, 126, 143, 147, 153, 155 (in Russian); RGAE, Russian State Archive of Economy. Fond 1562, opis 329, delo 16, 19, 20, 21, 22, 23, 26, 49, 56, 58, 83, 107–111, 125, 132, 134, 167, 190, 256, 260, 267, 268 (in Russian).

41 TSU USRR [Tsentralnoye statystycheskoe upravleniye USRR (Central Statistical Board of the UkrSSR), 1927–1932. *Pryrodnyi rukh naselennia (liudnosty) Ukrainy: 1924–1929* [Vital Statistics of Ukraine's Population 1924–1929] (Statystyka Ukrainy 106, 117, 154, 169, 193, 213) (Kharkiv: TSU USRR and Hospodarstvo Ukrainy) (in Russian); TSU SSSR [Tsentralnoye statisticheskoye upravleniye S.S.S.R. (Central Statistical Board of the U.S.S.R.)], 1928. *Estestvennyoe dvizheniye naseleniya Soyuza SSR: 1923–1925, t. 1* [Vital Statistics of the U.S.S.R.: 1923–1925, vol. 1] (Moscow: TSU SSSR) (in Russian); Yurii Korchak-Chepurkivskyi, *Tablytsi dozhyvannia i spodivanoho zhyttia liudnosti USRR 1925–1926* [Life Tables and Life Expectancy of the UkrSSR 1925–1926] (Kharkiv: TSU USRR, 1929) (in Ukrainian); F.N. Lebedev, *Smertnost i prodolzhitelnost zhizni naseleniya Uraliskoyi oblasti* [Mortality and Life Expectancy in the Ural Region] (Sverdlovsk: Uralska *oblast* Statotdela, 1929) (in Russian); Gosplan USSR, *Smertnost i prodolzhitelnost zhizni naseleniya S.S.S.R., 1926–1927: Tablitsy smertnosti* [Mortality and Life Expectancy of Population of the USSR, 1926–1927: Life Tables] (Moscow and Leningrad: Plankhozgiz, 1930) (in Russian); Arsen Khomenko and Rosa Kolner, *Suchasna smertnist nemovlyat v Ukraini* [Contemporary Infant Mortality in Ukraine] (Kharkiv: Hospodarstvo Ukrainy, 1930) (in Ukrainian); Kachibek A. Aliev, *Naseleniye Kirgiskoi S.S.R. i razvitiye narodnogo khozyaystva* [The Population of the Kyrgyz S.S.R. and the Development of its National Economy] (Frunze: Kyrgyzstan, 1980) (in Russian); Goscomstat USSR, *Tablitsy smertnosti i ozhidaemoy prodolzhitelnosti zhizni naseleniya* [Mortality Tables and Life Expectancy] (Moscow: Goskomstat S.S.S.R., 1989) (in Russian). O. Rudnytskyi, 'Demohrafichni naslidky holodu 1932–1933 rr. v Ukrainskii R.S.R.' ['Demographic Consequences of 1932–1933 Famine in the Ukrainian S.S.R.'], in *Istoriia narodnoho hospodarstva ta ekonomichnoyi dumky Ukrainskoyi RSR* [History of National Economy and Economic Thought of the Ukrainian SSR] (Kyiv: Naukova dumka, 1990, 22–26) (in Ukrainian); Sergei Adamets and Vladimir Shkolnikov, 'O dovoyennykh tablitsakh smertnosti S.S.S.R.' ['About the U.S.S.R. Pre-war Life Tables']. *Conference on the U.S.S.R.'s Population in the 1920s–1930s in Light of Newly Classified Documentary Evidence* (Toronto: University of Toronto, 1995) (in Russian); RGAE, Russian State Archive of Economy. Fond 1562, opis 329, delo 16, 19, 20, 21, 22, 23, 26, 49, 56, 58, 83, 107–111, 125, 132, 134, 167, 190, 256, 260, 267, 268 (in Russian); RGAE, Russian State Archive of Economy. Fond 1562, opis 336, delo 604 (in Russian).

42 Yurii Korchak-Chepurkivskyi, *Smertnost i prodolzhitelnost zhizni naseleniia g. Samarkanda v 1938–1939* [Mortality and Life Expectancy of the Population of Samarkand in 1938–1939]. Manuscript (Archives of Korchak-Chepurkivskyi, Institute for Demography and Social Studies, National Academy of Sciences of Ukraine, 1947) (in Ukrainian); Rima M. Dmitrieva, 'Tablitsy smertnosti i sredney prodolzhitelnosti zhizni naseleniya Sredney Aziyi' ['Life Tables and Life Expectancy of Central Asia'], in *Trudy vsesoyuznoy mezvusovskoy nauchnoy konferentsiyi po problemam narodonaseleniya Sredney Aziyi* [Report Presented at the All-Soviet Mezvusovskoy Academic Conference on Population Issues of Central Asia], ed. M.K. Karakhanov (Moscow: Moscow State University, 1965), 333–335 (in Russian); RGAE, Russian State Archive of Economy. Fond 1562, opis 329, delo 16, 19, 20, 21, 22, 23, 26, 49, 56, 58, 83, 107–111, 125, 132, 134, 167, 190, 256, 260, 267, 268 (in Russian).

43 Andreev *et al.*, *Demograficheskaya istoriya Rossiyi: 1927–1959* [Demographic History of Russia: 1927–1959].

44 Aleksandr Kokurin and Nikita Petrov, 'Gulag: Struktura i kadry' ['Gulag: Structure and Staff'], *Svobodnaya mysl* 3 (2000), 105–123 (in Russian); Russian Academy of Sciences, *Naseleniye v Rossiyi v XX veke: Istoricheskie ocherki v 3-h tomakh, T. 1, 1900–1939* [Population of Russia in the 20th Century: Historical Essays in 3 Volumes, 2000, vol. 1, 1900–1939] (Moscow: ROSSPEN, 2000) (in Russian).

45 Z.B. Abylkhozhyn, M.K. Kozybaev and M.B. Tatimov, 'Kazakhstanskaya tragediya' ['Kazakhstan tragedy'], *Voprosy istoriyi* 7 (1989), 53–71 (in Russian); Alekseenko, 'Naseleniye Kazakhstana v 1926–1939' ['The Population of Kazakhstan in 1926–1939'].
46 Niccolo Pianciola, 'The Collectivization Famine in Kazakhstan, 1931–1933', *Harvard Ukrainian Studies* 25(3–4) (2001), 237–251.
47 Zhiromskaya, *Demograficheskaya istoriya Rossiyi v 1930-e gody: vzgliad v neizvestnoye* [Demographic History of Russia in the 1930s: A Look into the Unknown].
48 Durdiev and Kadyrov, *Turkmeny mira* [The Turkmen of the World]; M. Tatimov, 'Tragedy of the Great Steppe: Demographic Catastrophe in Kazakhstan in the 1930s', *Mysl* 6 (2009), 55–60 (in Russian).
49 See also Robert W. Davies and Stephen G. Wheatcroft, *The Years of Hunger: Soviet Agriculture* (New York: Palgrave Macmillan, 2009), 411.
50 Pianciola, 'The Collectivization Famine in Kazakhstan'.
51 Pianciola, 'The Collectivization Famine in Kazakhstan'; Davies and Wheatcroft, *Years of Hunger*; Snyder, *Bloodlands: Europe Between Hitler and Stalin.*
52 Rudnytskyi, *Urban-Rural Dynamics of the 1932–1933 Famine Losses in Ukraine.*
53 Davies and Wheatcroft, *Years of Hunger*.
54 Alekseenko, 'Naseleniye Kazakhstana v 1926–1939' ['The Population of Kazakhstan in 1926–1939'], 9–26; Andreev *et al.*, *Demograficheskaya istoriya Rossiyi: 1927–1959* [Demographic History of Russia: 1927–1959]; Zhyromskaya, *Demograficheskaya istoriya Rossiyi v 1930-e gg.* [Demographic History of Russia in 1930].
55 U. Korchak-Chepurkivskyi, 'Sproba analizu perepysnykh chysel malykh ditei na Ukraini' ['Attempt of Analysis of the Number of Children in Ukraine According to the Census'], *Visnyk statystyky Ukrainy* 2 (1928), 153–158 (in Russian); O. Rudnitskyi, *Informatsionnye problemy izucheniya dinamiki gorodskogo i selskogo naseleniya Ukrainy v 1926–1939 gg.* [Information Problems in Studying the Dynamics of Urban and Rural Population of Ukraine in 1926–1939]. *Migratsiya i urbanizatsiya naseleniya (na materialah Ukrainy i Pol'shi)* [Migration and Urbanization of Population (Based on Materials from Ukraine and Poland)] (Kyiv: Naukova dumka, 1991) (in Russian); Alekseenko, 'Naseleniye Kazakhstana v 1926–1939' [The Population of Kazakhstan in 1926–1939].
56 I.G. Venetskyi, *Matematicheskiye metody v demografiyi* [Mathematical Methods in Demography] (Moscow: Statistics, 1971), 296 (in Russian).
57 Russian Academy of Sciences, *Vsesoyuznaya perepis naseleniya 1939 goda. Osnovnye itogi* [1939 General Population Census. Basic Results] (Moscow: Nauka, 1992) (in Russian).
58 Andreev *et al.*, 'Istoriya naseleniya S.S.S.R. 1920–1959' ['History of Population of the U.S.S.R. 1920–1959'].
59 Ibid.
60 Ibid.
61 Andreev *et al.*, *Demograficheskaya istoriya Rossiyi: 1927–1959* [Demographic History of Russia: 1927–1959].
62 Ibid.
63 J.B. Simchenko, *Perepis 1939 goda. Dokumentalniye istochniki TSGANH S.S.S.R.* [The 1939 Census. Documentary Sources of the TsGANKh S.S.S.R.], part 1, hh. 18–19 (Moscow, 1990), 24–25 (in Russian).

9 The uses of hunger

Stalin's solution of the peasant and national questions in Soviet Ukraine, 1932 to 1933

Andrea Graziosi

Introduction

In 1931 to 1934 approximately six million people perished from hunger in the Soviet Union: some four million of that number died in Ukraine, with another 1.3 to 1.5 million in Kazakhstan, and several hundred thousand in the northern Caucasus and Volga region. Suffering and starvation affected the entire USSR, save for a few key cities, but even in those major urban centres life became grim and miserable.

Until 1986, when Robert Conquest's *Harvest of Sorrow* was published, research on the Ukrainian famine was almost non-existent.[1] While survivor and witness testimonies were not wanting, the few Western historians who did mention a Soviet 'man-made famine' did not analyse its Ukrainian or Kazakh peculiarities. Indeed, an overwhelming majority of scholars ignored this issue entirely, resulting either in books that made no reference to it at all and even a few that questioned if it had actually occurred. It was not until 1956 that historians in the USSR were permitted to use the term 'food difficulties' in reference to this period and, even then, there was a prohibition against using the word 'famine'. In fact, it was not until 1987 that the word 'famine' was voiced officially in reference to the early 1930s.[2]

The impact of Conquest's book, the collapse of the Soviet Union in 1991, the possibility of gathering more testimonies, and a substantial if only partial opening of former Soviet archives have subsequently altered radically our understanding of what occurred in 1931 to 1934. The accumulation of evidence, and the collective effort of scores of scholars from many countries, have furthered greatly an appreciation of the causes, the dimensions, the dynamics, the responsibilities and the geopolitical variations of what we now know to have been the Soviet *famines* of 1931 to 1934, among which the 1932 to 1933 *Holodomor* – a term coined early in 1988 by the Ukrainian writer Oleksa Musiyenko, who fused the words *holod* (hunger, famine) and *moryty* (to destroy by starvation) – and the 1931 to 1933 Kazakh tragedy, stand out.[3]

There is now a growing consensus over the number of victims and an appreciation of the fact that the *Holodomor* and the Kazakh famine were two quite distinct phenomena rather than just regional variations of a pan-USSR famine, even if they share a common background.[4] Increasingly, there is also agreement over the fact that to understand the uniqueness of the *Holodomor* it is necessary to treat both the social (that is, the peasant) and the national (that is, the Ukrainian) factors together, bridging the divide between those scholars who offer an interpretation based largely on one or the other perspective. Certainly, in Stalin's mind, the two were linked: the crucial December 1932 decree that reversed pro-Ukrainian national, linguistic and educational policies was entitled 'On Grain Procurements in Ukraine, Northern Caucasus and the Western region'.[5]

This chapter, which draws on some of my previous work, attempts to reconstruct what happened in Soviet Ukraine between 1928 and 1933 and to do so from a comparative perspective, making reference both to the overall Soviet situation and to these 'regional' or, more precisely, to these national tragedies.[6] Since appreciating the importance of the 'Ukrainian Question', particularly for the leadership of the Communist Party of the Soviet Union, requires reference to the events of 1917 to 1927, the chapter begins with that period, concluding with a discussion about whether the *Holodomor* was an act of genocide and about the need for widening the focus of future research to include the *Holodomor*'s consequences for Ukraine, both in the Soviet and post-Soviet periods.

Prologue, 1917 to 1927

The Ukrainian national movement – headed principally by socialist parties – demonstrated its strength during the revolutionary upheavals, struggle for independence and Civil War of 1917 to 1922, as evidenced by great peasant insurrections and repeated occupations of Kyiv and other Ukrainian cities by forces mainly raised, sustained and sallying forth from Ukraine's countryside.[7] Grasping this fact, the Bolsheviks, who for tactical reasons supported peasant demands for land, peace and bread, were able to briefly harness the Ukrainian national movement to their own ends, in 1918. The advantage they so gained was, however, squandered by 1919, undone by Bolshevik requisitioning and their pro-Russian policies, provoking an often violent reaction against Soviet rule. This setback had a telling effect upon Lenin. He responded by resuscitating his initial support for national movements and adopting an anti-imperial, and implicitly, therefore, an anti-Great Russian chauvinism stance, especially, if not solely, in Ukraine.[8]

This shift laid the basis for the adoption, in 1923, of a policy known as *korenizatsiya* (indigenisation, from *koren*, meaning root). It was supposed to shape how the Party and Soviet state would behave when dealing with the component nationalities of the newly established USSR. So extensive were the rights and privileges conceded to the formerly oppressed nationalities of the Tsarist Russian Empire that Terry Martin would describe the USSR of the 1920s as 'an affirmative action empire'. Unsurprisingly, republican communist elites eagerly seized upon and attempted to expand the entitlements they were granted, trying to forge societies simultaneously socialist and national in nature rather than 'national in form and socialist in content', the latter remaining Moscow's preferred prescription.

For a time, 'the Centre' allowed these republican leaderships significant leeway, hoping to cast the Soviet republics of Ukraine, Belarus, and those being set up in Central Asia, as models for the anti-Polish (and thus anti-Versailles) movements of the West and for the anti-imperialist ones of the East. Furthermore Iosif Stalin's wish to secure the support of republican-level cadres during his struggle against Leon Trotsky, Lev Kamenev and Grigory Zinoviev also played a crucial role, the more so since they, collectively known as the 'Left Opposition', often took a centralist stand, disparaging the national leaderships.

As the Party's main expert on the national minorities, furthered by his experience as Commissar for Nationalities during the Civil War, Stalin actually had a rather sophisticated grasp of the 'nationalities question' and of its importance for the new Soviet state. In 1923, reflecting upon the features of the newly 'developed' national republics, he recognised the importance of Turkestan (soon to be divided into separate union republics) and of Ukraine as templates for the oppressed nationalities of East and West. However, he also stressed the dangerous weaknesses of these Soviet republics, noting that their Party cadres were 'remote from the language and manner of life of the people'. Originally, he seems to have intended to rectify this failing through indigenisation. Eventually he would choose a very different and far more brutal course.[9]

By 1925 Stalin had also explicitly linked the peasant question with the national one, showing a clear understanding of both the opportunities and the dangers this combination represented for communists and their agenda. As he wrote:

> [T]he national question [is], in essence, a peasant question. Not an agrarian but a peasant question, for these are two different things. It is quite true that the national question must not be identified with the peasant question, for, in addition to peasant questions, the national question includes such questions as national culture, national statehood, etc. But it is also beyond doubt that, after all, the peasant question is the basis, the quintessence, of the national question. That explains the fact that the peasantry constitutes the main army of the national movement, that there is no powerful national movement without the peasant army, nor can there be. That is what is meant when it is said that, *in essence*, the national question is a peasant question.[10]

Opportunities, however, seemed more immediate than perils, and – also because of the internal fight against the 'Left Opposition' – Moscow continued to support Ukrainisation, as shown by Stalin's 1925 decision to dispatch to Ukraine, as general secretary of the Soviet Ukrainian Party, one of his most trusted henchmen Lazar Kaganovich, charged with speeding up *korenizatsiya* (Stalin would deploy Kaganovich in Soviet Ukraine again, in 1932, but in this latter instance it would be for the purpose of imposing ferociously anti-Ukrainian policies).

The same Party that, in 1919, had shut down many of the Ukrainian publishing houses founded in 1917/1918, and that had up until 1923 rejoiced over the 'convergence' of the Ukrainian and Russian languages, now began to strongly favour publications and education in Ukrainian: by 1927 a majority of the children in Soviet Ukraine's primary schools were taught in Ukrainian, as were 40 per cent of city students. Meanwhile, because of what was being done with dictionaries, the alphabet and the lexicon, the Ukrainian language began to further diverge from the Russian one, while some Ukrainian communist intellectuals went so far as to denounce the 'colonial' situation of their country vis-à-vis Moscow: the Centre, they said, absorbed local revenues, but invested them elsewhere, preferring the Urals or western Siberia to the Donbas. Senior republican officials even began discussing the need for creating the economic basis for 'true statehood'.[11]

Attitudes towards Ukrainian indigenisation began to change by 1926. Ukrainian functionaries dispatched to set up soviets in Ukrainian-speaking areas located in Soviet Russia (often along the Russian side of the border) were accused of trying to create *khokholands* (the stereotypical Ukrainian Cossack style of haircut, *khokhol*, is a Russian pejorative for ethnic Ukrainians). In April, Yury Larin, a top Bolshevik leader who, in 1917, had sung the praises of the war economy and hyper-centralisation, formally raised 'the Russian Question in Ukraine' during a meeting of the USSR's Central Executive Committee, maintaining that Ukrainisation in the cities was nothing but a 'Petlyurite policy' (Symon Petlyura had headed a Ukrainian national movement that politically and militarily contested the Bolshevik occupation of Ukraine from 1918 to 1922). Attending Soviet Ukrainian leaders protested Larin's charges. Hryhoriy Petrovsky, who served as People's Commissar for Interior Affairs between November 1917 and March 1919, and so knew how the political police operated, rejected Larin's claims, saying they were based on dubious secret police sources. In addition, Mykola Skrypnyk tellingly reminded his audience that Larin had opposed Lenin's desire to form a federation of nationalities, instead advocating a unitary state organised around Russia.[12]

Confirmed as the Party's general secretary, Stalin, who in 1922 also opposed the establishment of a federal structure for the USSR, only to eventually give way to Lenin's preferences, was more worried about what was happening in the countries bordering the Soviet Union, and over what Soviet Ukraine's communist leaders were up to, than about the specific fate of the Russian minority in Ukraine. But he noticed how, in the spring of 1926, the Soviet Ukrainian national-communist elite, after having first successfully removed some of Moscow's most faithful representatives from the governing organs of Soviet Ukraine, had even begun agitating for Kaganovich's replacement, accusing him of opposing the request, advanced in March by Oleksander Shumsky, that Ukrainisation be extended into the country's mostly Russian-speaking main cities. Shumsky also doggedly supported Mykola Khvylovy, Ukraine's most important communist writer, who railed against those whom he felt were denigrating Ukrainian culture. Ukraine, Khvylovy insisted, must turn to the West, towards Europe, instead of orienting itself on Moscow and the culture of Russia.

Simultaneously, the success of Marshall Józef Piłsudski's May 1926 coup brought into power a Polish leader whom Moscow regarded as a dangerous enemy, especially given Piłsudski's vision of a federal Poland, a state potentially capable of extending its frontiers eastward, which could only happen at the expense of the Soviet Union's western borderlands. Now it was Moscow's turn to see 'its' Ukraine threatened by a hostile and potentially expansionist neighbour. Not surprisingly, Petlyura, whose forces had temporarily allied in 1919 with Piłsudski's forces, was assassinated by a Soviet agent in Paris on 25 May 1926, ostensibly in retaliation for pogroms perpetrated by some of his troops, but more likely because of the potential for a renewed alliance between the Polish state and an anti-Soviet and pro-independence Ukrainian national movement.

When, in this new situation, the Communist Party of Western Ukraine (that is, of Polish-controlled Galicia and Volyn) endorsed Shumsky's position, Stalin understood that the mechanism of *korenizatsiya*, crafted in the hope of attracting supporters in the Ukrainian and Belarusian territories lost to Poland after 1920, had begun to malfunction, that indeed the compromises reached with the nationalities and the peasantry that lay at the heart of the New Economic Policy (NEP), were now becoming increasingly counterproductive. At the beginning of 1927 he therefore ordered Shumsky's removal from Ukraine. To avoid alienating his still-powerful Ukrainian comrades, however, particularly during the final stage in his fight against Trotsky, Stalin remained cautious and appointed Mykola Skrypnyk as Soviet Ukraine's new Commissar for Education, a post the latter would hold until 1933, using his authority during those years to further Ukrainisation, at times vigorously.

The assault upon the peasants and the move against nationalities, 1928 to 1931

Stalin launched his attack on the countryside, utterly undoing the NEP in January 1928, just two weeks after Trotsky's final defeat. It was decided that a 'tribute' would be imposed upon the countryside, the bounty so collected to be used for speeding up heavy industrialisation and the rearmament of the Soviet state.[13] This wealth was to be extracted forcibly from more than 20 million peasant households, subjecting them to cruelties reminiscent of the Civil War period. These requisitions immediately provoked both passive and active resistance. Many peasants fled to the cities or reduced the areas of arable land they cultivated, laying the foundations for future problems; on occasion, peasants even physically resisted the requisitioning of their grain reserves by the special detachments deployed for that purpose. According to the intelligence reports compiled at the time, rural acts of mass opposition increased from 63 in the first eight months of 1927, to 564 in the corresponding period of 1928. 'Terrorist acts' and political killings also grew in number, while Red Army conscripts were reportedly deluged with demoralising letters from their home communities complaining about the hardships brought about by these new measures. Reportedly, the 5,000 soldiers of the Novocherkassk garrison received thousands of such letters in a single day.[14]

Stalin's initiative even met with resistance within the Party, leading to a temporary halt to the requisitioning, in the late spring of 1928.[15] This brief respite did not, however, substantially alter the course of events. In a matter of months the 'Right Opposition' was defeated, leaving Stalin free to again pursue his former policies, which he did with a renewed vigour.

Stalin thus consciously decided to reopen the conflict with the peasantry that the NEP had quelled. The exclusion of peasant households from rationing, reintroduced in 1928/1929, was by itself an indirect declaration of his intentions, which the Soviet leadership likely understood, even if they could not then foresee how the struggle would develop, nor be decided.[16] For instance, when at the Central Committee plenum of July 1928, Nikolai Bukharin (the leader of the 'Right Opposition'), challenged those present to imagine 'a proletarian state in a petit-bourgeois country that forcibly drives the peasants into communes', Kliment Voroshilov interrupted him with 'as in 1918–1919', only, in turn, to have Bukharin retort: 'Then you shall get a peasant insurrection.'[17] Tellingly, Stalin knew that excessive requisitions combined with large industrial investments financed by massive exports of grain could, in short order, provoke an 'artificial' famine. He seems to have even said so in December 1925, during a polemical exchange at the Fourteenth Party Congress in which he accused the hyper-industrialising policies promoted by the Opposition of possibly resulting in just such an outcome.[18]

In 1929 a more concerted wave of requisitions met with a more active, if desperate, resistance (reported peasant disturbances grew in number to 1,300 that year), while the needs of industrialisation – in the spring of 1929 the Party approved the most extreme variant of the first Five-Year Plan – made it imperative to seize as much grain and other products as possible. This led Stalin, now free to act as he pleased, to officially launch his 'revolution from above', based on the speedy and mass collectivisation of peasant households, preceded by the 'liquidation' of the Party's enemies in the countryside, the latter branded as *kulaks*. The guiding idea was the neutralisation of the peasantry through the annihilation of its elite (*dekulakisation*) accompanied by the gathering of the greatest possible number of families into relatively few and large collective units that could more easily be controlled and exploited by the state (collectivisation). Furthermore, *kulak* properties made for attractive booty in a land that, at the end of 1929, was otherwise being stripped bare: the State seized 22.4 per cent of the crop, as against the 12 to 14 per cent in the NEP years, and according to the *Jewish Telegraph Agency*, 'everything that could be exported or sold abroad' had already disappeared from Soviet Ukraine.[19]

At first, the national-communist leaderships, including the Soviet Ukrainian cadres, supported Stalin's anti-peasant about-face, somehow blind to its centralist and anti-national implications. No doubt the disillusionment these elites had experienced with their own peasantry during the Civil War played a role in this. Many hoped that an accelerated programme of industrialisation and urbanisation would build a much firmer basis for the national effort while solving, once and for all, the 'accursed' problem of the colonial character of the republic. It was anticipated that 'ethnic' (that is, Ukrainian) peasants moving into the cities from the surrounding countryside would transform the still dominantly Russian character of Ukraine's urban centres.

Ukrainian national communists were also reassured by the fact that while indigenisation policies did change, they were not discontinued completely. The assault launched in 1929 against the Ukrainian *intelligentsia*, often of bourgeois origin, seemed balanced by the extension of Ukrainisation even to Ukrainian communities in the Volga region, the Soviet Far East, Kazakhstan, and above all in the Kuban, in the northern Caucasus. Here districts, including hundreds of thousands of inhabitants, were being organised along Ukrainian lines; Stalin himself had sung the praises of Ukrainisation during a grandiose festival held in Moscow celebrating Ukrainian culture.[20]

However the Centre continued to ever more thoroughly extend its power throughout society. In 1929, for example, control over institutions of higher learning was transferred from the republican to Moscow-based commissariats. While Mykola Skrypnyk was assured that this would not result in Russification, and even though the percentage of students of Ukrainian origin continued to grow, the longer term trend was unmistakable. Above all, the attack on Ukraine's top intellectuals, and the challenge to their pro-European orientation, did not abate. In July 1929 Serhii Efremov, an important literary critic, was charged with membership in the 'Union for the Liberation of Ukraine' (SVU), a non-existent group concocted by the political police to provide a convenient catch-all for perceived enemies. In September the GPU 'uncovered' a similar organisation in Soviet Belarus. By the end of the year more than 700 alleged SVU members had been arrested. Even the great historian, Professor Mykhaylo Hrushevsky, who had been the first president of the Ukrainian National Republic, and whom Soviet Ukraine's national communist leaders had convinced to return to Kyiv from abroad, was subjected to increased harassment, finally being forced to emigrate to Moscow.

In January 1930 Stalin wrote personally to the Ukrainian Politburo demanding a prompt trial of the SVU's members and detailing the grounds upon which the proceedings were to unfold: the accused were to be charged with preparing an insurrection aimed at exposing Soviet Ukraine to foreign invasion, of committing acts of terrorism, and with scheming to poison senior communist leaders, with doctors to be implicated in this supposed plot. Stalin also insisted that the trial be afforded maximum publicity, and not just in Soviet Ukraine. The pressure put on the arrested – forced to confess to imaginary crimes and to incriminate others – was intense, and as it grew so too did the number of arrests. At about the same time the Ukrainian Autocephalous Orthodox Church was forced to disband, and many members of the Ukrainian Academy, historians, scientists, doctors, former leaders of the Ukrainian socialist parties and other influential members of Ukrainian society were jailed.

Over the following two years the Ukrainian national-communist leadership slowly, but decidedly, recoiled against this new wave of centralism and the resulting havoc wrought upon the countryside, particularly as it became evident that the Ukrainian 'ethnic' element was bearing the brunt of *dekulakisation* and collectivisation. *Dekulakisation* would come to involve the arrest and sometimes even the 'liquidation' of all men included in the first of the three categories into which the approximately one million *kulak* families of the Soviet Union were divided. Remaining family members in this 'first category' would be deported to Siberia and other remote regions. All members of families in the 'second category' were also exiled. Those in the third category were also removed from their home villages but were at first allowed to remain within their region of origin.

Dekulakisation was executed with great determination and rapidity between November 1929 and February 1930. The official balance sheets list thousands of people repressed, or even killed, in the very first weeks of that year, including 381,000 families, totalling 1.8 million people, deported from 1930 to 1931. Of that number 64,000 families came from Ukraine, 52,000 from western Siberia, 30,000 from the lower Volga, and 28,000 from the Urals. Their destinations were the 'special villages' administered, after 1931, by the OGPU.[21]

Next came collectivisation, which reached its first peak in February 1930, by which time nearly eight million families had been collectivised. Violence and terror were the usual method for accomplishing this purpose, a fact that is not disputed: OGPU reports describing collectivisation do not differ markedly from descriptions left by the victims.[22]

By the end of February 1930, with some 60 per cent of peasant households already collectivised, the Soviet leadership thought success was near. At that point, however, under the stimulus of repeated requisitions and claims for tax arrears, villagers began uniting, overcoming their initial divisions, and actively opposing Soviet power.

This mounting wave of peasant resistance was well documented by the OGPU. Tasked with compiling data for the Party's top leadership, the secret police reported 13,754 peasant disturbances in 1930 (ten times the figure of the previous year) involving some 2.5 million participants in the 10,000 disturbances about which intelligence was gathered. Some 402 disturbances, four of them representing significant revolts, took place in January; 1,048, including 37 revolts, in February; 6,528, with 80 revolts, in March; and 1,992, with 24 revolts, in April 1930. To these uprisings and protests must be added approximately 4,000 acts of individual 'terrorism', including the murder of 1,200 Soviet officials. More than 7,380 of these disturbances were directed against collectivisation, 2,339 against the arrest or deportation of 'anti-Soviet elements', and 1,487 against the closing of churches. Lack of food (1,220), seizure of seed grain (544), and forced delivery of grain and other foodstuffs (456) were also reported officially as motivating rural resistance.[23]

The 'region' most affected by protests and uprisings was Soviet Ukraine, with 4,098 incidents recorded, in which well over a million people participated (29.7 per cent and 38.7 per cent of the respective totals). The Central Black Earth Region followed, including Tambov (the site of one of the Civil War's most important peasant anti-Bolshevik insurrections, the *Antonovshchina*), with 1,373 disturbances involving more than 300,000 people. The northern Caucasus witnessed 1,061 demonstrations with 250,000 rioters, while the Middle Volga, the Moscow region, western Siberia and the Tatar Republic, with more than 500 mass demonstrations each, came next. The influential role of women in these uprisings, and of women's revolts specifically (which the OGPU counted at 3,712), were regarded as being particularly worrisome.[24]

The similarities between these incidents of resistance and Civil War insurrections – and sometimes even the revolts of 1905 – and where they took place are striking, as OGPU officials duly observed. In their reports on what was happening in Soviet Ukraine, for example, we read that rebellious villages were often the very same places that Semen Budënny's Red cavalry had 'cut' (massacred) by some 50 per cent in 1920, while Iosif Vareikis, the Party Secretary of the Black Earth Region, noted that anti-collectivisation revolts were particularly strong in former Antonov strongholds. Interestingly enough, in the north, as well as in the Moscow and Leningrad regions, peasant resistance was less apparent, probably because these were grain-consuming areas, whose inhabitants lived off seasonal work in the cities and in industry, regions home to only a relatively few well-off peasants. Significant requisitions were not imposed here because Soviet officialdom knew full well how little could be secured from them.

The demands voiced by those who rose up were also strikingly similar to those of the Civil War period. Again, OGPU reports present us with an unequivocal picture: the peasants demanded the recovery of their collectivised and requisitioned goods, the return of deported families, the disbanding of *Komsomol* (the Young Communist League was widely considered to be an agency for spying on the villages), respect for religious beliefs and practices, free elections to the village soviets, a halt to requisitions, and free trade. From every quarter the secret police reported that the peasants were unified in denouncing any return to a new kind of 'serfdom', by which they meant the imposition of collectivisation.

Since peasants had been disarmed in previous years their demonstrations were mostly peaceful and the corresponding repressions, while harsh, were not as brutal as those carried out during the Civil War. Furthermore, given that tens of thousands of *kulaks* had already been shot, or arrested and deported, resistance was further muted. Nevertheless, hundreds of people were killed in Soviet Ukraine, possibly even thousands if the northern Caucasus is included, and arrest followed by deportation certainly involved hundreds of thousands more. While this was different from what had occurred in 1918 to 1922, a certain continuity was evident in the fact that many of the Civil War-era Bolsheviks did duty again in 1930 (for example, Vsevolod Balitskii in Soviet Ukraine and Efim Evdokimov in the northern Caucasus, where he led the internal security troops of the Dzerzhinsky Division). In general, these special units were employed to quell rural revolts, regular troops being deployed only on rare occasions, there being doubts about the willingness of conscripts drawn from the countryside to obey commands to repress people of the same class origins.

In Soviet Ukraine, as in other non-Russian areas, nationalist slogans were heard in the resistance's strongholds. In Central Asia – where *basmachi* (the fighter-bandits of the Civil War period) reappeared – and in the northern Caucasus (Chechnya in particular), armed skirmishes occurred: the three largest Kazakh incidents, for instance, witnessed between 2,000 and 4,500 insurgents taking the field in anti-Soviet actions. From the perspective of Moscow, however, what happened along the western borders of Soviet Ukraine was far more important, since in that region local revolts had managed to effectively displace Soviet power, sometimes for weeks. Reports about peasants singing the praises of Ukrainian independence only served to confirm in Stalin's eyes the soundness of his belief that a natural reservoir of regime-challenging nationalism reposed in Ukraine's villages. When peasants of Polish ancestry organised entire villages, like Sulomna, and led marches west, towards the border with Poland, even as thousands of other Soviet citizens fled to neighbouring countries, the Politburo reacted by ordering the immediate deportation of *kulak* families from these western districts, starting with those of 'Polish nationality'.[25]

For Moscow, these developments involved more than just a question of losing face – after all, official Soviet propaganda maintained that socialism was being built in a happy countryside. What worried Stalin most was the prospect of a repetition of 1919: large peasant revolts again opening up the way for external enemies, in particular for Piłsudski, whose forces had once allied with those of Petluyra and had even taken Kyiv in early May 1920. This time Stalin feared such an invasion might secure British and French support. Yet, even though Warsaw knew quite well that the Ukrainian peasants hated Bolshevism, and possibly longed for a revival of the Ukrainian People's Republic, Marshall Piłsudski also recognised that he did not have the military might needed for such an operation, and that most of the supposedly active underground Polish and Ukrainian nationalist organisations exposed by the GPU were, in reality, non-existent, phantoms conjured up to justify Stalinist repression.

This spectre of a major Ukrainian revolt that would tempt hostile foreign powers to invade the USSR nevertheless became one of the main motives behind Stalin's decision, in early March 1930, to bring forced collectivisation to a halt, albeit temporarily. He even went so far as to accuse local cadres of being the perpetrators of 'excesses', although he had actually demanded they do exactly what he now condemned. That it was a fear, born out of his own earlier experiences, that was troubling Stalin is further suggested by the fact that he insisted upon such conspiratorial charges being made a central pillar of the SVU trial, which opened in Kharkiv's opera theatre in March 1930 and involved 45 defendants. *Pravda* devoted scores of articles to these proceedings, transforming the trial into a symbolic indictment of the dangers of nationalism, thus establishing the boundaries that national-communist leaders in all of the republics must not trespass if they wished to avoid being repressed. In March, a seriously worried Skrypnyk begged Stanislav Kosior, the Party Secretary for Soviet Ukraine, to make sure that at least the positive aspects of the Ukrainian Academy's activities were mentioned at the trial.[26] His request was denied, signalling Moscow's intention to undermine any prospect of an autonomous and high Ukrainian culture that could challenge Russian predominance.

At this very time, and for the first time since the 1920 war with Poland, the regime also began using Russian nationalism as a tool of social control, seeing it as an essential centripetal force for a Soviet state increasingly unsettled, economically, socially and psychologically. This appeal to Russian pride, which Stalin formalised in a speech to economic executives in February 1931, resonating as it did with the themes and words of Mussorgsky's *Khovanshchina*, thereafter became a stable component of state policies and Stalinist ideology.[27] This implied a retreat from support for indigenisation, a policy that had itself upset many Russians living outside the RSFSR, who now found themselves being extolled by Moscow for playing the pivotal, indeed the dominant, role in Soviet society.

Even so, in primary education and in promotions from the ranks, Ukrainisation continued, and even, for a while, expanded: the publication of books in Ukrainian, which had started to grow in 1923, reached a peak in 1931 (77 per cent of all titles), although it started to decline after that. In 1931 the percentage of Party members of Russian origin in Soviet Ukraine, which in 1922 accounted for 72 per cent of its cadres, dropped to 52 per cent, while the number of 'ethnic' Ukrainians living in cities, or working in industry, grew rapidly, proving in the eyes of national-communist leaders the virtues of Stalinist industrialisation. In addition, by 1932, ethnic Ukrainians for the first time had passed the 50 per cent residency mark in a majority of Soviet Ukraine's cities. In the sphere of culture, however, and not only in the elite circles already disrupted by the SVU trial, the promotion of Ukrainian culture was increasingly being circumscribed.

Other minority nationalities in Soviet Ukraine did not fare much better. The attack against the NEP, and the liquidation, and often arrest, of *nepmen*, translated in Ukraine into an attack against diaspora communities (in Ukraine in 1926 more than 40 per cent of traders, artisans, shopkeepers and small industrialists were of Jewish, Armenian or Greek nationality). Jews, in particular, also suffered because of the 1927 to 1930 campaign against religion, which saw the closure of synagogues and the removal of rabbis, even as their *shtetls*, that traditionally survived by providing services to villagers, were economically devastated by the pauperisation of those same Ukrainian peasants.

It is thus possible to maintain that while Stalin dismantled the NEP's existing arrangements with the peasants and bourgeois specialists, as well as the currency and market reforms associated with the policy, he did not cancel the accommodations reached with the various nationalities in 1923 (indigenisation). Instead, he emasculated them with varying degrees of severity across the entire Soviet Union. How indigenisation was adapted and applied varied across the union republics according to the Centre's geopolitical considerations. Since Moscow's fears were focused in the USSR's western borderlands, and in particular within Soviet Ukraine, the new strictures were most rigorously imposed there, while in the Caucasus, Central Asia or the far north – regions geographically remote from the sources of perceived threat – indigenisation officially continued in effect.

Stalin's March retreat, and the good crop of 1930 (three to five million tons larger than in 1929, even given the disruptions caused by collectivisation) seemed to calm the situation. However, a few months after this harvest, as the peasants' reserve stocks shrank while rapid industrialisation continued to expand the state's needs, the contest between the village and the state – which had succeeded in taking almost 30 per cent of the crop, and was thus able to export 4.8 million tons of grain – reached new heights. Once more, Moscow focused its attention upon the grain-growing areas: at the end of 1930 Soviet Ukraine, the northern Caucasus and the Volga region were given the target of collectivising 80 per cent of peasant families by June 1931, while in the USSR as a whole their number was to double from 6.5 to almost 13 million, approximately 50 per cent of the total. And so a new wave of arrests, deportations, forced collectivisation, 'excesses', and mass and individual acts of resistance, both active and passive (the new *kolkhozniki* resisted by doing far less work than they had when they were independent peasants), spread throughout the countryside, and especially within the above mentioned 'regions', where the peasants were given a 'choice': either join a *kolkhoz*, and give it 30 to 60 per cent of their time and labour for no remuneration at all, or attempt to flee to the cities, to find work in the industrial sector.

The 1931 harvest was not a good one, although bringing in the crops did provide for a short lull in the struggle between the state and the countryside. Procurement operations soon became almost warlike, accompanied by violence and arrests, spreading fear throughout the rural areas and even raising concerns, and doubts, among local Party leaders. At the October plenum some openly suggested lowering procurement targets given that poor weather and the resulting crop failures were causing food shortages. Worried about feeding the cities and the army, and obsessed with hard currency problems and thus with export capacity, Stalin responded harshly to these calls, using Anastas Mikoyan as his proxy, to say that 'the question of how much is left to eat and for other needs is not important. What is important is to tell the *kolkhoz* that they have to meet the state's needs first; their own will have to wait.'[28] Procurements were thus to be conducted independently of the condition of the peasants and their toil was to be compensated only if something was left after the state took what it needed (which amounted to approximately 40 per cent of the harvest, even more so in grain-growing regions).

In 1932 the USSR was thus able to export almost five million tons of grain.[29] In the countryside, however, there was havoc caused not only by the liquidation of the ablest peasants, the *kulaks*, but by the loss of a large part of their livestock (peasants often slaughtered, sold or ate their animals rather than giving them to the *kolkhoz*), the consumption of existing grain reserves, all compounded by the poor organisation and malfunctioning of most of the collective farms. All of this, in turn, undermined deeply the productive capacity and the spirit of the rural population, and consequently production throughout the USSR.

The situation, however, had begun to diverge considerably across different areas. In grain-producing areas, where the Soviets concentrated their requisition efforts, food difficulties and peasant unrest were more intense, and, by the early spring of 1932, pockets of actual famine started to appear, just as they had in 1921 after the great requisition campaign of 1920. The first crisis would occur in Kazakhstan.

As the work of Niccolò Pianciola has confirmed, the terrible famine and associated epidemics that would exterminate at least one-third of the indigenous, semi-nomadic Kazakh population were not the outcome of compulsory 'sedentarization', since that campaign was never fully implemented. Rather, grain and livestock procurements were the prime factors causing this tragedy, as would be the case throughout the entire Soviet Union. The decision to seize most of the Kazakh herds – in part to replenish the stocks of the Russian and Ukrainian agricultural regions that had already been devastated by collectivisation – was of special importance. The similarities between the Kazakh and Ukrainian (or the northern Caucasus) famines did not stop at causes: as in Soviet Ukraine so too the Kazakhs were, at times, prevented from escaping famine-struck regions or seeking relief in cities or towns. Yet, there were also important differences: in the Kazakh lands collective farming as yet played but a minor role, and the fate of the indigenous population resulted more from indifference than intention given that local officials, generally Slavs, preferred their kin when it came to the distribution of scarce resources. Furthermore, Moscow never pursued a deliberately anti-Kazakh policy, the local national-communists were relatively weak, and there was no significant threat to the USSR along its borders with China, certainly nothing comparable to the dangers perceived to be lurking in the western borderlands of Soviet Ukraine.[30]

Crisis and *Holodomor*, 1932 to 1933

In early 1932 Moscow realised that peasants, and especially those in the grain-producing areas such as Ukraine, the northern Caucasus and the Volga region, were not doing what the state expected of them. True to form, Stalin interpreted their actions, which were a direct response to excessive requisitions, as a plot, orchestrated by enemies. The extensive lists of '*kulak* bandits' and 'leaders of *kulak* insurrections' whose death sentences were sanctioned by the Politburo in March and April 1932 are indicative of the repression that followed. In spite of the 1931 decision to curtail deportations they began anew, and grew: in April alone the Politburo decided to deport 38,300 families, 6,000 from Soviet Ukraine. Eventually, more that 70,000 peasants would be deported, followed by another 200,000 in 1933, meaning that between 1930 and 1933 some 2.25 million people officially suffered this fate, excluding those displaced within their own region. Among themselves the USSR's leaders referenced even higher figures: Stalin himself spoke of ten million exiled peasants, and, towards the end of his life, Molotov boasted of even higher numbers.[31]

Undeniable famine conditions did, at first, result in some ameliorative measures being adopted, patterned on the actions Lenin had authorised in the spring of 1921 under similar circumstances. At the end of March, for example, the Politburo prohibited the seizing of individual livestock, allowing peasant families to keep a cow, whose milk was essential for their children's survival. The state also lowered the procurement targets for meat and grain, and in early May the *kolkhozniki* were permitted to sell whatever they could *after* first fulfilling their obligations to the state. Since most peasants had very little, or nothing, to sell, these '*kolkhoz* markets', which were later to play an important role in Soviet history, barely functioned.

Stalin did consent to a limited amount of grain being bought in the Far East and from Iran, this aid being distributed to the peasants before the sowing of their own crops, suggesting that he knew what measures were needed in order to counter the crisis looming ahead. However, he authorised only the bare minimum of relief, without altering the basic course of his policies. Conditions therefore continued to deteriorate. Later in the spring, when even Slavic colonists began dying in Kazakhstan, the area being sowed in the most fertile agricultural areas shrank significantly, a result of the physical exhaustion and lack of motivation of the peasants, as well as of the great reduction in livestock (especially horses), exacerbated by the abysmally ineffective organisation of the collective farms.

By mid-May 1932 only eight million hectares had been sowed in Soviet Ukraine, as against the 15.9 million hectares of 1930 and the 12.3 million hectares in 1931. Local officials, village schoolteachers and Party cadres had already begun to inform the Centre about the seriousness of the famine conditions affecting the regions where the requisition brigades had concentrated their efforts. By May, rumours about the sale of human flesh in city markets circulated in Kyiv and in June the OGPU reported that sowing was taking place in extremely tense conditions, even recording how peasants were committing suicide in order to avoid a painfully lingering death by starvation, with cannibalism becoming more and more frequent.[32]

On 10 June 1932, Soviet Ukraine's premier, Vlas Chubar, wrote to Stalin and Vyacheslav Molotov, stressing how bad the situation was: at least 100 districts (*raiony*) desperately needed food aid, and there were growing difficulties in meeting the bread requirements of the cities. Soon afterwards, the Soviet Ukrainian president Petrovsky – who in April had written to Stalin about entire villages starving due to local requisition 'excesses' – informed the Ukrainian Party Secretary, Kosior, that the situation had become so dire that Stalin had to be told that procurements in Soviet Ukraine had to stop. Significantly, both Chubar and Petrovsky used the Russian word for famine (*golod*) in describing what was happening.[33]

This correspondence, and news about thousands of people starving to death, did prompt Stalin into authorising some concessions: on 26 June, for example, in a letter to Kaganovich, he mentioned the need to lower – 'for a sense of justice' – procurements in Ukraine's most famine-ravished areas, while keeping in mind the needs of the border districts. However, all such reductions – Stalin added – were only to be of a local and limited nature and duration.

More importantly, however, Stalin began to convince himself that the difficulties his anti-peasant policies were encountering in Soviet Ukraine were being stoked by local officials, treacherously abetting village resistance for 'national' reasons. As Terry Martin shows, Stalin was in fact the first person to give the famine a 'national interpretation'.[34] At first he did so in private, ranting against republican leaders whom he considered responsible for the crisis, insisting they had not met it with the necessary resolve. On 2 July, for example, he wrote to Kaganovich and Molotov, sharing his view that Chubar's 'corrupted' and 'opportunistic' personality, and Kosior's 'rotten diplomacy' and 'criminally frivolous' attitude towards his duties, were responsible for ruining Ukraine. It was therefore necessary, Stalin insisted, to impose a much firmer 'Bolshevik stand' at the Third Ukrainian Party conference, so confronting Petrovsky's and Chubar's hypocritical self-criticisms and Kosior's silence.[35]

In fact, given the desperation increasingly evident in the countryside, members of the Party in Soviet Ukraine grew increasingly disillusioned with Moscow. At the conference, which opened on 6 July in Kharkiv, many delegates, whose speeches were subsequently censored in the official minutes, described how requisition brigades forced peasants to sit naked in the snow in order to intimidate them into giving up all of their belongings, and spoke about people so bloated from starvation that they could no longer even stand to do work. Chubar pleaded with local cadres not to accept orders without considering their consequences, so implying that responsibility for the famine lay with Moscow's policies rather than with the republic's government or even the peasants' behaviour. Skrypnyk, who still headed the Commissariat for Education, was even blunter:

> What is the reason for our current failures, our current situation? How is it possible that Ukraine, in spite of a not particularly bad harvest ... has to deal with food difficulties in many districts? Since January I have driven through more than thirty districts ... I heard the following answer.... 'The communists are at fault for the non-fulfillment of the grain-procurement plan, for the poor food situation; the communists took the grain, and that is why there is no grain to live on ... that is why there is famine in certain localities.'[36]

As Stalin expected, however, the conference dutifully followed the line taken by Molotov and Kaganovich, who switched the focus away from complaints against Moscow to a reaffirmation of the duties all communists had towards the Soviet State. As Molotov was later to repeat, 'even if we have today to face, especially in grain-producing areas, the famine's ghost ... procurement plans must be respected at all cost', in order to avoid any repetition of the extensive food riots in industrial cities that had occurred in the spring while also honouring the need to repay German loans.[37]

The conference's final resolutions did not, however, fully placate Stalin, who suspected that the Ukrainians only formally complied with his wishes, an inkling confirmed by what Kaganovich reported on what was possibly the last recorded disagreement to occur in a Politburo meeting involving Stalin. On 2 August, someone, possibly Petrovsky, dared to object to Stalin's draft of what was to become, on 7 August, the draconian law on the defence of State property against theft. Criticism, also voiced by other leaders, focused on the law's second paragraph, which imposed the death penalty upon anyone found guilty of stealing *kolkhoz* property, reduced to a five- to ten-year forced labour sentence if mitigating circumstances existed. On the basis of this decree, which was eventually approved as per Stalin's initial text, more than 100,000 people would be sentenced in under five months, 4,500 to the death penalty (a figure suggesting that statistics about death sentences in the USSR are less than reliable). Some judges admitted that their own 'petit-bourgeois' prejudices caused them to agonise over sentencing a person to years in the Gulag camps for the theft of a few ears of grain.[38]

Stalin's suspicions about his Soviet Ukrainian comrades were further heightened by OGPU reports, such as one dated 22 August, which accused the Ukrainian communist cadres of being infected with nationalism, and even of acting on orders sent from the Polish General Staff. According to the political police, members of at least 50 Party district committees, including those of Kyiv and Dnepepetrovsk (formerly Ekaterinoslav but renamed to honour Petrovsky), had doubts about procurement policies, evidenced by local Party cadres voicing views such as: '(1) I will not carry out procurement plans. (2) It will be difficult to fulfil procurement quotas, but I know what to do: I will return my Party card and become a free man. (3) To force the population to starve is criminal. It's better to return my Party card, than to sentence peasants to death by starvation.'

On 11 August 1932, in what is now regarded as a crucial document, Stalin wrote to Kaganovich about how the situation in Soviet Ukraine had become the main issue facing him, about how the Republic's Party, State, and even political police organs teemed with nationalist agents and Polish spies, and about the real risk of 'losing Ukraine', which he demanded must instead be transformed into a Bolshevik fortress.[39] Since the USSR and Poland had actually signed a non-aggression pact on 25 July 1932, Stalin was exploiting a non-existent foreign threat to justify the liquidation of his internal enemies, using this tactic to further consolidate his position, as he had done in the past more than once, most famously against Trotsky in 1927.

Meanwhile, the harvest, and procurements, confirmed the seriousness of the situation. Out of approximately 60 million tons of grain, a figure only slightly inferior to that of 1931, the State was able to seize only 19 million tons, against the 23 million secured in the previous year, leaving most of the harvest to rot in the fields. Procurements were especially poor in Soviet Ukraine and in the northern Caucasus, providing Moscow with 60 per cent less than what had been delivered in 1931, declining respectively from 32 per cent to 23 per cent, and from 14 per cent to 10 per cent of the procurement totals. The situation was also bad in the Black Earth Region, ameliorated only by deliveries from western Siberia and the Volga region, which were subjected to severe requisitioning.[40]

The lack of grain and other agricultural products lowered exports, causing a crisis in the balance of payments. Hard currency was simply not to be had, forcing the State to suspend payments to foreign specialists and workers, many of whom then left. Their departure, in turn, compounded problems in the newly built factories, which still needed parts, machinery and the advice of those very same foreign experts. Essential raw materials could also not be imported in the required quantities, and many industrial complexes producing tractors, armaments, vehicles and other machinery had to stop production for weeks at a time, imperilling the Soviet industrialisation campaign.

In September/October 1932 the regime was almost on the verge of collapse, and obviously so: grain reserves were low, exports were at a near standstill, the German bills of exchange, used in 1931 to relaunch industrialisation following the 1930 crisis, were coming due, cities teemed with former peasants deeply inimical to the regime, and there was mounting discontent in the workers' ranks. Moscow feared what would happen if another cut in food rations was announced. In this perilous situation even men like Sergo Ordzhonikidze, Stalin's friend and the Commissar of Heavy Industry, despaired. Documents began surreptitiously circulating in Party circles attacking Stalin and his policies. Then, on 7 November, following the celebration of the October Revolution's fifteenth anniversary, Stalin's second wife Nadezdha Alliluyeva committed suicide, for reasons both private and political.

Against this background there loomed a coming famine. If in 1921/1922 famine had put an end to the Soviet State's first confrontation with the peasantry, the much more terrible hunger of 1932/1933 paradoxically allowed Stalin a chance to exercise his extraordinary self-confidence, cruelty and willpower. Despite all the setbacks he had so recently endured, Stalin determinedly deployed a prophylactic and collective model of repression against any and all national, social-national and political groups that he believed posed a threat to the Soviet regime and, in doing so, he rescued it from collapse.[41]

From the summer of 1932 even the Party's members were targeted, just as they had been during the fight against both the 'Right' and the 'Left' oppositions. However, it was the need to collect grain, and thus the situation in the countryside, and most particularly so in Ukraine, that topped Stalin's list of worries, especially after information about the new crop and procurements began to arrive. While, as late as September 1932, one could find references to starvation and cannibalism in the confidential reports for internal use only, all such intelligence disappeared after that because, as Kaganovich and others would observe, including any such 'photograph of reality' left Party cadres troubled, making them overly sensitive to human suffering and inclined to give the peasants bread. That could not be allowed. The cadres must instead be made to follow the Party's dictates without question, regardless of the consequences.[42]

On 22 October 1932 Stalin dispatched Molotov, Kaganovich and Pavel Postyshev to Soviet Ukraine, the northern Caucasus and the Volga region, each man tasked with fulfilling the quotas at all costs. Simultaneously, he telegraphed Filipp Goloshchekin in Kazakhstan, threatening drastic measures if grain-procurement plans there were not met. Stalin's servitors left Moscow with firm instructions about how the crisis was to be resolved and they did as they were told. Within a week Molotov had forced the Ukrainian Politburo to approve a resolution calling for the 'tightening of procurements', indicating that this was to be the Party's highest priority, with harsh punishments for any *kolkhoz* which did not fulfil its obligations. An even harsher treatment was inflicted by Kaganovich upon local officials in the northern Caucasus, and especially in the Ukrainian-settled Kuban. He said bluntly:

> Let me remind you that in 1921 we deported the Cossacks who fought Soviet power.... You do not like to work here, then we deport you. Someone may object: you cannot do this, it is illegal. Well, that's not true. It is legal. You take the side against Soviet power, you do not sow, therefore – in the name of state interests – Soviet power has the right to fight against your attitudes.... We shall achieve our aims, if not with you – dear comrades – then bypassing you.[43]

In early November 1932 Molotov and Kaganovich returned briefly to Moscow to report directly to Stalin about what they had seen. It was probably in those very days, around the time when Stalin's wife committed suicide, that the decision to use the emerging famine conditions as a weapon was decided. The idea was to teach an unforgettable lesson to anyone who refused the 'new serfdom', using a brutally simple method: those who would not work in the fields of the collective farms would not eat. Stalin hinted at his thinking in correspondence with the writer, Mikhail Sholokhov, in 1933.[44] Sholokhov had pleaded for relief for the Don region, which Stalin rejected, claiming that the 'esteemed grain-growers' there were engaged in a ' "secret" war against Soviet power', that 'they used hunger as a weapon', for which they would now suffer the consequences, namely famine. In other words, the famine was their own fault.

In the northern Caucasus, Kaganovich resorted to fines-in-kind to deprive peasants of meat and potatoes and 'blacklisted' entire areas, the goods and reserves of which were systematically removed, even as any new imports were forbidden.[45] Local famines, of an entirely artificial sort, were thus induced. Entire villages were deported. Eventually, about 60,000 Kuban Cossacks were exiled, while many more simply starved to death. Since Kuban Cossacks were, largely, of Ukrainian descent, these deportations acquired an unmistakably ethnic dimension. Villages whose inhabitants were deported were then repopulated with former soldiers, mainly non-Ukrainians.

Local communist cadres suspected of aiding or abetting the peasants were purged, because – as Stalin said – nobody believed their complaints about the lack of grain, and the State – not the village – took priority when it came to guaranteeing survival. At the end of November 1932 Stalin even maintained that, all things considered, the 'sabotage' of collectivisation and of the procurement campaigns was playing a positive role, allowing the Party and State to expose and expunge untrustworthy cadres. Kaganovich, for instance, divided rural communists into three categories: (1) Those unable to work, who because of their ignorance, or stupidity, fell easy prey to the bourgeois specialists' machinations. (2) The hypocrites who, in the name of compassion and great-heartedness, treated the peasants liberally. (3) Those who were in the service of the enemy.[46]

Eventually, 15,000 local communists were arrested in the northern Caucasus, 5,000 of them in Kuban, where those of Ukrainian descent – charged with being agents of Petlyura and Piłsudski – suffered the most. Approximately half of the *kolkhoz* Party secretaries were punished, and many were executed, at times for the crime of 'populism' (meaning that they had fed the starving).

In Ukraine an informal centre imposed and controlled by Moscow simply replaced the elected bodies of the Party and Soviet Ukrainian state, leaving Soviet Ukraine governed on what amounted to an emergency basis. On 18 November 1932 Molotov forced the local Central Committee to pass a resolution on the 'strengthening of procurements' which ordered peasants to return the meagre food advances they had earlier received in exchange for their labour.[47] In the following weeks he was thus able to squeeze another 90 million *pud* of grain out of the countryside, while – as in northern Caucasus – local officials who dared defend the peasants were fiercely purged. This negative selection rewarded the most brutal with promotion while the relatively more humane comrades were persecuted or committed suicide, as did a district president who, in a final letter addressed to Skrypnyk, wrote: 'I no longer have the strength to so shamefully abuse my own people.'[48]

Meanwhile Balitskii, dispatched to Ukraine with Molotov and made head of the republic's political police, used Stalin's 'national interpretation' of the famine to launch a massive campaign of terror: the primary aim, he said, was to promptly expose, and excise, any rebel and counter-revolutionary activity, a goal that would be achieved by the imposition of harsh punishments on the *kulak*, counter-revolutionary and Petlyurite elements allegedly sabotaging Party and Soviet policies in the countryside. More than 1,200 counter-revolutionary groups would conveniently be 'uncovered' as operating in the Republic's collective farms: in just one month (15 November to 15 December 1932), the Ukrainian GPU (whose leading *troika* enjoyed, for a time, the right to autonomously mete out the death penalty) arrested almost 16,000 people, busily destroying underground organisations of its own fabrication, accusing them of trying to exploit famine conditions to instigate insurrections, allegedly in concert with Poland and émigré Ukrainian nationalists. As a pleased Balitskii was to declare the following February, the GPU had thus defeated a well-prepared and coordinated plan whose aim had been to launch an armed revolt in the spring, an insurrection aimed at overthrowing Soviet power and re-establishing an independent Ukrainian republic (an obvious reference to 1919).[49] Postyshev resorted to similar, if not as equally harsh, measures in the Volga region during his December tour, even as the crisis gave renewed impetus to repression throughout the Soviet Union.[50] The political police arrested 410,000 people in 1932 and more than 500,000 in 1933, 283,000 of them for counter-revolutionary crimes (this figure is possibly an underestimate, given the arbitrariness of governance in the countryside).

In 1932/1933 Stalin's terror thus followed two principal lines, one linked to requisitions, and therefore concentrated in the grain-producing areas, and the other of a more directly political nature, which reached its heights in areas the regime considered particularly dangerous because of past rebellions, the strength of their national movements or their geostrategic location. Where just one of these 'worries' existed, the terror, albeit severe, was not as intense in comparison to where two or even three such considerations came into play. Soviet Belarus, for instance, though a western borderland, was not a major grain-producing region and its national movement was far weaker than that in Soviet Ukraine. Thus, while repression came to Soviet Belarus, it was nowhere near as intense as what would be focused on the Ukrainian Soviet Socialist Republic, where Stalin's 'worries' all coincided.

And so it came to be that Stalin – who explicitly linked the national question with the peasant one, and recalled only too well what had happened in Ukraine in 1918 to 1922, and again in 1930 – combined his anti-peasant policies with quite effective anti-national ones, inaugurating his campaign with the already-mentioned resolution on procurements in Ukraine, the northern Caucasus and the Western region of 14 December 1932. Six days later Kaganovich pushed the Ukrainian Politburo to accept even higher targets of grain procurements. Soon afterwards, he declared that the necessary precondition to reach them was the discovery, and confiscation, of family reserves, so opening the door to mass death.[51] Finally, on 22 January 1933, Stalin and Molotov ordered the OGPU to stop the exodus of peasants trying to leave Soviet Ukraine and the Kuban in search of food. The Central Committee and government, they wrote:

> Do not doubt that this flight of villagers, like the exodus from Ukraine last year, have been organized by enemies of Soviet power, socialist-revolutionaries and Polish agents who use the [fleeing] peasants to agitate against the *kolkhoz*, and more generally against Soviet power in Northern territories. Last year the Party, Soviet, and *Cheka* agencies of Ukraine missed this counter-revolutionary undertaking.... Last year's mistakes cannot be repeated this year.[52]

The *Chekists* and Party activists were thus given orders 'to prevent the mass flight of peasants' from Soviet Ukraine and the northern Caucasus, and to arrest those who attempted to flee. Since Ukrainian cities, while miserably supplied, did have some foodstuffs, they were cordoned off. Over the following months approximately 220,000 people, mainly starving peasants, were arrested and sent back to their villages, there to die. Areas stricken with famine were not extended any help until the spring of 1933 even as Litvinov, the Commissar of Foreign Affairs, publicly denied the famine's existence and the State 'ferociously fought' (in Kaganovich's words) to fulfil its procurement targets.

Famine – which, according to Stanislav Kulchytskyi, killed approximately 100,000 people in 1932 – took on, as a result of political decisions, a quality and dimensions far more extreme than it would have if nature had followed its course. It did not effect as wide a geographic region as the 1921/1922 famine, nor was drought its cause. In fact the 1932 crop, though quite low, was actually greater than the one that would be harvested in 1945, and the latter did not result in any comparable scale of hunger-related deaths.[53] We may therefore conclude that the famine of 1932/1933, which caused three to four times as many victims as that of 1921/1922, was essentially brought about by political decisions made by the Stalinist regime, aimed at saving it from the very crisis to which its own policies had led, assuring the victory of the 'great offensive' launched four years previously.

Also as a consequence of political choices, the 1932/1933 famine took on profoundly – and at times radically different – features in each of the Soviet republics and regions. It is therefore necessary to distinguish between the general conditions of suffering and hardship observed throughout the USSR (the pan-Soviet famine) and the 'local' and far more terrible mass-starvation famines that occurred in specific territories. It is just as important to distinguish between what happened in the cities as compared to what took place in the countryside, both at a pan-Soviet level and in the most-stricken rural areas.

In the major Soviet cities, Stalin's choices took on features that, as extreme as they may seem, cannot be compared with what was done in the grain-producing and predominantly non-Russian rural areas. At the end of 1932, for example, in order to strengthen control over urban and industrial centres, and to prevent any repetition of the unrest that had been evident that spring, the Politburo launched a mass 'cleansing' of major urban-industrial centres. This was done by reintroducing, only for urban residents, an internal passport system, akin to the one that had existed in Tsarist times, and whose abolition had once been vaunted as one of the great victories of the October Revolution.[54]

In January 1933 Moscow, Leningrad and Kharkiv, then Soviet Ukraine's capital, were the first cities to be 'passportized'. Kyiv, Odesa and Minsk, all major urban centres situated within 100 kilometres of the western border, and industrial boom towns such as Magnitogorsk, underwent the procedure in the spring. Everywhere, thousands, and often scores of thousands, of vagrants, 'unreliable elements', people with 'a suspicious past', were removed from the cities in which they had been living and working. The comparatively lucky were dropped off in the countryside, 100 kilometres or so from their previous residences. Those less fortunate were exiled to hinterland locations where, at times, they met a fate even more terrible than that of *dekulakised* peasants.[55]

Since the regime provisioned the 'cleansed cities' far better than others, the internal passports, a necessary (but not sufficient) precondition for securing a residence permit, represented a coveted entitlement. Moscow and Leningrad were thus only slightly touched by famine: in the first quarter of 1933, for example, the Soviet capital received 165,000 tons of grain, plus 86,000 for the surrounding district. By contrast, the entire Soviet Ukrainian Republic, with a far larger population, received only 280,000 tons.[56] Even major cities in Soviet Ukraine witnessed starvation deaths, with Italian and Polish diplomats becoming accustomed to recording the daily removal of the emaciated bodies of those who had somehow bypassed the roadblocks, only to die in the streets of Kharkiv and Kyiv.[57]

The strategy elaborated in the autumn of 1932 was systematised and sanctioned at the Central Committee plenum of January 1933, where Stalin declared that it was no longer necessary to spur the USSR forward. Industrial investments were thus reduced, and factories were told to raise productivity by reducing the labour force. In the countryside special 'political sections', charged with controlling the collective farms and their *kolkhozniki*, were established in the Machine and Tractor Stations (MTS). It was also decided to launch a general purge of the

Party, whose rural structures had already been reduced in previous months. Command over this effort rested with Nikolai Ezhov, an uncultivated Stalinist henchman who, under his master's guidance, was to transform this purge into what came to be known as the 'Great Terror' in 1936 to 1938. Meanwhile Postyshev, accompanied by hundreds of cadres, was dispatched from the Centre, entrusted with 'normalising' the Ukrainian Party, the latter being deemed to be a special case requiring especially careful treatment.

Soon after the plenum, at the first congress of collective farm workers, held in February 1933, Stalin stated that the main difficulties of the past had been overcome, and that existing problems were not as bad as what had gone before. Possibly, from his perspective, this was true: he was indeed winning his war against the countryside. In the villages, however, and especially in Soviet Ukraine, the tragedy was just then reaching its acme. As Kosior reported on 15 March 1933, so confirming that hunger had been deliberately used to teach the population a lesson, 'the unsatisfactory course of sowing in many areas' showed 'that famine still [hadn't] taught reason to many *kolkhozniki*'.[58] New repressive measures were thus adopted, such as prohibiting the sale of meat and grain on the *kolkhoz* market, no longer being made available even to those who had fulfilled their quotas if they lived in areas that had not completely complied with the requisitioning agenda. In March a new law on seasonal work restricted any chance of peasants leaving their home districts, making it necessary for them to first obtain a permit from the *kolkhoz* authorities. A resolution was also passed which redefined as a *kulak* any peasant unable or unwilling to fulfil his labour and procurement obligations towards the State.[59]

This measure opened up the prospect of another round of mass deportations similar to those of 1930/1931. However, such plans, while they were drafted, were not executed. Even so, in March, still fearing peasant uprisings, Moscow decided to remove from Soviet Ukraine, the northern Caucasus and the central Black Earth Region anyone who had been sentenced to more than two years, so eliminating every potential danger. Throughout 1933 another 270,000 peasants were deported. Even the Gulag administration complained about the condition of these deportees (as many as 3 per cent died during transport). The situation was likewise dire in the 'special villages'. Some 90,000 of the 1.3 million people living in them died in 1932, and in 1933 the number of deaths, generally caused by starvation, passed the 150,000 mark. It is also reasonable to assume that many of the 200,000 registered as having escaped from their 'special' villages actually died of hunger or exposure, a fact local administrations were unwilling to admit.[60]

In the early months of 1933 people starved to death in many regions across the Soviet Union, more so in the smaller centre than in larger cities, and especially so in the prisons, Gulag camps and special settlements. Above all, however, people perished in the rural areas, where between 25 and 30 million peasants suffered severe food shortages. In Soviet Ukraine, the northern Caucasus and the Volga region the extraordinary requisitions launched in November 1932 deprived villagers of their food reserves, supplies essential to carry these communities over the winter and into the next harvest. While hiding food allowed some to survive for a time, once those stocks were depleted the population foraged for whatever else was edible – dogs, cats, fish, rats, small animals, roots, tree bark, even weeds. By mid- to late January 1933 death from starvation became ubiquitous. Possibly 80 per cent of the more than four million Ukrainians who perished during the *Holodomor* did so in the compressed period of time between March and May 1933, the most intense mass extermination to occur in the twentieth-century history of Europe, a fact still unrecognised.

Throughout the USSR the months of April and June 1933 witnessed extensive mortality, with as many as five million deaths occurring (one or more million deaths, previously attributed to the period between late 1932 and early 1933, were actually people who had died in the previous two years). Aside from the losses in Soviet Ukraine, 1.3 to 1.5 million people died in Kazakhstan (where the dying was most intense in 1932, exterminating between 33 and 38 per cent of the Kazakhs and 8 to 9 per cent of the Slavic/European population), along with several hundred thousand victims in the northern Caucasus (where the father of the future CPSU general secretary, Mikhail Gorbachev, lost three of his brothers) and, on a lesser scale, in the Volga region.[61]

Other Russian regions, larger cities and major industrial centres also suffered, with deaths in such places numbering in the thousands, the deaths generally occurring among people living outside the 'special regime' (that is, outside the passportised areas). In Transcaucasia the crisis hit far less harshly. Local leaders – traditionally hostile to the Slavic penetration of their homelands – were more worried about halting the inflow of refugees from the famine-blighted lands.

If we consider annual mortality rates per thousand inhabitants in the countryside for the USSR as a whole, and make 1926 equal to 100, we see an increase during 1933 to 188.1 across the USSR and an increase to 138.2 in the RSFSR (which then included both Kazakhstan and the Kuban, meaning that the figure for Russia proper is lower). The increase in Soviet Ukraine rose to 367.7, almost triple what was happening elsewhere in the Soviet Union. Life expectancy at birth dropped from 42.9 years for men and 46.3 for women registered in 1926 to, respectively, 7.3 and 10.9 in 1933 (it was 13.6 and 36.3 in Ukraine in 1941). In addition, in Ukraine there were 782,000 births in 1932 but only 470,000 in 1933, compared with an average of 1.153 million per year for the period from 1926 to 1929.[62]

As we know, differences in the severity of the death-tolls over the entire USSR are explained by the famine's different course, for which the varying policies Moscow imposed were largely responsible. The same applies to the variation in the intensity of the famine in Soviet Ukraine, the northern Caucasus and the Volga region. Here, too, large cities and industrial centres suffered far less than villages, while border areas were known to have received better supplies, for strategic and political reasons. Death rates were thus unevenly distributed, even within Soviet Ukraine, with regions such as Kyiv, Cherkasy, Kirovohrad, Dnipropetrovsk, Zaporizhia and Kharkiv suffering a decline in population of 25 per cent or more, as was the case in the Kuban. Northern regions, bordering

Soviet Russia, fared better, as did the Donetsk mining and heavy industrial area.[63] As the Army Political Directorate reported to Voroshilov in 1933, the most terribly affected areas were those in which the Bolsheviks had traditionally encountered 'special difficulties in the class war'.[64] Here the famine took on unmistakably deliberate features.

Mortality thus depended on residency, urban or rural, and not explicitly on nationality, meaning that people living in the countryside suffered regardless of their ethnic background. Yet one cannot forget that the rural areas of this Soviet republic remained overwhelmingly Ukrainian-populated. Meanwhile, the better-supplied cities largely preserved their Russian, Jewish and Polish character. Thus, the countryside was targeted for the purpose of breaking the peasants because they were understood to represent the spine of the Ukrainian nation, the core of its resistance to Soviet rule.

What did Stalin know of the consequences of his decisions, and how did he respond to the information he received? Documents exist confirming that key local leaders – such as Turar Ryskulov and Stanislav Kosior – sent Stalin detailed information about the famine, as did writers like Sholokhov who, on 4 April 1933, addressed him a 16-page letter describing the procurement operations being carried out in the Don region:

> I will never be able to forget what I saw. By night, under a cruel wind, in the frost, when cold made even dogs hide, the families evicted from their houses lit fires in the street and gathered around them. Children wrapped in rags lay on the earth the fire had thawed.... A woman with an infant went from house to house asking for shelter. To let her in was forbidden, and in the morning the infant was dead in his mother's arms.[65]

Sholokhov recorded painstakingly the methods used to intimidate the peasants: mass beatings, naked people left to freeze outdoors, feigned executions, torture with red-hot irons, suffocation, and similar cruelties. In addition, he informed Stalin that these brutalities were carried out on instructions received from above rather than being excesses indulged in by misguided local activists. Stalin also received OGPU reports which did not pretend that 'enemy' machinations were somehow at the root of the problems existing in the countryside. Instead these memoranda accurately described the famine, the resulting mass mortality and cannibalism, and the corresponding growth of anti-Soviet sentiment. Towards the end of 1932 Stalin also received rather precise data about the famine's demographic effects.[66]

However, as Khlevniuk has noted, Stalin not only rejected the idea that he was in any way responsible for the famine (the very existence of which would repeatedly be denied publicly) but he even circulated a contrary explanation for what was happening, built upon a mixture of lies and clever reinterpretations of reality. First of all, any link between his policies and mass starvation was rejected: the responsibility for famine, Stalin insisted, lay with enemy sabotage and with the opposition, combined with the thievery and ignorance of the peasants, who did not understand the need to put the State's interests before their own. These very same malignant and maligning elements also purposely exaggerated the famine's real dimension: all reports of famine were nothing, in other words, but tools in the fight against Soviet power. By claiming that the real culprits were the very peasants actually dying from the famine, and insisting that all accounts deliberately inflated its real scale, Stalin freed himself from any obligation to help the starving.[67]

It is known that in the summer of 1932 Moscow held grain reserves (1.4 million tons) sufficient to feed approximately four million people for one year. Those stocks were never deployed to feed the hungry. Instead, in 1933, 1.4 million tons were exported and no food was imported, nor was any proffered foreign aid accepted. Mass death from starvation could have been averted but was not because the Stalinist regime did not, as yet, wish to end the famine, because it served their geopolitical ends.

In the early spring of 1933, even despite their catastrophic situation, some peasants were still resisting. As the Italian vice-consul in Novorossiisk reported to Rome in April:

> The terms of the struggle remain the same: the rural masses passively but effectively resist; the Party and the government are determined to suppress their resistance.... The peasant revolt (it cannot be called otherwise) is too vast to be effectively controlled and suffocated, and has disrupted the *kolkhoz*. Yet, force is but on one side: peasants are just an amorphous, clearly powerless mass. Starving peasants are completely destitute, and no organization, certainly not the persecuted church, keeps their spirit and resistance alive, yet their resistance is not sapped. To a well-equipped and resolute army, villages do not oppose an army of their own, not even the bands and the brigandage that have always accompanied rural revolts. Perhaps here lies the peasants' strength, or, rather, the reason of their enemies' failure. The well-armed and very powerful Soviet apparatus cannot look for victory in the open field; the enemy does not regroup, is everywhere, and the battle – that cannot be joined – is rather reduced to a never-ending series of very small, minimal operations: an un-weeded field here, a few quintals of grain hidden there, tractors that do not work properly, go around in circles, or are maliciously broken everywhere.[68]

In those very same weeks, however, hunger was 'winning' the war. As a senior Soviet official wrote following a tour in the Don region, 'in most villages the "conspiracy of silence" [peasants had stopped talking to local authorities] has been broken. People speak again at meetings, and they do so to ask for bread, promising that once food will come, work will be properly done.'[69] He added that a small increase in the number of those reporting for work could be noted, even though 'generalized sabotage' was not yet over. The handing out of approximately 1.3 million tons of seed grain, and of more than 300,000 tons in food aid – a proportion reflecting the regime's priorities – sealed Moscow's victory. That summer, Germany's agricultural attaché, Dr Otto Schiller, returning after a road trip through parts of Soviet Ukraine and the Northern Caucasus, told Bernardo Attolico, the Italian ambassador to Moscow, that 'the secret of the Ukrainian agriculture's revival' lay precisely in the fact that 'peasants were not left with any other choice than working for the government in exchange for a minimum of food, or literally starving to death'. In those very weeks Piłsudski was forced to admit that the mass starvation of the Ukrainian peasantry represented a victory for Stalin. By the time these conclusions were reached, the Stalinist triumph was indeed complete. In July, Attolico reported to Mussolini what the German diplomat had told him, namely that 'stuck in their villages, and deprived of the possibility to beg for food in the cities', Ukrainian peasants had finally understood that the only way to survive was to work for the Soviet State.[70]

Of course, resistance and localised rebellions did not disappear entirely, and peasant labour did not become particularly efficient (laying the basis for Soviet agriculture's intrinsic weakness), yet the Bolsheviks finally realised their long-held dream of extracting from the countryside what they deemed they needed, without fairly compensating peasants for their industry.[71] After the summer of 1933, while Stalinist leaders gloated, the State was able to seize, without difficulty, more than 30 per cent of what proved to be a rather poor crop.[72]

National repression and terror

His understanding of the fact that in Ukraine and the Kuban the peasant question was also a national question strengthened Stalin's determination to 'solve' both as one. In order to make sure that the solution he imposed would be final it was complemented by a decision to purge the nation's elites, suspected, as they were, of abetting peasant resistance. On 14 and 15 December 1932, the Politburo passed two secret decrees that reversed, *but only in Ukraine*, the official nationality policies originally announced in 1923. Since the view from Moscow was that *korenizatsiya*, as implemented originally in Soviet Ukraine and in Kuban, had not undermined nationalistic feelings but had instead helped them grow, producing 'enemies with a Party card in their pocket', that situation must now be reversed. Peasants were obviously not the only ones responsible – they shared the blame with Soviet Ukraine's *intelligentsia*, its political and cultural elites, who would now be repressed.

A few days later, on 19 December, similar if less harsh measures were also imposed on Soviet Belarus, where – as in Ukraine – the peasant and the national questions largely coincided, and had caused problems during the Civil War, even if not on the same scale as in Ukraine. Here, too, in early March, the Republican Party was accused of abetting nationalism, resulting in local Party cadres and the Belarusian *intelligentsia* suffering for these 'crimes' even if there was no reversal of 'Belarusisation'.[73]

Working from this premise, Ukrainization programs were discontinued in the Soviet Russian Republic. Several million Ukrainians who, following the border delimitations of the mid-1920s, found themselves living in the RSFSR, lost the educational, press and communal rights which other nationalities continued to enjoy. As a result the 1937 Soviet census would reveal that only three million citizens of the RSFSR identified themselves as Ukrainian, compared to the 7.8 million who had done so in 1926 (at least part of this decline was caused when Kazakhstan, previously an autonomous republic within the RSFSR, became a union republic).[74]

Soon afterwards, an attack on the Ukrainian language was launched in Ukraine itself. Stalin was not, however, content with just the indirect consequences of his policies, which would have brought about the re-Russification of Ukraine's cities and would have long-term and significant consequences still evident in contemporary Ukraine. His aim was to simultaneously transform the Ukrainian language into a second-rate and subordinate one, which upwardly mobile people would abandon in favour of Russian. Thus policies were put into place aimed at bringing the Ukrainian language closer to Russian. As this happened, thousands of state officials who had earlier been tasked with promoting Ukrainisation lost their jobs, if not suffering even worse fates.[75]

While in Kharkiv, according to Italian diplomats, top GPU officials boasted of changing the 'ethnographic material' of the countryside, at the Central Committee plenum of February 1933 Skrypnyk was attacked because 'not only did he not wage a struggle against ... the bourgeois-nationalist line on the questions of creating Ukrainian scholarly terminology, he also facilitated this distortion of the line on the linguistic front'.[76] This was equated with 'separating the Ukrainian language from the Russian language'. Skrypnyk was also criticised for his 'theory of a mixed dialect', according to which children of ethnic Ukrainians who spoke *surzhyk* (an Ukrainian-Russian patois) were supposed to begin their schooling in the Ukrainian language, thus preparing for the transformation of Ukraine into a completely Ukrainian-speaking republic. In addition, he was accused of having introduced a scholarly-based, nationwide orthography of the Ukrainian language, which included the linguistic features of both Soviet-ruled Ukraine and western Ukraine. This orthography, confirming the separateness of the Ukrainian language, impeded the process of bringing it closer to Russian, and so was deemed unacceptable.[77]

Meanwhile, hundreds of middle and local cadres and intellectuals continued to be repressed, at times even sentenced to death for alleged sabotage or for having 'undermined agriculture and caused a famine in the country' (accusations that reflected reality much better than official propaganda which continued to deny the existence of famine conditions). Among them was Skrypnyk's secretary Esternyuk, born in Galicia and accused of being a member of another concocted body, the Ukrainian Military Organisation. While Skrypnyk energetically defended himself, Esternyuk, under duress, confessed to being involved in the counter-revolutionary activities of this clandestine organisation. Other 'Galician' intellectuals – often refugees from Poland, until recently called 'western Ukrainians' – were quickly arrested, while in both the Party and State a wave of de-Ukrainisation began, signalled among other things by a switch from the use of Ukrainian to the Russian language in many newspapers, journals and university classes. More than 2,000 officials of the Commissariat of Education –which had been the hearth of Ukrainization – were removed, including almost the entire senior management of the Commissariat's *oblast* directorates. The publication of Ukrainian dictionaries was also suspended, new editions began incorporating Russian terms and the 1928 Ukrainian orthography was abolished.[78]

Scores of Ukrainian writers were also arrested. Not surprisingly these measures precipitated deep angst among Soviet Ukraine's national-communist leaders and intellectuals. In May the most important Soviet Ukrainian writer, Mykola Khvylovy, committed suicide. Skrypnyk, who tried to answer the criticisms directed at his work by penning an essay on nationality policies, had his efforts rebuffed by the Ukrainian Politburo, and was mercilessly criticised on the eve of the Ukrainian Central Committee plenum of June 1933, where Postyshev once more attacked Skrypnyk's orthographic reforms and branded all attempts at promoting Ukrainian among the working classes as counter-revolutionary. In despair, but reportedly willing to say 'everything', Skrypnyk considered personally confronting Stalin but his wife convinced him not to, threatening to herself commit suicide if he did so. Thus, on 7 July 1933, he went to a Politburo meeting carrying a document acknowledging his guilt but then left the room and retired to his office where he took his own life. With the repression of thousands of its cadres, and the death of its leaders, the Soviet Ukrainian national-communist experiment that had emerged during the Civil War thus came to an end.

Skrypnyk's suicide ended his denigration in public (Stalin, almost respectfully, spoke about Skrypnyk's 'biblical fall') but the anti-Ukrainian purge continued. In November the Central Committee repeated that the most dangerous enemy lurking in Soviet Ukraine was Ukrainian nationalism, supporting, and itself shored up by, the threat of foreign intervention, a reversal of the view that the greatest hindrance to the emergence of 'Soviet man' was Great Russian chauvinism. Postyshev boasted of the purge of nationalistic-minded personnel in the educational system, which included the firing of 4,000 'hostile' teachers. Soon afterwards, at the Seventeenth Party Congress in January 1934, he confirmed that the Ukrainian Party organisation had been ruled directly and firmly from Moscow. A few weeks later, he asked the GPU, which was still engaged in 'uncovering' counter-revolutionary organisations, to evict from their apartments and deport to the north the families of all those who had been arrested or executed as nationalists, their relatives losing their jobs even as their sons were expelled from their schools.

This 1933/1934 anti-Ukrainian terror thus portended what would happen during the 'Great Terror' in 1936 to 1938, when some of the 'cases' the GPU had fabricated in Soviet Ukraine were reopened and used against senior leaders in Moscow, such as Georgy Piatakov. The Terror thus started in Soviet Ukraine, as Lev Kopelev maintained, and it is possible to say that Ukrainians – including those starving in the Kuban, or losing their national rights in the Soviet Russian republic – were actually the first nation to be 'punished' by Stalin.[79] This explains why Stanislav Kulchytskyi challenged Viktor Danilov's remark that Ukrainians suffered fewer losses than Russians in 1937/1938. Kulchytskyi noted, accurately, that Soviet Ukraine had *already* been visited by the Terror in 1932 to 1934, when the security organs arrested approximately 200,000 people, almost as many as the total of all those who would be victimised in later years.[80]

Conclusions: the question of genocide

It would be wrong, at present, to suggest that we know exactly or entirely what happened in 1931 to 1934: much remains to be learned from new research on the causes of the Soviet famines, their mechanics, geographical variations, chronology, and the long-term consequences of the enormous human suffering they caused, particularly to the psychological and spiritual well-being and subsequent social and political behaviour of the surviving millions. Yet much has been uncovered and, with a few exceptions, many past controversies about the nature, course and consequences of these famines have become the subjects of learned discourse rather than of polemical exchanges.

The effort to reach a consensus on at least the crucial features of the Ukrainian tragedy is still, however, hampered by difficulties not only of an intellectual or documentary nature. The definition of the *Holodomor*, its post-Soviet use in the process of Ukrainian nation building, and consequential Russian–Ukrainian arguments over responsibility – as groundless as they may be, given that both nations were victims of the Stalinist regime in the 1930s – still distort scholarly discourse, especially over the question of whether or not the famine in Soviet Ukraine was a genocide.

On the one hand, there is the 'genocide thesis' that sees in the events of 1932/1933 a famine organised in order to alter or destroy the Ukrainian nation's social and demographic fabric, a concerted effort aimed at undermining this nation's ability to resist the transformation of the USSR into what it became under Stalin: a despotic empire. Given what happened up until the autumn of 1932, this variant of the genocide thesis is inadequate.

On the other side, there are historians, including V. Danilov, R. Davies, S. Wheatcroft and V. Kondrashin, who, though acknowledging the criminal nature of Stalin's policies, deem it necessary to study the famine as a 'complex phenomenon'. They maintain that the famine was the *unplanned* result of Stalin's catastrophic anti-peasant policies; that the regime used it to force peasants to work for the *kolkhoz;* that the famine had *regional* peculiarities which determined its scale and consequences, being intense in the areas of full collectivisation, where the State faced the reactive resistance of the peasantry and the threat of an agricultural collapse; that the situation in Soviet Ukraine was defined by its role as grain provider, by the extent of peasant opposition, and by the measures taken to eradicate this resistance to prevent the collapse of the *kolkhoz* system; that the Ukrainian crisis did give the Stalinist regime a pretext for also tackling national problems, but, they insist, the famine was not engineered to resolve the national question but was instead a consequence of the problems of the *kolkhoz* system, an economic and political crisis resolved using brutal methods reflecting the personality of the leader; and, finally, they point out that the famine did not distinguish among people of different nationalities. As such they conclude that there was no genocide but rather a more widespread tragedy involving the Soviet countryside as a whole, obviously including Ukraine and Russia.[81]

While all of the above observations are partially true, these historians ignore Stalin's view of 'the national question' being 'in essence a peasant question'. As a result, they focus on the 'pan-Soviet' phenomena and largely ignore the different outcomes of Stalin's policies at the national level. Above all, they do not fully appreciate the crucial turning point which took place in the autumn of 1932 when, in Soviet Ukraine, the Kuban, the northern Caucasus and the Volga region, a 'spontaneous' famine was made into a politically orchestrated one that would continue to ravage the rural communities of Soviet Ukraine and adjacent lands well into the summer of 1933.

In short, Stalin transformed a famine that his policies had inadvertently caused into a weapon of state power. Instead of ameliorating an existing famine in Soviet Ukraine, as he could have done, Stalin instituted what has come to be known as the *Holodomor*. Did he intend to eradicate the entire Ukrainian nation? No. But he did wish to emasculate it through the decimation of its peasantry, the purging of its *intelligentsia* and the cowing of its Republican Party cadres, all accompanied by the undoing of Ukrainisation.

Stalin's strategy attained some of his designs. While the Soviet famines of 1931 to 1933 had essentially different consequences in each of the different Soviet republics and regions where they occurred, there was also a common, and Union-wide, experience of hunger, suffering and want during this period. Thus, throughout the USSR, the political use of hunger broke peasant resistance; guaranteed Stalin's victory; opened the door to the subsequent Terror; allowed, by means of the subjugation of the most important republic, the de facto transformation of a avowedly federal state into an empire; and left a dreadful legacy of grief in a multitude of Ukrainian families who were prevented from hallowing their dead or recalling what they had endured as long as the official taboo against any mention of the 1932/1933 famine prevailed, as it would for several decades, even as the Stalinist myth about life having become 'more joyous' was promoted.

In Soviet Ukraine and in Kazakhstan famine took on unparalleled dimensions. Kazakhstan's traditional society was seriously disrupted. In Soviet Ukraine not only the nation's rural core but society's elites were destroyed or subjugated, significantly impeding and distorting the process of Ukrainian nation building.[82] The crippling of this nation involved more than just blunt repression. Postyshev often wore Ukrainian embroidered shirts, he raised monuments to Ukraine's national bard Taras Shevchenko, he allowed the publication of Ukrainian books and magazines (albeit in much reduced print runs) and even oversaw, in 1933, Kyiv becoming Ukraine's capital city. But none of these gestures evidenced any genuine sympathy for what may be described as the Skrypnyk brand of Ukrainisation. Instead, a 'Bolshevik' style of indigenisation came to the fore, the main pillar of which remained the promotion of communist cadres of Ukrainian origin provided that they accepted Russification, the Ukrainian-turned-Russian Leonid Brezhnev being a most notable embodiment of the end-product of this process. In many urban centres, where the proportion of 'ethnic' Ukrainians continued to grow, almost reaching the 60 per cent mark nationally by 1939 (although, in the major cities, this figure was much lower), cultural Ukrainisation was halted even as two linguistic spheres coalesced, one Russian, the other Ukrainian, the former enjoying pre-eminence, as Ukrainian language use came to be identified with rural backwardness and social inferiority.

Only from this perspective can one explain the much weaker presence in 1941 to 1945 of any organised Ukrainian national movement in eastern Ukraine, in the very region where just such a force had played a vital role during the revolutionary and insurrectionary years of 1917 to 1922 (while, in western Ukraine, namely Galicia and Volyn, which had not been part of the USSR until late September 1939, a nationalist insurgent movement would vigorously contest Soviet power well into the 1950s). Then came the famine of 1946/1947, once more ravaging a large swathe of Soviet Ukraine.[83] The memory of these two tragedies, together with the suffering caused by collectivisation, widespread deportations, the war and the oppression of the late Stalin period, coalesced into an almost uninterrupted *continuum* of extreme hardship between 1929 and the year of Stalin's death, 1953, affecting negatively the psychology of a large proportion of Ukraine's population over several decades.

The *Holodomor* left its most discernible imprint on the Ukrainian nation's demographic structures. As another chapter in this volume underscores, over four million people died in Soviet Ukraine in 1933 alone, most of them in the first six months of that year.[84] The French demographers France Meslé and Jacques Vallin previously noted that Ukraine's population without the *Holodomor* would have been 52 million in 2007 instead of the 46.5 million recorded. Without the subsequent devastation of the Second World War, and of the 1946/1947 famine, Ukraine's populaton would have been 65.7 million. These statistics expose the intensity and scale of the Ukrainian nation's losses over a time-span of less than two decades, a crippling legacy that continues to resonate within today's Ukraine. Intriguingly, Stalin hinted that he knew what he was doing when he used famine as a tool of national destruction. In 1952 he told a Ukrainian Politburo delegation: 'the history of mankind knows many tragic cases in which entire nations died out because of lack of bread, and were thus cancelled from history.'[85]

A final note. Both the *Holodomor* and the Kazakh tragedy share an important feature, namely that the regime bearing responsibility for them succeeded for decades in concealing the truth about what had happened. As a consequence our historical memory of the 1930s, and more generally about the twentieth century, was crafted without reference to these Soviet famines, which this author considers genocidal.[86] That helps explain the harshness of the debates over this period in Soviet history, arguments that were integral to the difficult process that has led to our present-day understanding of the extraordinary dimensions and consequences, moral and interpretive ones included, of what the Soviet regime was, and what it did. To bring awareness of the *Holodomor* into the collective discourse about Europe's immediate past we must radically revise the previously received and widely accepted story. That will require time, and it will not be painless.

Acknowledgement

I am grateful to Professor Lubomyr Luciuk for his editorial comments and assistance with several earlier drafts of this chapter.

Notes

1 Robert Conquest, *The Harvest of Sorrow: Soviet Collectivization and the Terror-Famine* (Oxford: Oxford University Press 1986), complemented by the findings of the US Commission on the Ukrainian Famine (James E. Mace (ed.), *Investigation of the Ukrainian Famine, 1932–33: Report to Congress* (Washington, DC: Government Printing Office, 1988)) and by those of the International Commission of Inquiry into the 1932/1933 Famine in Ukraine, reproduced in Lubomyr Y. Luciuk and Lisa Grekul (eds), *Holodomor: Reflections on the Great Famine of 1932–1933 in Soviet Ukraine* (Kingston: Kashtan Press, 2008), 245–351.

2 Among published memoirs see: Viktor Kravchenko, *I Chose Freedom: The Personal and Political Life of a Soviet Official* (New York: Scribner's, 1946); Semen O. Pidhainy (ed.), *The Black Deeds of the Kremlin: A White Book*, vol. 2, *The Great Famine in Ukraine in 1932–1933* (Detroit, MI: Globe Press, 1955), and Miron Dolot, *Execution by Hunger: The Hidden Holocaust* (New York: W.W. Norton, 1985). In the mid-1960s Dana G. Dalrymple reviewed the available sources in 'The Soviet Famine of 1932–1934', *Soviet Studies* 15(3) (1964), 250–284; 16(4) (1965), 471–474. Diplomatic reports started to be published in the 1980s, including Marco Carynnyk, Lubomyr Y. Luciuk and Bohdan S. Kordan (eds), *The Foreign Office and the Famine: British Documents on Ukraine and the Great Famine of 1932–33* (Kingston: Limestone Press, 1988); Dmytro Zlepko (ed.), *Der ukrainische Hunger-Holocaust* (Sonnenbühl: Verlag Helmut Wild, 1988); Andrea Graziosi (ed.), '"Lettres de Char'kov": La famine en Ukraine et dans le Caucase du Nord à travers les rapports des diplomates italiens', 1932 to 1934, *Cahiers du monde russe et soviétique* 1–2 (1989), 5–106. See also the more complete *Lettere da Kharkov: La carestia in Ucraina e nel Caucaso del Nord nei rapporti dei diplomatici italiani, 1932–33* (Torino: Giulio Einaudi, 1991), and Athanasius D. McVay and Lubomyr Y. Luciuk (eds), *The Holy See and the Holodomor: Documents from the Vatican Secret Archives on the Great Famine of 1932–1933 in Soviet Ukraine* (Kingston: University of Toronto, 2011). Historians who mentioned the famine include Naum Jasny, *The Socialized Agriculture of the USSR: Plans and Performance* (Stanford, CA: Stanford University Press, 1949); Alec Nove, *An Economic History of the USSR* (Harmondsworth: Penguin, 1969; 3rd edn, 1992); Moshe Lewin, '"Taking Grain": Soviet Policies of Agricultural Procurements before the War' (1974), now in *The Making of the Soviet System: Essays in the Social History of Interwar Russia* (New York: Methuen, 1985), 142–177; and Zhores A. Medvedev, *Soviet Agriculture* (New York: W.W. Norton, 1987).

3 Sergei Maksudov [A. Babyonyshev], *Poteri naseleniia SSSR* (Benson, VT: Chalidze, 1989); Feliks M. Rudych *et al.* (eds), *Holod 1932–1933 rokiv na Ukraïni: Ochyma istorykiv, movoiu dokumentiv* (Kyiv: Vyd-vo politychnoï literatury Ukraïny, 1990); Stanislav V. Kulchytskyi (ed.), *Kolektyvizatsiia i holod na Ukraïni, 1929–1933* (Kyiv: Naukova Dumka, 1992); Stanislav V. Kulchytskyi (ed.), *Holodomor 1932–1933 rr. v Ukraïni: Prychynyi naslidky* (Kyiv: Instytut istorin Ukraïny NAN Ukraïny, 1995); Nikolai A. Ivnitskii, *Kollektivizatsiia i raskulachivanie* (Moscow: Magistr, 1996); Andrea Graziosi, *The Great Soviet Peasant War, 1918–1933* (Cambridge, MA: Harvard University Press, 1996); M.K. Kozybaev *et al.*, *Nasil'stvennaia kollektivizatsiia i golod v Kazakhstane v 1931–33 gg* (Almaty: XXI vek, 1998); Nikolai A. Ivnitskii, *Repressivnaia politika sovetskoi vlasti v derevne (1928–1933 gg)* (Moscow: Institut rossiiskoi istorii RAN, 2000); V. Danilov, Roberta Manning and Lynne Viola (eds), *Tragediia sovetskoi derevni: Kollektivizatsiia i raskulachivanie*, vol. 3, *Konets 1930–1933* (Moscow: Rosspen, 2001); Terry Martin, *The Affirmative Action Empire: Nations and Nationalism in the Soviet Union, 1923–1933* (Ithaca, NY: Cornell University Press, 2001); Yury Shapoval and Valery Vasylyev, *Komandyry velykoho holodu: Poïzdky V. Molotova i L. Kahanovycha v Ukraïnu ta na Pivnichnyi Kavkaz, 1932–1933 rr.* (Kyiv: Heneza, 2001); Robert W. Davies, Oleg V. Khlevniuk and Edward A. Rees (eds), *The Stalin–Kaganovich Correspondence, 1931–36* (New Haven, CT: Yale University Press, 2003); Viktor Kondrashin and D'Ann Penner, *Golod: 1932–1933 gody v sovetskoi derevne (na materiale Povolzh'ia, Dona i Kubani)* (Samara: Samara University Press, 2002); Volodymyr M. Lytvyn (ed.), *Holod 1932–1933 rokiv v Ukraïni: Prychyny ta naslidky* (Kyiv: Naukova Dumka, 2003); Robert W. Davies and Stephen G. Wheatcroft, *The Years of Hunger: Soviet Agriculture, 1931–1933* (New York: Palgrave Macmillan, 2004); Niccolò Pianciola, 'Famine in the Steppe: The Collectivization of Agriculture and the Kazak Herdsmen, 1928–1934', *Cahiers du monde russe* 45(1–2) (2004), 137–192. Some of these sources were compiled by Bohdan Klid and Alexander J. Motyl (eds), *The Holodomor Reader: A Sourcebook* (Toronto: CIUS Press, 2012).

4 Population loss estimates have been calculated by the demographers France Meslé and Jacques Vallin in *Mortalité et causes de décès en Ukraine aux XXe siècle* (Paris: Cahiers de l'INED, 2003), translated into English as *Mortality and Causes of Death in 20th Century Ukraine* (Dordrecht: Springer 2012). More recently their calculations have been refined further. See Omelian Rudnytskyi *et al.*, Chapter 8, this volume.

5 Martin, *Affirmative Action Empire*; Larisa S. Gatagova *et al.* (eds), *TsK RKP(b)-VKP(b) i natsional'nyi vopros*, kniga 1, *1918–1933* (Moscow: Rosspen, 2005), 696–698.

6 Graziosi, *Great Soviet Peasant War*; Andrea Graziosi, 'The Soviet 1931–33 Famines and the Ukrainian *Holodomor:* Is a New Interpretation Possible and What Would its Consequences be?', in *Hunger by Design*, ed. Halyna Hryn (Cambridge, MA: Harvard University Press, 2008), 1–20 (originally published in Ukraine in 2005); Andrea Graziosi, *L'Urss di Lenin and Stalin* (Bologna: Il Mulino, 2007); Andrea Graziosi, 'Why and in What Sense Was the *Holodomor* a Genocide?', in *Holodomor: Reflections on the Great Famine of 1932–1933 in Soviet Ukraine*, ed. Lubomyr Y. Luciuk (Kingston: Kashtan Press, 2008), 139–158; Andrea Graziosi, '"Nezruchnyj klass" u modernizacijnykh proektakh', *Ukraina Moderna* 6 (2010), 9–17; my contribution to a forum discussing Norman Naimark, *Stalin's Genocides* (Princeton, NJ: Princeton University Press, 2010), *Journal of Cold War Studies* 14(3) (2012). Most recently, Andrea Graziosi, Lubomyr A. Hajda and Halyna Hryn, 'Introduction', in *After the Holodomor: The Enduring Impact of the Great Famine in Ukraine*, ed. Andrea Graziosi, Lubomyr A. Hajda and Halyna Hryn (Cambridge, MA: Harvard Ukrainian Research Institute, 2013), xx.

7 Arthur E. Adams, *Bolsheviks in the Ukraine: The Second Campaign, 1918–1919* (New Haven, CT: Yale University Press, 1963); Andrea Graziosi, *Bol'sheviki i krest'iane na*

Ukraine, 1918–1919 gody (Moscow, AIRO XX, 1997); Stephen Velychenko, *State Building in Revolutionary Ukraine, 1917–1922: A Comparative Study of Governments and Bureaucrats, 1917–1922* (Toronto: University of Toronto Press, 2011). Both Mikhail Bulgakov, *White Guard* (New Haven, CT: Yale University Press, 2008) and Alexander Barmine, *One Who Survived: The Life Story of a Russian under the Soviets* (New York: Putman's, 1945) vividly describe the entrance into Kyiv of Ukrainian peasant detachments in 1918/1919.

8 See e.g. Lenin's theses of November 1919, written to dictate the policies to be followed in Ukraine after its reoccupation, in Richard Pipes (ed.), *The Unknown Lenin: From the Secret Archive* (New Haven, CT: Yale University Press, 1996).

9 'Draft Platform on the National Question for the Fourth Conference, Endorsed by the Political Bureau of the Central Committee', 9–12 June 1923, in *Works*, vol. 5, *1921–23* (Moscow, 1952–1954), 297–348; Andrea Graziosi, 'Vneshniaia i vnutrennaia politika Stalina: o natsional'nom voprose v imperskom kontekste, 1901–1926', in *Istoriia stalinizma: itogi i problemy izucheniia*, ed. E. Iu. Kondrashina *et al.* (Moscow: Rosspen, 2011), 215–235.

10 Iosif V. Stalin, 'Concerning the National Question in Yugoslavia', *Bol'shevik* 7 (15 April 1925), in *Works*, vol. 7, *1925*, 69–76.

11 James E. Mace, *Communism and the Dilemmas of National Liberation: National Communism in Ukraine, 1918–1933* (Cambridge, MA: Harvard University Press, 1983); Bohdan S. Krawchenko, *Social Change and National Consciousness in Twentieth-century Ukraine* (New York: Macmillan, 1985); Martin, *Affirmative Action Empire*; Graziosi, *Urss di Lenin e Stalin*, 223–226; TsK *RKP(b)-VKP(b) i natsional'nyi vopros*, kniga 1, *1918–33*.

12 Martin, *Affirmative Action Empire*, 89–98.

13 Yuri G. Fel'shtinskii, 'Konfidentsial'nye besedy Bukharina', *Voprosy istorii* 2–3 (1991), 182–203; Graziosi, *L'Urss di Lenin e Stalin*, 228–252.

14 Andrea Romano and Nonna Tarkhova (eds), *Krasnaia armiia i kollektivizatsiia derevni v SSSR, 1928–1933. Sbornik dokumentov iz fondov RGVA* (Napoli: Istituto universitario orientale, 1997).

15 Moshe Lewin, *La paysannerie et le pouvoir soviétique, 1928–1930* (Paris: Mouton, 1968); Graziosi, *L'Urss di Lenin e Stalin*, 241.

16 While it is true that during the First World War Europe's peasants had been excluded from rationing, no state attempted to take their land and animals or to systematically rob them of the greater part of their produce. In the conditions prevailing in the USSR during the 1930s this exclusion, maintained up until the abolition of rationing at the end of 1934, effectively meant that the Soviet State formally decided not to consider the peasantry as full citizens of Soviet society.

17 Miklos Kun, *Bukharin, ego druz'ia i vragi* (Moscow: Respublika, 1992), 247.

18 'Iz 'Pis'ma k Fedoru', *Politicheskii dnevnik* 25 (October 1966), 148ff. In the summer of 1928 the fact that Stalinist policies could precipitate a famine was discussed openly (in Fel'shtinskii (ed.), 'Konfidentsial'nye', 198).

19 Marco Carynnyk, 'Day for Night: The Death and Life of Oleksandr Dovzhenko', *Kino-Kolo* 22 (2004).

20 Martin, *Affirmative Action Empire*, 100.

21 Viktor N. Zemskov, *Spetsposelentsy v SSSR, 1930–1960* (Moscow: Nauka, 2003); Ivnitskii, *Kollektivizatsiia i raskulachivanie*; J. Otto Pohl, *The Stalinist Penal System: A Statistical History of Soviet Repression and Terror, 1930–1953* (Jefferson, NC: McFarland, 1997); Pavel Polian, *Against Their Will: The History and Geography of Forced Migration in the USSR* (Budapest: CEU Press, 2003).

22 Compare the OGPU reports published by Danilov with the testimonies collected in *Black Deeds of the Kremlin*.

23 V.P. Danilov and Alexis Berelowitch, 'Les documents des VČK-OGPU-NKVD sur la campagne soviétique, 1918–1937', *Cahiers du monde russe* 35 (1994), 633–682.

24 *Tragediia sovetskoi derevni*, vol. 2, *Noiabr' 1929-Dekabr' 1930*; Andrea Graziosi, 'Collectivisation, révoltes paysannes et politiques gouvernementales à travers les rapports du GPU d'Ukraine de février-mars 1930', *Cahiers du monde russe* 3 (1994), 437–632; Lynne Viola, *Peasant Rebels under Stalin: Collectivization and the Culture of Peasant Resistance* (New York: Oxford University Press, 1996); Isabelle Ohayon, *La sédentarisation des Kazakhs dans l'URSS de Staline: Collectivisation et changement social, 1928–1945* (Paris: Maisonneuve & Larose, 2006).

25 Timothy Snyder, 'A National Question Crosses a Systemic Border: The Polish-Soviet Context for Ukraine, 1926–1935', paper presented to the *Società Italiana per lo Studio della Storia contemporenea*, Bozen/Bolzano, 2004.

26 Martin, *Affirmative Action Empire*, 249–260.

27 I.V. Stalin, 'The Tasks of Business Executives: Speech to the First All-Union Conference of Leading Personnel of Socialist Industry', 4 February 1931, in *Works*, vol. 13 (Moscow, 1954), 31–44.

28 Viktor Kondrashin, 'La carestia del 1932–33 in Russia e Ucraina: analisi comparativa (cause, dati, conseguenze)', in *La morte della terra. La grande carestia in Ucraina nel 1932–33*, ed. Gabriele De Rosa and Francesca Lomastro (Rome: Viella, 2005), 44.

29 Graziosi, *Great Soviet Peasant War*, 44; Robert W. Davies, Mark Harrison and Stephen G. Wheatcroft (eds), *The Economic Transformation of the Soviet Union* (Cambridge: Cambridge University Press, 1994), 285.

30 Niccolò Pianciola, *Stalinismo di frontiera. Colonizzazione agricola, sterminio dei nomadi e costruzione statale in Asia centrale, 1905–1936* (Rome: Viella, 2009); Ohayon, *Sédentarisation des Kazakhs*; Sarah Cameron, 'The Hungry Steppe: Soviet Kazakhstan and the Kazakh Famine, 1921–1934', unpublished Ph.D. dissertation, Yale University, 2011. Of special importance is Turar Ryskulov's detailed letter to Stalin of 9 March 1933, in *Sovetskoe rukovodstvo: Perepiska, 1928–1941* (Moscow: Rosspen, 1999), 204–225.

31 Winston S. Churchill, *The Second World* War, vol. 4, *The Hinge of Fate* (New York: Bantam, 1962); Feliks Ivanovich Chuev (ed.), *Molotov Remembers: Inside Kremlin Politics: Conversations with Felix Chuev* (Chicago, IL: I.R. Dee, 1993).

32 *Tragediia sovetskoi derevni*, vol. 3, 420–422.

33 Martin, *Affirmative Action Empire*, 296–299; Yury Shapoval, 'La dirigenza politica ucraina e il Cremlino nel 1932–33: i coautori della carestia', in De Rosa and Lomastro, *La morte della terra*, 92.

34 Martin, *Affirmative Action Empire*, 273–308.

35 *Stalin-Kaganovich Correspondence*, 152.

36 Now in Klid and Motyl, *Holodomor Reader*, 237.

37 Quoted in N.A. Ivnitskii, 'Golod 1932–33 godov: kto vinovat', in *Golod 1932–33 godov* (Moscow,1995), 59.

38 *Stalin–Kaganovich Correspondence*, 134, 256, in the original Russian edition; Peter H. Solomon, *Soviet Criminal Justice under Stalin* (Cambridge: Cambridge University Press, 1996), 111–129.

39 *Stalin–Kaganovich Correspondence*, 273–274, in the original Russian edition.

40 O. Chlevnjuk (Khlevniuk), 'Stalin e la carestia dei primi anni Trenta', *Storica* 11(32) (2005), 27–40.

41 In a 2004 letter to this author, Khlevniuk pointed out that many of Stalin's policies had what could be called 'genocidal' features. 'No matter what problem arose in the country, it was solved through the application of violence directed at specific and well-defined socio-cultural or national groups of the population.' These groups and the treatment inflicted upon them, from preventive measures to liquidation, varied over time according to the internal and international situation and the despot's own beliefs. The *Holodomor* must be understood against this background.

42 Chlevnjuk, 'Stalin e la carestia dei primi anni Trenta'.

43 Loris Marcucci, 'Il primato dell'organizzazione. Biografia politica di L. Kaganovich', unpublished Ph.D. dissertation, Università di San Marino, Scuola Superiore di Studi Storici, 1991, 282–283; Shapoval and Vasylyev, *Komandyry velykoho holodu.*
44 Yuri G. Murin (ed.), *Pisatel' i vozhd': Perepiska M. A. Sholokhova s I.V. Stalinym 1931–1950 gody* (Moscow: Raritet, 1997).
45 Shapoval and Vasylyev, *Komandyry velykoho holodu.*
46 Ibid.
47 Ibid.
48 Graziosi *et al.*, 'Introduction', in *After the Holodomor*, xx.
49 Yury Shapoval, 'The Holodomor and its Connection to the Repressions in Soviet Ukraine, 1932–1934', in *After the Holodomor: The Enduring Impact of the Great Famine in Ukraine*, ed. Andrea Graziosi, Lubomyr A. Hajda and Halyna Hryn (Cambridge, MA: Harvard Ukrainian Research Institute, 2013), xx.
50 Krawchenko, *I Chose Freedom*; Kondrashin and D'Ann Penner, *Golod: 1932–1933 gody v sovetskoi derevne.*
51 *Tragediia sovetskoi derevni*, vol. 3, 603, 611.
52 Now in Klid and Motyl, *Holodomor Reader*, 254.
53 Graziosi, *Great Soviet Peasant War*, 60.
54 V.P. Popov, 'Passportnaia sistema v SSSR (1932–1976 gg)', *Sotsiologicheskie issledovaniia* 8 and 9 (1995), 3–14, 3–13; 'Izmeneniia pasportnoi sistemy nosiat printsipial'no vazhnyi kharacter', *Istochnik* 6 (1997), 101–122; Gijs Kessler, 'The peasant and the town: rural–urban migration in the Soviet Union, 1929–1940', unpublished Ph.D. thesis, European University Institute, 2001; Graziosi, *Urss di Lenin e Stalin*, 343–345.
55 Nicholas Werth, *Cannibal Island: Death in a Siberian Gulag* (Princeton, NJ: Princeton University Press, 2007).
56 Graziosi, *Great Soviet Peasant War*, 63.
57 Robert Kuśnierz, 'Głod na Ukrainie w latach 1932–1933', *Dzieje Najnowsze* 2 (2007), 129–159; R. Kuśnierz (ed.), *Pomór w 'raju bolzewickim'* (Toruń, 2008); *Lettere da Kharkov*, 170.
58 Ruslan Pyrih (ed.), *Holodomor 1932–1933 rokiv v Ukraïni* (Kyiv: Instytut Istorii Ukrainy NAN Ukrainy, Vyd. Dim Kyievo-Mohylians'ka akademiia, 2007), 771.
59 Ivnitskii, *Repressivnaia politika sovetskoi vlasti v derevne.*
60 Oleg V. Khlevniuk, *The History of the Gulag: From Collectivization to the Great Terror* (New Haven, CT: Yale University Press, 2004); V.N. Zemskov, 'Spetsposelentsy', *Sotsiologicheskie issledovaniia* 11 (1996), 6.
61 Kondrashin and D'Ann Penner, *Golod: 1932–1933 gody v sovetskoi derevne.*
62 Meslé and Vallin, *Mortalité et causes de décès en Ukraine.*
63 The rate of population decline in various Ukrainian regions is shown on the map 'Political Geography of the *Holodomor*', in Luciuk (ed.), *Holodomor: Reflections*, 32. More recently, cartographic work on the demography and geography of the famine has been undertaken at the Harvard Ukrainian Research Institute. See the map of direct losses by *oblast* and accompanying text found in this volume as well as the complementary chapter by Rudnitskyi *et al.* (Chapter 8, this volume)
64 In *Krasnaia armiia i kollektivizatsiia derevni v SSSR.*
65 *Tragediia sovetskoi derevni*, vol. 3, 717–718.
66 Chlevnjuk, 'Stalin e la carestia dei primi anni Trenta'.
67 Ibid.
68 *Lettere da Kharkov*, 157–164.
69 Nicolas Werth and Gaël Moullec, *Rapports Secrets Soviétiques, 1921–1991* (Paris: Gallimard, 1994), 155.
70 *Lettere da Kharkov*, 192–194. Schiller's 23 May 1933 report is reproduced as Document 36 in Carynnyk *et al.*, *The Foreign Office and the Famine*, 258–268.

71 Andrea Graziosi, 'Stalin, krest'ianstvo i gosudarstvennyi sotsializm, 1927–1951 gg', in *Istoriia stalinizma: krest'ianstvo i vlast'*, ed. A.K. Sorokin (Moscow: Rosspen, 2011), 12–32.
72 Graziosi, *Great Soviet Peasant War*, 69.
73 Elsewhere, in Central Asia, as in the Far North or the Far East, there was also a turn in national policies, but on a much lesser scale. The percentage of 'indigenous' leading cadres went down at the senior levels but not so much at the medium and lower ones, where it continued to grow; most languages were switched back from a Latin to a Cyrillic alphabet and the unifying role of Russian was extolled. See Martin, *Affirmative Action Empire*, 344–393.
74 *Vsesoyuznaia perepis' naseleniia 1937 g. Kratkie itogi* (Moscow: Institut istorii SSSR AN SSSR, 1991).
75 See the above-mentioned forum on N. Naimark's book, in *Journal of Cold War Studies*, 165.
76 *Lettere da Kharkov*, 168.
77 See Hennadii Efimenko, 'The Kremlin's Nationality Policy in Ukraine after the Holodomor of 1932–33', in *After the Holodomor: The Enduring Impact of the Great Famine in Ukraine*, ed. Andrea Graziosi, Lubomyr A. Hajda and Halyna Hryn (Cambridge, MA: Harvard Ukrainian Research Institute, 2013), 69–98; Yury Shapoval, 'The Holodomor: A Prologue to Repressions and Terror in Soviet Ukraine', in *After the Holodomor: The Enduring Impact of the Great Famine in Ukraine*, ed. Andrea Graziosi, Lubomyr A. Hajda and Halyna Hryn (Cambridge, MA: Harvard Ukrainian Research Institute, 2013), 99–122.
78 The short-term consequences of the *Holodomor* – that is, of the way Stalin chose to deal with the Ukrainian question on both the social and the national front – acquired crucial long-term implications whose effects are still evident today, as shown by the importance and the regional peculiarities of the language question in contemporary Ukraine.
79 Lev Kopelev, *The Education of a True Believer* (New York: Harper & Row, 1980).
80 Stanislav Kulchytskyi, 'The Holodomor and Its Consequences in the Ukrainian Countryside', in *After the Holodomor: The Enduring Impact of the Great Famine in Ukraine*, ed. Andrea Graziosi, Lubomyr A. Hajda and Halyna Hryn (Cambridge, MA: Harvard Ukrainian Research Institute, 2013), 1–14.
81 Viktor Kondrashin, *Golod 1932–1933 godov: tragediia rossiiskoi derevni* (Moscow: Rosspen, 2008).
82 Graziosi, 'The Soviet 1931–1933 Famines and the Ukrainian *Holodomor*', 10.
83 Vladimir F. Zima, *Golod v SSSR 1946–1947 godov: proiskhodzhenie i posledstviia* (Moscow: Institut istorii SSSR AN SSSR, 1996); Olexandra Veselova's contribution in *After the Holodomor* (forthcoming).
84 O. Rudnytskyi, N. Levchuk, O. Wolowyna and P. Shevchuk, 'Famine Losses in Ukraine in 1932 to 1933 Within the Context of the Soviet Union', in *Famines in European Economic History: The Last Great European Famines Reconsidered,* ed. D. Curran, L. Luciuk and A. Newby (London: Routledge, forthcoming) (Explorations in Economic History).
85 Valerij Vasylyev (ed.), *Politicheskoe rukovodstvo Ukrainy, 1938–1989* (Moscow: Rosspen, 2006), 168.
86 On the question of genocide see Graziosi, 'The Soviet 1931–33 Famines and the Ukrainian *Holodomor*', 11. For the 1948 *United Nations Convention on Genocide* go to the *Yearbook of the United Nations* (New York: Department of Public Information, 1948–1949), 959. See also Raphael Lemkin, *Axis Rule in Occupied Europe* (Washington, DC: Carnegie Endowment for International Peace, 1944), 82. Lemkin's speech, 'Soviet Genocide in the Ukraine' (New York, 1953) is reproduced in Luciuk (ed.), *Holodomor: Reflections*, appendix A, 235–242. While the 1932/1933 famine was neither an expression of Russian nationalism nor a premeditated plan on Stalin's

part to destroy the Ukrainian nation – though he did gain politically from the harrowing consequences of his policies to subjugate and emasculate Ukraine, its peasants and its intelligentsia – I accept Lemkin's position that 'generally speaking genocide does not necessarily mean the immediate destruction of a nation … it is intended rather to signify a coordinated plan of different actions aiming at the destruction of essential foundations of the life of national groups.' Considering (1) the substantial difference in mortality rates across the different Soviet republics, (2) the millions of Ukrainians who were forcibly Russified after December 1932, including Ukrainian peasants who took refuge in the Soviet Russian Republic, (3) the fact that approximately 20 to 30 per cent of the Ukrainian nation either perished or were subjected to Russification, and remembering that (4) these losses were caused by a political decision, unquestionably subjective, that occurred when Stalin fused an anti-Ukrainian purpose to an existing famine, and that (5) without such a decision the death-toll would have been, at most, in the hundreds of thousands, and remembering, finally (6) the widespread liquidation of the Soviet Ukrainian Republic's political, religious and cultural elites coupled with deliberate measures adopted to distort the development of the Ukrainian language and culture, then 'yes' is the answer to the question '*Was the Holodomor a genocide?*', as Lemkin himself affirmed. Of course the Ukrainian nation was not extirpated. Stalin well understood that orchestrating such an erasure was both improbable and unnecessary. That said, Ukrainian society still bears the negative demographic, spiritual and political consequences of the Stalinist agenda, being what Professor James Mace once described as a 'post-genocidal society'. See 'Spadshchyna holodomoru: Ukraina iak posthenotsydne suspilstvo'. Available at: www.msmb.org.ua/books/thematic_bibliography/292/ (accessed 1 October 2014).

Index

Page numbers in *italics* denote tables, those in **bold** denote figures.

For Product Safety Concerns and Information please contact our EU representative GPSR@taylorandfrancis.com
Taylor & Francis Verlag GmbH, Kaufingerstraße 24, 80331 München, Germany

www.ingramcontent.com/pod-product-compliance
Ingram Content Group UK Ltd.
Pitfield, Milton Keynes, MK11 3LW, UK
UKHW021011180425
457613UK00020B/895
* 9 7 8 0 3 6 7 8 6 7 4 8 5 *